Encyclopedia of
Exotic
Plants
for Temperate
Climates

Encyclopedia of
Exotic Plants
for Temperate Climates

Will Giles

Foreword by Fergus Garrett

Timber Press

Title page

Two of Will Giles's cats on the front steps of his home at the Exotic Garden in Norwich, Norfolk, England

Published in 2007 by
Timber Press, Inc.
The Haseltine Building
133 S.W. Second Avenue, Suite 450
Portland, Oregon 97204-3527, U.S.A.
www.timberpress.com
For contact information regarding editorial, marketing, sales, and distribution in the United Kingdom, see www.timberpress.co.uk.

Designed by Dick Malt
Printed in China

Library of Congress Cataloguing-in-Publication Data
Giles, Will.
  Exotic plants for temperate gardens : an encyclopedia / Will Giles ; foreword by Fergus Garrett.
    p. cm.
  Includes bibliographical references and index.
  ISBN-13: 978-0-88192-785-6
  1. Gardening–Encyclopedias. 2. Exotic plants–Encyclopedias. 3. Tropical plants–Encyclopedias. I. Title.
SB450.95.G55 2007
635.903–dc22
                    2007010380

A catalogue record for this book is also available from the British Library.

All photographs by Will Giles except those appearing on pages 2–3, 12, 18–19, 23, and 26–7 by David Clarke; pages 277–8, 279 (left), 280 (right), 282 (lower), 283 (lower right), 284 (left), 285 (right), 287, 289, 290 (upper), 293, 296, and 297 (upper right & lower right) by Paul Craft; pages 35 (upper left), 39, 44–5, 105 (upper), 106 (lower left), 109, 113 (upper), 116 (right), 117, 121, 124, 133–5, 136 (right), 164 (lower right), 165, 167 (upper right & lower), 176, 178, 180–1, 183, 184 (right & lower left), 185, 187 (upper left), 190, 192, 195, 200, 211 (bottom), 212, 215 (upper left), 221 (upper left), 224, 228, 231, 234–5, 239, 241–2, 250 (left), 251, 254 (lower), 264 (left), 267 (upper left), 280 (left), 332, 339 (upper), 347 (lower), 359 (lower right), 360, 369, 371, 380–1, 384–5, 387 (upper left & upper right), 388, 392 (upper left), 393 (right), 394 (left), 395, 405, 406 (upper), and 412 by Global Book Publishing Photo Library; pages 37, 42 (left), 43 (top right), 94, 123 (upper), 127, 138, 154 (right), 164 (upper left), 168, and 171 (upper left) by Terry Moyemont; pages 281, 284 (right), 285 (left), 286, 290 (lower) by Robert Lee Riffle; and pages 54, 55 (upper left, upper right, & lower left), 56–7, 58 (left), and 59–73 by Paul Whittaker.

Contents

Foreword

The mysterious world of the exotic has captured the imagination of gardeners young and old since the Victorian era. The word alone conjures up images of another world—a world of steamy jungles dripping with vegetation evoking the deafening noises of the existence around you, intoxicating the senses and leaving you hallucinating deep in the womb of Mother Earth. Paintings of Henri Rousseau come to mind with bizarre and animated tigers stalking amongst lush vegetation.

Plants from exotic places have hypnotic qualities, and opening your mind to them makes gardening mouthwateringly exciting. And it's not just about jungle giants; the variety of material is endless, from delicate ferns with filigree fronds to bolder beasts with leaves several feet across. Anybody who has travelled into the jungle knows what a treasure chest it is for the plantaholic. Many plants in faraway places are unfamiliar to us and out of our growing range, needing conditions of high humidity and hot temperatures that we simply cannot replicate outside in our gardens. But some are old friends that have played a part in our landscape for centuries. And others although unfamiliar fall within the scope of the adventurous gardener. They are there to experiment with and to learn from, through trial and error.

Whether old or new, all the plants selected for this book have one thing in common—they have a feel of exoticism. With our palettes continually enriched, years of pleasure lie ahead, pushing the boundaries and taking risks. But when dabbling with the unusual, be prepared for the unexpected. Tread carefully and expect failure, and when times are low remember your successes. The sheer thrill of experimenting can, and will, outweigh all that goes wrong. Understanding your conditions and your materials will get you a long way. Do your homework: be hungry for information and keep your eyes and ears open.

Exotics can be incredibly rewarding. And once bitten by the bug you will find it difficult to go back. Life as a gardener just wouldn't be the same without the paddle-shaped leaves of *Ensete ventricosum*, or the matte-black marbled foliage of the moody and mysterious *Colocasia esculenta* 'Black Magic'. Their contribution in shape and in character cannot be equalled. Begonias, cannas, dahlias, gingers, palms, cycads, and tree ferns—the list goes on. These are the movers and shakers of the plant world.

So the future is exciting. But in everything we do we have to take into account the shrinking resources of this planet we live on. Contrary to popular belief, exotic

gardening need not be extravagant in using those resources. Again it comes down to understanding and making careful choices. And remember, not everything with an exotic look comes from the misty forests near the equator. Many hardy plants from harsher climates like fatsias, catalpas, and paulownias do an excellent job of mimicking their tropical cousins. These may have cold blood running through their veins but the impression is quite the opposite. Making the right choice is where expertise makes a difference and reading this latest work from Will Giles will give you just that.

Left
Geranium maderense

Fergus Garrett
Head Gardener, Great Dixter
East Sussex, United Kingdom

Acknowledgments

During the writing of this book I met many people who garden with exotic plants, not only in the United Kingdom but also in North America, Germany, and probably other locations I have forgotten about with the passage of time. To those I have not mentioned, thank you for our conversations. I also wish to thank the many visitors to my "exotic garden" in Norwich, Norfolk, who have often passed me gems of wisdom and information on their growing conditions and experiences.

I would like to thank the following (in no particular order) for their input and patience with me over the years that it has taken me to assemble all the information within the covers of this book. There have been many times when I felt like giving up, but my good friends and colleagues have gone out of their way to help me.

First, I would like to thank Anna Mumford for her calm patience as she gave me extra time on so many occasions and for her gentle guidance, enthusiasm, and confidence in me. Also, a big thank you to her assistant, Erica Gordon-Mallin, for all the e-mails that flew back and forth and for her diligence in collating all the text and pictures, sometimes in a very hot office! Another big thank you to Mindy Seale Fitch at Timber Press in Oregon for editing this book while pregnant and working on it till almost the last moment and also to Lorraine Anderson for her patience and gardening knowledge while completing the editing.

A big thank you to my oldest friend, Vaughan Fleming, who diligently checked much of the text, burning the midnight oil to make sure that everything was correct. Thanks to Paul Sprakelin, owner of a fantastic garden on the Essex Riviera, for his tremendous input to the cacti and succulent section, as well as to the bromeliad section, which would have been very thin without his help—he is a veritable mine of information. Peter Reed gave me most of the material on growing cycads outside, from his experiences growing them in his coastal garden in southern England.

To Martin Gibbons of the Palm Centre, a big thank you for almost rewriting the palm section, giving me the benefit of his years of experience and wisdom. Thanks to Martin Rickard for his assistance with the fern section, with his strong passion for these wonderful green and luscious plants. John Eddy at Trevena Cross Nurseries in Cornwall helped me by sharing his knowledge of growing restios in southwestern England. Much gratitude must be given to David Constantine of KobaKoba for his invaluable assistance with the ginger and banana sections, and also to Keith Haywood of Hart Canna for his vast knowledge of growing cannas and their problems.

Thanks to Paul Whittaker, the king of bamboo and colleague on BBC Radio Norfolk Saturday morning garden phone-ins, who gave me much wisdom and input on the bamboo section and also supplied many wonderful photographs to illuminate the text.

Much appreciation must be given to Terry Moyemont of Mesogeo Nursery on Bainbridge Island, Washington, United States, for his knowledge of gardening in the Pacific Northwest. Without having met me, he supplied some excellent photographs of plants and gardens. We also had many long transatlantic phone calls about the vagaries and pleasures of gardening in his region.

I also thank Paul Craft and Robert Lee Riffle for their generous and timely contribution of photographs of palms.

I would like to thank Alice Harris at Karchesky Canna in Pennsylvania, United States, for her advice on growing brugmansias. I would also like to give a big thank you to Monika Gottschalk in Germany for checking all the rather confusing information that I sent her and getting it all in order.

A big thank you to Ian Roofe and Craig Knight for keeping the "exotic garden" going while I feverishly worked on my computer, for cheering me up when I felt low, and for pushing me on to get the book finished so that I could join them in the garden! An extra thank you must be given to Craig for helping me collate much of the information and photographs for this book. Andrew Mott helped me with the original plant content list, suggesting many interesting plants from the Southern Hemisphere. He also helped me start collecting bamboos and introduced me to the illustrious Paul Whittaker. I must not forget Liam Tobin for introducing me to a vast range of eclectic music while I was glued to my computer.

Matt Biggs of "Gardeners' Question Time" on BBC's Radio 4 has been a good friend, often comparing notes with me on the frustrations of writing books in solitude and battling with deadlines.

Anna Mumford asked me to choose a well-known gardener to write the foreword to this book. I was originally going to ask Christopher Lloyd, creator of the exotic garden at his home in Great Dixter. Alas, he passed away on 27 January 2006, at age 84. With his demise I could not think of anyone better suited to undertake the task than his head gardener, Fergus Garrett, and Christo's closest friend.

Introduction

Strictly speaking, any plant that is not native to a particular region is an exotic simply because it hails from somewhere else. Cannas in British Columbia, eucalypti in India, and cacti in England are all examples of exotic plants. So far so good, but by this definition a large number of familiar plants that have become part of temperate landscapes could also be described as exotics: the common horse chestnut (*Aesculus hippocastanum*), widely cultivated throughout the temperate world but native to the Balkans in southeastern Europe; the common or garden buddleia or butterfly bush, familiar coloniser of scrubby ground and railway sidings in the British Isles, but introduced from the Americas, Asia, and South Africa; and that pernicious weed and bane of all gardens, ground elder (*Aegopodium podagraria*), thought to have been introduced into Britain from southern Europe by the Romans. In reality we are surrounded by a plethora of exotic plants that we do not think of as exotic because they are so common in our gardens or so mundane in appearance.

In contrast, the exotic plants you will find described in this book are anything *but* mundane in appearance and either originate from or are characteristic of places that are foreign to us. Here you will find plants that are subtropical or tropical in appearance but in fact originate in cooler climatic regions of the world, as well as true tropicals and subtropicals that, for various reasons, flourish in temperate gardens and in some cases are able to withstand several degrees of frost.

Why Grow Exotics?

The garden is a place of escape from the everyday world of earning money and feeding the kids (or in my case, a pride of cats), and the exotic garden, with its otherworldliness, provides the best escape of all. Whether you are a fair-weather gardener or the type who will work in the garden all through the winter whatever the sky throws at you, this style of gardening is absorbing and innovative, as much experimentation is involved. You may not always be successful, but when you are, the results are astounding. There is also tremendous joy in growing something in your garden that isn't supposed to be hardy! And for the exotic enthusiast, growing something different from the neighbours is irresistible.

There is something for everyone in this style of gardening, from those who require

Left

Will Giles's home and garden, where he set out to grow something different from the neighbours. On the house, the climber *Parthenocissus tricuspidata* 'Veitchii' has free rein. To the left of the gravel path, the gigantic leaves of *Musa basjoo* tower over the fat, pale green flower spikes of *Eucomis bicolor* and the variegated leaves of *Phormium cookianum* subsp. *hookeri* 'Cream Delight'; *Miscanthus sacchariflorus* is the tall grass in the background. To the right of the path, *Canna* 'Durban' pops out in front of the common sunflower and the windmill palm, *Trachycarpus fortunei*; *Setaria palmifolia* edges the path with its broad straplike leaves, and *Verbena hastata* sends up purple flower spikes to the far right.

Exotics such as brugmansia, hibiscus, and *Clerodendrum bungei* knit together in the author's garden to provide an explosion of colour and texture quite different from the cottage-garden look.

their gardens to look good year-round to those who want to make a big splash in summer with flamboyant bedding. This latter aim is particularly well suited to parts of the United States that have cold winters and hot summers, where most of the more tender exotics—such as cannas, gingers, and colocasias, to name only a few—can grow exceedingly quickly in one season, speedily knitting together and forming an impenetrable jungle of foliage and flowers. In this environment, the choicer plants are generally overwintered in a frost-free basement, cool-room, or garage.

In my view, for plants to be considered exotic, they have to dramatically improve or change their surroundings. Many of the plants included in this book will do just that; whether they are trees, shrubs, or exotic-looking annuals, they are all architectural in some way, through their shape, texture, or colour. They might have tropical-looking flowers, brightly coloured foliage, or huge leaves. They all give a very different feel from the more traditional cottage-garden lupins, roses, and summer-bedding geraniums (pelargoniums), and are far more exciting than a backyard full of grass!

The prevalence of gardening programs covering exotics in recent years has brought many new plants to the attention of gardeners. This combined with a veritable explosion of outlets selling exotic plants means it has never been easier to start an exotic garden. Whether your garden is large or small, you can always create a wonderful oasis that will please you and your plants. Exotics fit well in a variety of different contexts, so whether your garden is overshadowed by high buildings in a bustling city or nestled in open countryside, you will always be able to find exotic-looking plants that suit the site perfectly.

Much experimentation has been carried out over the last decade or so by individuals and dedicated nursery owners who have made new discoveries and improved the availability of many new exotic plants that will not only survive but also thrive in your garden. Numerous new hybrids and cultivars are becoming more readily available as well, greatly enlarging the number of accessible plants that will transform your garden or yard into a veritable paradise. There are countless trees, shrubs, and herbaceous plants, whether evergreen or deciduous, that although hardy still give a truly exotic feel to the garden.

The scope for planting is huge, ranging from a palm grove, consisting of the many different hardy palms that are now readily available, to a Victorian-style fernery with a rich tapestry of moist, lush greens planted under a forest of giant tree ferns, creating an almost prehistoric atmosphere. Or how about your own banana plantation with a palm-frond-thatched jungle hut or tree house, where you can overlook your own personal heaven with gin and tonic in hand? Then again, perhaps you have a penchant for a typical Mediterranean or California-style garden with architectural shapes and soft silvery planting, with lots of container and potted plants, and maybe a cooling waterfall to reflect the heat.

You might desire more spiky architectural plants that would give the garden structure and attitude, and thus you might use the more drought-resistant plants from the succulent and cactus world. These xerophytes can live for months without water, reveling in the searing heat of high summer. The plants required for this style of garden are often far hardier than might have been thought, seeing as many of them hail from desert areas that often freeze during the winter months. On the other hand, some gardeners will prefer a mainly green garden with plants that give a moist, lush feel. These could be plants that grow at high elevations in the tropics, where the nights can also be decidedly cool. The wonderful *Brugmansia* species and hybrids fit into this category well with their enormous, often highly scented flowers preferring cooler maritime summers.

Exotics bring a welcome note of surprise to a huge range of environments. A few days ago I was driving down a leafy suburban road that I had never travelled before, counting the plants that give an exotic appearance. One front garden in particular stood out like a beacon, having a large range of mature exotics of all sizes and forms almost bursting at the seams. It was a gravel garden stuffed to the gunnels, defiantly standing out from the mundane neighbouring gardens. What a sight!

History of Exotic Gardening

Gardening as a hobby became popular during the Victorian era, and not just as a private pastime. This was the age of the Industrial Revolution, when squalid slums spread through towns and cities. During this period municipal authorities in many of the major cities made a concerted effort to provide extensive public gardens, creating

The seed heads of *Pennisetum glaucum* 'Purple Majesty' (front) and the foliage of *Canna* 'Durban' (middle) and hybrids of *Colocasia esculenta* (back) function as architectural elements in the garden at the Urban Jungle in Norwich, Norfolk.

Bananas mingle with palms in the author's garden: *Ensete ventricosum* 'Maurelii' (foreground) and *Musa basjoo* (toward the back) are interplanted with *Trachycarpus fortunei* and *Cordyline australis*.

open areas for pleasure and recreation. This apparently benevolent action, sponsored by the wealthy industrialists of the time, was not without private interest as the benefactors believed that access to public gardens would decrease drunkenness and improve the manners of the lower working classes. The upper classes and intellectuals of the period also thought that encouraging gardening would minimise antisocial behaviour by creating tranquil settings that would engender a sense of pride and respect for public spaces.

The exotic garden style reached its heyday during the mid-nineteenth century in Britain. The seemingly endless expansion of the British Empire opened up all the corners of the globe to the new avid gardeners. Intrepid botanical explorers were constantly bringing back new species, a task made easier by the invention around 1829 by Dr. Nathaniel Bagshaw Ward (1791–1868) of a small portable glass structure called a Wardian case. Use of these structures turned the trickle into a veritable flood of new exotic plants that were subsequently housed in large glasshouses or domes. Virtually every major European capital, however chilly its climate might be, managed to create a display of exotica from around the world.

In Britain, the repeal of the glass tax in 1845 and the growth of new industries producing cheaper glass started a massive boom in glasshouse, or greenhouse, production. These fanciful new structures housed collections containing a wide range of exotica, including such recently introduced plants as orchids, bromeliads, ferns, and palms. Cities vied for the best collections; visitors flocked by the thousands to see spectacular plants with huge leaves and exotic flowers. During this period an increasing number of plants became available and public interest in them quickly developed. At the same time, hothouses—large intricate structures of glass and iron, often called stoves or winter gardens—started to appear. Glass was relatively cheap, as was labour to care for the hothouse plants and fuel to heat the structures. Kept at a minimum temperature of 21°C, these hothouses recreated the humid, damp atmosphere of the plants' native habitats, producing lush, verdant growth.

The Royal Botanic Gardens, Kew, was opened to the general public in 1841, and the famous Palm House at the Kew Gardens, a gigantic greenhouse some 110 m long and 18 m wide constructed with the latest manufacturing techniques, was opened in 1848. It stands to this day as a marvel of Victorian construction containing a large range of tropical plants from around the globe. So also does the oldest existing public conservatory in the Western Hemisphere, the Conservatory of Flowers located in San Francisco's Golden Gate Park, opened to the public in 1879.

The stately monkey puzzle (*Araucaria araucana*) became one of the "must-have" trees of Victorian society, planted in large and small gardens; many towering specimens survive to this day. This venerable plant was first introduced from Chile to the British Isles in 1795 by Archibald Menzies (1754–1842), a Scottish physician and naturalist. He allegedly pocketed some fertile monkey puzzle seeds when they were given to him as a dessert while he was dining with the governor of Chile on a global circumnavigation. He sowed the seeds on the ship during his return voyage to England; only five seedlings survived the journey and were given to Kew Gardens, where one survived until 1892. The monkey puzzle remained a rarity until the 1840s, when William Lobb rediscovered it on a plant-hunting expedition to South America, thus starting the Victorian-era explosion of interest.

Bananas and cannas, used in Victorian-era exotic gardens, grace Will Giles's garden. *Canna* 'Pretoria', to the left, complements the showy leaves of *Ensete ventricosum* 'Red Stripe', to the upper right. The thin central plant with purple flowers is *Verbena bonariensis* and to its right is the filamentous *Cyperus papyrus*. At the bottom left and right are the large leaves of *Colocasia esculenta*.

A craze had begun for planting exotics outside as well as inside. Fabulous displays were created in the larger cities, with massed beds of flamboyantly coloured plants laid out in intricate, often geometric patterns. One of the earliest Victorian proponents of the new style of bedding was John Gibson, who produced large foliage displays in Battersea Park, one of London's best-known public gardens. He used, as well as the more familiar bedding plants, a dazzling array of exotics such as bananas, cannas, and tree ferns, all bedded out for the summer months. The park was laid out between 1846 and 1864 to the grand designs of James Pennethorne and John Gibson.

In 1871 William Robinson's *The Subtropical Garden* appeared, discussing the use of many different types of tropical and subtropical plants that could be successfully planted out during the warmer months of the year. Robinson, and later Gertrude Jekyll (1843–1932), disliked the formal, regimented planting style then in vogue and preferred the more naturalistic look. He also maintained that exotic-looking gardens could be created using hardy plants that had the appearance of their more tender subtropical counterparts—plants that would be visually pleasing but survive throughout the year and revel in Britain's cool maritime winters.

Gardeners in general soon discovered from the likes of Robinson that many exotic plants would actually thrive in temperate gardens with a mixture of hardy exotics and the more tender summer bedding, with the larger subtropical species and their cultivars kept under glass for the cold winter months. One of the benefits of this style of gardening was that it greatly lengthened the garden's season of interest. Plants of this nature could be enjoyed for a far longer period than those in the traditional cottage garden, which comes to a flowering peak in June; the new style carried on through high summer to autumn, often creating an explosion of riotous colour and large leaves with the use of such plants as cannas and gingers.

This sumptuous style of planting started to wane toward the end of the nineteenth century with the loss of the larger estates and their patrons, who paid for their rather expensive upkeep. The once-praised greenhouses became far too expensive to run, with labour costs spiralling and the price of fuel soaring. Well-known gardeners like Gertrude Jekyll praised the virtues of the cottage garden style, hailing the end of bedded-out plants, and hence the fashion for exotics came to an end.

After World War II, fairly low-growing, regimented bedding plants such as blue lobelia, red salvia, white alyssum, heliotrope, and bedding begonias started to be used again; these were employed especially by parks and gardens with the odd well-spaced, solitary canna thrown in. These plants were comparatively cheap and could be grown from seed, creating a splash of colour fairly quickly.

In the latter part of the twentieth century the use of exotics slowly started to re-emerge as a style of gardening, boosted since the 1960s by the ease of air travel to the Mediterranean and farther-flung parts of the world. Travelers somewhat bored with traditional herbaceous borders and prissy summer bedding saw many exotic plants and wanted to recreate what they saw in some small part of their gardens. By the mid-to-late 1990s and into the twenty-first century it had become very fashionable to have a garden designed by somebody else, invariably with a standard set of plants that are generally considered exotic or subtropical looking. While the use of exotics unquestionably adds flare to the garden, you will probably be happier if you make the choice of plants yourself. I hope that this encyclopedia will be an invaluable tool for you in that endeavour.

Pushing the Boundaries of Hardiness

Many of the exotic plants grown in temperate gardens today were until fairly recently considered viable only in the warmer southwestern parts of the British Isles and the more southerly parts of the United States. Climate change has been a significant factor in changing the contents of our gardens, along with encouragement to experiment with plants traditionally thought of as warm-zone or hothouse plants. This follows an established tradition: when camellias were first introduced into England they were grown in large greenhouses, and it was only when heating became more expensive and glasshouses fell into ruin that they were discovered to be actually hardy!

A number of exotic plants introduced from the colder extremities of the tropical regions of the world adapt especially well to gardens in the temperate northwestern United States, which runs in a band along the seaboard stretching from Oregon through Washington to southern British Columbia in Canada, as well as many parts of the British Isles and northern Europe. These are hardy exotics, meaning they have a subtropical appearance but take cool summers and relatively cold winters well. It

surprises many gardeners to find that palms, for instance, are hardy in a maritime climate. In the last decade or so, windmill palm (*Trachycarpus fortunei*) has been popping up everywhere from private gardens to parks and municipal gardens, even roundabouts, as it is hardy in all but the coldest locations. Bamboos are also enjoying a revival, with many of the noninvasive species and cultivars being suitable for smaller gardens as well as containers, where they give a very Asian feel with their fabulous culms and frothy foliage. And the false castor-oil plant (*Fatsia japonica*), with its large, palmate, glossy evergreen leaves, has a subtropical appearance but hails from cool areas in eastern Asia and thus is hardy in temperate gardens.

Numerous cacti and some succulents take considerable amounts of frost in their native habitats and work well in the garden provided you are aware of their need for exceedingly well-drained soil. Many cacti, for instance, will take lows of −10°C for weeks or months in the wild where it is very dry or where they have a blanket of snow over them, but they will not tolerate the damp cold or slushy rain of a maritime climate. If these frost-tolerant plants are grown on excruciatingly well-drained soils or have a canopy put over them to keep out winter rain, or alternatively are planted in the lee of a south-facing building, they will not only survive but also thrive, with a modicum of care and attention.

A collection of succulents and cacti in pots adorns a south-facing wall, where the plants stay warm enough to survive a frosty winter.

A mixture of houseplants, including Philodendron, Guzmania, Tillandsia, Aspidistra, Asplenium, Maranta, and an orchid grow under an old pear tree at the Exotic Garden.

Over the last few years I have been experimenting with plants more strictly described as houseplants, including many bromeliads as well as *Chlorophytum*, *Monstera*, *Tradescantia*, and *Platycerium*. Some visitors to my garden look at these and say, "You can't grow those outside—especially on the supposedly chilly east coast of England!" Luckily, though, the so-called houseplants do not know this, happily taking root and growing vigorously through our warmer months (a style much used by the Victorians), apparently unaware of the fact that they should really be sitting on a window ledge in my house.

Tradescantia species and hybrids (wandering Jew), although normally considered nonhardy, have become naturalised in my garden in recent years, dying down to the ground in autumn and returning in late spring. According to many authoritative reference books, they will take a minimum of 5°C! I discovered their hardiness through trial and error. This is one of the best and most exciting ways to garden. When I planted out my first root-hardy *Musa basjoo* (banana) some quarter of a century ago, scant information was available at that time regarding their cultivation and hardiness, apart from the classic book *The Exotic Garden* by Myles Challis (published in 1988 and sadly out of print). I had no idea whether it would survive, but with some experimentation with different types of protection, I now have several *M. basjoo* grown to perfection and forming a large clump reaching 5.5 m tall or more every year. They give a spectacularly architectural effect with their giant paddlelike leaves. In the last

Above

A young *Musa basjoo* grows to the left of the author's front steps. A couple of *Agave americana* 'Marginata' in pots grace the top step on either side. Note also the silvery leaves of *Plectranthus argentatus* to the left of the bottom step and the straplike leaves of the tall *Cordyline australis* to the far right.

Below

Microclimates are affected by sloping ground, exposure to sun, and proximity to bodies of water, amongst other factors. This water feature in the author's garden, situated on a sunny south-facing slope and sheltered from prevailing winds by tall trees, supports a variety of exotic plants.

few years I, along with many other exotic enthusiasts, have discovered that with our recent comparatively mild winters, they haven't needed any protection at all! Even if a hard winter cuts them down to the ground, they will vigorously reshoot the following spring.

One of the most important factors in this style of gardening is your garden microclimate. Microclimates are climatic variations that occur in comparatively small areas. Factors that influence microclimates in a garden can include sloping ground, exposure to sun or the lack of it, proximity to large areas of concrete or bodies of water, and prevailing winds. A garden surrounded by a wall or hedges and/or in a city is likely to be much warmer than those in the open countryside. There are even mini-microclimates within gardens; for example, plants grown near a south-facing wall pick up its latent heat and thus tender selections that might not survive in a more exposed area of the garden will thrive there. A shelterbelt of trees or tall buildings will also protect your choice plants. For instance, palms like *Trachycarpus fortunei* have a tendency to becoming rather tatty in exposed gardens, while those surrounded by other trees become more lush and verdant and develop larger, healthier fronds.

My Philosophy

You can take many different paths with this style of gardening. Whatever anyone says to you, there are no rules, only those of common sense and an awareness of your plant's provenance and requirements for healthy growth. I have found over many years of visiting exotic gardens that their creators each have their own styles, their own preferences for plants and ways to arrange them. In fact, there is no set style, only personal choice and enthusiasm. The garden, after all, is a place of escape, and the exotic garden should be a place of fulfilment and fun, a personal oasis of pleasure and contemplation.

I personally learned my gardening skills through experience and experimentation over several decades, discovering which plants are hardy and which need protection or have to be brought under cover for the winter months, and which annuals produce a wonderful effect in just one season. In my case I discovered many plants to be hardy by just plain forgetting to take them inside in autumn, only to discover them happily returning the following spring!

I am lucky enough to have a garden in Norwich, England, of about an acre with an excellent microclimate due to its being part way down a south-facing hillside, surrounded by shrubs and trees on the western, northern, and eastern sides that slow down the prevailing chilly winds of winter and trap the heat of the sun in summer. I also have plenty of space to overwinter some of the more tender plants, as I have mentioned, but most gardeners do not have these facilities and have to go down the hardy route, using those plants that look exotic although they do not necessarily come from the tropics. With this in mind, I have included in this book hardy plants to fit most sites, including specimens that are small, tall, wide, and thin.

I believe it is a good idea to start a new garden with plants that will have year-round appeal, creating a strong backbone through evergreen foliage or interesting bark or even precious flowers that bloom in the depths of winter. All gardens can look rather bare at this time of year, so it is absolutely essential to have a good structural

backbone to carry the garden through the dimmest and most desperately grey days of winter. Then you can add in herbaceous plantings, and finally incorporate the more tender species and varieties to give a boost during the summer months—a bit like putting the icing on the top of a cake. Palms, cordylines, bamboos, phormiums, fatsias, palms, and tree ferns can provide the backdrop to more tender plants such as cannas, gingers, and even more tender papyrus, and the dark-leaved Abyssinian banana, *Ensete ventricosum* 'Maurelii', which are planted out in late spring when the nights have warmed up. An exotic effect can also be created comparatively cheaply with annuals like *Ricinus communis* (castor-bean plant) with its huge, often dark purple leaves on large, tall, strong plants, or an old Victorian favourite, *Amaranthus caudatus* (love-lies-bleeding), with its soft green leaves and myriads of long purplish-red tassels in abundance in high summer. *Cobaea scandens* (cup-and-saucer vine), a fast-growing climber with purple or white flowers, will cover a fence or shed in one season.

The point is that what you have in your own exotic garden is a matter of personal choice. My style of gardening is high maintenance—much has to be protected during the winter months or dug up and stored in several polytunnels. All this effort to get a fabulous show from July to October might seem to some ludicrously daunting. If it

Ricinus communis 'New Zealand Purple', grown as an annual, produces a dramatic effect in just one season. Here it is mixed with *Ensete ventricosum* (far left), *Hedychium coccineum* 'Tara' (bottom right), *Ensete ventricosum* 'Maurelii' (far right), and the variegated foliage of *Brugmansia* ×*candida* 'Maya' (top right).

seems so to you, do not attempt it. Working within the limits of your own time, energy, and garden microclimates, you can still create an exotic garden that pleases you.

Using This Book

I have employed an all-embracing approach to my selection of exotic plants for inclusion in this encyclopedia, though I am sure some purists will disagree with my choices. The field of exotics is very subjective, as are the people who grow them! Personal choice is everything; there are no rules as to how you as an individual should interpret your ideas through planting. As long as you can provide an exotic plant with what it needs to grow and thrive, you can include it in your garden.

The purpose of this book, then, is to tell you what you need to know about a large range of both tender and hardy exotics in order to discover which ones you can provide a good home to. Plants are like children; they are dependent on you for their success or failure, and definitely so in their juvenile stages of growth, often need-

In the author's garden, the evergreen *Magnolia grandiflora* at centre top provides a structural backbone, while the more tender *Ensete ventricosum* 'Maurelii' (far left), *Alocasia odora* (below left), *Musella lasiocarpa* (centre bottom), and *Hedychium greenii* and *Colocasia esculenta* 'Mammoth' (centre right), sheltering a low-growing *Codiaeum variegatum*, provide a summer show of colour and texture.

ing much cosseting. Having an awareness of a plant's provenance—that is, where it originates, the temperatures and soil types it is used to in the wild, even the altitude at which it naturally grows—is essential to its success, as is a knowledge of its requirements, whether full sun or shade, damp or arid, acid or alkali. An awareness of its ultimate size is also essential; that eucalyptus you bought as a 50-cm juvenile whip is now a huge monster at 24 m, filling up your entire front garden and heavily shading your neighbour's garden to boot!

The entries in this encyclopedia give information on a plant's ultimate height and spread as well as its cultural requirements and climatic needs. Plants are organized into logical groupings, either by family (as in the case of aroids, for instance), super-family (as for bananas and their relatives—cannas, strelitizias, and gingers), or similar forms (bulbs and tubers, climbers and scramblers, for example). A general description of the entire grouping is followed by descriptions of species grouped by genera. The family is indicated for each genus, followed by common name (if any), place of origin (if a generalisation can be made about this for all species listed in that genus), and a general description of the genus. Entries at the species level give synonyms (if any), common name (if any), hardiness level and light requirements, and size and cultural information, and mention place of origin if different from others in the genus. Measurements and temperatures are indicated in metric units; tables at the back of the book provide metric-U.S. conversions.

Hardiness information is given for each plant. In general, the ranges of minimum temperatures for plants of varying degrees of hardiness are as follows:

hardy	tolerates −15°C (5°F) and below
frost-hardy	survives down to about −5°C (23°F)
half-hardy	survives down to 0°C (32°F)
semi-tender	damaged by temperatures below 5°C (41°F) unless protected
tender	must be overwintered indoors at 7°C (45°F) or higher, depending on provenance

The hardiness ratings I assign are based on my own experience in the British Isles. If you live in a temperate climate with hotter summers like the ones in much of the United States, you may find that the exotics you grow are hardier than I indicate. This may be due to the fact that the root mass grows larger during warmer summers and thus the plant is able to withstand cooler winter temperatures than it would were its root mass smaller.

I have deliberately avoided discussing the hardiness zones established by the U.S. Department of Agriculture (USDA) in the United States as I want to encourage you to push against boundaries, experiment with different care and maintenance regimes, and make the most of microclimates in your garden. Gardeners in a wide range of zones may be able to provide for an exotic plant's cultural requirements using any number of methods, the most extreme of which is overwintering indoors or under cover. Proving my point, it is interesting to note that a growing number of members of the Pacific Northwest Palm and Exotic Plant Society, based in British Columbia, live in USDA hardiness zones 5 (minimum temperatures −20° to −10°F or about −29°C to −23°C) and 7 (minimum temperatures 0° to 10°F or about −18°C to −12°C), with a few members having success even in zones 3 (minimum temperatures −40° to −30°F or about −40°C to −35°C) and 4 (minimum temperatures −30° to −20°F or about −35°C to −29°C)!

The best way to determine how cold your garden gets in winter is to purchase a "maximum-minimum" thermometer and place it in different parts of your garden, measuring the warmest and coldest spots, especially during the night. The warmest areas are invariably near the wall of a building. A south-facing wall will always be warmer than a north-facing one.

Many of the plants included in this encyclopedia are generally available at your local garden centre, and a good number can be found at specialist nurseries dealing in exotics (some of which deal in only one or two plant families; see "Where to Find Exotics" at the back of this book). Most specialist nurseries have a Web site where you can purchase plants online and have them delivered to your door, from locations all over the British Isles and the United States. Buying plants from abroad via the Internet is fairly easy, though comparatively expensive because of the often-hefty shipping costs and the necessity of purchasing a phytosanitary certificate so that they can legally enter the country. For those who aren't computerised, the annual *RHS*

Plant Finder is an essential book listing more than seventy thousand plants and where to buy them, a great source for those difficult-to-find must-haves. Finally, some plants you can only obtain through who you know. Making friends in the exotic world is a sure way to expand your exotic garden while at the same time adding like-minded people to your circle.

You should note that some exotic plants, like tree ferns, can be rather expensive acquisitions, as they have been transported from the Southern Hemisphere. They are also slow growing, taking many decades to get up to a reasonable height. Nevertheless, tree ferns are still worth every penny as they dramatically change the feel of the garden with their rugged trunks and delicate palmlike fronds. Some of the other plants mentioned in this book, such as eucalyptus, should be bought as small 45-cm whips, as they will soon overtake larger specimen plants and grow more rapidly, at a fraction of the cost.

If you want to know what other exoticists are growing in your country, it is a good idea to visit exotic gardening chat groups, boards, and forums on the Internet. In the British Isles there are several such cyberspace meeting places, such as the UK Oasis, where all types of exotic plants are discussed in great depth. In the United States there are likewise many forums dealing with exotic plants to a greater or lesser degree. You will find a list of such sites in the "References and Further Reading" section near the back of this book.

Aroids

Aroids (the common name for plants in the family Araceae) are among the most important plants to grow in the temperate exotic garden as they impart a truly tropical feel. This family includes some of the more unusual and bizarre plants from around the world. They can be exquisitely beautiful or ugly, depending on your point of view. The distinguishing feature of aroids is their inflorescence of tiny flowers blooming around the lower region of a fleshy column, known as the spadix, which is largely hidden by the frequently flamboyant, cowl-like spathe that surrounds it. The spathe may be very small, as in water lettuce (*Pistia*), or exceedingly large, as in *Amorphophallus titanum*, which can be even taller than a person.

This family of herbaceous monocots consists of 106 genera and approximately 3000 species, ranging from free-floating aquatics through terrestrial, climbing, and epiphytic species. Most appear in the New World tropics. Well-known examples include calla lily (*Zantedeschia*), cuckoo-pint (*Arum*), elephant's ear (*Colocasia* and *Alocasia*), skunk cabbage (*Lysichiton*), arrow arum (*Peltandra*), and the common houseplants dumb cane (*Dieffenbachia*), Swiss cheese plant (*Monstera deliciosa*), and flamingo flower (*Anthurium*).

They vary from the ridiculously tender to those hardy enough to grow in any temperate garden year-round. Some of the half-hardy varieties can be grown outside permanently in warmer locations with a thick mulch, while others can either be planted out for the frost-free months or grown in containers. Most will survive only under warm, moist greenhouse conditions, as they originate in tropical rainforests, but if you have a warm area in the garden with protection from desiccating winds, you can use members of the following tropical genera for summer bedding: *Alocasia, Anthurium, Caladium, Epipremnum, Monstera, Philodendron, Spathiphyllum*, and *Syngonium*. There are many aroids worth trying in the garden and as container plants, of which this is only a small selection.

Left
Zantedeschia aethiopica

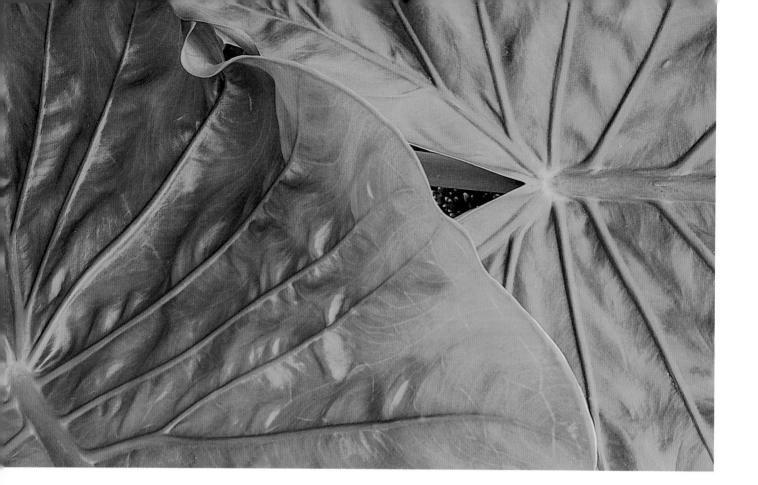

Alocasia
macrorrhiza,
leaf detail

Alocasia (Araceae)

Elephant's ear
Tropical Asia, Australia

There are seventy species of *Alocasia*, usually having glossy shield-shaped leaves that often dominate the areas they inhabit, whether in the wild or in the garden. Unfortunately they do not grow very well outside in a temperate climate, preferring constant humidity, with warm daytime and nighttime temperatures. Although some temperate areas can get hot days in summer, the nights are generally too cool for Alocasia; hence it is advisable to grow them as container plants under glass or to bring them out only for the summer months in warm, sheltered locations. If it becomes too cool, they go into dormancy, which can be difficult to break. If purchased as large plants from abroad, they will not retain their stature and tend to become smaller with age. For several years an *Alocasia macrorrhiza* specimen came into leaf in June on a compost heap in my garden and attained 46 cm in height before autumn, whereas in its native habitat it would grow to massive proportions.

The problem with low or freezing temperatures is that the rhizomes tend to rot, although they may take colder temperatures if kept dry. I would therefore suggest using *Alocasia* only as container plants that are brought under cover during the winter and kept at a minimum of 5°C or warmer. Many of the *Alocasia* species I describe here are listed in U.S. plant catalogues as hardy down to −14.9°C, but in the British Isles their hardiness is mostly borderline. The general consensus is that many of them grow much larger rootstock in the United States with its summers that are considerably warmer (hotter, even) and longer than in Britain with its relatively cool maritime climate. All require well-drained soil rich in organic matter and appreciate regular moisture and humidity.

Alocasia cucullata

Chinese taro, Chinese ape
Semi-tender to half-hardy / Sun or dappled shade

Tuberous clump-forming perennial with roundish green stems 60 cm long or more, with heart-shaped glossy midgreen leaves up to 30 cm long and 17 cm wide, though usually much smaller in cool-temperate climates. Forms a fairly compact plant. Reportedly takes low temperatures for short periods.

Alocasia gageana

Semi-tender to half-hardy / Sun or dappled shade

Tuberous perennial with shield-shaped bright green leaves with prominent veins and a pronounced wavy margin. Similar to but smaller than *A. macrorrhiza*, growing up to 1 m tall, reportedly taking fairly cold temperatures.

Alocasia macrorrhiza

Giant elephant's ear, giant taro
Semi-tender to half-hardy / Sun or dappled shade

Enormous alocasia that reaches 4–5 m tall, with green leaf blades that are bluntly triangular, 1–1.2 m long, in its native habitat. 'Variegata' is a slightly smaller variegated form. In cool-temperate climates, both are considerably smaller.

Alocasia odora

Semi-tender to half-hardy / Sun or dappled shade

Rhizomatous perennial, similar to *A. macrorrhiza*, with vertical 60-cm stems supporting upright or spreading large, green, waxy, crinkled, arrow-shaped leaves. Leaf blades up to 1 m in its natural habit but much less in cool-temperate climates. Grows fairly well as a container plant. 'Yunnan' is similar to *A. odora* but with blue-tinged stems and blue veins, coming from regions with reportedly cold, dry winters down to 0°C.

Alocasia 'Portodora'

Semi-tender to half-hardy / Sun or dappled shade

Robust rhizomatous perennial hybrid of *A. portei* and *A. odora*, with stout, erect, brownish stems to 1.5–1.8 m. Leaves are large, green, upright, deeply lobed, and glossy, with an ovate-sagittate form and prominent veins, in similar proportions to stems. Quite spectacular if grown well.

Alocasia macrorrhiza

Alocasia odora

Alocasia odora,
flower detail

Alocasia sanderiana

Tender / Dappled shade

Rather spectacular rhizomatous perennial growing up to 2 m tall in the wild, though more like 60 cm or less as a houseplant. Can be grown outside after all danger of frost has passed and the nights are warmer, doing best in warm summers. Leaves shield-shaped, pointed at the tip, highly glossy, very

*Alocasia
sanderiana*

dark rich green, with silver-white raised midrib and lateral veins, and with deeply lobed and silvery margins; underside is normally green, though in 'Gandavensis' is dark purple. Must be overwintered at a minimum of 10°C or higher. Requires a moist, shady position. This plant is really only for the adventurous!

Alocasia wentii

Semi-tender to half-hardy / Sun or dappled shade

Fairly fast-growing, tightly clumping, rhizomatous perennial with glossy green to bronzy green leaves that are said to attain more than 1 m in length, though usually much less in temperate climes. May also take cooler temperatures as it hails from mountains in a remote region of New Guinea.

Alocasia wentii

Amorphophallus (Araceae)

Tropical Asia, Africa

Ninety species of terrestrial herbaceous perennials that are predominantly tuberous plants belong to this genus. Their size and shape vary dramatically from species to species. The inflorescence is usually produced before the leaves and is described as either attractive or grotesque, but never less than extraordinary. Inflorescences vary considerably in shape, size, and colour and are composed of a spadix surrounded by a spathe that is pollinated by bees or flies. They produce odours that can be pleasant or repulsive, like rotting meat. The leaves are usually single and sometimes enormous, on exquisitely patterned stalks. *Amorphophallus titanum* is often described as the largest flower in the world, with a spadix reaching 3 m. (*Amorphophallus* literally means "misshapen phallus.")

Many make excellent seasonal foliage plants with a very exotic appearance for the greenhouse or conservatory or for summer bedding. Some are hardy enough to be grown permanently in the garden, where they should be planted at least 26 cm deep in spring and covered during the winter months when they are dormant with at least 16 cm of straw and then with polythene or similar material to keep the straw dry. If you grow them in a container, use a very free-draining mix with grit added and keep them bone dry in the winter or they will quickly succumb to rot.

British Victorians were fascinated by these strange and rather bizarre plants and often used them in their planting schemes, as spot plants in parks and gardens. Interest in them has recently been rekindled, with many growers in the United States such as Plant Delights Nursery of Raleigh, North Carolina, leading the way. Only a few are mentioned here, though there are many more worth trying.

Amorphophallus bulbifer

Tender / Dappled shade

Grey-green inflorescence with a distasteful odour, flushed pink with a pink spadix, appears in late spring up to 40 cm tall. Fleshy, heavily mottled

Amorphophallus bulbifer

Amorphophallus konjac habit and stem detail

stems up to 1 m high emerge in early summer, with a large solitary handlike leaf made up of numerous leaflets up to 1.5 m across. Sometimes will skip a year without producing foliage. Worth trying outside if planted deep, mulched well, and kept dry in winter; otherwise dig up and store in frost-free conditions.

Amorphophallus konjac

Tender / Dappled shade

Inflorescence the colour of raw liver, with a distasteful odour, can grow up to 70 cm tall in spring, followed by a leaf stalk up to 1.75 m tall, marbled green and dull purple-pink, randomly flecked with white spotting, topped by a single leaf consisting of leaflets spanning up to 2 m though usually less in temperate gardens. One of the easiest to grow outdoors if well mulched and kept dry in winter; otherwise can be used as summer bedding, brought inside when the foliage dies down, and stored dry. Tubers can become large with age, weighing up to 3 kg.

Amorphophallus napalensis

Tender / Dappled shade

Green inflorescence with a pale yellowy green spadix appears on a 46-cm stalk, followed by a solitary tan-and-black-marked 76-cm stem topped by a green palmate leaf.

Amorphophallus paeoniifolius

Elephant foot yam
Tender / Dappled shade

Grown in India for its tubers, which can weigh up to 10 kg and are eaten after boiling or roasting. Phallic inflorescence appears first and has a red-purple spathe that can grow up to 40 cm across, with a spongy dark purple spadix and a strong odour of carrion. Fleshy stem is marbled green, with a nodular surface, growing to 2.5 m tall. Enormous dark green leaf, of similar proportions, creates a large canopy. Makes an excellent conservatory plant, as it needs a lot of heat to grow to these palmlike proportions.

Anthurium (Araceae)

Flamingo flower
Tropical America and the West Indies

There are more than seven hundred species of *Anthurium*, ranging from evergreen perennials to climbers. Here we are dealing with the most commonly available species, *A. andreanum*, and its many forms.

Anthurium andreanum

Semi-tender / Dappled shade

Large, leathery, stiff, elliptical, lance-shaped leaves are usually held upright on stiff green stems. Stunning inflorescence is a shield-shaped spathe, normally bright red though there are many hybrid forms from green to pink, surrounding a perturbing spadix. Looks quite unreal, as though made of plastic! Aerial roots are often produced. Prefers humus-rich soil in dappled shade and tolerates cool summers well, though flowers more profusely in hot summers. Overwinter indoors or under glass at a minimum temperature of 5°C. Works particularly well outside in a moist, sheltered corner. Commonly available as specimens.

Arisaema (Araceae)

Mexico, North America, the Himalaya, China, and Japan

Plants in this genus of some 170 tuberous perennials are grown for their large, often bizarre, hooded spathes that usually enclose an erect pencil-shaped spadix, followed by spikes of fleshy red fruit in autumn before they die down. Arisaemas resemble carnivorous plants, but the flies and other insects they attract are required only as pollinators. They are becoming more popular, especially in the United States. All prefer moist, well-drained soil with added organic matter; they are half-hardy to fully hardy in part sun to dappled shade, though the more tender forms are best grown in dry shade. They should be planted deeply for winter protection and thereby fully protected from surface temperatures down to −15°C. The following is only a small selection of small- and large-leaved forms.

Arisaema candidissimum

Frost-hardy to hardy / Sun or dappled shade

Produces a very attractive, sweetly scented pale pink spathe, usually grey-green at the base and striped with translucent white vertical lines, growing up to 45 cm tall in late spring to early summer. A splendid solitary trifoliate, broadly ovate, green leathery leaf on a stem up to 80 cm tall emerges as the flower begins to fade and hides the flower completely as it withers. Prefers good drainage but adapts to most humus-rich soils, where it will produce offsets and create small colonies. Mulch deeply in winter.

Arisaema fargesii

Frost-hardy to hardy / Sun or dappled shade

Another spectacular arisaema that is both vigorous and easy, growing to 60 cm tall with large trifoliate leaves (similar to *A. candidissimum*). Form called 'Big Momma' has a leaf 90 cm across. The inflorescence appears at the same time and is wine red with dramatic white stripes. Mulch deeply in winter.

Arisaema flavum

Frost-hardy to hardy / Sun or dappled shade

Tuberous perennial growing up to 45 cm tall with two pedate green leaves divided into five to eleven oblong-lanceolate pointed leaves, topped by a small dull yellow inflorescence that appears in early summer and is 2–3.5 cm long and often held under the foliage. Forms colonies when mature. Mulch deeply in winter.

Arisaema griffithii

Cobra lily

Frost-hardy / Shade

Dramatic wide spathe 8–16 cm tall is deeply hooded, rolled, yellowish green, heavily patterned in liver-maroon colouring, with purple-black coiled spadix extending like a threadlike tongue, up to 60 cm long, from late spring to early summer. Flared spathe and protruding spadix look like a cobra about to strike, giving the plant its common name. Foliage is up to 50 cm tall, with two green stems heavily spotted black-green and leathery trifoliate leaves with purple-painted veins on the underside. Inflorescence and leaves appear at the same time. Grow in dry shade and mulch heavily in winter; otherwise can be grown in a container.

Arisaema griffithii

Arisaema sikokianum

Frost-hardy / Shade

Fleshy stalk grows to 30 cm tall in spring with two five-lobed palmate leaves, divided into five broadly ovate oblong-elliptic pointed leaflets. Inflorescence is a dark brownish purple spathe outside, with a snow white inner funnel containing a swollen club-headed spadix of pure white. Grow in dry shade and mulch deeply in winter.

Arisaema tortuosum

Frost-hardy / Shade

Grows to 1.5 m tall with a mottled stalk with two or three pedate leaves divided into five to seven leaflets, each 15–20 cm long. Inflorescence is carried above the foliage. Hooded green-to-maroon spathe, 10–18 cm long, appears from spring to early summer. Described as tortuous because of the extremely long, curling green or purple spadix that curves out of the mouth of the spathe tube and bends back and upward, tapering to a fine tip, like the tail of a thin snake. Grow in dry shade and mulch deeply in winter.

Arisaema tortuosum with spathe tube and spadix

Arum italicum
'Marmoratum'

Arum (Araceae)

Cuckoo-pint, lords-and-ladies
Mediterranean region, eastern Europe, and Turkey,
 with one species native to the British Isles

This genus contains twenty-five species of tuber-ous perennials commonly called cuckoo-pint and lords-and-ladies, although the native species has acquired more popular names than almost any other in the British Isles. These plants are grown for their ornamental leaves, striking spathes, and unusual appearance. Curiously, they exhibit ther-mogenesis, generating heat in cold weather to dis-perse volatile oils and thus attract pollinating flies. All species are fully hardy to half-hardy in a dry winter situation and require sun to partial shade in moist, well-drained, humus-rich soil, mostly prefer-ring a high pH.

Arum creticum

Frost-hardy / Full sun

Tuberous perennial with dark green leaves up to 26 cm long appearing in early autumn on 35-cm stems. The pleasantly musky-sweet scented inflores-cence appears above the foliage in spring. The yel-low spathe (occasionally cream) is up to 35 cm long. As it ages the tip of the spathe becomes backswept,

revealing the prominent orange spadix. Requires full sun to grow well in very well-drained gritty soil.

Arum italicum

Hardy / Dappled to full shade

Most commonly cultivated arum in temperate gardens, very hardy and exotic, especially when in fruit, making an excellent plant for the winter gar-den. The sagittate leaves, up to 35 cm long, green or variegated with pale yellow-green veins, emerge in late winter and remain until late spring, when they die down. In late summer the green fruit ripen to a bright orange-red and last for several months. Pale green-white spathe contains a dull yellow to brown-ish spadix to 30 cm long that is almost insignificant compared to the stunning leaves. 'Marmoratum' has conspicuous cream veining; several other fine cultivars are available as well.

Arum maculatum

Hardy / Dappled to full shade

Arrow-shaped leaves up to 26 cm long by 19 cm wide appear from late winter to early spring. Long, pale green spathe is often purple-tinted with a darker edge. A purple spadix appears in late winter followed by spikes of green fruit that turn red in summer.

Arum purpureospathum

Half-hardy to frost-hardy / Sun or dappled shade

Arum with the longest name and the most intense colour; most recent addition to the genus, becoming the twenty-fifth species known upon its discovery on Crete in 1983 by my old pal Vaughan Fleming. Midgreen, sagittate leaf with fine purple edge, 14–22 cm long by 11–17 cm wide. Spathe 22–30 cm long, very deep dark purple until caught by sunlight from behind, at which time it blazes an electric red-purple. Will thrive in a protected corner of the garden if well mulched and is well worthwhile for its exceptional qualities.

Caladium (Araceae)

Tropical America

Members of this genus of seven species of deciduous, tuberous perennials are grown for their stunning variegated leaves, splashed with a kaleidoscope of bright colours. Most varieties are derived from *Caladium bicolor*. They are naturals in beds with ferns or coleus or in pots to accent shady spots. Being tropical plants, they don't like temperatures much below 15°C, hence tend to perform better in hot summers or warmer parts of the world; otherwise treat them as container plants that can be brought under cover when the nights become too cool for them. They prefer humus-rich, moist soil. When the leaves start to die down in autumn, dry out and store the tubers at a minimum of 12.5°C.

Caladium bicolor

syn. *C. hortulanum*
Angel wings, elephant's ear
Tender / Sun or shade

Grows to 60 cm high by 30 cm wide in ideal conditions, though usually less in cool-temperate cultivation. Varieties available include 'Carolyn Whorton', which has a large upright habit and leaves with pink blotches, red veining, and green mottling, and which tolerates sunny conditions well; 'Florida Cardinal', medium-sized plant and leaves edged with grey-green and with a bright red blotch in the middle;

Caladium bicolor 'Carolyn Whorton'

Caladium bicolor 'White Christmas'

'Rosebud', leaves with pink in the middle and following the veins, surrounded by white and then a green edge; 'White Christmas', leaves white with green veining.

Colocasia (Araceae)

Elephant's ear
Tropical Asia (probably India)

Six species of tuberous perennials belong to this genus. *Colocasia esculenta* has been grown in tropical and subtropical Asia for around seven thousand years and is one of the oldest cultivated crops in the world, now no longer found in the wild. If consumed uncooked, the tubers cause discomfort because of the thousands of microscopic needles within; therefore, they need to be thoroughly cooked before eating. Cultivated forms fall into two categories: the eddo type, *C. esculenta* var. *antiquorum* (syn. *C. antiquorum* var. *globulifera*), which have a small main corm surrounded by relatively large and numerous cormlets, and the dasheen or taro type, *C. esculenta* var. *esculenta*, with a large corm, up to 30 cm long and 15 cm in diameter, and a few

Colocasia esculenta 'Mammoth'

smaller cormlets. Despite the large number of varieties, most forms of *C. esculenta* are similar in general appearance. More unusual varieties can be bought from specialist nurseries, while the more common edible forms are available very cheaply from Asian food shops.

All become dormant in winter when the temperature remains lower than 7°C and will usually defoliate. The taro types are less sensitive to cooler temperatures. In cultivation the genus is generally water loving, though the eddo types are more tolerant of drought. They prefer free-draining compost containing peat moss or similar with added bark to keep the mixture open. Keep moist during the growing season. For the biggest leaves, feed regularly with a nitrogenous fertiliser or mulch with well-rotted manure.

Colocasia affinis var. *jeningsii*

Dwarf elephant's ear
Tender / Sun or dappled shade

Small tuberous rooted perennial that grows in dense clumps to 46 cm tall, native to the tropical eastern Himalaya. Leaves are rounded, pointed at the tip,

and velvety in texture, with grey-green colouration and a distinct light silvery blotch in the middle that follows the dark veining to the edges of the leaf. Glaucous underneath.

Colocasia esculenta var. antiquorum 'Illustris'

Black leaf illustris, Egyptian taro, imperial taro
Tender / Sun or dappled shade

Emerges in late spring when grown in the ground, reaching 1.5–1.8 m tall, though smaller in maritime climes. Upright stems are pale green with brown markings. Leaves are rich apple green with large dull blackish emerald green blotching between the veins, looking very spectacular.

Colocasia esculenta 'Black Magic'

Black leaf elephant's ear
Tender / Sun or dappled shade

Much-praised tuberous perennial that grows on dark maroon stems, 1.5–1.8 m, with similar spread in ideal conditions, though usually much less in cool-summer gardens. Dramatic leaves are heart-shaped with a pointed tip, solid matte grey-black, and up to 60 cm long. 'Black Ruffles' is a sport of 'Black Magic' growing to 1.2–1.8 m with similar leaves that are distinctly wavy along the edges. Considered difficult to overwinter in cooler climates.

Colocasia esculenta 'Black Runner'

Black runner elephant's ear
Tender / Sun or dappled shade

Introduced in the early 2000s, 'Black Runner' is a mutation of 'Black Magic' with leaves that are more of a black-purple and leaf edges that are much more ruffled. Growing to around 1.8 m tall, clumping, with leaves up to 60 cm long, it produces long runners that readily root in moist soil, creating new plantlets.

Colocasia esculenta 'Black Magic'

Colocasia esculenta 'Chicago Harlequin', stem detail

Colocasia esculenta 'Chicago Harlequin'

Tender / Sun or dappled shade

Tuberous perennial growing to 1.5–1.8 m high, though usually less in cool-summer areas. Discovered by John Joicus of the Brookfield Zoo circa 1993 in a batch of normal *C. esculenta*, this stunning

Above

Colocasia esculenta
'Fontanesii'

Above right

Colocasia esculenta
'Mammoth'

colocasia has dark grey-green upright stems that are vertically striated with lighter shades of green to pale yellow. Large green typical leaves are blotched with random light green sections. Spreads by means of aboveground rhizomes, especially in moist areas.

Colocasia esculenta 'Elepaio'

Elepaio elephant's ear
Tender / Sun or dappled shade

A fairly short colocasia named after a Hawaiian fly-catching bird. Grows to around 1 m high with correspondingly smaller leaves. Green foliage is heavily spotted and patched with white flecks. Being an unstable chimera, it often has some leaves that are half green, half white, as a result of the variegated patterns.

Colocasia esculenta 'Fontanesii'

Black stem elephant's ear
Tender / Sun or dappled shade

Tuberous perennial that grows to 1.5–1.8 m tall, less in cooler areas. Stems are shiny purple-black, topped with large green heart-shaped, pointed leaves with a shiny black cast up to 1 m long. In late summer, the plant produces yellow aroid-type flowers to 30 cm long with a fragrance of papayas.

Colocasia esculenta 'Mammoth'

Tender / Sun or dappled shade

One of the largest colocasias for the garden. Large apple green leaves, frequently reaching 1 m long by 60 cm wide by late summer, sit atop thick pale yellowish green stems. In hot-summer climates this wonderful colocasia often reaches even bigger proportions. I have been growing this gem for many years, with plants regularly growing up to 2 m tall by late summer if ludicrously well fed and watered.

Colocasia esculenta 'Nancyana'

syn. *C. esculenta* 'Nancy's Revenge'
Tender / Sun or dappled shade

Introduced at the 2000 International Aroid Society meeting in Florida, this dazzling elephant's ear growing to 2.75 m became the most sought-after plant at the meeting. Discovered in the Caribbean, it was imported by Jerry Kranz, who later named the plant for his business partner, Nancy McDaniels of Florida. Leaves 60 cm long or more emerge pure light green and turn bright creamy yellow in a central blotch that radiates out along the veins. During the summer it sends out side stolons that root in moist soil; these can also be cut off and potted.

Colocasia esculenta 'Red Stem'

syn. *C. esculenta* 'Rhubarb', *C. esculenta* 'Burgundy Stem'

Tender / Sun or dappled shade

Tuberous-rooted perennial growing to 1.2 m tall on thin burgundy-coloured stems. Pointed, heart-shaped midgreen leaves have lighter veining. Like many colocasias, this form makes a good pond plant for the warmer months.

Colocasia esculenta 'Ruffles'

Colocasia esculenta 'Nancyana' and leaf detail

Colocasia esculenta 'Ruffles'

Tender / Sun or dappled shade

Spectacular form "discovered" by Hayes Jackson in a garden in Anniston, Alabama. Vigorously grow-ing, tightly packed, clump-forming plant growing to 1.8 m with pale stems carrying 1-m leaves, with regularly scalloped edges.

Colocasia fallax

Silver leaf elephant's ear

Frost-hardy / Dappled shade

Short, clump-forming colocasia that grows to 46 cm high, at home in Thailand and Vietnam. Leaves are rounded, medium green, velvety, and highlighted with a wide silvery streak down the centre vein and with smaller veins radiating to the leaf edge.

Colocasia fallax

Spreads fast in wet soil. Reportedly endures lows of −8°C if well protected.

Colocasia gigantea

Tender / Sun or dappled shade

Eaten in Japan, where it is called *hasuimo* (lotus potato) because of its leaf stalks, which are hollow like lotus roots. Also widely used as pig fodder in Asia. Perennial growing to 3 m in ideal conditions, much less in cooler climates, as it needs a hot summer. Resembles an alocasia as the leaves are held at right angles to the glaucous leaf stalks. Leaves are large, 60–76 cm long and about two-thirds as wide, silver-veined, and greyish green with distinct rippled edges. When the plants mature, the tip of the leaf arches downward and each leaf develops bizarre appendages on the underside.

Dieffenbachia (Araceae)

Dumb cane
Tropical America

Plants in this genus of about twenty-five species of evergreen highly ornamental perennials are grown for their colourfully patterned foliage. Although tropical, they perform well as long as nighttime temperatures stay above 7°C during the summer months. They prefer dappled shade and well-drained, moist soil that doesn't dry out. During the winter they should be kept at this temperature and preferably higher, and allowed to dry out between waterings.

Dieffenbachia seguine

Dumb cane
Tender / Dappled shade

Evergreen plant with a thick, fleshy stem and large green leaves with pointed tips, growing 1–1.8 m high with a spread of 45–60 cm in its native habitat but half this size when purchased as a houseplant. The many variegated cultivars include 'Camille', one of the best known, with creamy yellow leaves bordered in rich green; 'Rudolph Roehrs', with creamy yellow leaves with white spots and dark green veins

Dieffenbachia seguine

and margins; and 'Tropic Snow', with wide-spreading, dark green leaves blotched in creamy white along the veins, tolerant of lower light levels than most other dieffenbachias. Unfortunately, there is usually little selection at garden centres. These are very poisonous plants—avoid getting the sap in your mouth as it causes the tongue to swell, giving it its common name.

Dracunculus (Araceae)

Mediterranean region, northwest Africa

This genus contains three tuberous perennials that produce foetid-smelling spathes. *Dracunculus canariensis* is endemic to Madeira and the Canary Isles, *D. muscivorus* is found in Corsica, Sardinia, and the Balearic Islands, while *D. vulgaris* is found from Corsica to southern Turkey. The latter is the best, largest, and hardiest species for the exotic garden. All prefer well-drained, humus-rich soil.

Dracunculus vulgaris

Dragon arum
Frost-hardy / Full sun

Reminiscent of *Amorphophallus*, exuding the pungent stench of rotting meat, so plant away from kitchen windows or outside seating areas! In late winter pointed shoots appear from the large tubers that grow into stout mottled stems up to 1 m tall by spring. The two dark green pedate leaves have eleven to fifteen lanceolate segments to 20 cm long. The inner spathe is a deep, velvety maroon, ruffled at the edges and up to 45 cm long by 18 cm wide, containing a glossy, very dark purple-black spadix, much loved by flies. Can reach 1–1.5 m tall.

Epipremnum (Araceae)

syn. *Scindapsus*
Southeast Asia and the western Pacific

About fifteen species and numerous hybrids, all of which are evergreen, root-clinging climbers with juvenile and adult stages, belong to this genus. Most of the plants obtained from your local garden centre will invariably be juvenile and may be sold under their former name, *Scindapsus*. These exotic plants are grown for their attractive leaves and climbing habit.

Epipremnum aureum

syn. *Scindapsus aureus*
Golden pothos, devil's ivy
Tender / Dappled shade

Sturdy climber growing up to 12 m high in the wild though more like 1–3 m in cultivation. On juvenile plants, midgreen leaves are heart-shaped, bright, waxy, to about 12–20 cm long, variegated with irregular yellow or cream marbling. On large mature vines, the leaves become much larger at 30 cm or more long, with deep lobes. Trunks of tree ferns make a perfect support for this fabulous climber, which is somewhat suggestive of philodendron. Bring in when nighttime temperatures regularly drop below 7°c and overwinter at this temperature or higher. Many hybrids are available; for instance, 'Exotica' has dark green leaves mottled silver, 'Marble Queen' has mostly white leaves randomly streaked with cream, yellow, and green, and 'Tricolor' has off-white stems and green leaves variegated white.

Lysichiton (Araceae)

Skunk cabbage
Northeastern Asia, western North America

Lysichiton is a genus of two species of vigorous marginal aquatics, grown as herbaceous perennials for their attractive inflorescences and foliage. As for all Araceae, the flowers appear first. The two species are easily identified by the colour of their spathes, but there is also an intermediate cream-coloured hybrid between the two species. *Lysichiton* is commonly called skunk cabbage because of the heavy musky scent it produces to attract pollinating insects in spring. Both are very exotic, dramatic, tropical-looking plants that are suited to pond margins or bog gardens in sun or dappled shade. They can also

Left

Lysichiton americanus

Right and below

Monstera deliciosa

be grown in large containers if the soil is kept muddy at all times. *Lysichiton americanus* is the best known of the two species.

Lysichiton americanus

Skunk cabbage

Hardy / Sun or dappled shade

Marginal, aquatic, clump-forming perennial, growing to 1 m tall and 1.2 m wide, with rosettes of ovate-oblong, strongly veined, leathery, glossy, midgreen to dark green leaves, 50–120 cm long. Ovate to narrowly ovate bright yellow spathes, up to 40 cm long (with a very odd foxy odour) are borne in early spring before the leaves appear.

Lysichiton camtschatcensis

White skunk cabbage

Hardy / Sun or dappled shade

Marginal, aquatic, clump-forming perennial, growing to a height and spread of 0.75 m, with rosettes of ovate-oblong, veined, leathery, glossy, midgreen to dark green leaves 50–100 cm long. In early spring, produces ovate to broadly lance-shaped, usually pointed, white spathes up to 40 cm long.

Monstera (Araceae)

Central and South America

Members of this genus of twenty-two species of evergreen climbing and epiphytic tropical plants are usually grown as medium to large houseplants. The leaves often have large holes or slits in them. They are exceedingly tropical looking plants and grow well in our cool-summer climates.

Monstera deliciosa

Swiss cheese plant

Tender / Full shade

Ridiculously exotic scrambling climber, growing to 15 m high by 6 m wide and more in the wild, often growing up the trunks of trees. Leaves can get up to 1 m long, though more like 20–30 cm in temperate gardens. In the wild produces delicious, edible, cone-shaped fruit. Considered exceedingly tender, grows well in the garden during the summer months in a cool-summer climate. Because they are comparatively cheap, it is possible to have a thicket of them on the ground or tied to the side of a tree fern. Plant out in late spring, after the last frosts have passed. Prefers moist, humus-rich soil in a shady position, where it will romp away. Tolerates cool nights well and takes temperatures near freez-

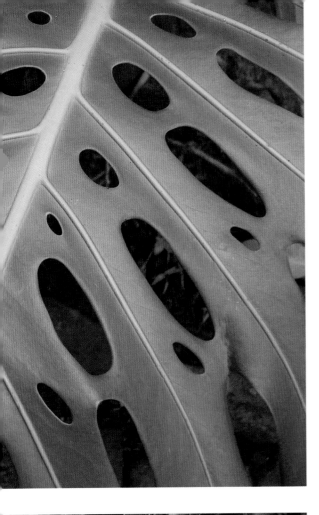

ing for short periods but must be brought back into frost-free conditions for the winter or reused as a houseplant. Overwinter at a minimum of 5°C.

Philodendron (Araceae)

West Indies and tropical America

Members of this genus of about five hundred species are climbing and twining plants, often epiphytic, with prominent aerial roots. Many have a juvenile phase, with leaves that are quite dissimilar to those on mature plants. Potted plants are often at this stage of growth. They have arrow- to heart-shaped leaves that are frequently thick, leathery, and dark glossy green, with some hybrids bronzy purple. Often as houseplants they are grown on moss poles with their aerial roots growing into the moss. The large leaves are redolent of the tropics and add great impact to the temperate exotic garden. I have not mentioned any specific plants here as you are generally limited to the species or cultivars commercially available at your local houseplant retailer.

They are best grown outside in a sheltered corner of the garden that can be kept moist at all times and will benefit from being sprayed with water daily, to raise the humidity around the plant. They prefer humus-rich soil in dappled shade out of direct sunlight. They must be brought inside well before frosts begin and stored over the winter at a minimum of 10°C, kept on the dry side.

Remusatia (Araceae)

Tropical Africa and from Indian state of Himachal Pradesh through the Himalaya to Taiwan

Members of this genus of four species of tuberous ground-growing to epiphytic plants are found at an altitude of 1000–2500 m in subtropical forests, often on moss-covered rocks or in crevices. They have heart-shaped peltate leaves, somewhat similar to *Colocasia esculenta*. Both the following are marginally hardy, so should be thickly mulched in autumn or dug up and stored frost-free during the winter months. Grow in moist, well-drained, humus-rich soil.

Remusatia pumila

Tender to half-hardy / Dappled shade

Leaves emerge grey-green with silvery veining that turns a darker green with age, sometimes attractively blotched with purple. Inflorescence consists of a golden yellow spathe to 20 cm long surrounding a purple spadix and appears under the foliage. Occasionally epiphytic in its natural habitat but grows well in humus-rich soil.

Remusatia vivipara

Tender to half-hardy / Dappled shade

Usually epiphytic in the wild, though it grows well in humus-rich soil with plenty of organic matter. In late spring the usually solitary glossy green leaf appears, reaching 60–92 cm long. When the tuber is mature a solitary inflorescence is occasionally produced after dormancy. In late summer, stolons (aerial shoots) are produced that arise from the tuber. These grow erect, spreading or hanging to 25 cm long, and produce clusters of hooked tubercles (bulbils), which can be propagated.

Sauromatum (Araceae)

Voodoo lily, monarch of the east
Indian Himalaya, eastern and western Africa

Plants in this genus of two species of spring-flowering tuberous perennials, found growing in woodland areas and on shady cliffs in their native range, will flower without soil and before the leaves appear. The most commonly grown is *Sauromatum venosum*, which is often sold as a windowsill oddity, though it must be planted to produce leaves. It can be grown either as a container plant or permanently planted in the garden, where it will bulk up readily, forming a colony with time.

Sauromatum venosum

syn. *S. guttatum*

Half-hardy to frost-hardy / Sun or dappled shade

Inflorescence, 30 cm tall, precedes foliage in spring, in the form of a large spathe that is brownish green on the outside and cream, heavily spotted purple-brown, on the inside, with a central, long, tapering, pale brown spadix, the whole giving off an acrid smell of rotting meat, which attracts flies and other insects for pollination. Inflorescence lasts only a few days, followed by a large, handsome, lobed green leaf up to 46 cm and more across, on a green and black mottled stalk 30–46 cm tall. Hardy to −5°C and lower if mulched during the winter months. If you are unsure, dig up in autumn after the leaves have died down and store dry. The tubers can become quite large and produce many offsets, which can then be propagated. Grow sheltered from wind in moist, humus-rich, well-drained soil that stays dry in winter. Grows well in containers, requiring free-draining, gritty compost.

Plant Delights Nursery in Raleigh, North Carolina, United States, stocks 'Indian Giant', similar to the typical species except that the tropical-looking leaves are about twice as large, reportedly growing to a staggering 1.2 m across, on a tall stalk that is dusty light green, with fewer but much larger black patches, hence much more dramatic than the typical form; so far, it has proven equally hardy.

Spathiphyllum (Araceae)

Tropical North, Central, and South America, the Caribbean, Indonesia, and the Philippines

Tender / Dappled shade

Spathiphyllum is a genus of about forty species of rhizomatous evergreen perennials mostly found growing in moist tropical forests. In cultivation they are grown for their majestic, long-stemmed white spathes, which contrast well with their alluring dark green foliage. They are popular as houseplants because they adapt well to different conditions; you can easily obtain them in garden centres and supermarkets, where they are invariably labelled only with the genus name. Although considered delicate,

Sauromatum venosum

they grow surprisingly well if planted out during the warmest months of the year in a moist, shaded position and protected from desiccating wind.

Syngonium (Araceae)

Central and South America

This genus includes some thirty species of evergreen root-climbers native to tropical woodlands, grown for their lush foliage. Though tender, they take cool summers well if grown in a humid, moist, shady corner of the garden protected from sun and desiccating wind. They can also be used as ground cover.

Syngonium podophylla

Tender / Dappled shade

Most commonly available species, with many hybrids. Sparsely branched climber that can be trailing and rather floppy in habit. Leaves are dark green with pale greyish green markings radiating from the veins, heart-shaped when juvenile and becoming more arrow-shaped when mature, up to about 30 cm long, though usually less in cool-summer climates. 'Variegatum' has green leaves splashed creamy white.

Xanthosoma (Araceae)

Cocoyam, elephant's ear, malanga ape, tannia, yautia
Tropical America

This genus of about fifty species of rhizomatous or tuberous rooted perennials, some cultivated for their edible stems, tubers, and leaves, is closely related to *Caladium* and *Colocasia*. *Xanthosoma sagittifolium* has become a staple food in many areas of the tropics and is the second most important food crop after *Colocasia*. Although tropical in nature, a few can be bedded out for the summer months or used as container specimens. They need humus-rich, moist soil.

Xanthosoma nigrum

syn. *X. violaceum*
Tender / Dappled shade

Grows to 1.5–2.5 m tall in ideal conditions and around 1 m tall in cooler climates. Slightly rolled leaves emerge faintly tinged with lavender-purple and age to bluish green on stems that have a glaucous, lavender-purple bloom.

Xanthosoma sagittifolium

Half-hardy / Sun or dappled shade

Rhizomatous perennial growing to 2 m tall or more, though only half that in cool-summer climates. Fleshy stems to 1 m with glaucous leaves, broadly ovate, sagittate, to 1 m, with attractively prominent veining underneath. Spathe greenish white, 25 cm

Xanthosoma sagittifolium

long, with a white spadix. Becomes dormant below 7°C. Reportedly hardy down to −14.9°C in the United States though of doubtful hardiness in the British Isles. A fine plant for summer bedding and as a container plant brought into frost-free conditions over the winter.

Zantedeschia (Araceae)

Arum lily, calla lily
Southern Africa

This genus contains six species of summer-flowering tuberous perennials that are usually evergreen in warmer climates and are very popular garden plants. Formerly classified in the genus named *Calla* by Carl Linnaeus and still commonly called arum lilies or calla lilies, zantedeschias are neither arum (genus *Arum*), calla (genus *Calla*), nor lily (genus *Lilium*, family Liliaceae). The genus *Zantedeschia* is named after Francesco Zantedeschi, an Italian botanist born in 1797. The leaves of zantedeschias are evenly green or speckled and spear-shaped. The flowers are funnel-shaped with a spadix. Zantedeschias are semi-tender to frost-hardy and make excellent container plants.

Zantedeschia aethiopica

Frost-hardy / Sun or dappled shade

Rhizomatous perennial growing up to 1 m tall and with a 35–45 cm spread. Lush and lustrous dark green leaves are arrow-shaped. Inflorescence appears in spring and on into summer, with the odd flower at any time. In the wild it forms colonies in marshy areas. 'Crowborough' is identical to the type but with greater hardiness in cooler temperatures. 'Green Goddess' is a robust form bearing a succession of green spathes, each with a large radiating central splash of white; it grows up to 1 m tall.

Zantedeschia elliottiana

Golden arum lily
Frost-hardy / Sun or dappled shade

Tuberous plant reaching a height of 60 cm–1 m with semi-erect basal leaves with random, conspicuous transparent markings. Although considered half-hardy in England, they have overwintered without protection in my Norwich garden for more than a decade with lows of −8°C (though they do not always flower).

Zantedeschia hybrid cultivars

Half-hardy to frost-hardy / Sun or dappled shade

A large range of zantedeschias, referred to in the trade as callas, in a dazzling array of exciting colours, add greatly to the exotic garden. Many new hybrids, created through crossing many of the smaller species, are coming onto the market and are worth trying. Generally compact with white-spotted leaves, sturdy stems, and showy flowers, these are bestowed with some of the following evocative names: 'Cameo' (peachy yellow petals with a dark purple throat), 'Crystal Blush' (the white spathe acquires a slight pinkish blush once the pollen is shed), 'Firebird' (orange with golden tones), 'Flame' (beginning yellow with red and then turning flame red in maturity), and 'Garnet Glow' (bright hot pink blooms with a slightly darker eye). Planted in groups, they make excellent container plants. Mulch in winter.

Zantedeschia aethiopica
'Green Goddess'

Below left

Zantedeschia 'Flame'

Below

Zantedeschia hybrid

Bamboos

Bamboos are mysterious plants that have always been thought of as quintessentially Asian in nature, evoking raked pebble gardens, temples, and stone lanterns. Today, though, they have become very popular in Western gardens, either to create an Asian style or to change the feel of the garden with tall, waving stems that give stature and volume. They are also perfect for adding a tropical, lush effect to the exotic garden, and they look good throughout the year whatever the weather throws at them. With their beauty, style, and gentle movement, bamboos give a soothing, harmonious, and tranquil dimension to any garden, from the smallest to the largest.

For many years bamboo was thought to be a primitive grass, but recent DNA testing has shown it to be one of the most highly evolved forest grasses. There are more than twelve hundred forms of bamboo in a broad range of colours, from the familiar green and gold to burgundy, blue, black, and various striped combinations. Some tropical bamboos can grow up to 30 cm a day and ultimately reach a staggering 40 m tall, while the smallest cultivar attains a height of only 15 cm.

Bamboo has more than fifteen hundred documented uses, ranging from flooring to acupuncture needles and from agricultural fodder to musical instruments. In India bamboo plants are commonly called "the wood of the poor" and in China "the friend of the people." Bamboo is a symbol of long life, strength, and versatility in many cultures of the world. Unravelling its mysteries is a continuing source of enjoyment. When you know how to grow bamboo, you'll find that your love for the plant grows as fast as the plant does!

Unluckily for bamboo, it has a reputation for being an invasive plant, growing from running rhizomes. Although this is true for some cultivars, the most cold-hardy plants don't run at all but grow from well-behaved clumps with well-established root systems. For the invasive forms, it is advisable to sink a barrier around them that goes down into the soil at least 46 cm to prevent the inevitable invasion of your and your neighbour's garden, lawn, and greenhouse! Or better still, buy the right plant for the right place: if you have a large enough garden, bamboo can romp away to its heart's content, creating groves of beautiful culms with luxuriant foliage that gently sways in the breeze, where you can cut secret pathways. (Until they are cut, bamboo stems are properly called culms and not canes.)

Two considerations in growing bamboo successfully are air and water. All true bamboos are grasses and won't grow in saturated soils. They also need air circulation.

Most of the information in this section was supplied by Paul Whittaker, owner of PW Plants, a nursery in Kenninghall, Norfolk, where his collection of bamboos has been rigorously tested over the years. He is the author of the ultimate reference book, *Hardy Bamboos: Taming the Dragon* (2005).

Borinda albocerea,
stem detail

species identified, only three are available, in speciality nurseries: *B. albocerea*, *B. boliana*, and *B. fungosa*. (This number may soon be out of date, as some new species are on the way, although much of this genus is still confused with *Fargesia*.) Of these, *B. albocerea* is the most gardenworthy. All borindas appreciate well-drained soil in a sheltered situation.

Borinda albocerea

Frost-hardy / Dappled shade

A tidy, clump-forming bamboo, lax in youth but gracefully arching when mature, reaching 3–4.5 m tall and 0.8–1.5 m wide in ten years. Culms reach a maximum diameter of 2 cm and are sky blue when young, maturing to yellow. Leaves are small to medium, narrow, willowlike, and 15 cm long by 1 cm wide. Although new culms are produced in profusion, they often rot in adverse conditions; however, if given time and a sheltered location, *B. albocerea* should be a very gardenworthy bamboo. Hardy to −13°C.

Chimonobambusa (Poaceae)

Southern and eastern Asia

This genus contains about forty species of bamboo with running rhizomes, typically found growing in deciduous woodlands and on cool forest floors at elevations not exceeding 1600 m. They are small to medium bamboos, often bushy and dense, with a strong running habit, making them excellent candidates for hedges and screening. You can allow them to wander if you have the space. They prefer fertile, humus-rich, moist, well-drained soil, preferably in dappled shade and sheltered from cold, drying winds. They can take drier conditions once established.

Borinda (Poaceae)

Yunnan Province, China; Nepal

The hardiest borindas are often deciduous in their native habitats; hence there is no need to be alarmed if they lose their leaves, as fresh new growth returns quickly in spring. Out of more than a dozen

Chimonobambusa quadrangularis

syn. *Arundinaria quadrangularis*

Shiho-chiku, shikakudake, square-stemmed bamboo

Hardy / Dappled shade

Vigorous, spreading, rhizomatous bamboo, hailing from southeast China and Taiwan and naturalised in Japan, forming loose clumps with erect culms up to 9 m tall, averaging 4 m tall by 1–2 m across, with attractive, pendent, lance-shaped, dark green leaves up to 20 cm long, produced from prominent culm nodes. New culms are purple and become square in cross-section, especially at their base, producing culms 5 cm in diameter when mature. 'Suow', hardy to −11°C, grows to 2.5–6 m by 1–4 m in ten years, spreading slowly, with pale yellow culms randomly striped green up to 2.5 cm in diameter.

Chimonobambusa tumidissinoda

Chinese walking stick

Frost-hardy / Dappled shade

Vigorous, aggressively spreading bamboo (though very attractive), native to small areas in Yunnan Province, China, reaching 3–6 m tall and averaging 3.5 m by 3–10 m in ten years, with culms 3 cm in diameter. Narrow, willowlike foliage with dainty rich green leaves up to 10 cm long. New shoots appear in late spring, turning into arching culms.

Chimonobambusa tumidissinoda and stem detail

Saucerlike swollen nodes are very prominent on the culms; hence they are used in China for making walking sticks and tobacco pipes. Barriers do not seem to contain it, so be prepared to control its rampant spreading habit by cutting back the rhizomes. Hardy to −13°C.

Chusquea culeou
and stem detail

Chusquea (Poaceae)

Mexico to Chile

This genus of at least two hundred species of ever-green clump-forming bamboos naturally occurs in temperate, cloudy, high-rainfall upland regions, especially in Chile, up to 4270 m and down to sea level, though we are interested only in the mountain forms here. They differ from other bamboos in that they have solid pith-centred, rather than hollow, culms. Chusquea also have a unique branching system, forming multiple branch buds around the nodes. Chusquea leaf sheaths do not drop and are bristly with leaflike outgrowths that are known as auricles. Because many of these bamboos grow at high elevations in cloud forest, they are used to fairly cool, moist conditions, although many will take drought, but only for short periods if lush plants are desired. They prefer humus-rich, leafy, moist but well-drained soil in sun to partial shade, sheltered from cold, dry winds. They are excellent bamboos for woodland gardens or as solitary specimens if you have the room.

Chusquea culeou

Hardy / Sun or dappled shade

Graceful, erect bamboo forming dense clumps of glossy, cylindrical, yellow to olive green culms 4.7–5 m, averaging 6 m by 1.5 m or more in ten years, with culms up to 3 cm in diameter. Clustered branches, 10–80 cm long, arise alternately and almost encircle the white-waxy nodes, and bear many midgreen linear leaves up to 7 cm long. As old leaves fall, branches and leaf stalks persist, giving a whiskered look to the lower culms. Takes drought well once established.

Chusquea gigantea

syn. *C. breviglumis*
Hardy / Sun or dappled shade

Outstanding truly giant bamboo with deep rhizomes; forms a slowly spreading grove of very upright olive green culms, 6–16 m in its native habitat, though more like 10 m in cool-summer climates, with a spread of 2–5 m in ten years, still making this

one of the thickest culmed bamboos that can be grown in temperate gardens. Central branches can be more than 1 m long. Leaves midgreen, up to 30 cm long by 1 cm wide.

Fargesia (Poaceae)

Central China to the northeastern Himalaya

These fairly compact, clump-forming bamboos are indigenous to damp upland wooded areas, mainly in Gansu and Sichuan provinces, China, at 900–4200 m, making them some of the hardiest bamboos available. They prefer moisture-retentive, moderately fertile soil.

Fargesia denudata

Hardy / Sun or dappled shade

Densely clump-forming, slightly weeping bamboo reaching 3–5 m tall and 0.75–1 m wide in ten years, with culms up to a maximum diameter of 1.5 cm. Mature culms ripen to a glorious, rich, burnished yellow in full sun. Leaves pale green, 5–1.5 cm, contrast beautifully with the yellow culms when planted singly or in groups. Hardy to −23°C.

Fargesia murielae

Fargesia murielae

Umbrella bamboo

Hardy / Sun or dappled shade

Grows at elevations up to 3000 m in its native habitat, Hubei Province, China. Dense, clump-forming bamboo growing to 4 m tall, averaging 3 m tall and 1.2 m wide in ten years, with graceful, billowing,

Fargesia robusta

Fargesia nitida

fountainlike growth. Culms white-powdery yellowish green, leaves bright apple green with tapering tips, up to 15 cm long, much loved by pandas. Deciduous leaf sheaths downy, greenish purple, becoming hairless and pale brown with age. Hardy to −29°c.

Fargesia nitida

Hardy / Light to half shade

Clump-forming, upright, squat, tidy bamboo growing to 3–4 m tall, averaging 3 m tall by 0.6–1 m wide in ten years. (Some forms and cultivars are flowering.) Culms dark purple to a maximum diameter of 1.5 cm. Leaves greyish green, short, and slim to about 5 by 1.5 cm. A very refined bamboo, with its mass of frothy, lightly arching foliage giving a highly graceful appearance. On all forms, the new culms remain leafless until their second year, rising

vertically through the existing foliage. Makes a fine specimen plant and can be used for screens and hedging as well. Because many cultivars and clonal variations exist, two plants in different gardens may be labelled *Fargesia nitida* but contrast greatly in their presentation. Hardy to −29°c.

Fargesia robusta

Hardy / Sun or dappled shade

Clump-forming, strong, upright habit, growing to 4–6 m tall, averaging 5 m tall by 0.75–1.5 m wide in ten years. New shoots hairy and rusty red upon emergence from the ground in early spring. Culms up to 2.5 cm in diameter, deep green with white culm sheathes and red branch sheaths; leaves dark green, long, and narrow, 2 cm by 13 cm. Excellent spot plant or for making narrow screens. Hardy to −18°c.

Fargesia rufa

Hardy / Sun or dappled shade

Broad, clump-forming bamboo growing to 2–3.5 m tall, averaging 2.5 m tall and 0.75–1.5 m wide after ten years, with orangish-red or dark shrimp-pink culms and branch sheaths. Culms up to 1 cm in diameter, with narrow, wavy, pale green leaves 8 cm by 0.75 cm. Arching, delicate appearance makes it a very useful bamboo for smaller gardens or court-yards. Hardy to −20°C.

Fargesia utilis

Hardy / Sun or dappled shade

Tight, clump-forming bamboo with a huge, cascading, fountainlike crown, reaching 4–6 m tall, averaging 4.5 m by 0.75–1.2 m. Pale green culms, up to a maximum of 2.5 cm in diameter, darken with age. Young plants are less congested, hence in the sun are glowing claret-red on the upper reaches. Persistent straw-coloured sheaths, leaves pale green, 9 cm by 1.5 cm. Because of its enormous crown, not suitable for small gardens and best used as a solitary bamboo that can be seen in all its glory. Old culms should be removed yearly to prevent congestion once established. Hardy to −18°C.

×Hibanobambusa (Poaceae)

A hybrid with characteristics of both *Phyllostachys* and *Sasa*, this is one of the most beautiful, versatile, and weather-tolerant bamboos. The genus includes one species and one cultivar.

×Hibanobambusa tranquillans 'Shiroshima'

Hardy / Sun or dappled shade

Bold, rounded, often flat-topped dense bush, with occasionally well-spaced culms to 2.5–5 m tall, averaging 3.5 m by 0.75–1.5 m in ten years. Culms pale green to a maximum diameter of 2 cm. Leaves pointed and brightly variegated, striped green and cream, giving a silvery effect from a distance; the brightest leaves of any variegated bamboo. Hardy to −22°C.

Himalayacalamus (Poaceae)

India and the Himalaya

This genus of fifteen species is native to the cool and relatively moist forests of the Himalaya. Most withstand maritime winters but will not tolerate dry air, making them difficult to maintain in drought conditions in summer gardens. They can be razed to the ground in excessively freezing winters but usually reappear in the following spring. Above all they need to be planted in a cool, moist part of the garden and protected from desiccating winds. They work well in cool coastal gardens with little winter frost.

Himalayacalamus falconeri 'Damarapa'

Candy cane bamboo, pink-striped bamboo
Frost-hardy / Sun or dappled shade

Beautiful clump-forming bamboo that is well worth trying, being the easiest of this less hardy genus, if given protection from other taller bamboos or shrubs. Culms striped in shades of cream, yellow, pink, and green, holding dense branches of

Himalayacalamus falconeri 'Damarapa', stem detail

bunched and layered feathery leaves. Paul Whittaker's 'Damarapa' rarely exceeds 1.5 m, so he has to stoop down low to see the culms under the leaf canopy but reckons it's well worth the potential backache! A specimen planted at the Portland, Oregon, Classical Chinese Garden in 1998 had grown to more than 6 m tall by 2005. Hardy to −9°C for short periods only.

Indocalamus (Poaceae)

China, Japan

This genus of twenty-six species has much promising hardiness, but unfortunately, only five species are obtainable from nurseries so far. Most grow at relatively low altitudes, with only one or two species found above 1000 m, occurring on low hillside slopes or as an understorey in broad-leaved forests. All *Indocalamus* species are classed as spreading, though they are more refined than *Sasa*, staying within bounds for many years. They have a very tropical appearance with their lusciously long leaves and grow well in temperate gardens as long as they have some shade from hot summer sun.

Indocalamus hamadae

Hardy / Dappled shade

Bold, erect, and slightly running, growing to 2–5 m tall, averaging 3 m tall and 0.75–1.5 m wide in ten years. Culms lustrous deep green to a maximum diameter of 1.5 cm. Leaves long (longest of any temperate bamboo) and narrow to 60 cm by 8 cm, hanging rigidly downward. Young plants take time to establish, often looking rather ragged for a while, but improve with age, especially if older culm branches and leaves are removed. Hardy to −20°C.

Indocalamus tessellatus

Hardy / Sun or shade

Usually short with a distinctive weeping habit, to 1–3 m tall, averaging 1.5 m by 0.75–1.5 m in ten years. Culms thin and matte green with thin brown sheaths, to a maximum diameter of 0.6 cm. Leaves very large, up to 45 cm by 8 cm, with pale creamy

yellow to green central vein on new growth, making this by far the best bamboo for an exotic tropical look in a cool garden. Also works well in containers as it is so cold tolerant. Hardy to −25°C.

Phyllostachys (Poaceae)

Eastern Asia

This is the most important genus for use in the exotic garden, containing more than eighty medium to large species with some of the best and most versatile ornamental bamboos available. They are also much used as commercial and cultivated crops worldwide. They are widely dispersed throughout the temperate and subtropical zones in eastern Asia, mostly from lowland areas in eastern China. The key identification feature of *Phyllostachys* is the indented sulcus or groove that runs longitudinally down each culm internode on alternate sides. Growth habits of individual phyllostachys vary widely, though all are arborescent, with mighty stature, good culm colour, and elegance in leaf and branch, as well as being evergreen. They are almost forestlike in their Chinese homeland, where there are hot summers and cold winters. In cooler temperate cultivation, with shorter summers, they are usually more restrained and better behaved, forming tight clumps.

Phyllostachys aureosulcata

Hardy / Sun or dappled shade

Evenly spreading bamboo, clump-forming in cooler areas, growing to 4–9 m tall, averaging 6 m tall and 1.2–3 m wide in ten years, vase-shaped when young, upright when mature. Culms matte green with soft yellow sulci to a maximum diameter of 4 cm in warm areas. Some culms kink randomly at about forty-five degrees before returning to the vertical. The long and narrow leaves are 17 cm by 1.5 cm and darker green than on most *Phyllostachys* species. Hardy to −26°c.

Phyllostachys aureosulcata f. aureocaulis

Hardy / Sun or dappled shade

Loosely clumping, fairly upright bamboo, growing to 4–7.5 m tall, averaging 5 m tall and 1.2–2 m wide in ten years. Culms golden yellow often tinted reddish brown on the sunny side of new growth, with a maximum diameter of 4 cm; occasionally zig-

Phyllostachys aureosulcata, stems

zag but not as much as others. Leaves fresh green, occasionally striped yellow, 17 cm by 1.5 cm. A very elegant bamboo that looks stupendous with its glowing yellow culms on grey days in winter. Hardy to −26°c.

Phyllostachys bambusoides

Hardy / Sun or dappled shade

Typical bamboo of Asian drawings, forming an open grove of stout culms with long rigid branches, looking very bold with foliage arching from the culm tips. Grows to height of 6–20 m, averaging 8 m by 1–4 m in ten years. Culms glossy green to a maximum diameter of 15 cm, though considerably

*Phyllostachys
bambusoides,
stems*

less in cool-summer climates; needs a long hot summer to grow to perfection. Leaves large for a *Phyllostachys*, particularly at branch tips and on juvenile plants, to 19 cm by 3.5 cm in a shade of lustrous green. Hardy to −18°C.

Phyllostachys bambusoides 'Allgold'

syn. *P. bambusoides* 'Holochrysa'

Hardy / Sun or dappled shade

Open, though clumping, bamboo growing to 4–9 m tall, averaging 6 m tall and 1–3 m wide in ten years, forming a V shape when juvenile, becoming more vertical with age. Culms translucent bright golden yellow, deeper golden orange in shade, with occasional faint striping, to a maximum of 6 cm in warm areas, less in cool areas. Leaves rich green,

occasionally finely striped, 15 cm by 3.5 cm. Excellent for brightening up dull areas, especially in light woodland with a dark backdrop. Hardy to −15°C.

Phyllostachys bambusoides 'Castillonis'

Hardy / Sun or dappled shade

Impressive, almost vertical bamboo growing to 4–10 m tall, averaging 6 m by 0.75–2 m in ten years, forming a slightly V-shaped plant. Only a few new

Phyllostachys
bambusoides
'Castillonis' and
detail of stems

culms are produced each year compared to most of the others and are bright golden yellow, with green grooves, to a maximum diameter of 6.5 cm in warm areas. Leaves pale green with some faint creamy striping, 15 cm by 3.5 cm, making this another impressive bamboo that looks excellent with a darker background to show off the attractive culms. Hardy to −15°C.

Phyllostachys bambusoides 'Castillonis Inversa'

Hardy / Sun or dappled shade

Imposing, stately, almost vertical bamboo that is generally open with well-spaced culms, though rarely invasive, growing to 4–10 m tall, averaging 6 m by 1–3 m in ten years. Culms deep dark green with deep yellow sulci, while the older culms become pale to soft green, to a maximum diameter of 6.5 cm in warm areas. Leaves green, to 18 cm by 3.5 cm. Branches are long and distribute the bowing weight of the foliage evenly. Hardy to −18°C.

Phyllostachys
bambusoides
'Castillonis
Inversa' and
stem detail

Phyllostachys dulcis, stem and new shoot

Phyllostachys dulcis

Hardy / Sun or dappled shade

Stately, architectural, mostly upright bamboo with some culms twisting and turning before becoming vertical, forming an open grove, to 6–12 m tall, averaging 8 m tall and 1.5–4 m wide in ten years. Culms matte green with white rings at the nodes, to a maximum diameter of 7 cm in warm areas. New culms curve outward toward the sun before resuming to the vertical and are often thick at the base. Leaves matte green and drooping, to 12 cm by 2 cm. Often grown in China for its tasty shoots early in the season. Hardy to −18°c.

Phyllostachys nigra

Hardy / Full sun

Usually tightly clump-forming and well behaved, forming a V shape or vertical, arching with age, growing to 4–12 m tall, averaging 6 m by 0.7–1.5 m in ten years. Culms green when juvenile, then mottling, aging to jet black, with a maximum diameter of 5 cm in warm areas, usually plentiful in production, with culm thickness varying according to height. Leaves small for *Phyllostachys*, green, to 8 cm by 13 cm, forming a dense canopy. Has become the most popular bamboo in recent years, though now rare in the wild. Hardy to −18°c.

Phyllostachys nigra, stems

Phyllostachys nigra 'Boryana', stem

Phyllostachys nigra 'Boryana'

Hardy / Sun or dappled shade

Clumps or runs, forming a tight grove to 5–15 m
tall, averaging 7 m by 1–4 m in ten years. Culms
green with dark brown blotching, to a maximum
diameter of 10 cm in warm areas though usually
much less. New culms emerge green, changing
toward the end of the season with brown or purplish black uneven spotting. Leaves green, to 9 cm
by 1.5 cm. Hardy to −18°c.

Phyllostachys nigra f. henonis

Hardy / Sun or dappled shade

Tidy, upright, open, clump-forming habit, to 6–20
m tall, averaging 8 m by 1.5–3.5 m in ten years.
Culms fresh green, turning pale yellow, to a maximum diameter of 10 cm though usually much less.
Leaves deep shiny green and matte bluish green on
the underside, small and massed, to 9 cm by 1.5 cm.
A beautiful and architectural bamboo that makes a
good screen. Capable of maturing to great size so
should be carefully positioned. Hardy to −26°c.

Phyllostachys vivax and stem detail

Phyllostachys vivax

Hardy / Full sun

Very upright, slowly spreading bamboo, growing to
6–20 m tall, averaging 8 m by 75 cm–2 m in ten
years. Produces shoots early in spring, growing dark,
lustrous, rich green culms with pale nodes. Older
culms pale with age, contrasting well with new ones.
Foliage and branches well spaced, with leaves up to
13 cm by 2.5 cm or more, elegantly arching from the
culms. In warmer climates, produces culms with a
maximum diameter of 13 cm. Originally obtained
as a division from a mature clump in the garden of
the renowned Peter Addington at Stream Cottage.
Hardy to −23°c.

*Phyllostachys
nigra* f. *henonis*,
stem

Phyllostachys vivax
f. aureocaulis

Hardy / Full sun

Described by Paul Whittaker as the eighth wonder of the world in his nursery catalogue. More vigorous than the species, slowly spreading, sometimes clumping, growing to 6–20 m tall but averaging 8 m tall and 1–3 m wide over ten years. Best colouration, with great ornamental appeal, is visible on the lower sections of the culms, being bright yellow with green stripes of random varying thickness around the circumference, to a maximum diameter of 13 cm in warm countries. Hardy to −21°C.

Sasa (Poaceae)

Korea, China, and Japan

This genus contains forty to fifty species of small to medium bamboos with running rhizomes, found growing in damp hollows and woodlands in their native habitats. They are mostly small, fast-spreading species, often with relatively large, broad, ribbed leaves and arching culms. They are very useful for giving a jungle effect, but beware—they can easily take over your garden if you turn your back! Hence it is advisable to put them in a position where they can run free, or contain them with a barrier (mine are surrounded by an impenetrable flint wall); or if you have little room, you can grow them in large containers. They are extremely cold-hardy, as their natural habitat extends further north than any other bamboo, to the Kuril and Sakhalin islands at an altitude of up to 2770 m. They prefer fertile, humus-rich, moist, well-drained soil, though take dry conditions as well, in full sun to deep shade.

Sasa kurilensis

Hardy / Sun or shade

Fast-growing, evenly spreading, invasive bamboo growing to 2–3 m tall and 1–4 m across in ten years. Slender culms curve out of the ground, turning sharply vertical, emerging green but soon turning pale olive-yellow, with a maximum diameter of 2 cm. Leaves medium to large, 20 cm by 5 cm, glossy,

Phyllostachys vivax f. *aureocaulis* and detail of stem

midgreen, held in palmate formation at the tops of the culms and branches. 'Shimofuri' is a beautiful, spreading, variegated clone that grows to 3 m tall in Paul Whittaker's Norfolk garden. It prefers to be grown in partial shade because the handsome, finely white-striped leaves are subject to burning in hot sun. The most northerly bamboo. Hardy to −30°C.

Sasa nipponica

Hardy / Sun or shade

Slowly running, spreading bamboo growing to 20–40 cm tall, averaging 30 cm by 1–3 m in ten years. Culms dark green with a maximum diameter of 0.5 cm. Leaves fresh green, narrow and thin, to 15 cm by 2 cm. Being one of the short species, it is ideal for use as a ground cover, looking especially attractive when the leaves become uniformly bleached around the edges in winter, giving it a variegated appearance. It is essential to mow or cut down the old growth before the new growth appears in spring. Hardy to −25°C. 'Nippon-Kisuji' has some yellow striping on the leaves, providing summer colour that is lacking in the species.

Sasa palmata f. nebulosa

Hardy / Sun or dappled shade

Growing to 1.5–3 m tall, averaging a spread of 1.5–6 m in ten years, forming an upright marching grove, eventually becoming invasive. Culms green, mottled brownish black, with a maximum diameter of 1.25 cm. Leaves very large, up to 30 cm by 10

cm, held up high on the culms and upper branches. Although this is one of the most invasive bamboos you can grow, it has a tropical appearance like no other temperate bamboo. If you are worried about it taking over your garden, try growing it in large containers and thinning out the older culms occasionally. Hardy to −30°C.

Sasa veitchii,
foliage and detail

Sasa veitchii

Hardy / Sun or dappled shade

Short, slowly running, colony-forming bamboo growing to 1–1.5 m tall, averaging 1.2 m by 1–4 m, having a highly ornamental appearance with its dark green leaves, to 25 cm by 6 cm, bleaching uniformly around the edges in winter. Culm purple when visible, to a maximum diameter of 0.6 cm. Most attractive when allowed to romp freely, forming a variegated undulating carpet. Very adaptable, growing in most soils, whether moist or dry. Very useful for stabilising banks and eroded areas. Also works well in large containers. Hardy to −25°c.

Semiarundinaria (Poaceae)

Japan, China, Korea, and Taiwan

This genus has only six species of plants, running in their native habitats but usually densely clump-forming in cooler climates. They are indigenous to deciduous woodlands, upland slopes, and ravines. They work well as woodland plants, specimens, or informal screens. They prefer moderately fertile, humus-rich, moist but well-drained soil in full sun to dappled shade. The very obvious culm sheaths of this genus stay attached to the new emerging culms slightly longer than on *Phyllostachys*. They are robust enough to be used as hedging and windbreaks.

Semiarundinaria fastuosa

Hardy / Full sun

Tall, stiffly vertical, stately bamboo forming a large grove with time, growing to a height of 6–10 m eventually and to an average of 7 m by 1–3 m in ten years. Culms midgreen, sometimes fading to purple with age, with pale cream sheaths. Older culms often fade with a patchwork of blotches and stains with subtle tints of red, buff, and purple. Leaves midgreen and narrow, to 15 cm by 4 cm. Fairly restrained in habit, tending to spread only in very warm areas. Grows well in gardens near the sea. Excellent for screening purposes. *Semiarundinaria fastuosa* var. *viridis* is by its very name a variety with viridian colouring. Culms are glaucous and dark green, maintaining this colour with age, with leaves that are slightly smaller and also deeper green. Hardy to −25°c.

Semiarundinaria fastuosa, stem

Semiarundinaria kagamiana

Hardy / Sun or dappled shade

Forms rigid colonies in an open grove of stout vertical culms with tight branches to a height of 5–10 m, averaging 6.5 m by 1–3 m in ten years. Culms turn a pale shade of red or purple in full sun, to a maximum diameter of 4 cm. Regular thinning is necessary on mature stands to prevent overcongestion, as it is capable of producing many culms annually. This is the bamboo of classical Japanese illustration. Although tolerant of shade, better grown where the colour can be seen. Hardy to −18°c.

Semiarundinaria yashadake

Hardy / Sun or dappled shade

Mostly clump-forming and usually vertical but bushy, to a height of 3–7.5 m, averaging 4 m by 1–2.5 m in ten years. Culms deep green, to a maximum diameter of 4 cm. Leaves dark green and glossy, to 14 cm by 1.25 cm. A very reliable bamboo, tolerant of a broad range of aspects, and at home in moist or dry soils, although it is more widely spreading in sandy soils. Hardy to −22°c.

*Semiarundinaria
fastuosa* var.
viridis

Thamnocalamus crassinodus 'Kew Beauty', new shoots and stem detail

Thamnocalamus (Poaceae)

Tibetan Himalaya, with one African species

This genus contains only a few species, found growing in broad-leaved and coniferous forests in Tibet at elevations above 2500 m, making them well suited to cool-temperate gardens. In warmer climates, they may require shelter from strong sun and desiccating winds. The culms are generally thicker than those of *Fargesia* and the nodes are more pronounced. The culm sheaths, which can remain attached for much of the growing season, are usually hairy. Culm sheath blades are erect and pointed, not curved backward as in other genera. Although perfectly hardy, young juvenile plants benefit from being given some protection from scathing winds and hot sun. They will mature quickly as a reward for this extra care.

Thamnocalamus crassinodus 'Kew Beauty'

Hardy / Dappled shade

An exceptionally attractive and graceful clump-forming bamboo with upright culms slightly arching at the tips, to a height of 3.5–5.5 m, averaging 4 m with a spread of 0.75–1.2 m in ten years. Culms pale sky blue and glaucous when young, with pink sheaths, fading to brownish red with red branches. Culms on mature plants take five to six weeks to reach their final height and then produce branches and leaves, with a maximum culm width of 2 cm. Green leaves are very small, 6 cm by 0.5 cm. Hardy to −15°C.

Thamnocalamus crassinodus 'Lang Tang'

Hardy / Dappled shade

Clump-forming and squat bamboo with an open V-shape, sometimes wider than high, growing to a height of 2.5–4.5 m, averaging 3.5 m by 0.75–1 m in ten years. Culms pale blue when young, becoming brighter with age, to a maximum diameter of 2 cm. Light green leaves are very small, to 6 cm by 0.5 cm. From a distance, the mass of leaves, which are usually the smallest of the species, create a froth

Thamnocalamus crassinodus 'Lang Tang' and stem detail

yellow with pink tints in good light, making a vivid contrast to the darker new culms. Leaves soft green, to 15 cm by 1.25 cm. A beautiful bamboo, if a little slow to establish. Foliage arches in layers from the long branches on immature plants, while older plants are more vertical. Hardy to −18°C.

Yushania (Poaceae)

China, Taiwan, India, and Africa

This is a large genus of many species of medium-sized mountain bamboos found mostly in the Chinese Himalaya at moderate to high altitudes, with some in Taiwan and India, and one nonhardy form in Africa. The culm structure is usually quite strong, with vertical branches that point upward tight to the culm, before arching under the weight of a normally luxuriant mass of foliage.

Yushania anceps

Hardy / Sun or dappled shade

Reasonably clump-forming bamboo with vertical culms and plumes of elegant weeping foliage to a height of 3–5 m, averaging 4 m by 1–3 m in ten years. Culms fresh green, to a maximum diameter of 2 cm. Leaves fresh green, long and narrow, to 13 cm by 1.25 cm. One of the first bamboos introduced into England, in 1865; subsequently widely planted and revered for its delicate-looking habit and speedy growth. Culms can arch dramatically at the tops of the bamboo, being pulled over by the mass of small leaves, creating a layered, plumelike effect that is very alluring. Hardy to −18°C.

Yushania maculata

Hardy / Sun or dappled shade

Open and slowly spreading with strong vertical culms and graceful arching foliage to a height of 3–5 m, averaging 3.5 m by 1–2.5 m in ten years. Young culms are bloomy bluish grey with the darkest of culm sheaths, varying in colour from rich red-purple to dusky dark brown. In the second year, culms lose their bloom and turn a dark shade of olive green, while sheaths pale to the colour of old

Thamnocalamus spathiflorus leaves

of tumbling pale greenery from a vigorous branching habit at the extremities of the culms. Hardy to −15°C.

Thamnocalamus spathiflorus

syn. *T. aristatus*
Hardy / Sun or dappled shade

Clump-forming bamboo with graceful arching culms to a height of 4–8 m, averaging 6 m by 0.75–1.5 m in ten years. Culms green, aging to soft

Yushania anceps
and stem detail

parchment. Leaves narrow and willowy, to 13 cm by 1.25 cm. A very suitable bamboo for windy gardens, staying fresh throughout the seasons. Hardy to −18°C.

Bananas and Their Relatives

Several tropical plant families are related to the Musaceae, or the banana family. All are contained within the order Zingiberales, which includes eight families of tropical and subtropical perennial plants, ranging from the diminutively small to the very large: the Cannaceae, Costaceae, Heliconiaceae, Lowiaceae, Marantaceae, Musaceae, Strelitziaceae, and Zingiberaceae. This section deals only with plants from the families Cannaceae, Musaceae, Strelitziaceae, and Zingiberaceae, as these contain the majority of the Zingiberales that can be grown in temperate gardens.

Bananas

The family Musaceae contains a very interesting and essential range of plants for the exotic garden, giving a very lush tropical feel, adding impact and stature. Banana plants are often referred to as trees, which they are not; in fact, they are the largest herbaceous plants in the world, differing from trees in one fundamental characteristic, that the pseudostem (or false trunk) does not contain woody tissue or lignin. The plant is a gigantic herb basically consisting of a pseudostem made up of leaf sheaths with an inflorescence pushing through the sheaths. Bananas are closely related to gingers and heliconias.

Much experimentation is being carried out by avid gardeners endeavoring to find out which bananas make gardenworthy plants on the edge of hardiness. Although bananas are usually thought of as ridiculously tender, several now available can be grown permanently in a temperate garden with little or no protection. These bananas usually come from mountainous areas at higher elevations where the nights are much colder. Also included here are some that are not hardy or are on the borderline of hardiness. These are nevertheless essential plants for a truly exotic feel and can easily be overwintered with minimal heat or in frost-free conditions. The hardier species can be grown as herbaceous perennials that are cut down to the ground each year. Alternatively, with adequate protection the soft trunks can be saved from freezing during the colder months. This method insures that they will grow on from the tops of the trunks, making a much larger plant the following summer.

It is advisable to grow bananas in the lee of a house or hedge, as most bananas shred very easily in wind. They perform to perfection when well fed and irrigated.

A general fertiliser should be used in spring to help boost them out of dormancy. An organic mulch spread around established plants in spring is also beneficial. Use compost or, preferably, well-rotted farmyard manure to a depth of approximately 15 cm.

Ensete (Musaceae)

India, Southeast Asia, and Africa

From the tropics of the Old World, ensetes have large leaves formed on a short trunk (pseudostem) made of overlapping leaf sheaths. These plants are monocarpic (dying once they have flowered), so new material has to be grown from seed. The ensete suckering situation is confusing, but essentially ensetes do not sucker unless the growing point dies or is damaged, whether deliberately or accidentally.

Ensete glaucum

Elephant hip banana, giant Nepal banana, snow banana

Semi-tender / Sun or dappled shade

Highly ornamental species with huge, glaucous, midgreen leaves that have a pale green midrib and appear like a shuttlecock on a long trunk. Grows in mountainous regions of China, India, Vietnam, and Thailand, where the large trunks are used for pig fodder, especially in Yunnan Province, China. Shows promise as a new introduction although its behaviour in cultivation in temperate regions as an ornamental is not yet known and much experimentation with its hardiness is taking place; it may be that different provenances will result in significantly different levels of cold hardiness. Worth trying if you have more than one plant and live in a virtually frost-free location; otherwise bring it inside before it gets too cold and store it over the winter at a minimum of 5°c.

Ensete superbum

Semi-tender (?) / Sun or dappled shade

New to cultivation, with hardiness unknown. In the wild in India, Burma, and Thailand, reaches 3–3.65 m high. Pseudostem 1.5–1.8 m tall with an enlarged base; leaves bright green. In the wild this plant dies down in the dry season and returns again in the wet season. Might be hardy to 0°c for short periods, but I would recommend storing it at a minimum of 6°c.

Ensete ventricosum

Abyssinian banana

Semi-tender / Sun or dappled shade

From central and eastern Africa, probably the biggest banana that can be grown in the garden. Produces massive paddlelike leaves up to 3 m long by 60 cm wide on mature specimens. Leaves bright green; with maturity sometimes has a red leaf stalk and central midrib. Grows very quickly from seed (fresh seed is essential) and will reach 1–1.8 m in the first season, especially if well fed with a high-nitrogen fertiliser. In the subsequent seasons it will become enormous, with a trunk up to 30 cm in diameter. Unless you have a tall greenhouse, you will need to take the drastic measure of removing all the leaves, including a section of the trunk if necessary, to a height that you can accommodate over the winter. Very tolerant of cold but not of freezing, so should be brought inside for the winter at a minimum of 5°c and kept on the dry side. Variable in nature as well as in cultivation, due partly to natural seedling variation but also to seed of difference provenances being offered commercially.

Ensete ventricosum 'Maurelii'

Red Abyssinian banana

Tender / Sun or dappled shade

Absolutely stunning, if not jaw dropping; much sought after; an almost essential addition to the exotic summer border. Grows to proportions similar to *E. ventricosum*. Base colour is green, suffused with shades of red to purple that are so deep that some parts can look almost black. Leaf edges and midribs are a shade of rich deep red, as is the trunk. Rarely blooms in temperate gardens. Hailing from Ethiopia and Angola, it requires slightly warmer winter temperatures than the species and must be kept dry in winter, as it tends to rot or get a condition commonly known as the strangles, where the central leaf stalk becomes twisted. When this happens the plant can be cut to the ground and kept dry; small pups will then appear around the base, which can be propagated by removing with a section of the base plate. Normally grown from micropropagated material.

Ensete ventricosum 'Montbeliardii'

Tender / Sun or dappled shade

Recent introduction to the British Isles by Koba-Koba Nursery in Somerset. Very elegant, sometimes mistaken for 'Maurelii' though it is quite distinct. Forms a much more stiffly upright plant with longer petioles (leaf stems) and large leaves that have more purple tones. A very gardenworthy banana that should be grown more often, though rarely offered in the trade.

Musa (Musaceae)

Southern and eastern Asia to Australia

The name of this genus of about sixty species is derived from *mauz*, *mouz*, or *moz*, the Arabic word for the fruiting parts of the plant, and also considered by Linnaeus to be a fitting tribute to Antonius Musa (63–14 BC), physician to the first Roman emperor. All edible bananas originate in whole or in part from *Musa acuminata*, which is native to the Malay Peninsula and adjacent regions. A triploid form of this species is considered to be the parent of the edible desert banana, and a hybrid with *M. balbisiana* gave rise to the plantain or cooking banana, *M. ×paradisiaca*. Musas are clump-forming plants that can be propagated by removing new shoots with a sharp knife from the parent plant with a piece of root attached or a section of the base plate.

Musa balbisiana

Semi-tender / Sun or dappled shade

Clump-forming in its natural habitat (Indomalaysia, the Philippines, Java, and China). Pseudostems green or yellowish green, robust, up to more than 6 m high, commonly at least 30 cm in diameter at the base. Leaf sheaths and petioles glaucous, sometimes heavily so. A recent introduction to the expanding number of bananas available; hence, little evidence for hardiness exists yet, though it could be tried outside with winter protection. If you live in a cold area, grow it as a container plant or bedded out for the summer.

Musa basjoo

Japanese fibre banana, Japanese root-hardy banana

Frost-hardy / Sun or dappled shade

Probably the hardiest of all bananas and the best known, hailing from the volcanic islands in the Ryukyu archipelago, formerly Chinese and now Japanese, stretching between southern Japan and northern Taiwan in the western Pacific Ocean. Although the common name Japanese fibre banana is applied to *Musa basjoo* and it was introduced to the British Isles from Japan, *M. basjoo* is not Japanese and it's not grown for fibre; it was introduced to Japan from China and has only ever been grown in Japan as an ornamental.

Excellent garden plant, with midgreen leaves with a pale green midrib growing about 2.5 cm a day in summer, reaching up to 1.8 m long or more, 0.5 m wide. Pseudostem can reach 2.7 m tall, making large plants up to 5.4 m high and 3.65 m across, with long arching leaves. Clump-forming/spread-

ing, multistemmed with time. With age each stem produces drooping pale yellow flowers with brownish bracts, followed by small green inedible fruit. Fruiting stems die after fruiting and are replaced by many new pups around the base. Stem takes several degrees of frost (with protection, −10°C and lower), though leaves tend to burn at −2°C. Trunk if killed will reshoot from the ground in spring, hence the name Japanese root-hardy banana. Grown from root division or micropropagation.

Musa (AAA Group) 'Dwarf Cavendish'

syn. *M. cavendishii*
Tender / Sun or dappled shade

Named after the family name of the Duke of Devonshire, whose gardener, Joseph Paxton, in 1836 managed to get this clone to flower in his greenhouse. The clone came from south China via Mauritius and was distributed from Britain all over the Empire. The French introduced a different clone to the Canaries and again disseminated it to their colonies. 'Dwarf Cavendish' is derived from *Musa acuminata* but it is not *M. acuminata*, which is a wild species. Many clones of 'Dwarf Cavendish' exist, some with brown markings on their leaves. Some clones flower at about 1.4 m, though up to 2.5 m is more usual. This readily available banana is often sold in garden centres and supermarkets as hardy, which it definitely is not! It works well planted out for the summer or grown in large containers that can be brought in for the winter months; otherwise grow in a conservatory at a minimum of 7°C, though for fruiting I would recommend more like 10–15°C.

Musa 'Rajapuri'

Half-hardy / Sun or dappled shade

Small plant (classified as a semidwarf), attaining a height of only 2.5 m. Heavier leaved and more like 'Dwarf Cavendish' in habit, with a white bloom on the trunk and underside of the leaves. Hardiest fruiting banana available, coming from high altitudes in India; could be tried in the ground permanently with winter protection, or alternatively as an attractive summer bedding plant or in a container. Thrives in cool summers and is easy to overwinter in a cool greenhouse. Has been used for a number of years as bedding by parks departments in the United States.

Musa sikkimensis

syn. *M. hookeri*
Half-hardy / Sun or dappled shade

Strong and vigorous plant from Sikkim, with tougher and more upright leaves than *Musa basjoo*, making it more resistant to shredding winds. Leaves dark green, shiny, often flushed with ruby red tints especially when young, usually reverting to plain green with age; undersides flushed maroon. Suitable for large containers or growing in the border with winter protection. Can be grown from root division or seed.

Musa velutina

Pink velvet banana
Tender / Sun or dappled shade

Highly ornamental small banana from Assam in northeastern India, fast growing to about 1.5 m high by 1 m wide. Lush dark green leaves up to 60 cm long have paler undersides and a striking red midrib. Once plant is established, red bracts with white or yellowish flowers are followed by clusters of inedible velvety pink bananas in late summer. When ripe, bananas' skins split open at the tip revealing white flesh. Interesting in borders or as a container plant.

Musa 'Yunnan'

syn. *M. itinerans*
Half-hardy (?) / Sun or dappled shade

Dwarf banana endemic to the cold tropical mountains of Xishuangbanna in the south of Yunnan Province in China, growing to about 3.5 m tall. Another recent introduction to cultivation, with promising but as yet unknown hardiness. Leaves somewhat similar to though more slender than *Musa basjoo*, midgreen, glaucous and silver-green on the underside, with a bluish trunk.

Right
Musa sikkimensis with a small *Cordyline australis* specimen (bottom left) and the large leaves of *Tetrapanax papyrifera* (bottom right)

Far right
Musa sikkimensis, leaves

Right
Musa velutina, fruit

Far right
Musa velutina, leaves

Musella (Musaceae)

Yunnan Province, China

The genus *Musella* is closely related to the genus *Musa* and includes one or possibly two species. *Musella lasiocarpa* (now thought to be extinct in the wild) was discovered by Abbé Delavay in 1885 at an altitude of approximately 1200 m in Yunnan and was first described by Franchet in 1889, who named the plant *Musa lasiocarpa*. DNA studies show that the plant is more closely related to *Ensete* than to *Musa*, and in fact it was classified in the genus *Ensete* between 1947 and 1960, but in 1978 the new genus *Musella* was created to accommodate the plant. A potential second species has been identified in Vietnam but may turn out to be no more than a Vietnamese specimen of *Musella lasiocarpa*.

Below
*Musella lasiocarpa,
flower detail*

Below right
Musella lasiocarpa

Musella lasiocarpa

China yellow banana, golden lotus banana
Frost-hardy / Sun or dappled shade

Shrubby, forming a dense clump 1.2–1.5 m high with a similar spread. Leaves paddlelike, stiff and upright in habit, matte greyish green. Flower head exceptional, looking somewhat like a globe artichoke flower head in a shade of rich ochre yellow. Because of its size, ideal for restricted space or as a container plant. Most are grown commercially from tissue culture. Mature plants can be divided in late spring once they have started growing. In China the whole plant is used as pig fodder. Hardy to −8°c with protection.

Cannas and Strelitzias

Cannas are among the most essential plants for the exotic border. They are big, brash, and bright, and give an exotic look in one season, as they grow ridiculously fast if fed well and watered copiously. Strelitzias are extremely beautiful plants that are well known for their huge leaves and inflorescence that resembles an exotic bird's head. Neither genus is particularly hardy, but both are well worth growing for the dramatic accent they add to a temperate garden.

Canna (Cannaceae)

Tropical and subtropical Americas
Tender / Full sun

Canna is a genus of approximately ten species, all of which are native to the tropical and subtropical Americas, especially the West Indies and South America. They are often referred to as lilies, probably due to their luscious growth and flowers. The common name for *Canna indica*, Indian shot, is derived from the fact that the hard, round, black seeds resemble lead shot used in eighteenth- and nineteenth-century shotguns. The seeds are also used for making jewelry in tropical parts of the world. Cannas can be classified as species cannas, which are the wild types; water cannas, which thrive in boggy conditions; large-flowered cannas, divided into those with green, purple, or bronze leaves; and finally, variegated cannas.

Cannas vary considerably in size and stature, from the very small such as *Canna* 'Lucifer', which grows to no more than 45 cm high, to giants like *C*. 'Musifolia', which can easily reach 3 m or more in an average season. Most cannas are green leaved, though a good percentage of plants have leaves in various shades of pewter-purple-maroon and a few are truly spectacular with vivid variegation as in 'Pretoria' and 'Durban'. Flowers on the

Above

Canna
'Black Knight'

Above right

Canna 'Cleopatra'

species cannas tend to be small, whereas many of the cultivars have large blowsy flowers in many shades from yellow to pinks to red to white, and many are bicoloured.

Cannas are now grown worldwide and are considered a weed in some countries. They have been developed over the years mainly in the temperate climate of Europe, and hence are ideal for temperate gardens. They are clump-forming plants that are easy to grow and will perform well with a modicum of care and attention. Their requirements are simple: plenty of water and copious amounts of organic matter in the form of a mulch of well-rotted manure. They are similar in culture to dahlias, with the added bonus that they do not need staking!

Cannas are considered to be tender perennials, although many growers in favorable locations leave them in the ground, only mulching with the dead foliage or some straw. This is only advisable in light soil or areas that have a warm winter microclimate. If you live on clay or soil that becomes waterlogged

through the winter, I would recommend digging them up and storing the tubers in an airy frost-free location. Canna rhizomes can be started off in a cool greenhouse in late winter to early spring and finally planted out in late spring to early summer, and will normally start flowering by midsummer. They also make spectacular container plants.

Cannas can be attacked by two viruses: bean yellow mosaic and canna yellow mottle, both of which are widely present in canna stocks. Any distorted foliage, streaking, or stunting should be viewed as possible signs of a virus infection. Infected plants should be destroyed, ideally by burning. It is preferable to buy cannas as growing plants, because then you can see if they are healthy. If you are buying dormant rhizomes, buy from a reputable specialist canna grower. Avoid buying dry rhizomes from general bulb suppliers, garden centres, and other general outlets. Any new stock from unknown sources should always be grown separately to be sure of its health. Also keep cannas free of aphids, whitefly, and red spider mite, which are thought to transfer the disease. When dividing the plants in spring, break the clumps apart; if you do use a knife for cutting, sterilise it between plant divisions.

Since the nineteenth century more than a thousand cultivars have been produced (and many new hybrids are being bred in the United States), but today there are approximately three hundred canna varieties available. Many of these have been covered in great detail in *The Gardener's Guide to Growing Cannas* (2001) by Ian Cooke. Additional information for this section was provided by Keith Haywood of Hart Canna. Here we will be dealing with a small selection of the gardenworthy forms and the most readily available. Heights are indicated for each, either short (up to 1 m), medium (up to 1.5 m), or tall (above 1.8 m).

Canna 'Alberich'

Short, very stout canna with thick, fleshy, spoon-shaped, dark green leaves and reddish-black stems, bracts, and seedpods. Large peach-apricot flowers, very well shaped. Among the best cannas for flower and foliage.

Canna 'Assaut'

Tall, graceful canna; the French for "assault" is a rather harsh name for such. Deep red-pink flowers are large and flat, occasionally as much as 150 mm from petal tip to petal tip. Foliage pale bronze and very stately.

Canna 'Black Knight'

Choice medium-tall plant with elegant darkly bronze leaves. Flowers deep red and large, contrasting well with the foliage. Excellent as a specimen or used in mass plantings.

Canna 'Cleopatra'

This medium canna is a chimera—it can't decide what colour it wants to be. Some flowers are yellow with red spots, while others are all red, and some are a mixture of both! Often, petals are half red

Canna 'Durban' with virus

and half yellow-spotted. The foliage is also indecisive—usually green but occasionally streaked with purple. Despite the confusion, this is an excellent and very exotic canna.

Canna 'Durban'

Medium-tall, probably the most ridiculously variegated of all the cannas, making it an absolute must for the summer garden! Foliage red-plum, striped and feathered with strawberry pink. Large flowers are bright mandarin orange. Excellent as a container plant. (Note: Stock of this cultivar was introduced to the British Isles under this name from South Africa in 1994. Trials of this alongside 'Phasion' and 'Tropicanna' have proved that they are identical.)

Canna 'Extase'

Short-medium, big and stocky, green leaved, topped with large wavy-petalled salmon pink flowers. Similar in stature to 'President'. Exquisite plant that should be more widely grown.

Canna 'Florence Vaughan'

Tall and stately, growing to 2 m or more. Leaves very large and pale green. Large flat flowers have an orange blotch in the middle and orange blobs changing to a rich yellow border.

Canna indica 'Purpurea'

Very tall, growing to 2 m or more. Bronze foliage is slender and points upward rather than sideways (fastigiate). Flowers small and orange, held up above the foliage.

Canna iridiflora 'Ehemanii'

Tall, exotic species canna, growing to 1.8–2.4 m or more. Long tubular cerise-pink flowers hang in panicles above large light green leaves. Plant spreads out at the top, creating a vase shape. An impressive plant when grown as a specimen or background. Prefers moist conditions, though it will grow in drier situations if watered regularly.

Canna 'Louis Cayeux'

Medium-tall, big, bold, and brash! A large plant with bright green foliage topped off with a large salmon pink flower. An old variety.

Canna 'Louis Cottin'

Short, classic canna with pewter green leaves topped by large copper-yellow flowers that are well-shaped and have the exquisite texture of bone china. One of the very few cannas that has a yellow flower (albeit dark yellow).

Canna 'Margaret Strange'

Medium, very bushy. Deep bronze foliage combined with strong orange flowers borne in abundance. A new introduction in 2003 bred by Jim Ranger in England.

Canna 'Musifolia Grande'

Tall and large. *Musifolia* means "bananalike" and refers to the leaves, which are very big, growing up to 1 m long and 30 cm across. Their colour is green brushed with red and a distinct red-purple border. Stems are thick and like a broom handle. Small red flowers, rarely produced in areas such as the British Isles as the summers are not long enough.

Canna 'Panache'

Medium-tall, delicate in both colour and form. A slender plant with narrow green foliage and small soft-apricot flowers shading to pink. Flowers continuously from late spring to autumn. Excellent as a conservatory plant.

Canna 'Picasso'

Short, with bright green leaves and large yellow flowers uniformly and densely spotted dark red. If it's a spotty canna you want, there's no better plant. Shorter than 'En Avant' and earlier flowering, with a squarer flower shape and darker spots.

Canna 'President'

Medium-tall, the good old standby of public parks and gardens, where it has been grown as an herbaceous bed spot-plant for many years. Keeps its shape well, with foliage right down to ground level. Very large fleshy matte green leaves topped by large bright red flowers, sometimes with a fine yellow thread at the edge.

Canna 'Pretoria'
syn. *C.* 'Bengal Tiger', *C.* 'Malawiensis Variegata', *C.* 'Striata'

Medium-tall and stunning, with green leaves striped yellow in a bold herringbone pattern. Foliage is topped with large blowsy tangerine-orange flowers. Similar to 'Durban' in shape, size, flower, and stripes, differing only in foliage colour.

Canna 'Roi Humbert' with *Musa basjoo* behind and a stem of *Arundo donax* var. *versicolor* to right

Canna 'Roi Humbert'

syn. *C.* 'Red King Humbert'

Very tall with bronze foliage, topped with large deep orange-red flowers that always remain slightly cupped and tulip-shaped. One of the classic centrepiece cannas traditionally used in parks and gardens.

Canna 'Stuttgart'

Tall, growing up to 3 m with narrow upright powder green leaves irregularly splashed and streaked with creamy white. White portions of the foliage tend to burn in sun, so light shade and plenty of moisture is necessary. Always, in maturity, some white stripes turn brown, but by then the plant is so majestic that it doesn't matter. Small apricot flowers are carried very high above the foliage.

Canna 'Robert Kemp'

Medium-tall with bright green foliage. Smallish orange-red flowers are carried very high. Somewhat like species cannas, grows and reproduces very prolifically, and for this reason is often substituted for larger-flowered varieties in mail-order and garden centre prepacks—whatever picture is shown on the packaging, you may get 'Robert Kemp'!

Canna 'Tchad'

Medium-tall and stately, with bronze foliage and large deepest-velvet-red flowers. Flowers are like 'Black Knight', but with darker foliage. A classic canna and one of the best reds.

Canna 'Wyoming'

Canna 'Wyoming'

Tall, with deep-bronze-brown foliage that when grown well has an exotic dark leathery texture. Large brilliant tangerine-orange flowers are carried very high. For best effect should be grown in a thick clump.

Strelitzia (Strelitziaceae)

Crane flower, bird-of-paradise
Subtropical regions of South Africa

Strelitzia is a genus of four or five large, very architectural, evergreen, clump-forming, palmlike perennials grown for their showy flowers and elegant foliage. Unfortunately, these beauties are not hardy, taking only short spells of light frost if you forget to bring them inside. Nevertheless, they are well worth growing as summer bedding plants or as container-grown specimens that can be brought in for the winter and kept at −5°c or higher. All make excellent conservatory plants that enjoy living outside in a sunny position during the summer months.

Keep on the dry side during the coldest months. Do not repot too frequently, as pot-bound plants flower more freely. All three species described here are fairly drought tolerant once established. They tend to flower from late autumn to spring, so are excellent plants to overwinter indoors.

The name *Strelitzia* was given to honour Queen Charlotte (wife of King George III of England), who was from the house of Mecklenburg-Strelitz.

Strelitzia alba

White bird-of-paradise
Semi-tender to half-hardy / Full sun

Clump-forming perennial growing to 10 m by 3 m in its native habitat, though considerably less in cool-temperate cultivation. Oblong to lance-shaped leaves grow up to 2 m by 60 cm wide on long stalks. Flowers are white with a light blue "tongue" sitting in a purplish boat-shaped bract. The only problem with this size is winter storage! Needs to be brought in before the first frosts and stored at a minimum temperature of 4°c.

Strelitzia nicolai

Strelitzia nicolai

Giant bird-of-paradise
Semi-tender to half-hardy / Full sun

Evergreen perennial, eventually producing a stout trunk, forming thickets in the wild. Growing to a massive 10 m high by 5 m wide, with stiff, dark greenish-grey, leathery leaves, up to 1.5 m long or more, in tropical regions. In a cool-summer climate, though, expect a container plant to grow to around 2–4 m, with proportionately smaller leaves. Inflorescence is a beaklike sheath with white and pale blue flowers in a boat-shaped, dark purple bract, resembling the head of a bird. The problem with such plants is the space required for winter storage!

Strelitzia reginae

Bird-of-paradise
Semi-tender to half-hardy / Full sun

This must be one of the best-known plants in the world. Evergreen, clump-forming perennial growing to 1.2 m tall, with long-stalked, blue-green,

Strelitzia reginae

tough, leathery leaves. Beaklike sheath inflorescence has three brilliant orange sepals and three vivid purple-blue petals in boat-shaped, red-edged bracts from winter to spring. More commonly available than *S. nicolai* but equally bold and architectural.

A wonderful plant to grow outside during the summer months; needs very little attention and stands neglect well. Can be grown from seed, flowering in three to five years, or from root division, flowering in two to three years.

Gingers

Gingers are becoming increasingly popular in temperate gardens and deservedly so, as many are far easier to grow than might be thought. These stunning plants are usually associated with the tropics because of their lush foliage, amazing symmetry, and delicious scent. A substantial number come from high altitudes in tropical zones, making them exceptional plants for temperate gardens. Many will grow well with a little protection of some straw or similar material spread over the crown in frosty weather. In areas with frosty winter nights, the foliage is cut to the ground.

Gingers are fast-growing and rewarding plants that give the garden a very tropical look. All are clumping in habit, producing substantial plants after a few years. As a rule they prefer rich, well-drained soil with plenty of organic matter and moisture. Free-draining soil is essential if they are to overwinter successfully outside. If you want an early show of flowers the following year, you can overwinter most evergreen gingers in a cool greenhouse at around 5°c, where they will stay in leaf until the following spring and will flower up to two months earlier than if left in the ground.

For more in-depth information on this fabulously exotic family of plants, please refer to the excellent *Hardy Gingers* by T. M. E. Branney (2005).

Alpinia zerumbet,
flower detail

Alpinia (Zingiberaceae)

Tropical Asia and Polynesia

Members of this genus are usually tall and fast growing in their native habitat, preferring very moist conditions and high heat. Some can be overwintered outside in maritime climates, though they will come into leaf late and will not have enough time to flower before the winter returns. They need high nighttime temperatures to grow well.

Alpinia zerumbet

Shell flower / Shell ginger
Semi-tender / Sun or dappled shade

One of the grandest of all gingers. In a warm, frost-free climate this is a tremendous plant, growing in large, towering thickets. Waxy white or pinkish shell-like flowers are borne in terminal, pendent clusters on stems 2.75 m or more tall. Unfortunately the attractive flowers are only borne on the previous year's growth; hence a frost-free environment over the winter is essential. We can still enjoy the glossy dark green foliage and stems, which will grow to around 1.8 m. Can be grown as a container plant brought out for the summer months, or bedded out in the garden, then dug before the first frosts in autumn and stored at a minimum winter temperature of 5°C.

Alpinia zerumbet 'Variegata'

Variegated shell ginger
Semi-tender / Sun or dappled shade

A spectacular form, growing to 2.75 m or more tall in a tropical or subtropical climate, though more like 1–1.2 m in a maritime climate. Like many of the more tropical gingers, it needs warm nighttime temperatures to really get going, so only does well during a hot summer. Although it will not flower in a cool summer climate, it is still worth growing for its stunning, highly decorative, green-and-yellow-striped foliage. As with the species, best overwintered in frost-free conditions.

Cautleya spicata,
flower detail

Cautleya (Zingiberaceae)

Himalayan Kashmir, Nepal, Sikkim, Bhutan, and Tibet to Yunnan and Sichuan provinces of China

This small but botanically confused genus (botanists disagree on the precise number of species) is from the Himalayan foothills and hence contains some of the hardiest gingers. Closely related to *Roscoea*, members of this genus are fully deciduous and naturally found growing in damp woodland valleys and also epiphytically on trees. They are some of the most reliably hardy flowering gingers for the garden, preferring dappled shade to partial sun in a protected location that doesn't get too hot or cold.

Cautleya gracilis

Frost-hardy / Dappled shade to partial sun

Small and slender, found in cool, moist woodland valleys in the Himalayan foothills at fairly high elevations, growing to around 40 cm tall, with narrow arching leaves up to 30 cm long. Leaves are green above, with a reddish purple colouration underneath, somewhat reminiscent of *Hedychium greenii*. Inflorescence lax in habit, with two to ten yellow to orange-yellow or primrose-yellow flowers, displayed clear of the foliage and opening in succession over several days in late summer. Hardy to −10°C with mulch.

Cautleya spicata

Frost-hardy / Dappled shade to partial sun

Very desirable ginger hailing from northeastern Himalayan foothills to Yunnan in China, growing up to 1 m in height, with broadly lance-shaped, dark green leaves up to 35 cm long on contrasting red stems. Inflorescence contains red bracts that show off the rich yellow flowers well. Variety *lutea* (syn. *C. lutea*) has brilliant yellow flowers with red bracts, which appear in succession over a period of several weeks in summer. Hardy to −10°C with mulch.

Curcuma (Zingiberaceae)

Tropical and subtropical Asia, with one species in northern Australia and the South Pacific

Members of this genus of some fifty species of deciduous perennials with rhizomatous roots have only recently started to appear in the British Isles. Curcumas emerge from dormancy from spring to summer, depending on soil temperature. All require moist, humus-rich, free-draining soil and dislike wet or waterlogged soils. The foliage can be extremely ornamental, with large paddlelike leaves, often heavily ribbed and veined, sometimes with colouration on either side of the midrib. Many require a long growing season to flower and hence are often shy to flower in cool summer climates, but they are nevertheless worth growing.

The flowers are borne on separate leafy stems that arise from the rhizome, in an open conelike head that develops brightly coloured bracts, largely enclosing three-petalled flowers, often before or at the same time as the foliage emerges or in late summer and autumn. Although not considered hardy, several are worth trying in the garden permanently in the warmest areas; otherwise they should be bedded out for the summer months. Plants overwintered outside usually appear late in the season and are small, often only a third the size of curcumas that are planted out in late May. They also make excellent container plants for the conservatory or brought out for the summer.

Many *Curcuma* species are used as culinary spices; *Curcuma longa* rhizomes when dried provide the well-known spice turmeric. Others have medicinal applications.

Curcuma amada

Mango ginger
Tender / Dappled shade

Known as mango ginger because it smells like green mango. Also used in India in the production of pickles and chutneys as well as curries. Produces flowers before leaves; purple-pink inflorescence appears from the base of the rhizome to about 20–25 cm tall, followed by broad, large leaves up to 1 m in length. Worth growing for their lush foliage alone; leaves are prized by florists for their excellent vase life. Deep yellow flowers emerge from large pink-white bracts produced in late summer. Best grown as summer bedding in maritime climates; can also be grown as a container plant, brought outside in summer and overwintered in frost-free conditions.

Curcuma angustifolia

Half-hardy / Dappled shade

One of the largest species in the genus, growing up to 1.8 m tall in warm climates, though much less in cool-temperate areas. Purple-pink inflorescence appears from the base of the rhizome followed by large leaves up to 60 cm long, probably the best foliage of all the curcumas for the garden. Possibly hardy to around −5°C in warm gardens with a heavy mulch; otherwise lift in autumn and store in frost-free conditions.

Curcuma aromatica

Half-hardy / Light shade

Inflorescence consists of creamy yellow flowers aris-ing from bracts shading from green to red in spring, followed by lightly variegated green leaves. Height 1 m. Possibly hardy to around −5°C in warm gar-dens with a heavy mulch; otherwise lift in autumn and store in frost-free conditions.

Curcuma zedoaria

Half-hardy / Light shade

Floral bracts light green fading to deep pink at the top, to about 20–25 cm tall in spring, followed by decorative leaves that have a deep purple-brown line down the centre. Grows to about 1.5 m. Pos-sibly hardy to around −5°C in warm gardens with a heavy mulch; otherwise lift in autumn and store in frost-free conditions.

Hedychium (Zingiberaceae)

Garland flower, ginger lily, Kahili ginger
Himalaya and tropical Asia

This genus contains approximately fifty species, from moist and lightly wooded areas of the Hima-laya and tropical Asia, growing to 1.2–1.8 m high. Hedychiums are the most popular gingers, as many have decorative and highly scented flowers. In the ground, they are usually late in breaking their win-ter dormancy, requiring a good period of warm weather to trigger growth, usually in May. They make excellent container plants. All prefer moist, humus-rich soil and respond well to feeding and watering during the growing season. Late-flower-ing hybrids are best grown under glass in maritime climates. Many are reportedly hardy to between −5°C and −10°C. The following are only a few of the many species and hybrids worth trying.

Hedychium coccineum

Orange bottlebrush ginger, red ginger lily
Frost-hardy / Sun or dappled shade

Variable, erect, herbaceous perennial with stems

1–2 m tall or more, bearing glaucous, green, lance-shaped leaves 30–50 cm long. Orange-red flowers have prominent dark stamens borne in dense ter-minal spikes of fragrant (sometimes not) flowers up to 30 cm long from early to late summer, depend-ing on temperature. 'Tara' is one of the best forms, with glaucous, bluish green leaves and large termi-nal spikes of scented, bright, vivid orange flowers. Hardy to −10°C with a thick straw mulch. Variety *aurantiacum* is another form with tall stems, up to 2.5 m, with terminal racemes of delectable deep-flame-orange-red flowers and no scent.

Hedychium densiflorum

Frost-hardy to hardy / Sun or dappled shade

One of the hardiest gingers, easily taking −10°C and lower in its stride with a heavy mulch. It has been growing in my garden for well over a decade, rapidly forming a large clump. Grows to 1.2 m tall with arching stems and green leaves. Variable in flower colour, with densely packed racemes of yel-low to orange flowers. 'Assam Orange' is similar,

Above

*Hedychium
densiflorum*
'Assam Orange',
flower spike

Above right

Hedychium densiflorum
'Assam Orange' with
Trachycarpus fortunei
(behind), *Ensete
venticosum* (left), and
Phyllostachys nigra (far left)

Right

Hedychium densiflorum
'Sorung', flower spike

but with orange honey-scented flowers. A flower
stem broken in half gives off a strong smell of cam-
phor. Two scents for the price of one! One of the
first gingers to break through the ground in spring,
shooting up to 1.5–1.8 m and flowering in August. A
second display of bright red berries is produced in
autumn, so don't cut them down too soon. Another
cultivar named 'Stephen' has larger, more open
flowers in warm apricot with burnt-orange stamens
and a delicious scent. 'Sorung' is a fairly new introduction by Edward Needham, similar to 'Stephen'
but with spikes of alluring salmon pink, fragrant
flowers; very desirable.

Hedychium 'Elizabeth'

Frost-hardy / Sun or dappled shade

Hybridised by Tom Wood in the United States, probably the tallest hedychium that can be grown outside in a cool-summer climate. In a hot summer, reaches 3 m tall, topped with clusters of unique salmon-red flowers with a scent redolent of honeysuckle. Reportedly takes a low of −10°c with a heavy mulch. Well worth trying in maritime climates in a warm corner of the garden.

Hedychium ellipticum

Shaving-brush ginger
Frost-hardy / Sun or dappled shade

A very exotic hedychium reaching 1–1.5 m tall, though usually shorter in cool-summer areas. Stems grow upward and when mature lean outward with the weight of the foliage, thereby displaying the flower spikes clear of the leaves. Magnificent terminal inflorescences are densely packed with creamy white flowers with conspicuously long, spidery, orange filaments in early autumn. A truly stunning ginger and one of my favourites. Frost-hardy to about −5°c for short periods only, with a very thick mulch. If you are at all dubious about its hardiness, it is best bedded out for the summer months or grown as a container plant, overwintered frost-free.

Hedychium flavescens

Frost-hardy / Sun or dappled shade

Once thought to be a form of *H. coronarium* but now considered a species in its own right. A tall ginger, growing up to 2 m with greyish green leaves. Produces a conelike spike of strongly lemon-scented yellowish cream flowers from late summer to autumn, when the flowers can be hit by early frost. Hardy to about −5°c if kept dry, with a good mulch. Start in a heated greenhouse to increase flowering chances, bedding it out each summer or growing in a container, which can then be overwintered in frost-free conditions.

Hedychium forrestii

Frost-hardy / Sun or dappled shade

A robust, handsome ginger growing to about 1.5 m and higher, with bold, glossy, midgreen leaves 30–50

cm long. From late summer to early autumn, bears tall terminal spikes up to 30 cm long, of pure white, slightly scented flowers, with pale-yellow stamens, from midsummer to early autumn. Soon forms a spreading clump, making it a good choice for the exotic border. Hardy to at least −10°c with a good mulch.

According to David Constantine of KobaKoba Nursery in Somerset, the plant that everyone grows as *H. forrestii*, with a yellow stamen, is not *H. forrestii*. No one knows what it is or where it originated, but he does know that it was sent to the British Isles from Hawaii by Joseph Rock labelled as *H. gardnerianum*. Until he knows what it is, he calls it *H. forrestii* hort (meaning "of gardens").

Hedychium gardnerianum

Kahili ginger

Frost-hardy / Sun or dappled shade

One of the most spectacular gingers that can be grown in temperate gardens; until recently considered suitable only for greenhouse culture or bedded out for the summer months. Thick stems are 1.2–1.5 m high with large shiny-leathery leaves. Flower heads up to 30 cm tall by 15 cm wide, highly scented, with masses of intense yellow flowers with greatly extended orange-red stamens. Flowers are borne from late summer to early autumn. There is quite a bit of variability in *H. gardnerianum*, with some forms seeming much more floriferous than

others. Although deciduous in our gardens, it is evergreen in the wild. Hardy to about −8°c for short periods if heavily mulched with straw. Usually late breaking ground, often not until June; alternatively, can be grown in containers and stored frost-free during the winter months to induce flowering earlier the following season.

Top and above

Hedychium gardnerianum and flower detail

Hedychium greenii

Frost-hardy / Sun or dappled shade

Highly ornamental evergreen ginger growing to 1–1.2 m tall or more, with exquisite dark green leaves that are rich maroon on the underside and on the stems. Short, fairly small, conelike terminal spikes have individual bright orange-red flowers with a large, showy lip, borne from summer to early autumn depending on the temperature. Unfortunately, this beauty is unscented. Hardy down to −8°c for short periods with a heavy mulch. Grown as an evergreen container plant stored frost-free, it will flower by midsummer. Forms small plantlets or bulbils from the inflorescence once the flowering has finished. These can be collected and brought in for the winter, and propagated.

Hedychium spicatum

Frost-hardy / Sun or dappled shade

A variable species with some indifferent forms about but also some very good collections, such as 'Singalila'. Deciduous, to 76 cm to 1.2 m tall, with rather thin, glossy, midgreen leaves. Loose spikes of scented, large, individual, pure white spidery flowers up to 5 cm across are borne in midsummer, followed in autumn by abundantly produced fruit. These seedpods give the bonus of a second season of interest, the capsules splitting open to reveal their orange linings and bright scarlet arils (fleshy coating around the seeds) in late autumn. Hardy to −10°c with protection.

Hedychium thyrsiforme

Pincushion ginger
Frost-hardy / Sun or dappled shade

A delectable evergreen ginger that has arching stems to 1.5 m high, with ribbed-crumpled, broad, glossy, dark green leaves. The flowers appear rather late in

the season but are nevertheless worth growing, as they are highly scented and pure white with massively extended creamy white stamens, giving the plant its common name. Hardy to −10°C with protection. As this is a very late flowering plant, often in November or even December, it is worth growing in a container that can be brought in before the winter so the flowers can be appreciated when little else is in bloom. That's if it flowers at all!

Roscoea (Zingiberaceae)

Kashmir through the Himalaya to Assam, and southern China to northern Vietnam

This genus of about eighteen species of relatively small gingers, typically 30–60 cm tall, was named after William Roscoe (1753–1831), a founder of the Liverpool Botanic Garden and a leader of the movement for the abolition of the slave trade in Liverpool. They are tuberous rooted perennials, cultivated for their highly attractive and very exotic orchidlike flowers. In their native habitats, these gingers thrive in cool regions, preferring shady,

Roscoea
unnamed cultivar

damp, lightly forested areas, as well as grasslands and slopes often at high altitudes; hence, some of them are almost alpine in nature and thus tolerant of cold. In cultivation, they prefer to be grown in cool dappled shade in moderately fertile, humus-rich, moist, well-drained soil. Unlike the other gingers, they have been fairly popular garden plants for some time, though until recently not particularly common in local garden centres; this is slowly changing as their beauty and ease of growth is realised.

Roscoea auriculata

Frost-hardy / Dappled shade

Very desirable species growing 25–40 cm tall with three to ten broadly lance-shaped, dark green leaves up to 25 cm long. Attractive rich purple-violet flowers have a contrasting white throat, to 3.5 cm across, produced from the upper leaf axils from summer to autumn. Hails from Nepal, Sikkim, and Tibet. Often confused with *R. purpurea*, which is somewhat similar. 'Floriade' is larger in all parts than the species, with similarly coloured flowers.

Roscoea cautleoides

Frost-hardy / Dappled shade

Another highly desirable, sturdy, quickly spreading *Roscoea*, this one from Sichuan and Yunnan provinces, China. Grows 25–50 cm tall by 15 cm across, with strongly upright, lanceolate, deep green leaves up to 40 cm long, though shorter at flowering time. Most cultivated forms produce a succession of delicious pale-yellow to primrose-yellow flowers up to 4 cm across, borne from the upper leaf axils from late spring to summer. There are also white- or purple-flowered forms that are equally desirable. Several cultivars are available with names like 'Kew Beauty', 'Purple Giant', and 'Yeti'.

Roscoea humeana

Frost-hardy / Dappled shade

A relatively well-known and magnificent species reaching 15–25 cm tall and 15 cm across, native to Sichuan and Yunnan provinces, China. Sturdy plant with ovate to lance-shaped, deep green leaves

up to 22 cm long, though only partially developed at flowering time. From the upper leaf axils, up to ten pale-to-rich-purple flowers 4 cm across are borne in early summer. Forms good clumps with time. Several cultivars are available with names like 'Purple Streaker', 'Rosemoor Plum', and 'Snowy Owl'.

Roscoea purpurea

Frost-hardy / Dappled shade

Another popular species, hailing from the Indian Himalaya through Nepal to Bhutan, reaching 25–40 cm tall and 15 cm wide with four to eight lance-shaped, deep green leaves up to 25 cm long. Purple-lavender to lilac flowers are produced in succession from the upper leaf axils from early summer to midsummer. Occasionally the flowers can be white or bicoloured. Another good clump former. Several cultivars are available with names like 'Brown Peacock', 'Nico', and 'Polaris'.

Zingiber (Zingiberaceae)

Asia and northern Australia

This genus of more than eighty species of tropical and subtropical, evergreen, rhizomatous, clumping, herbaceous perennials gives its name to the ginger family (Zingiberaceae). The rhizome of *Z. officinale* is the source of the culinary ginger root, and the most commercially important member of the Zingiberaceae. (Being a tropical species, it is not gardenworthy or particularly interesting as a plant, though it can be grown more out of curiosity as a pot plant, growing to about 60 cm high, with fairly narrow leaves.) Most species are semi-tender, although a few show hardiness.

Zingiber mioga

Myoga ginger
Frost-hardy / Dappled shade

Traditional Japanese vegetable, grown for either spring shoots or the edible summer- or autumn-produced flower buds, which are used in soups and tempura, pickled, and as a spice. Hardiest member of the genus, found growing naturally in moist,

shady woodlands in mountainous valleys of southern China and Japan. Reaching 60–80 cm tall, with narrow, lanceolate, pale green leaves up to 35 cm long. Inflorescence borne on separate short stems, emerging directly from the rhizome from late summer to early autumn, consisting of a loose cone, at or just above ground level, of pale green bracts that open to reveal a succession of pale creamy yellow orchidlike flowers with a conspicuous lip. Naturally deciduous, breaking dormancy mid-to-late spring, depending on soil temperature. Must be grown in very free-draining soil to avoid winter rotting. Hardy to about −10°c with a good mulch.

Zingiber mioga 'Dancing Crane'

Variegated Japanese ginger
Frost-hardy / Dappled shade

Growing to about 60 cm with stout upright stems, broad pale-to-midgreen leaves with eye-catching, irregular creamy white streaks. Small, light yellow, orchidlike flowers peek out from the base of the plant at ground level from late summer to early autumn. Not as hardy as the species, though it might take a few degrees of frost if well mulched and kept dry on free-draining soil. Makes an excellent container plant, kept in frost-free conditions during the winter months.

Zingiber zerumbet 'Darceyi'

Half-hardy / Dappled shade

Grows to 60 cm and taller, with fairly narrow green leaves with irregular bands of creamy white along the margins and occasionally slashes across the surface. Of doubtful hardiness, so grow as a container plant brought in for the winter and kept in frost-free conditions. Otherwise plant out in the mildest gardens with a deep winter mulch and keep it on the dry side.

Bromeliads

Native to the Americas from eastern Virginia in the United States to the southern tip of Argentina, the bromeliad family (Bromeliaceae) comprises more than twenty-one hundred species, and new species are still being discovered. They grow in situations ranging from arid regions to cool forests and tropical jungles and can be very small to very large. Bromeliads give a really tropical feel to the garden and many make excellent summer plants for either bedding out in moist, shady areas or growing in containers. They also make good conservatory plants, flowering well and often becoming substantial with age.

Approximately half the species are air plants or epiphytes. Many epiphytic and some terrestrial bromeliads, sometimes known as tank bromeliads, are capable of holding water in their specially constructed leaf rosettes. They absorb nutrients, from rainfall and debris caught by their cupped shape, through special scales on their leaves. Many epiphytic bromeliads work well and look good tied or pinned to the trunks of tree ferns, to moss poles, or to tree branches and trunks. Many require moist conditions to thrive well so should be sprayed regularly to keep the ambient humidity up. Those from arid areas, known as xerophytes, require drier conditions, usually in full sun.

Unfortunately, the choice of bromeliads in garden centres in the British Isles is quite small; a much wider choice of named bromeliads is available in the United States. Paul Spracklin, on the Essex Riviera, is at the forefront of bromeliad hardiness trials in Great Britain. Much of the hardiness information that follows comes from him. Bromeliads are also discussed in great detail in Andrew Steens's encompassing book *Bromeliads for the Contemporary Garden* (2003).

Left

Group of bromeliads growing near the entrance to the Madeira Botanical Garden, Funchal, Portugal

Aechmea (Bromeliaceae)

Argentina, Brazil, northern Amazonia, Central America, southern Mexico, and the West Indies

This genus contains some two hundred species as well as a range of more than five hundred stunning hybrid bromeliads, popular as houseplants. Three species are mentioned here, including the most commonly available and best-known bromeliad, *Aechmea fasciata*. All prefer moist, well-drained soil. A number of other *Aechmea* species display enough cold tolerance for milder climates and are currently undergoing evaluation in the British Isles.

Aechmea distichantha

Semi-tender to half-hardy / Dappled shade

Large, spiky plant up to 1.5 m tall in its native habitat. One of a few species of *Aechmea* that displays enough cold tolerance to be grown outside in milder climates, having taken −5°c in the British Isles with no damage under light overhead cover.

Aechmea fasciata

Semi-tender / Dappled shade

Best-known bromeliad, with its classic vase shape and broad dark green leaves banded with silver-white. Inflorescence consists of shocking-pink bracts containing blue flowers, a dazzling combination. Use epiphytically or on the ground. Tolerates cool temperatures well but should be dug up and stored at a minimum temperature of 5°c before the first frost.

Aechmea recurvata

Half-hardy to frost-hardy / Dappled shade

With a smallish rosette 40 cm in diameter, the whole plant flushes reddish brown at flowering time. Inflorescence is a cushion of magenta bracts from which cerise flowers are thrown periodically. Probably the hardiest of the aechmeas, having survived six Essex winters and repeated lows of −5°c with no damage. Hybrids with *A. recurvata* blood seem to inherit its cold tolerance; one example is *A.* 'Sueños', another veteran of six Essex winters. Of the several forms, variety *benrathii* is probably the best, as it is very compact.

Ananas (Bromeliaceae)

South and Central America

This genus of approximately seven species includes the pineapple, *Ananas comosus*, an important food crop throughout the tropics. *Ananas* species appreciate regular moisture and fast-draining soil.

Ananas comosus

Tender / Full sun

The original edible pineapple species, *Ananas comosus*, has relatively small fruit, so has been superseded by 'Smooth Cayenne', which is the main pineapple in cultivation today. Produces large rosettes up to 1 m wide. The tuft at the top of the fruit can be carefully removed and planted in a sandy mix, then placed in a propagating frame or flowerpot covered with a plastic bag. Once rooted, it can then be planted in a larger pot in well-drained compost. English Victorian gardeners used to grow them on beds of manure under glass, the manure creating heat at the roots. *Ananas comosus* var. *variegatus* is a spectacular plant with green leaves vertically striped in ivory-white along the leaf margins, with the edge spines sometimes tinged pink. Fruit starts out bright red. Looks good grown in terracotta pots, placed outside for the summer months in a position with full sun.

Above right

Ananas comosus

Right

Ananas comosus var. *variegatus*

Billbergia (Bromeliaceae)

Northeastern and central South America, Central America, and southern Mexico

Billbergia is a genus of about sixty species of tank-type epiphytes that can also be grown successfully in soil that is humus-rich, moist, and free-draining. They are clump-forming but are individually distinctive in having few leaves, in tall, slender vases that are often barred with silver or maroon or spotted cream and pink. The flower spikes are usually pendulous and very showy, if only for a few weeks.

Billbergia distachia

Half-hardy / Shade or sun

Has dark green leaves when grown in shade, which change to a reddish green in full sun. Has survived −5°c outside with overhead cover.

Billbergia nutans

Frost-hardy / Dappled shade

Most commonly available. Dark green leaves, often marked with greyish silver in tight tubular rosettes. Flowering stem is erect, arching at the tip; flowers greenish yellow with purple-blue margins and pink bracts in spring. Works well as a potted plant, quickly filling the pot. Makes a good garden bromeliad in dappled shade on well-drained soil, where it will soon form a large clump. Protect when colder than −5°c. The variegated version of this, 'Variegata', seems only slightly less hardy.

Dyckia (Bromeliaceae)

South America

This genus of more than 120 species of usually clump-forming terrestrial bromeliads comes from harsh arid areas in South America. The leaves usually have a waxy-glossy appearance, edged with hard, sharp spines. Plants are half-hardy to frost-hardy in full sun; they will take a few degrees of frost if kept dry during the winter months outside, in a south-facing position, on well-drained soil. I have been growing *Dyckia cinerea* this way successfully for some years.

If grown in a pot make sure it is a large one, as they have an extensive root system, and overwinter in a cold greenhouse. *Dyckia velascana* has 30-cm silvery rosettes and lemon yellow flowers and has endured −5°c with no damage, as has *Dyckia* 'Morris Hobbs', which in the higher light intensity of summer flushes with burgundy overlaid with a silvery patina and orange flowers. Dyckias produce their flowers from the axillary buds at the side of the plant, rather than the centre as happens with most bromeliads, so the same rosette can flower year after year.

Fascicularia (Bromeliaceae)

Chile

This genus comprises some five species of evergreen xerophytic, epiphytic, or terrestrial bromeliads found growing in coastal regions up to 400 m high. Some make excellent and very attractive garden plants. They are fascinating plants that are tougher than originally thought and are stunning when in flower. They can be used in desert gardens and raised beds, planted with other spiky-looking plants, and also work well as container plants. All prefer fairly poor, sharply drained, gritty soil and are good for hot situations where other plants struggle to survive. Although they are considered semi-tender, I have been growing them in my Norfolk garden for more than fifteen years. Short, sharp frosts seem to do them no damage, though sustained periods of −5°c and lower can cause white blistering on the leaves, which will be covered by new foliage in the spring. For colder periods, straw or similar materials can be pushed into the rosettes.

Fascicularia bicolor

Frost-hardy / Full sun

Rosetted terrestrial bromeliad growing to a height of 45 cm by 60 cm with stiff, spiny-edged, glaucous, deep green leaves up to 50 cm long, silver-grey and scaly underneath. Innermost leaves become bright red at flowering time in late summer. Mature rosettes bear inflorescences with tight clusters of pale powder blue flowers, surrounded by silvery white bracts.

Left

Dyckia 'Morris Hobbs'

Fascicularia bicolor subsp. *bicolor*

Frost-hardy / Full sun

Looks similar to subspecies *canaliculata*, but floral bracts are shorter and flowers are slightly darker blue. Hardy to −3°C, sustaining light damage at −5°C from which it will speedily recover. Makes an excellent container plant.

Fascicularia bicolor subsp. *canaliculata*

Frost-hardy to hardy / Full sun

Forms dense clumps or mounds of thin, leathery, arching, heavily serrated, dark greyish green leaves in tight rosettes. In late summer central leaves turn brilliant red at the base, surrounding a dense cluster of pale blue, three-petalled flowers offset with bright yellow pollen. Hardy to −7°C with marking on the leaves below −10°C.

Fascicularia pitcairniifolia

Frost-hardy / Full sun

Rosetted, terrestrial bromeliad growing to a height and spread of 1 m with glaucous, midgreen leaves up to 1 m long, edged with short spines, whitish grey and scaly on the underside. Inner rosette leaves turn bright red around the inflorescence of powder blue, tightly packed flowers.

Greigia (Bromeliaceae)

Chile

Of the two species in this genus, *Greigia sphacelata* is most often encountered. This mysterious Chilean plant more strongly resembles a hard-leaved *Eryngium pandanifolium* than a bromeliad, and like *Dyckia* it produces its flowers from axillary buds. There are two long-established colonies of this in Queen Mary's Public Gardens in Falmouth, Cornwall, and it would seem to be hardy to −5°C and lower in full sun.

Guzmania (Bromeliaceae)

Tropical rainforests of South America

This genus comprises about 185 tank-type epiphytic species, with a few terrestrials, only a few of which are in cultivation. Many hybrids exist, though, produced by the millions in the Netherlands. They are widely available at garden centres though are unfortunately rarely named. The leaves are usually green with smooth edges, though there are some variegated forms. Their flower spike can be found in a wide range of colours and lasts for months. They can be used as summer bedding or attached to the trunk of a tree fern in dappled shade. They can also be grown in containers that are brought in before the first frost, or treated as an annual.

Neoregelia (Bromeliaceae)

Southeastern Brazil, with a few species from the upper Amazon

This genus of about a hundred species and countless hybrids, which are tank-type epiphytes or terrestrial, has some of the most diverse leaf colour in the bromeliad family, having stripes, spots, and blotches or banding. Most have flat rosettes, though a few are vase shaped. I have been growing *Neoregelia carolinae* for some years in the shade of an old pear tree, leaving a few out during the winter months to test their hardiness. The parent plants become rather tatty, though new pups are protected by the parent plants, surviving well at temperatures down to −3°c. *Neoregelia carolinae* f. *tricolor* also works well in this situation. Otherwise dig up and store at a minimum of 5°c, keeping on the dry side during the coldest months.

Nidularium (Bromeliaceae)

Brazil

A few of the forty-five species in this genus are known to have some cold tolerance. They are ground-dwelling, shade-loving plants, and this could facilitate their chances outside if they are grown under an evergreen canopy, which will keep off the most penetrating frosts. So far one species, *Nidularium fulgens*, has overwintered well through −5°c.

Ochagavia (Bromeliaceae)

Central and southern Chile

This genus comprises four species native to harsh environments, which therefore make excellent garden plants, especially when planted with other xerophytes. They make dense clumps of rosettes that do not retain water.

Ochagavia carnea

Frost-hardy / Sun or dappled shade

Leaves are arching, narrow, stiff, spiny-edged, grey-green. Stemless, globular inflorescence consists of

Ochagavia carnea

as many as fifty pink-petalled flowers surrounded by pink bracts. My plant was given to me by Mike Nelhams, curator of the Abbey Garden on the island of Tresco, part of the Isles of Scilly in southwest England, where frosts are quite rare. In my garden, where it grows on free-draining soil that is dry in winter facing south under a large tree, it has survived −5°c with little damage.

Ochagavia elegans

Half-hardy to frost-hardy / Full sun

A slightly smaller plant, clump-forming, with dense rosettes of stiff, spiny-edged green leaves. Inflorescence contains up to forty reddish purple flowers, surrounded by small red bracts. Hardy to −3°c and probably lower if kept dry during the winter months. Unfortunately, extremely rare in cultivation.

Puya (Bromeliaceae)

South America

This genus of more than 160 species grows at altitudes above 2000 m in its native habitat, where the conditions can be desertlike with snow, and hence all have good hardiness. Some form trunks. All require well-drained soil that is on the dry side during the winter months. They tend to rot in the centre in prolonged winter rain. A sheet of glass or plastic overhead during the winter months is beneficial.

Puya alpestris

Half-hardy to frost-hardy / Full sun

Has arching green leaves up to 1 m long in the wilds of the Chilean Andes, forming large tight clumps; smaller in cultivation. Flower stems produced when mature are stunning to say the least, with flowers in a shade of metallic blue that changes in the light as you look at them. Hardy to −5°c for short periods.

Puya berteroniana

Frost-hardy / Full sun

Chilean plant that seems to take the cold a little better than *Puya alpestris*, remaining unmarked through repeated lows of −5°c. Resembles *P. alpestris* almost exactly in appearance but half as big again in every dimension. Flowers share the same unearthly shade of metallic turquoise.

Puya chilensis

Half-hardy to frost-hardy / Full sun

From central Chile, a trunk-forming species with narrow, arching, heavily toothed leaves forming dense rosettes. Known to trap mammals with its vicious recurved spines. Flower spike can attain a height of up to 3.5 m, with yellow flowers. Hardy to −5°c for short periods.

Left

Puya alpestris

Above right

Puya berteroniana

Right

Puya chilensis

Puya coquimbensis

syn. *P. gilmartiniae*

Frost-hardy / Full sun

Rosettes are 0.75 m high, with leaves overlaid with a silver-gilt patina, rather than plain silver, and widely spaced marginal teeth. Seems to take −5°c in its stride.

Puya mirabilis

Half-hardy to frost-hardy / Full sun

Clump-forming, with thin, silvery green, arching, slightly toothed leaves in tight rosettes. Flower spike on mature plants can grow to 1 m high, with scented greenish-white flowers. Hardy to −5°c for short periods with overhead cover; in the open garden, the leaves can be lost at −3°c though regrowth is quick the following year, with the plant behaving almost herbaceously.

Puya raimondii

Half-hardy to frost-hardy / Full sun

Produces the largest inflorescence in the world, growing to 9.5 m and more at a hundred years old. Considerably smaller plant in temperate climates. Hardy to −3°c for short periods. Not in general cultivation, though collected at Kew and Tresco and by a few exoticists. Unfortunately, now rare in the wild.

Tillandsia (Bromeliaceae)

Southeastern United States to southern Argentina

This large genus contains more than five hundred species, with the majority xerophytic, found growing in scrubby areas to woodlands.

Tillandsia aeranthos and T. bergeri

Frost-hardy / Sun or dappled shade

Two very similar species differing mainly in their flower colour; one is pink, the other pale blue. Both are undemanding plants and will take −5°c in the garden with overhead cover. Can be attached to a tree branch and left to their own devices.

Tillandsia cyanea

Half-hardy / Sun or dappled shade

Relatively small bromeliad, growing to about 25 cm high. Hails from Ecuador, where it scrambles over rocks, often covering quite large areas. Leaves dark green, narrow, forming small, open rosettes that clump up quickly after flowering. Beautiful inflorescence is sword-shaped with pink overlapping bracts from which rich purple flowers appear in summer, lasting several months. Excellent plant for the temperate garden; looks especially good attached to tree ferns and other trees or grown in a rock garden. Keep moist during the summer months for the freshest growth, although it takes dry conditions. Hardy to about −3°c for short periods; otherwise bring into a cold or cool greenhouse for the winter, keeping on the dry side.

Tillandsia usneoides

Spanish moss

Tender / Dappled shade

Grows on trees, from southeastern United States to Argentina and Chile, as silvery-grey, threadlike

Tillandsia usneoides growing on *Quercus virginiana*

masses to 7.5 m long, densely covered by grey scales, which serve instead of roots to receive and hold atmospheric moisture. Tiny axial flowers change colours from yellowish green to blue. Usually purchased in a plastic bag as a length of plant, which can be draped from tree branches in a shady moist area of the garden and occasionally misted to keep up the humidity. Best used as an annual, as it is rather difficult to overwinter.

Vriesea (Bromeliaceae)

Central and South America

This genus of more than 250 species with countless hybrids comprises mainly tank-type epiphytes, some of which reach large proportions. They grow in similar habitats to guzmanias, in tropical forests, and often have very striking foliage, making a strong exotic statement in the temperate garden. The flower spike is usually sword-shaped and often branched, staying in flower for several months. A small number of *Vriesea* species are said to exhibit cold tolerance, though few have been tested in the British Isles. *Vriesea philippo-coburgii* has survived −5°C intact with overhead cover and should make an interesting plant in milder gardens as it is a full-fledged tank bromeliad that looks extremely tropical.

Vriesea splendens

Flaming sword

Tender / Dappled shade

One of the most popular vrieseas, growing to about 30 cm high. A rosette-forming plant with arching, wide, strap-shaped, olive green leaves, banded with purple to reddish-brown markings. Inflorescence produces yellow tubular flowers between bracts from summer to autumn. Works well in the ground in humus-rich soil, or attached to the side of a tree fern. Must be brought under cover and kept at a minimum of 7°C during the winter months.

Vriesea splendens

Bulbs and Tubers

Often novice gardeners think of bulbs as purely a springtime spectacle, as tulips and daffodils are, unaware that many bulbs and tuberous plants flower during the summer months. Included here are both well-known and lesser-known species and hybrids that fit in with the exotic garden style, with unusual or flamboyant flowers, scented or not. Most of the following will mix beautifully with your existing perennials and shrubs, often brightening up a dull corner. Many also make excellent container plants. I always have a selection of lilies growing in black plastic containers that can be placed in the border among other perennial plants, thus hiding the pots. When they have finished flowering I can then remove them and replace them with new plants. Tigridias are fabulous planted near a doorway or window where their beauty can easily be seen, as their flowers open for a single day only. The hardy tuberous begonias are another must for dappled shade with their exotic leaves and pale pink to white flowers.

Left

Alstroemeria hybrid

Above

Alstroemeria
hybrid

Above right

Alstroemeria ligtu

Although frost-hardy, alstroemerias should be mulched during the winter months in cold areas. They prefer well-drained soil in a sunny, sheltered aspect that is moist during the growing season. They may need staking, as they become rather top-heavy. Some can become invasive; left undisturbed, established clumps will spread freely by means of fleshy, brittle roots. Deadhead after flowering to prevent them from setting seed and appearing all over the garden. They are easy to grow from seed, performing best from the second year onward.

Alstroemeria (Alstroemeriaceae)

Peruvian lily, lily of the Incas
South America, often growing at altitude

This genus, named by Linnaeus after his pupil Claus von Alstroemer (1736–1794), includes about fifty species of normally summer-flowering, vigorous, fleshy, tuberous-rooted perennials grown for their exotic, long-lasting, showy, multicoloured flowers, much used in the cut flower industry as they last well in water. Alstroemerias have been hybridised extensively over the years; many named and unnamed hybrids in numerous beautiful colour forms are offered in the marketplace. They will also hybridise in your garden, producing many new colour breaks if you let them go to seed. The flowers range from white to pink, purple, red, yellow, and orange, and some even have green markings, all flowering through the summer months.

Alstroemeria aurea

syn. *A. aurantiaca*
Golden lily of the Incas, golden Peruvian lily
Frost-hardy / Full sun

Tuberous-rooted, clump-forming perennial growing to a height of 90 cm, bearing narrow, lance-shaped, twisted leaves, topped with loose heads of bright orange flowers that are tipped with green and red streaks on the two upper petals. Foliage yellows after flowering, causing them to look untidy in the border, so plant in a situation where this does not matter, or place behind other plants that will grow up and screen them.

Alstroemeria ligtu

Frost-hardy / Full sun

Tuberous-rooted, clump-forming perennial growing to a height of 60 cm, hailing from Argentina and Chile. Flowers are white through yellowy-cream, to lavender and magenta, normally with a yellow throat with reddish brown flecking.

Alstroemeria pelegrina

syn. *A. gayana*
Frost-hardy / Full sun

Tuberous-rooted, clump-forming perennial growing to a height of 30–60 cm with narrow, lance-shaped, green leaves. Each stem has up to three white flowers, flushed pink through mauve, yellow in the middle of the upper petals and spotted with brownish purple markings.

Alstroemeria psittacina

syn. *A. pulchella*
Frost-hardy / Full sun

Tuberous-rooted, clump-forming perennial, hailing from Brazil, with green foliage, growing to a height of 60 cm. Flowers in the form of loose heads are red-flushed green, with maroon flecking.

Amaryllis (Amaryllidaceae)

South Africa

This genus of one species of deciduous, late autumn-flowering, bulbous perennial hails from rocky places on the coastal hills in the southwestern Cape area of South Africa. The species provides colour, especially when grown en masse, at a time when not much else in the garden commands attention.

Amaryllis belladonna

Belladonna lily, Jersey lily, naked lady
Frost-hardy / Sun or dappled shade

Produces attractive, stout, dark purple, often slightly green stems topped with loose heads of six or more scented, funnel-shaped, rich pink flowers 6–12 cm long. Fleshy, strap-shaped leaves, 18–38 cm long, appear after the flowers. Many interesting hybrids are available, especially in the United States, of which these are only a few: 'Barton' with dark rose-pink flowers; 'Cape Town' with deep rose-red

Amaryllis belladonna

flowers; 'Hathor' with flowers that are pink in bud, opening to white with a yellow throat; 'Johannesburg' with up to twelve deep rose pink, widely flaring flowers with a white throat; 'Kimberley' with deep carmine-pink flowers and a white throat; and 'Purpurea Major' with up to six fragrant pink flowers, all facing in one direction. Though the plant is hardy down to −5°c and lower, it should be mulched over the winter in colder areas.

Begonia (Begoniaceae)

Tropical and subtropical regions worldwide

This genus of about nine hundred species of perennials, shrubs, and climbers includes a great diversity of plants with root systems that can be fibrous, rhizomatous, or tuberous, grown for their foliage and/or flowers. Several are hardy enough to survive most winters in the warmer parts of cool-temperate areas if the soil is kept dry. The so-called houseplant (tender) forms are dealt with in the later section "Houseplants Outside." Several of the hardy forms described below have been discovered recently on plant-hunting expeditions in Taiwan and other parts of Asia by Bleddyn and Sue Wynn-Jones of Crûg Farm Plants in northern Wales. Most prefer well-drained, moist, humus-rich soil, though some take dry conditions well.

Above

Begonia grandis subsp. *evansiana*

Right

Begonia grandis subsp. *evansiana* with flowers

Begonia grandis subsp. *evansiana*

Frost-hardy / Dappled shade

Clump-forming tuberous begonia from which red branched stems emerge, from mid to late spring, rapidly growing up to 50 cm tall with 30 cm spread by midsummer. Broad, fleshy leaves on red leaf stalks are pale green above and flushed red with prominent veining underneath. Pink flowers, 1.5–2.5 cm, are produced from the leaf axils in nodding clusters from midsummer onward. *Begonia grandis* subsp. *evansiana* var. *alba* is an attractive white-flowered form.

Begonia grandis subsp. *evansiana* 'Pink Parasol'

Frost-hardy / Dappled shade

Bleddyn and Sue Wynn-Jones of Crûg Farm Plants, in northern Wales, collected this from Shikoku, Japan, where it grows to a height of 90 cm, having luxurious, palmate leaves and bearing sprays of pink flowers opening from reddish buds. Adventitious tubers form in all its joints, falling to the ground and rooting by the following spring in its natural habitat. Flowering from midsummer to first frost. A very promising hardy begonia.

Begonia grandis 'Sapporo'

Frost-hardy / Dappled shade

A very hardy form of this species from Sapporo, the capital city of Hokkaido, the northern island of Japan, where the winters can be severe. Grows to a height of about 90 cm in its native habitat, on

erect stems that are red at the nodes, which in turn produce bulbils in autumn. Distinctive in foliage and form, with large, palmate, dark green leaves that are dark red underneath. Pink flowers are borne in terminal sprays, opening from reddish buds in late summer to first frost.

Begonia palmata

Frost-hardy / Dappled shade

Collected as a dormant rhizome from the Lachung Valley, northeastern Sikkim, where it is locally hardy to −5°C. Large, deeply lobed fleshy leaves to 40 cm long, on darkly mottled stems. Bears auxiliary cymes of pink flowers. Height to 60 cm, flowering from midsummer to first frost.

Begonia ravenii

Frost-hardy / Dappled shade

Collected at high altitude in the central mountains of Taiwan; reportedly hardy to −9°C. Grows to a

height of 90 cm from deep rhizomes. Leaves are large, obliquely ovate, almost succulent, to 30 cm long. Pink flowers from early summer to first frost.

Begonia sinensis 'Red Undies'

Frost-hardy / Dappled shade

Similar in habit to its Japanese bulbil-bearing counterpart *Begonia grandis*, this woodland perennial from China grows to a height of 30 cm, but with smaller narrowly palmate leaves on more upright stems and with earlier pink flowers held above the foliage from midsummer to first frost. Leaves dark red on their undersides.

Begonia sutherlandii

Half-hardy / Dappled shade

Dense, branching, clump-forming, tuberous begonia from South Africa and Tanzania, growing to a height and spread of 46 cm. Leaves bright green, slightly toothed, ovate, lance-shaped, up to 15 cm long,

Begonia palmata

often with red veining. Throughout the summer, freely produces panicles of pendent orange flowers up to 2.5 cm across. Bulbils are formed in the leaf axils, which should be collected for growing the following year. Unless you live in a virtually frost-free area, store the tuber in frost-free conditions during the winter months. Makes an excellent container or hanging-basket plant.

Bulbine (Asphodelaceae)

South Africa and Australia

Bulbine comprises some thirty-five species of succulent and nonsucculent, occasionally bulbous or tuberous rooted, perennials. The larger species have succulent, somewhat grasslike leaves. They are easy to cultivate, requiring humus-rich, moist, well-drained soil in full sun, and will tolerate poor soils once established. They are hardy to about 5°c and lower if kept on the dry side during the winter months.

Bulbine frutescens

Semi-tender to half-hardy / Full sun

Hails from South Africa into Mozambique. Branching, succulent, and slightly woody-stemmed near the base; growing to about 45 cm tall or more by 60 cm wide when in flower. Succulent leaves are light green, linear, semicylindrical. Forty or more star-shaped yellow flowers are borne above spikes. 'Hallmark' is a more compact form with shorter, often flopping, spikes, and orange star-shaped flowers fading to yellow in the centre.

Cardiocrinum (Lilaceae)

Himalaya to Japan

The three species in this genus develop quickly after winter dormancy, the most commonly grown being *Cardiocrinum giganteum*. With its large leaves and enormous flower spike, this is a spectacular plant for dappled shade in woodland gardens on permanently moist soil with added humus.

Cardiocrinum giganteum

Hardy / Dappled shade

From western China. Forms plants up to 1 m tall, when well grown, often in clumps; mature bulbs produce large, heart-shaped, soft, leathery green leaves up to 45 cm long and almost as wide. Leafy, very sturdy flower stem grows up to 3 m tall, topped with long, fragrant, slightly pendent, creamy white flowers, up to 20 cm long, with red-purple streaks inside. Flowers in early summer, followed by large brown seedpods that split open in midautumn. Grows in drier situations but will be correspondingly shorter. Bulb dies after flowering but produces several offsets that will bloom in three to four years, whereas growing from seed can take up to seven years before reaching flowering age. Prone to slug damage.

Crinum (Amaryllidaceae)

Tropical regions of the world, including South Africa

Found growing as marginals on stream and lake banks throughout tropical regions of the world, the approximately 130 species of *Crinum* include evergreen and deciduous bulbous perennials, with large bulbs and leaves, that are semi-tender to hardy. All require humus-rich, well-drained soil sheltered from wind, and all like plenty of water in the growing season.

Crinum americanum

Half-hardy / Full sun

Large, small-necked bulbs native to the southern United States produce green, strap-shaped, semierect, basal leaves, up to 1 m long. Tall stems bear three to six creamy white, fragrant flowers, with narrow petals tinged green or purple, and prominent stamens in pink or red. Best grown in pots, stored in frost-free conditions during the winter months, and kept on the dry side if kept cool.

Crinum asiaticum

Half-hardy / Full sun

Very leafy plant, 90 cm to 1.5 m tall and 1 m across. Broad, dark green leaves up to 1.2 m long appear from large, long-necked bulbs. Thick flowering stem bears up to thirty showy, long-tubed, fragrant white flowers, with narrow petals and long red stamens from spring to summer. Hardy down to −3°c with protection, so should only be planted in the warmest gardens. Makes a good container plant that should be brought into frost-free conditions during the winter months and kept on the dry side

if kept cool. Variety *sinicum* (syn. *C. pedunculatum*) has even larger leaves and a taller flowering spike.

Crinum bulbispermum

syn. *C. longifolium*
Frost-hardy / Full sun

Large, long-necked bulbs from South Africa giving rise to arching, strap-shaped, semi-erect, wide greyish green leaves, up to 90 cm long, grouped at the neck tops. Flower stem grows up to 1 m tall, topped with up to eleven fragrant, long-tubed, white to pinkish red flowers, with darker pinkish red stripes. Hardy to −10°c if covered with mulch.

Crinum bulbispermum

Crinum moorei

Frost-hardy / Full sun

Very large, long-necked bulbs from South Africa give rise to long, broad leaves, with a height and spread of foliage up to 70 cm by 60 cm. Flower spike up to 1 m tall bears up to twelve trumpet-shaped, fragrant, white to deep pink flowers in summer. Hardy to −5°c when mulched.

Crinum ×powellii

Crinum ×powellii

Cape lily

Frost-hardy / Sun or slightly dappled shade

Well-known, large-necked, bulbous plant, hybrid of *C. moorei* and *C. bulbispermum*, growing up to 1.2 m tall with similar spread. Bulbs can be as much as 18 cm in diameter. Leaves are green, broad, arching, straplike, to 1 m. Tall spikes are topped with clusters of eight to ten trumpet-shaped pink or white flowers. 'Album' has pure white flowers. Will take lows of −10°C if well mulched. Works well in large containers, which should be brought into a cold or frost-free greenhouse for the winter months.

Crocosmia (Iridaceae)

South Africa

Hardy / Sun or dappled shade

This genus of seven species of clump-forming cormous perennials in the iris family is native to grassland areas in South Africa. Crocosmia are grown for their handsome appearance and brightly coloured flowers, which appear from early summer to autumn, depending on variety. Countless hybrids and cultivars are available, in a vast range of colours and flower shapes; I will only cover a handful of my favourites here. Most are hardy, preferring well-drained moist to dryish soils. The name *Crocosmia* comes from the Greek *krokos* for saffron and *osme* for smell and refers to the way the dried leaves of these plants smell when rubbed. The genus is often called *Montbretia*, after Antoine François Ernest Conquebert de Monbret, a botanist who accompanied Napoleon on his Egypt campaign in 1798.

Crocosmia ×crocosmiiflora

Vigorous, sometimes invasive, hybrid cross between *C. aurea* and *C. pottsii*, growing to a height and spread of 50–60 cm. Leaves pale green, slender, arching, up to 70 cm long. Spikes of orange flowers, occasionally branching, appear in summer.

Crocosmia 'Emberglow'

Grows to a height of 60–70 cm, with midgreen, upright, slightly arching leaves. Flowers, dark red-orange, 5–8 cm long in summer.

Crocosmia 'Emily McKenzie'

Grows to a height of 60 cm, with midgreen, upright leaves. Flowers appear on branched spikes, often downward-facing, broad-petalled, brilliant orange with a dark orange-brown throat, up to 5 cm long, in late summer.

Crocosmia 'Lucifer'

Grows to a height of 1–1.2 m, with midgreen, upright, pleated leaves. Flowers brilliant flame-red, up to 5 cm long, produced on slightly arching, sparsely branched spikes in early summer; one of the earliest crocosmias to flower.

Crocosmia masoniorum

Grows to a height of 60–100 cm, with pleated midgreen leaves. Flowers, upward-facing, up to 5 cm long, in a shade of reddish orange on normally unbranched spikes.

Crocosmia 'Solfatare'

syn. *C.* 'Solfaterre'

Grows to a height of 60 cm, with alluring bronze leaves and apricot-yellow flowers up to 3 cm long on arching branched stems in midsummer.

Crocosmia 'Star of the East'

One of the most spectacular forms, growing up to 70 cm tall, with upright, midgreen leaves. Flowers are horizontal-facing, light orange, with a some-what paler centre, up to 3.5 cm long, on branching spikes, from midsummer to early autumn.

Crocosmia
masoniorum

Crocosmia
'Solfatare'

Dahlia (Asteraceae)

Mexico and Central America

This genus of about twenty-seven species and more than twenty thousand cultivars of bushy, normally tuberous perennials, named after Swedish botanist Andreas Dahl, is native to mountainous areas of Mexico and Central America. Grown for their distinctive flower heads and sometimes dark foliage, which looks especially good in the exotic garden, dahlias can be dwarf to tree-sized. Most dahlias are immediately recognisable by their pinnate to tripinate foliage, produced from hollow stems.

Dahlias, like many garden flowers, have fallen in and out of fashion during their two hundred years of cultivation; but they are now back in fashion, especially the many new forms with bronze and dark purple leaves, which tend to be more compact than most of the older varieties. The most common hybrids are the products of crossing *Dahlia coccinea* with *Dahlia pinnata*. They prefer to grow in moist, fertile, humus-rich, well-drained soil. They can be successfully overwintered in the ground, if they do not freeze or become waterlogged; otherwise dig up the tubers after frost has blackened the leaves in autumn and store the tubers in a dry, frost-free place during the winter months. Some of the bedding strains can be grown from seed and will flower in the first season. Most dahlias will flower from early summer to frost if they are deadheaded regularly. Tall dahlias, especially those more than 1 m tall, should be well staked at planting time.

For more extensive information on dahlias, see *The Gardener's Guide to Growing Dahlias* by Gareth Rowlands (1999).

Dahlia species

Dahlia coccinea

Half-hardy / Sun or dappled shade

One of the main parents of the garden dahlia, native from Mexico to Guatemala, where it grows up to 3 m high, though more like 1–1.2 m in temperate gardens. Dark glossy green foliage is often tinged purple. Inflorescence consists of clusters of

two to three simple, star-shaped, single scarlet flowers (which can be somewhat variable in colour) with brilliant yellow centres on long stalks.

Dahlia imperialis

Half-hardy / Sun or dappled shade

Largest of all the dahlias, growing to a height of 5–8 m on thick, bamboolike stems in its native habitat, though closer to 2–3 m tall in temperate gardens. Very large and graceful, much-divided grey-green leaves are widely spaced up the thick, woody stems. Clusters of pinkish-lavender, slightly cupped, star-shaped flowers appear from late autumn to winter; hence these rarely flower in cooler climates, as they are cut back by autumn frosts before flowering. Although not grown for its flowers in these gardens, it nevertheless makes an excellent foliage plant and conversation piece! To keep height for the following season, should be dug up before the first frosts and stored in frost-free conditions during the winter months.

Dahlia merckii

Frost-hardy / Sun or dappled shade

Hailing from Mexico, grows to a height of 2 m or more, with a spread of 1 m. A somewhat lax, scrambling dahlia that likes to be supported by other shrubby plants. Leaves are green, finely divided, with a slight reddish tint, up to 40 cm long. Flowers are graceful, simple, saucer-shaped, pale lilac-pink, with yellow anthers on wiry stems to 76 cm in late summer. *Dahlia merckii* compact is a dwarf version of this fairly hardy species with a tighter growth habit, with many more shoots that are less straggly. Hardy to −10°c.

Dahlia hybrids

Half-hardy / Sun or dappled shade

Following are a few popular varieties that fit in well with other exotic plants, usually because they have dark leaves, making a good contrast to their own flowers and the foliage of other plants. They are fast growing.

Dahlia 'Arabian Night'

Classical-style, decorative dahlia growing to a height of 1.2 m with sultry, dark green foliage. Flowers, from early summer to frost, are fully double, dark wine-red, with gold-green bracts between the petals, which are slightly incurved. In certain light conditions, the flowers almost look black!

Dahlia 'Bednall Beauty'

Like a smaller version of 'Bishop of Llandaff', without having to be staked, as it only grows to a height and spread of 60 cm, making it ideal for the front of the border. The cut-leaf foliage is rich, dark purple and the flowers, from midsummer to frost, are semidouble, shaded deeper red toward the base of the petals, up to 9 cm across.

Dahlia 'Bishop of Llandaff'

Grows to a height of 1 m with a spread of 45 cm, with foliage bronze-black in full sun. Flowers held above the foliage, double-petalled (peony-flowered), bright vivid red, 7.5 cm across. Can become straggly, especially if grown in a shady area, and hence should be staked well. Named after Bishop Hughes of Llandaff (now Cardiff), Wales, British Isles, in 1924; won the prestigious Award of Merit from the Royal Horticultural Society in 1928. Recently three new varieties have come onto the market, all reportedly growing to a height of 90 cm: 'Bishop of Auckland', dark bronze-black foliage with single-petalled, rich dark red flowers, 'Bishop of Canterbury', purple-black foliage with double-petalled, cerise pink flowers, and 'Bishop of York', dark foliage with single-petalled bright yellow flowers.

Dahlia 'Bednall Beauty'

Dahlia 'Bishop of Llandaff'

Dahlia 'Dark Desire'

Growing to a height of 80 cm, a variety with alluring, dark blood-red single flowers with slightly twisted petals on brownish-purple stalks above green-bronze foliage.

Dahlia 'David Howard'

Grows to a height of 75 cm with dark bronze-purple foliage and fully double, intense orange flowers up to 10 cm across. Each flower is light orange at the base of the petals and bright orange in the centre. Much used by Christopher Lloyd in his exotic garden at Great Dixter, Kent.

Dahlia 'Grenadier'

Old variety with dark green–blackish leaves and double scarlet flowers, with petals that turn back, giving it a spherical appearance. Grows to a height of 60 cm.

Dahlia 'Haresbrook'

Compact dahlia with blackish foliage and very large, deep purple, double flowers, growing to a height of 55 cm.

Dahlia 'Moonfire'

Grows to a height of 90 cm with rich bronze foliage and striking single flowers, creamy yellow with darker burnt orange near the centre.

Dahlia 'David Howard'

Dahlia 'Ellen Houston'

Grows to a height of 46 cm with purple-black foliage and vibrant orange-red flowers, making an excellent dahlia for the front of the border.

Dahlia 'Fascination'

Right

Dahlia 'Moonfire'

Semidouble, bright magenta-pink flowers contrast well with the deep bronze foliage, growing to a height of 50 cm.

Dahlia 'Preston Park'

Short bedding variety, growing to a spread and height of 45 cm, with very dark bronze, almost black, foliage. Single flowered, bright scarlet.

Dahlia 'Roxy'

Grows to 40 cm tall, a very floriferous form, with bushy, lustrous black foliage and attention-grabbing almost day-glow magenta flowers.

Dahlia 'Sunshine'

Looks similar to 'Moonfire' but only grows to 65 cm tall.

Dahlia 'Swanlake'

Dwarf form that grows to a height of just 25 cm with dark bronze foliage and semidouble white flowers that become creamy yellow toward the centre.

Dahlia 'Tally Ho'

Grows to a height of 75 cm with very dark, almost black foliage and single vermilion flowers.

Eremurus (Asphodelaceae)

Desert candle, foxtail lily
Western to central Asia

This genus of between forty and fifty species of fleshy-rooted and fleshy-stemmed perennials is found growing in dry grassland and dry rocky areas. They are statuesque in appearance, growing from basal clumps of linear, strap-shaped leaves, from which a towering leafless flower spike appears, up to 3 m tall, topped with a dense raceme of small, star-shaped flowers with conspicuous stamens, giving the inflorescence a soft appearance. The foliage dies back after flowering. They make excellent plants for the back of the exotic border, looking like exploding fireworks, and are available in a good range of colours. A cross between *Eremurus olgae* and *E. stenophyllus* has resulted in many free-flow-ering hybrid groups in shades of yellow, orange, amber, and pink to white. All *Eremurus* species are hardy to at least −10°c. They prefer humus-rich, well-drained, sandy soil in full sun in a sheltered position, as the tall stems have a tendency to fall over in windy spells.

Flower spikes of an *Eremurus* hybrid towering over *Agave angustifolia* var. *marginata*

Eremurus himalaicus

Frost-hardy / Full sun

Basal, tufted, strap-shaped, bright green leaves up to 30 cm in length give rise to majestic, long flower spikes 1.2–2 m tall topped with a raceme of numerous starry white flowers with golden yellow centres and protruding stamens, in early summer.

Eremurus robustus

Frost-hardy / Full sun

From Tajikistan, Kyrgyzstan, and Afghanistan. Basal, tufted, bluish green, strap-shaped foliage, up to 1 m long, gives rise to a flower spike 2–3 m tall, with a dense raceme of pale peachy pink star-shaped flowers up to 5 cm across, in early summer. Many exciting hybrids are available in an assortment of colours.

Eremurus stenophyllus

Frost-hardy / Full sun

Eucomis autumnalis

Basal, tufted perennial, with lance-shaped, midgreen leaves up to 30 cm in length, from which the flowering spike grows to a height of 1.5 m, topped with a raceme of brilliant yellow star-shaped flowers in summer, fading to brownish orange with age, giving a very pleasing two-tone effect.

Eucomis (Hyacinthaceae)

Pineapple lily
South Africa

This genus encompasses eleven species of summer- and autumn-flowering bulbous plants, grown for their lush leaves and showy spikes of flowers, which are topped with small tufts of pale green, leaflike bracts, resembling a pineapple. These easy plants for the exotic garden, first introduced into cultivation in the United Kingdom more than two hundred years ago, prefer a position with full sun in moist, well-drained, humus-rich soil that is drier during the winter months. They will take −5°c and lower in dormant season with a mulch of bark or grit. All make excellent container plants. Many hybrids are available.

Eucomis autumnalis

Frost-hardy / Full sun

Eucomis bicolor

From eastern South Africa, bulbous plant reaching 20–30 cm tall or more and 60–70 cm wide. Leaves semi-erect, strap-shaped, undulating, from a semi-erect basal tuft. Upright flower spike is topped with 15-cm racemes of densely packed, small, star-shaped white flowers aging to pale green, with leaflike bracts at the apex from late summer to autumn.

Eucomis bicolor

Frost-hardy / Full sun

Clump-forming bulbous plant, naturally growing in damp meadows and on stream banks. Leaves 30 cm long and 8–10 cm across appear from large part-submerged bulbs in spring and are light green, soft, undulating, and semi-erect, from a semi-erect basal tuft. Flower spike reaches 30–60 cm tall, topped with a flower head consisting of many loosely packed, pale green, star-shaped flowers with maroon edges, lasting for many weeks. Fetid scent attracts flies.

Eucomis comosa

syn. *E. punctata*
Frost-hardy / Full sun

From the eastern Cape and South Africa, bulbous plant growing to 70 cm tall and 30–60 cm wide. Green leaves, strap-shaped, undulating, with purple spotting underneath. Flower spikes purple-spotted, topped with a raceme of white to greenish white, often pink-tinted, flowers with bronze-purple ovaries and a tuft of bracts at the apex. 'Sparkling Burgundy' is a stunning variety, reaching 46–60 cm tall and up to 90 cm across when well grown. Strongest burgundy-red leaves and purple-red flowers and stems develop when grown in full sun; otherwise, greenish bronze when grown in a more shaded position. Flowers from late summer into autumn, followed by showy persistent seed capsules. Many new and interesting hybrids are available to the avid collector.

Eucomis pallidiflora

Giant pineapple lily
Frost-hardy / Full sun

Bulbous plant growing to about 75 cm, with a spread of up to 60 cm. Leaves sword-shaped, semi-erect, slightly undulating. Bears a yellow-green spike topped with densely packed, star-shaped, greenish-white flowers, creating a very pleasing effect.

Eucomis pole-evansii

Giant pineapple lily
Frost-hardy / Full sun

Largest species of the genus, with a flower spike reaching up to a staggering 2 m tall in ideal conditions, though usually less in cultivation. Flowers creamy white, ovaries green. Leaves green, up to 20 cm across and 1 m long, gently tapering toward the tip. Prefers wetland habitats in the wild, so is best grown in humus-rich, moisture-retentive soil; will grow in ordinary garden soil but will be smaller. Works well as a container plant. Flower spike has a tendency to bend so may need to be staked.

Eucomis comosa
'Sparkling
Burgundy'

Galtonia (Hyacinthaceae/Lilaceae)

South Africa

Right, top

Gladiolus callianthus, flower detail

Right, bottom

Gladiolus callianthus with *Canna* 'Durban'

The three species of bulbous perennials in this genus from moist grasslands are grown for their tall spires of nodding flowers, somewhat reminiscent of loose hyacinths, giving a light and airy feel when planted en masse. These late summer-flowering bulbs work well in the garden or as container plants. They prefer moist, well-drained soil in a position with full sun.

Galtonia candicans

Frost-hardy / Full sun

Bulbous perennial growing to 1.2 m tall by 30 cm across, with strap-shaped, fleshy green leaves up to 75 cm long. Dramatic, slender racemes of tubular, bell-shaped, pendent, slightly scented white flowers with green bases, up to 5 cm long, form in late summer. Hardy to −10°C and lower.

Galtonia candicans

Galtonia princeps

Frost-hardy / Full sun

Slightly smaller plant than *G. candicans*, hailing from the Drakensberg Mountains, growing to a height of 90 cm, with somewhat broader pillars of up to thirty tubular, pale green, hanging bells from mid-summer. Hardy to −10°C.

Galtonia viridiflora

Frost-hardy / Full sun

Bulbous perennial growing to a height of 60 cm or more, with lance-shaped, broad, greenish grey leaves up to 60 cm long. Often confused with *G. princeps*, though this is a more wonderful plant. In late summer produces racemes of waxy, pale lime green, with trumpet-shaped flowers, flushed white at the petal edges. Hardy to −5°C. In colder areas, dig up the bulbs and store in frost-free conditions during the winter months.

Gladiolus (Iridaceae)

Mostly South Africa, with some species in northwestern and eastern Africa, the Mediterranean, the Arabian Peninsula, and western Asia

This genus contains about 180 species of cormous perennial plants hailing from rocky areas and seasonally dry grasslands. Although most gardeners associate gladioli with the large blowsy hybrids, one species I like in particular is *Gladiolus callianthus*, which is still generally sold under its former name *Acidanthera bicolor*. And although some might think it rather trite to grow the many hybrids in an exotic situation, I would beg to differ. In Victorian times, they were often planted in between cannas, giving the illusion of early canna flower spikes before the main flowers appear later in the season. They look very attractive when thickly planted in containers. I won't mention any of the hybrids as there are so many to choose from—in shades from lime green to intense red—that it is a personal choice.

Gladiolus callianthus

syn. *Acidanthera bicolor* var. *murieliae*, *Acidanthera murieliae*

Peacock flower, Abyssinian gladiolus

Tender / Full sun

Erect perennial bulb from Ethiopia (formerly Abyssinia), reaching 60–90 cm tall from a flat, round, brown corm. Long, sword-shaped green leaves are up to 9 cm long, though usually less. Flowers fragrant, white with burgundy centre, in groups of three to six, up to 7.5 cm in diameter. Plant in groups in well-drained soil 10 cm deep and 5 cm apart in spring, or plant closer together in containers, for a fantastic midsummer display. Dig up the tubers and store in frost-free conditions for the winter.

completely recurved, undulating, bright scarlet-red petals that fade to claret and purple, yellow toward the base and the margins. Preferring moist, well-drained soil, it makes an excellent conservatory or greenhouse plant. Feed regularly during the summer. When the plant dies down in autumn, store the brittle tubers in a dry, frost-free place for the winter months.

Haemanthus (Amaryllidaceae)

South Africa

Twenty-one species of bulbous plants, of which some are evergreen, belong to this genus in the amaryllis family. In their native habitat they grow on grassy, rocky hillsides, where they bloom from summer to autumn and sporadically in winter. They are interesting plants that are fun to grow, looking somewhat like a shaving brush on a stalk, with dense heads of numerous small flowers with an attractive surrounding whorl of brightly coloured, waxy spathes. Normally the large bulbs produce only two large, thick, broadly elliptic, green to dark green basal leaves. The name is derived from the Greek *haema* (blood) and *anthos* (flower).

They are best grown as container plants that can be overwintered at a minimum of 5°C under glass. The bulbs should be planted with their necks just above the soil, in late autumn. They prefer well-drained, humus-rich soil-based compost that is kept moist during the growing season and on the dry side during the winter months. They flower best when pot-bound.

Haemanthus albiflos

Shaving-brush plant, white paintbrush
Semi-tender / Dappled shade

Evergreen, bulbous perennial with pairs of midgreen, semi-erect, then spreading, broadly strap-shaped leaves, which can reach a length of 40 cm in ideal conditions, though usually much shorter. Thick stems 20–30 cm tall, topped with brushlike heads 3–7 cm across, bear as many as fifty small white flowers with protruding stamens from autumn to winter.

Gloriosa superba 'Rothschildiana'

Gloriosa (Colchicaceae/Lilaceae)

Climbing lily, flame lily, glory lily
Africa, India

The one species belonging to this genus, *Gloriosa superba*, is often found growing by streams and rivers in woodland areas in the tropics. It is grown for its glamorous and colourful flowers.

Gloriosa superba

Tender / Sun to partial shade

Highly variable, climbing and scrambling, vine-like, tuberous perennial growing to a height of 1.8 m or more, with one or more stems. Leaves bright green, glossy, 5–8 cm long, with tendrils up to 5 cm long, from the leaf tip. Flowers are solitary, yellow, red, purple, or bicoloured, 10–13 cm across, on long stalks, emerging from leaf axils, from summer to autumn. 'Citrina' has yellow-striped maroon flowers; 'Grandiflora', large golden yellow flowers; the most commonly available, 'Rothschildiana', has

Haemanthus coccineus

Cape tulip

Semi-tender / Dappled shade

Deciduous, bulbous perennial, with dark purple-brown–streaked stems topped with heads 5–10 cm across, containing as many as a hundred miniscule flowers, with very prominent bright yellow stamens surrounded by rich scarlet bracts. Two (or sometimes three) semi-erect to prostrate, midgreen, strap-shaped, occasionally purple-marked leaves up to 45 cm long (though usually less) appear after flowering has finished.

Hymenocallis (Amaryllidaceae)

syn. *Ismene*

Spider lily

Southern United States, Central and South America

This genus of around thirty species of bulbous tropical and subtropical plants was once classified as *Ismene*, and the name still persists in horticulture. The very distinctive flowers have exquisite, thin, tapering, streamerlike petals, surrounding a narcissus-like central cup. This is a magnificently beautiful genus of plants that should be grown far more often. Although most are hardy down to 0°C, they are best grown in containers that can be kept at a minimum of 5°C.

The name is derived from the Greek words *hymen* (membrane) and *kallos* (beauty). The following require humus-rich, moist soil while growing and dry conditions during dormancy.

Hymenocallis × festalis

Half-hardy / Dappled shade

Deciduous, clump-forming, bulbous perennial, growing up to a height of 80 cm by 30 cm. Basal leaves semi-erect, oblong, mid to dark green, up to 90 cm long. Up to five scented flowers, 8–12 cm across, with long, narrow petals and flared cups, slightly yellow at the base inside, grow at right angles to the main stem. In temperate climates, flowers are usually produced in late spring; in their native habitat, at any time of year. Keep dry when dormant and store in frost-free conditions.

Hymenocallis littoralis

Tender / Dappled to full shade

Evergreen, clump-forming, bulbous perennial growing to a height of 70–90 cm in its native habitat, with evergreen leaves, tapering at both ends, up to 120 cm in length, though much less in temperate cultivation. Flowering stalk has four to eight long, white, streamerlike, deflexed petals surrounding a short, flattened cup.

Hymenocallis narcissiflora

Peruvian daffodil

Semi-tender / Dappled shade

Deciduous, bulbous perennial, hailing from the Peruvian Andes, where it grows in stony areas up to 300 m high. Grows to 50–60 cm tall. Basal leaves are strap-shaped, semi-erect, and dark green, to 60 cm long. Flowers are produced in loose cluster of

Hymenocallis littoralis

up to five deliciously scented white flowers, up to 10 cm across, occasionally with greenish-striped tubes. Overwinter at a minimum of 5°c.

Hymenocallis 'Sulphur Queen'

Half-hardy / Dappled shade

Bulbous perennial growing to 60 cm tall, with basal leaves that are strap-shaped, semi-erect, dark green, 25–60 cm long. Flowering stalks are topped with up to six fragrant, soft sulphur-yellow flowers, with a green star in the throat, up to 15 cm across.

Iris (Iridaceae)

Northern temperate regions

This genus comprises more than three hundred species of upright, rhizomatous, fleshy rooted perennials. I include only two here that fit in well with other exotic plants, even when not in flower, because of their unusual foliage.

Iris confusa

Frost-hardy / Sun or dappled shade

Vigorous, rhizomatous perennial iris from Yunnan Province, China, growing to about 90 cm high and slowly spreading. Branching flower stems produce up to thirty short-lived blooms in succession, which are white with purple or yellow spots around a yellow crest, up to 5 cm across. 'Martyn Rix' has ruffled blue flowers.

Iris japonica

Iris japonica

Frost-hardy / Dappled shade

Crested iris that grows in China and Japan in relatively wet grasslands on hillsides, or at the edges of open forests. Grows to a height of 45–60 cm with a spreading rhizomatous surface root system and produces many fans of strap-shaped, glossy, dark green leaves up to 45 cm long. In late spring up to four flattish, ruffled, white or pale lavender flowers with orange markings appear on branched stems. 'Variegata' (syn. 'Aphrodite') has stunning green-and-white-striped leaves.

Nerine (Lilaceae)

Guernsey lily / Spider lily
South Africa

This genus of about thirty species of bulbous perennials, naturally found in arid habitats, screes, and rocky areas in southern Africa, is grown for their exquisite flower heads, somewhat resembling small versions of *Amaryllis*. They have been much hybridised, creating some beautiful colour variations. They are very useful for late colour and fit well in a Mediterranean-style or arid garden, as they like to be baked during the summer months. The hardier forms are the most commonly available and the less hardy from specialist growers. They prefer to be grown in gritty compost, with their necks exposed, in containers kept in a frost-free place during the winter months. Keep dry while dormant.

Nerine bowdenii

Frost-hardy / Full sun

Commonly available and the most cold-hardy. Grows to a height of 40 cm, with broad strap-shaped leaves, up to 30 cm long, appearing after the flowers. In autumn, bears open heads of eight or more pink, faintly scented, funnel-shaped flowers, with recurved, undulating petals. Prefers well-drained soil in full sun, against a south-facing wall for added protection. In colder areas mulch well during the winter months. 'Pink Triumph' has rich deep pink flowers.

Nerine bowdenii

Nerine flexuosa

Frost-hardy / Full sun

Bulbous perennial growing up to 40 cm tall, with pink flowers in clusters of up to twenty blooms. Leaves are glossy green, up to 30 cm long, almost evergreen. 'Alba' bears white flowers occasionally flushed pale pink.

Nerine sarniensis

Half-hardy / Full sun

Bulbous perennial, producing clusters of ten or more stunning, iridescent crimson flowers with long conspicuous stamens in early autumn, on stalk up to 45 cm tall, followed by erect, strap-shaped leaves up to 30 cm long. Several varieties are available, including 'Cherry Ripe' (rose red), 'Early Snow' (white), 'Radiant Queen' (bright rose pink), and 'Salmon Supreme' (dark salmon pink). All will take lows of 0°C, and hence must be stored in frost-free conditions during the winter months.

Scadoxus (Amaryllidaceae)

Blood lily

Africa and the Arabian Peninsula

Nine species of bulbous and rhizomatous perennials belong to this genus, found growing in woodland and tropical regions of its native habitat. Cultivated for their stunning, spherical flower heads of cylindrical red flowers, borne on erect green leafless stems from spring to summer, they are closely related to *Haemanthus*, also sharing the common name blood lily. However, they differ from each other in their form and the arrangement of their leaves.

Scadoxus multiflorus

syn. *Haemanthus multiflorus*

Tender / Full sun

Large, bulbous, nearly evergreen perennial growing to a height of 50 cm with a slightly wider spread. Leaves are bright green, fleshy, oval to lance-shaped, growing in an upright branching rosette. Spherical heads of small star-shaped bright salmon-red florets with spidery stamens appear in summer. *Scadoxus multiflorus* subsp. *katherinae* (syn. *Haemanthus katherinae*) has green, wavy, undulating margined leaves and grows to 70 cm tall with a spread of 110 cm. Spectacular flower head is huge, reaching a diameter of 25 cm, spherical, consisting of up to two hundred flowers

held clear of the foliage at the end of a solitary stem. Each flower is pinkish orange-red with protruding stamens carrying bright yellow anthers. Each plant will produce only one flower head in a season.

Scadoxus puniceus

syn. *Haemanthus magnificus*
Half-hardy / Full sun

Striking bulbous perennial growing to a height of 50–60 cm with semi-erect, elliptic, wavy-margined, basal leaves to 30 cm long, with a stem often spotted with purple near the base. From spring to summer, conical heads of up to a hundred small, yellowish green to pink or scarlet flowers are borne within bracts that may be large and dark purplish red in colour, up to 15 cm across, followed by red berries. May survive below freezing if kept dry during the winter months; otherwise overwinter frost-free.

Sprekelia (Amaryllidaceae)

Central and South America

The single species in this genus is grown for its large showy flowers and is found on rocky slopes in areas that have dry winters followed by wet springs and summers. It dislikes root disturbance, so should be allowed to form a clump, which will flower freely. Although it will take temperatures down to 0°c for short periods if kept dry during the winter months, it is best grown as a container plant, in humus-rich, well-drained compost with the neck showing. It can be grown outside in mild areas, with a dry mulch in cold weather.

Sprekelia formosissima

Aztec lily, Jacobean lily / St. James lily
Half-hardy / Sun or dappled shade

Bulbous, usually winter-dormant plant growing to 30 cm tall by 20 cm across. Greyish green, semi-erect, straplike leaves grow in dense clumps on mature plants. Very showy, solitary flowers up to 12 cm across have six petals, three pointing up and three pointing down, in a shade of stunning, intense red in spring.

Tigridia (Iridaceae)

Mexico and Guatemala

Twenty-three species of bulbous plants, grown for their exotic flowers, belong to this genus in the iris family. *Tigridia pavonia* is the most commonly available and is relatively inexpensive. A pot full near a front door is a sight to behold.

Tigridia pavonia

Mexican shell flower, peacock flower, tiger flower
Semi-tender / Full sun or partial shade

Exquisite Mexican native growing to a height of 60 cm or more. Basal leaves, 30–50 cm long, are green and sword-shaped, with pronounced longitudinal veining. Flowers are borne on occasionally branched stems and are yellow to red with a heavily red-marked yellow cup; can also be pink to orange, red, yellow, or white, with usually contrasting central markings, 10–13 cm across. Well-drained soil and regular watering during the growing period is essential. They will survive in soil that does not freeze during the winter; otherwise dig up and store in frost-free conditions during the winter months.

Tulbaghia (Alliaceae)

Wild garlic
South Africa

This is a genus of semi-evergreen bulbous, clump-forming perennials in the onion family grown for their dainty flowers. The leaves and flowers can

be used to garnish salads and have a garlic-like fragrance when crushed. Considered borderline to hardy, they will survive in most gardens given a mulch. In colder areas they make excellent container plants that can be overwintered dry in a cold greenhouse, with a little heat if it becomes excessively cold. Most will take lows of −8°c for short periods overwintered this way. Native to areas that have summer rainfall, they grow well in a maritime climate. They flower during the summer months, spasmodically at other times, depending on local conditions. Many new and interesting hybrids have been created over the years. They prefer well-drained soil that is kept moist during the summer months and do well in deep containers, as they have an extensive fleshy root system.

*Tigridia pavonia,
flower*

Tulbaghia natalensis

Frost-hardy / Full sun

Small, bulbous perennial growing to a height of 20–30 cm with light green, linear leaves. Flowers are slightly fragrant, dark purple or white, from early to late summer.

Tulbaghia violacea

Tulbaghia simmleri

Frost-hardy / Full sun

Bulbous, semi-evergreen perennial growing to a height of 50–60 cm with comparatively broad, linear, greyish green leaves. Inflorescence has clusters of up to forty scented mauve flowers from spring to summer. 'Alba' is a white form.

Tulbaghia violacea

Frost-hardy / Full sun

Most commonly available *Tulbaghia* species. Vigorous, clump-forming perennial growing to a height of 45–60 cm, with grey-green linear foliage. Inflorescences are in clusters of up to twenty mauve-pink flowers, from spring to autumn and occasionally at other times of year, depending on situation. 'Silver Lace' (syn. 'Variegata') is a very attractive, slightly smaller variegated form with vertical creamy white striations.

Watsonia (Iridaceae)

South Africa

This genus comprises about fifty species of cormous, clump-forming plants in the iris family, with a somewhat sparse, crocosmia-like appearance, with more tubular flowers. Being on the borderline of hardiness, to 0°C, they are best grown in warmer parts of maritime climate zones and covered in a deep mulch in other areas, or grown as container plants that are brought into frost-free conditions for the winter and kept fairly dry. They prefer well-drained poor soil. They are beautiful plants that deserve to be grown more often.

Watsonia beatricis

syn. *W. pillansii*
Half-hardy / Full sun

Cormous, clump-forming, summer-flowering perennial growing to a height of 1 m with long, erect, sword-shaped green leaves. Stems carry dense, branched spikes of red-orange, narrow, curved, tubular flowers, up to 5 cm long.

Watsonia borbonica

syn. *W. pyramidata*
Half-hardy / Full sun

Robust, cormous, summer-flowering perennial growing to a height of 1–1.5 m with narrow, sword-shaped green leaves. Inflorescence consists of lightly scented, loose, branched spikes of exquisite pink to dark pink flowers with six lobes, from spring to early summer.

Watsonia fourcadei

Half-hardy / Full sun

Cormous, clump-forming, summer-flowering perennial growing to a height of 1.5 m with erect, sword-shaped green leaves. Inflorescence is in the form of a dense spike of tubular salmon-red flowers up to 8 cm across with six lobes.

*Watsonia
borbonica*

Watsonia meriana

Watsonia meriana

Half-hardy / Full sun

Cormous, clump-forming, summer-flowering perennial growing to a height of 1 m with erect, sword-shaped green leaves. Stem carries a loose spike of tubular pinkish red flowers, up to 6.5 cm long, with six spreading lobes.

Cacti, Succulents, Yuccas, and Other Spiky Things

True cacti are natives of the Americas, whereas succulents are found throughout the world from moist temperate to arid tropical regions. The term *succulent* simply means juicy. Most cacti are juicy succulents with prickles. These robust plants evolved under conditions where they had to survive prolonged drought by storing water in swollen leaves, stems, or roots. Spines on cacti developed as an effective method to ward off predators that would like to eat them. Succulents have developed protection either through colouration that blends into their surrounding habitats or by the production of noxious or toxic chemicals. Yuccas are viciously spiky plants. All add interest to the exotic garden with their bold forms and dramatic, if sometimes long-awaited and fleeting, blooms.

Cacti

When asked, the typical cactus grower will tell you that you can't grow cacti outside in a maritime climate: "They just rot in our wet winters." This is wrong! Surprisingly, many cacti take low and freezing temperatures well, provided they are planted in exceedingly free-draining soil or have a canopy over them to keep moisture out, as this does the most damage during the winter months. Adding coarse sand, grit, or other noncompacting aggregates to the planting area increases the rapidity of drainage and makes for healthier growth with far less damage during the winter months. Giving cacti full sun and good air movement is also essential. The following is a representative selection of those species that will grow—even thrive—in a maritime climate if these requirements are met.

Echinocereus (Cactaceae)

North, Central, and South America

These are generally small, ball-shaped cacti, forming slightly upright columns when mature. Several species are worth growing; here are a couple that are hardy to −15°c or lower.

Echinocereus reichenbachii var. baileyi

Hardy / Full sun

Small, solitary clumping plants from Oklahoma and Texas, up to 25 cm high, individually to about 4 cm across, with white spines and huge magenta flowers that often obscure the plant itself.

Echinocereus triglochidiatus

Hardy / Full sun

Clumping plant that reaches up to 40 cm high by 60 cm across in its native habitat (Nevada, Utah, and Colorado south to southern California, Arizona, New Mexico, Texas, and Mexico) in a relatively short period. Small scarlet to brick red flowers are occasionally produced in a warm summer.

Echinopsis (Cactaceae)

South and Central America

Unhelpfully, this genus has recently been swollen to the bursting point by taxonomists who have now lumped many defunct genera into it. This is a shame, as some of the more useful "garden cacti" that were previous identified by genera such as *Lobivia*, *Sohrensia*, *Trichocereus*, *Helianthocereus*, and so forth, are now all *Echinopsis* species, and not all *Echinopsis* species are winter-hardy! Also these classifications gave a clue as to their habits; as a rule *Trichocereus*, for example, were taller columnar cacti and *Sohrensia* could grow into substantial barrels in time. Regardless, any *Echinopsis* is worth trying—ultimately, growing cacti outside in a cool-temperate climate is very largely trial and error, and the errors will be fewer with *Echinopsis* than with most groups.

Echinopsis bruchii

syn. *Lobivia formosa* var. *bruchii*, *Soehrensia bruchii*, *Trichocereus bruchii*
Frost-hardy / Full sun

In time forms a basketball-sized barrel up to 50 cm high in its native habitat, with a dark green body and, generally, short yellowish spines. Takes lows of −5°c and probably lower.

Echinopsis huascha

Frost-hardy / Full sun

Variable plant forming a cluster of small snaking, branching dark green columns with small, thin, straw-coloured spines up to about 60 cm in length and 5–7.5 cm in diameter. Flower colour is variable, ranging from yellow through pink to deep red. Hardy to about −10°c.

Echinopsis pasacana

Frost-hardy / Full sun

Probably the easiest to grow of the tall columnar cacti, this is a visual replacement for the more familiar saguaro cactus of the deserts of southwestern North America. Slowly grows in the wild into an imposing column, 5 m by 50 cm in diameter, with thick ribs carrying prominent yellow spines. Perhaps the most alien-looking plant that it is possible to grow outside in a maritime climate. Flowers, should they occur, are nocturnally produced white trumpets the size of dinner plates. Possibly hardy to −8°c or lower, given perfect drainage and full sun.

Opuntia (Cactaceae)

Prickly pear
Southern Canada to southern South America, including the Galapagos and some of the Caribbean islands

This very variable genus contains about three hundred species from ground hugging to treelike in form that can be found growing from high altitude to temperate regions and tropical lowlands. For most people, these are either windowsill or green-

house plants, with maybe little interest. A large number of opuntias are hardy, but not many are worth growing: they are weeds, quickly outgrowing their allotted space and smothering their neighbours. The three plants described here are worth trying, though, because they look right in an exotic garden. They must have exceedingly well-drained soil with added grit or anything you can find that lets water pass through quickly. The worst thing for any cacti is having wet feet in winter or water dripping into the crowns, which soon turn to rot.

Opuntias naturally split into two groups. Although all have jointed stem segments, one group (often known as tunas) have flat padded segments, while the other (called chollas) have cylindrical segments (some authorities split this group off into *Cylindropuntia*). One or two species of tunas are important food crops, both for their sweet and edible but seed-filled fruits (*Opuntia ficus-indica* is one of these) and their pads, which, stripped of spines, form an important part of the vegetable diet in parts of Mexico.

Opuntia imbricata

Hardy / Full sun

One of the hardiest cholla opuntias, making a small tangled shrub up to 1 m tall comprised of a mass of finger-thin, jointed midgreen branches, extremely densely spined, in a criss-cross pattern of small white spines. Hardy down to −20°c if dry or snow covered as it would be in the wild.

Opuntia phaeacantha

Hardy / Full sun

Probably the pick of the hardier tunas for overall performance. Less inclined to flop, in a range of forms with varying spination, typically forming a congested, slow-growing shrub to about 1 m tall, with large pads up to 30 cm long by 20 cm wide, with sparse spination. Flower colour can vary but usually yellow. Hardy to −25°c or lower.

A tuna-type opuntia growing wild on a cliff edge in Madeira, Portugal

Opuntia robusta

Frost-hardy / Full sun

Large-growing species with very large, almost circular pads up to 50 cm in diameter, in a shade of bluish green. Hardy to −8°c, maybe lower, but a little more susceptible to rotting in damp winters. Can become rather floppy when more than four pads high, hence rather susceptible to being blown over by wind.

Opuntia robusta

Oreocereus (Cactaceae)

Old man of the Andes

Peruvian and Bolivian Andes

This genus contains small columnar cacti from high altitudes covered in fluffy hairs through which golden yellow spines protrude. There are a few species that are essentially the same apart from variations in the hair density and size. One favourite species is *Oreocereus trollii*, which slowly but surely grows to about 1.5 m tall and is hardy to at least −5°c, considerably lower with protection.

Aeonium arboreum

Winter-Hardy Succulents

The majority of succulents tend to be found in warmer climates where there is little chance of frost. The ones that are winter-hardy compared to cacti are limited in number. We have the choice of growing them in pots and containers that can be overwintered in a greenhouse, then brought into the garden when all fear of frost has passed, or limiting ourselves to the hardy species that are available and planting them out permanently. These include some agaves, aloes, beschornerias, dasylirions, lewisias, nolinas, sedums, and sempervivums.

Sempervivums, commonly known as houseleeks or hens-and-chickens, are especially hardy and commonly available with some very colourful hybrid forms. Many stonecrops or sedums are exceedingly cold tolerant, making them very suitable for cool-temperate gardens. Sedums, sempervivums, and many of the other cold-hardy succulents are excellent ornamentals that do well in diverse growing conditions. Sempervivums and sedums have become popular plants for living roofs, an alternative to more traditional roof coverings, being efficient, attractive, and changing colour with the seasons. Nigel Dunnett and Noël Kingsbury discuss the practice and techniques in detail in their book *Planting Green Roofs and Living Walls* (2004).

There has been much experimentation in recent years by avid enthusiasts, with good success. Much of the following information was supplied by one of them, Paul Spracklin, who gardens near the mouth of the River Thames Estuary, near to Southend-on-Sea, Essex. This part of England is hot, sunny, and very dry, with an average 500 mm of annual rainfall. Proximity to the sea and a south-facing, sloping site make the microclimate fairly benign, with winter lows of only −5°C in the past ten years—all of which adds up to a fairly interesting trial bed for succulent plants. Paul plants the succulents in raised beds filled with freely draining material. Currently his favoured material is coal residue mixed with ordinary garden soil to make up no less than 50 per cent of the volume—preferably a lot more. If he had to start all over again, he says, he would probably use just the clinker (or ballast/grit/limestone chips or whatever was at hand). He stresses that well-drained soil is absolutely essential, and full sun is preferred.

Aeonium (Crassulaceae)

Madeira and the Canary Islands, with some in
the Cape Verde Islands, northern Africa, and the
Mediterranean region

This genus includes some thirty species of ever-green perennials, often shrubby and woody-stemmed at the base, found growing mostly in the Canary Islands on hillsides and escarpments. They produce succulent rosettes of waxy leaves, generally at the ends of naked stems, often producing aeri-al roots. Depending on the plant and the species, the leaves can have attractive variegations. There are also some small stemless species that form flat ground-hugging rosettes at the ends of the stems. With their succulent appearance and texture, they make excellent summer bedding plants since their architectural shape contrasts well with most other bedding plants. Plant them out after last frost in moderately fertile, exceedingly well-drained soil in full sun. They can also be used effectively in pots and containers. Water these plants sparingly and let them dry out between waterings, especially in winter, because they are adapted to dry conditions and their succulent leaves store water for use during dry periods. Although they can take temperatures down to almost freezing for short periods, during the winter months they should generally be kept at a minimum of 5°c.

*Aeonium
arboreum
'Sunburst'*

Aeonium arboreum

Semi-tender / Full sun

Upright, perennial, succulent subshrub, growing to a height and spread of 2 m in its native habitat on the Atlantic coast of Morocco, though more like 30–90 cm in cool-temperate climates. Succulent branches bear tightly packed light green leaves in terminal rosettes 15–20 cm across. In spring and summer, bears large pyramidal heads of yellow flowers up to 30 cm long. 'Atropurpureum' has glossy bronzy-purple leaves, while 'Luteovariegatum' has green leaves with wide margins of light yellow. 'Sunburst' has attractive stripy green leaves with varying-width creamy yellow edges. 'Variegatum' has green leaves variegated with cream. 'Zwartkop' (syn. 'Schwarz-kopf'), whose name means "black head," is a very popular aeonium and deservedly so, with rich pur-plish black, narrow, spoon-shaped, polished leaves, much darker than 'Atropurpureum'. The stronger the sun, the blacker it becomes. Leaves become paler during winter.

Aeonium tabuliforme

Semi-tender / Full sun

Low-spreading aeonium from the Canary Islands (Tenerife) growing to a height of 8–10 cm with short unbranched stems bearing platelike rosettes of tightly packed light green leaves, hairy at the edges, up to 50 cm across in the wild but more like 15–26 cm in cultivation, especially if grown outside during the summer months.

Aeonium urbicum

Semi-tender / Sun to partial shade

Very upright aeonium from the Canary Islands with unbranched stems growing to 90 cm tall or more, with densely leaved, cup-shaped, open rosettes of bluish green, spatula-shaped leaves, often tinted purplish red on the edges, to 15 cm long or more. Produces creamy yellow flowers in summer and prefers moist, well-drained soil.

Aeonium arboreum 'Zwartkop'

Aeonium balsamiferum

Aeonium balsamiferum

Semi-tender / Full sun

Shrubby succulent perennial growing to a height of 1.5 m in the wild (Canary Islands—Lanzarote and Fuerteventura) but more like 30–46 cm in cool-temperate climates. Tightly packed, sticky, balsam-scented rosettes reach up to 12 cm across. Needs moderate water; tolerant of humidity in winter but needs good drainage.

Aeonium canariense

Semi-tender / Full sun

Short-stemmed perennial from the Canary Islands (Tenerife) growing to a height of 25 cm by 50 cm or more, with multiple stems, occasionally branched at the base. Terminal rosettes up to 38 cm across consist of spoon-shaped, greyish green, somewhat sticky leaves with dense white hairs on both surfaces, up to 20 cm long or more. Pale yellowish green or white flowers are borne in leafy pyramidal heads in late spring to summer.

Agave (Agavaceae)

North, Central, and South America and the
Caribbean Islands

This genus includes more than two hundred species of rosette-forming perennials found growing in desert and scrubby areas to mountainous regions in their native habitats. They usually have rigid fleshy leaves with sharp spines along the margins and a needle-sharp terminal spine. They are quintessential desert plants for the exotic garden, having a very architectural feel and adding dramatic impact whether grown in small to large containers, bedded out for the summer months, or permanently planted out in the garden. Many are amazingly tough plants that can take low temperatures well if grown in exceedingly free-draining gritty soils and kept dry in winter; their biggest problem is winter wet. They are monocarpic, meaning that the main plant dies after flowering, leaving new side shoots to grow on.

Agave americana
'Mediopicta'

Intrepid gardeners in the British Isles have been experimenting with their hardiness, with good success. They are commonly seen in gardens along the south coast of England, especially into Cornwall and the Isles of Scilly, where some astounding specimens can be seen. Their native sizes are given below, though they are usually considerably smaller in cool-temperate climates and rarely flower.

Agave americana
Frost-hardy / Full sun

Evergreen succulent species growing to a height of 2 m by 3 m in its native habitat in northeastern Mexico. Long lance-shaped, fleshy, bluish green leaves, with toothed edges and needle-sharp tips at the end of each leaf. Tall flower spikes are produced on mature specimens up to 8 m and taller, topped with large panicles of yellowish funnel-shaped flowers. Withstands hard frosts when mature but should be protected from severe frost and kept dry. Hardy to −8°c.

Variegated forms are somewhat smaller and correspondingly less hardy. 'Marginata' has leaves with yellow or white stripes on the margins. 'Mediopicta' has a central yellow variegated strip down each leaf.

spines. Central core also purses together interestingly, clasping around central new growth. One of a very few agaves that does not die after flowering, this event taking place via auxiliary buds. Takes damper conditions than some other agaves and handles frosts down to −6°c or lower.

'Mediopicta Alba' has a wide white band down the centre of each leaf. Hardy to −5°c if kept dry during the winter. One variegated cultivar, *Agave americana* 'Striata', is rarer but seems, unaccountably, as hardy as the plain species. Whole leaf brushed through with narrow pale yellow stripes and dashes—very unusual, very attractive, and worth seeking out.

Agave attenuata

Semi-tender / Sun or dappled shade

Evergreen succulent growing to 1 m tall by 2 m across in a warm climate, such as its native habitats in Mexico. Leaves are brittle, soft-leathery, powdery bluish lime green, without teeth or terminal spine. Arching spikes 2–4.5 m tall are produced in a warm climate. A most beautiful agave that has no tolerance for frost at all, and hence should be overwintered at a minimum temperature of 5°c. Beware of slugs!

Agave bracteosa

Frost-hardy / Full sun

Atypical-looking plant from northern Mexico, ultimately making a 70–80 cm rosette of narrow greenish leaves with no marginal teeth or terminal

Agave lophantha

Agave montana

Agave parrasana

Agave lophantha

syn. *A. univittata*
Frost-hardy / Full sun

One of the most widespread and variable agaves, up to 38 cm high by 50 cm across, typified by dark green leaves edged by a horny margin from which dark brown horny teeth emerge. Pale medial longitudinal stripe often decorates leaves. Leaf size, width, tooth size, and clustering habit vary from population to population in the wild, in southeast Texas and all the way south along the eastern side of Mexico to Veracruz. Seems to adapt to cool-temperate culture surprisingly well and appears to be hardy to about −8°c.

Agave mitis

syn. *A. celsii*
Frost-hardy / Full sun

Small to medium species of evergreen, clump-forming succulent, with individual rosettes growing to a height and spread of 69 cm in its native habitat, high altitude areas of eastern Mexico. Leaves are apple to bluish green, 30–60 cm long, 10–15 cm wide, and almost boat-shaped. Hardy to about −8°c if kept dry in winter, although more capable of tolerating damp conditions than some of the others. In the wild can be seen clinging to damp northern rock faces as well as brighter southern aspects, but always in damper areas.

Agave montana

Frost-hardy / Full sun

Relative newcomer, only discovered in northeastern Tamaulipas, Mexico, and described in the 1990s, but potentially the very best agave for growing in a cool-temperate garden. Spectacular plant forming a huge rosette 2 m across, comprising hundreds

of short, wide grey leaves, each beautifully marked and toothed, resembling a giant globe artichoke. In the wild grows as understorey and emerging species in oak and pine forests at an altitude of up to 3400 m, at which dizzy heights it regularly experiences heavy frosts, snow, ice, and damp mist for months on end during the winter, taking temperatures as low as −10°c and maybe −15°c, yet remains in pristine condition. Recent seed collections mean this plant is just starting to enter the European plant market.

Agave parrasana

Frost-hardy / Full sun

Indigenous to mountainous areas above 1200 m in northwestern Mexico. One of the more compact species, reaching a diameter of up to 60 cm when mature. Rosettes are comprised of a large number of very short, very broad leaves, measuring 20–30 cm by 15 cm, giving it a similar dense globe artichoke look to *Agave montana*. Leaf colour is typically pewter grey but colour and tooth size are variable. Very attractive agave that seems to handle damp conditions better than many. Hardy to −8°c or lower.

Agave parryi

Frost-hardy / Full sun

Evergreen succulent growing in the wild in Arizona, United States, to northern Mexico, to a height and spread of 60 cm with a dense, compact rosette of broadly oblong, spiny-edged, greyish blue leaves up to 30 cm long, with extended, vicious, needlelike terminal ends. Flower spike 3.5–6 m tall is topped

Agave parryi var. *truncata*

Agave parryi

Agave xylonacantha

with panicles of creamy flowers, tinged pinkish red in bud, on mature plants. Three recognised varieties are *couesii*, the largest and hardiest, with shorter, wider leaves and darker spines; *truncata*, the most desirable, with shortest and widest leaves though a little more tender; and *parryi*. Hardy to about −10°c.

Agave salmiana

Frost-hardy / Full sun

Most widespread of all agaves, having been cultivated for thousands of years in Mexico for its fibre and sap (brewed or distilled into the alcoholic beverage pulque or its distillate tequila, respectively). One of the most variable in appearance, ranging from dwarf, compact, wide-leaved plants reaching only 60 cm in diameter to narrow-leaved giants attaining 4 m across. Typically olive green and having an S-shaped curve to the top of the leaves. Most common form of *A. salmiana* in cultivation is variety

ferox (syn. *A. ferox*). This is one of the smaller varieties, reaching a still respectable 1.5 m diameter, but with extremely wide, beautifully puckered leaves that carry very large marginal teeth on even larger teats (bumps on the leaf margins). Leaves also have beautiful bud printing—imprint left on the leaf as it was tightly clasped around the emerging spear of new growth. Although not the hardiest agave, *A. salmiana* seems one of the most accommodating in terms of moisture tolerance. Hardy to −10°c, perhaps lower. An extremely rare variegated form exists that is highly desirable.

Agave xylonacantha

Frost-hardy / Full sun

Considered by some to be nothing more than an extreme form of *Agave lophantha*, having the same dark green leaves, often with a pale central line and carrying a pale brown horny margin. The teeth, however, set this species apart, looking like a ripsaw, set in twos, pointing backward and forward, creating a really menacing look. In the wild, in north-eastern Mexico, leaves can reach 90 cm in length. Hardy to −8°c or maybe lower.

Aloe (Aloeaceae)

Cape Verde Islands, tropical and southern Africa, Madagascar, and the Arabian Peninsula

This genus of some two hundred species of small to large, rosetted, evergreen perennials contains the well-known *Aloe vera*, valued for the medicinal properties of its sap. They can be low-growing, grasslike perennials, trees, shrubs, or climbing plants. This is a fascinating genus with many forms worthy for exotic gardens with their architectural shapes and colouration. Unfortunately, few are frost-tolerant, although many will endure low temperatures for short periods. They are best bedded out during the summer months or grown in pots and containers as specimens can become quite large. They prefer fertile, well-drained soil in full sun. Following is only a small number of aloes worth trying in temperate gardens or as container plants brought out for the summer months in colder areas.

Aloe arborescens

Candelabra aloe, octopus plant
Half-hardy / Full sun

Somewhat treelike, many-branched succulent reaching 2–3 m tall in its native habitat, though considerably smaller in cool-temperate climates. Rosettes of very fleshy, curved, tapering, bluish green leaves up to 60 cm long with wavy toothed edges produce terminal pyramidal spikes 30 cm long of cylindrical orange-red flowers in late winter to spring. Will take temperatures down to 0°c for short periods only; otherwise store in frost-free conditions. With rain shelter will take brief spells of −4°c or −5°c without too much damage. If left exposed or if the temperature becomes lower still, top growth will be cut back by frost, but plant can regrow from the roots if established; it won't take this kind of treatment for many consecutive

years, though. 'Variegata' is an attractive form with green-and-yellow-striped leaves. Both make excellent if rather big potted plants!

Aloe aristata

Frost-hardy / Full sun

Second hardiest of the African aloes. Clump-forming succulent growing to a height of 12.5 cm with an indefinite spread. Forms a mat of exotic, small, fleshy, densely leaved dark green rosettes, minutely toothed along edges and surface; whole plant takes

Aloe arborescens

Aloe aristata

Aloe ecklonis

Aloe ferox

on purplish red hues when frosted. Terminal heads of cylindrical, orange-red flowers are borne on spikes up to 50 cm long in autumn. Hardy to at least −5°C if kept dry in winter.

Aloe ecklonis

Frost-hardy / Full sun

One of a group of stemless aloes called grass aloes that are adapted to retreat underground to survive bushfires—a useful strategy employed to avoid harsh frost, too. Forms a small rosette up to 46 cm with midgreen strap-shaped leaves with toothed margins up to 40 cm long and a flower head of orange-green tubular flowers. Other grass aloes include *A. cooperi*, *A. dominella*, and *A. boylei*. Hardy to −8°C or lower.

Aloe ferox

Frost-hardy / Full sun

Single-stemmed somewhat treelike succulent growing to a height of 2–3 m in its native habitat, though considerably less in cool-temperate climates. Thick trunk is topped by rosette of fleshy, leathery, dull greyish green, broadly lance-shaped leaves with spines on the edges as well as on the top and underneath, up to 30 cm long when grown as a pot or container plant. Can also be bedded out for the summer months in well-drained soil. In summer produces erect spikes

of tubular scarlet-red flowers on mature plants, though rarely in temperate cultivation. Hardy down to about −3°C for short periods only; otherwise over-winter in dry, frost-free conditions.

Aloe maculata

syn. *A. saponaria*
Frost-hardy / Full sun

Variable plant, usually clumping but often solitary, forming small, short-stemmed rosettes up to 46 cm by 40 cm in its native habitat, consisting of wide, fleshy green leaves uniformly speckled with whitish markings, sometimes to the extent of almost producing banding. Hardiness varies with the clone, taking temperatures down to −8°C or lower, though leaf damage will occur below −2°C. Suckering forms can often regrow from beneath ground when cut back by harsh winters.

Aloe mutabilis

Frost-hardy / Full sun

Growing from vertical rock faces in southern Africa. Said by some to be just a northern form of *A. arborescens*, but this species is several degrees hardier than that one, having survived −5°C in open ground with no damage in cool-temperate gardens. Less inclined to form a tall trunk, remaining clustering, and may have bicoloured flowers of red and

Aloe striatula and
flower detail

creamy yellow in cultivated forms, while the wild species varies from bright yellow to greenish yellow. Unfortunately these are produced in winter and likely to be lost at the edge of its viability. Hardy to −6°c, maybe to −8°c if given some overhead protection to keep it dry.

Aloe pratensis

Frost-hardy / Full sun

Midsized aloe up to 40 cm tall forming a chunky, stemless rosette of leaves toothed on the margins and upper and lower surfaces. Leaves incurve attractively, making a tight ball of foliage. Leaf colour can vary from dark green to silvery blue. Bluer forms are a little hardier, taking lows of maybe −6°c to −8°c.

Aloe striatula

Frost-hardy / Full sun

Superb, upright to lax, many-branched aloe growing to a height and spread of about 86 cm when in flower in cool-temperate gardens. Fleshy midgreen leaves up to 18 cm long swirl around each stem. Conical heads of rich orange-yellow tubular flowers are borne in early summer. Unquestionably the hardiest aloe you can grow outside in cool-temperate gardens, taking lows of down to −7°c with little damage to top growth. At lower temperatures will

sprout from old wood at base. A mature plant has been documented as taking a staggering −18°c, resprouting from underground in late spring. Must be grown on exceedingly well-drained soil in full sun to prevent leggy growth and should be protected from desiccating winds in winter. Much liked by slugs and snails!

Beschorneria (Agavaceae)

Mexico

Named in honour of Friedrich Wilhelm Christian Beschorner (1806–1873), a German amateur botanist, this genus encompasses ten species of clumpforming, rosetted, perennial succulents that occupy semi-arid areas in their native habitat. They are grown in cultivation for their striking leaves and trifidlike racemes of tubular flowers. I have been growing *B. yuccoides* in my garden in Norfolk for more than ten years with temperatures dropping to −10°c for short periods with only minimal leaf damage. In areas that have sustained cold, I would suggest wrapping the leaves in straw and fleece;

otherwise these can be grown in large containers and brought into frost-free conditions for the winter. If you have room in your garden, they are well worth growing, and they will amaze your friends, too! They prefer sharply draining, humus-rich soil in full sun protected from cold winds.

Beschorneria septentrionalis

Frost-hardy / Full sun

A smaller species than *B. yuccoides*, with wider, greener leaves making a rosette to a height and spread of about 80 cm. When established, produces glossy red flower spikes up to 1.5 m tall adorned with pendulous flowers in exquisite beetroot red with green tips in spring. Hardy to about −12°C.

Beschorneria yuccoides, flowers

Beschorneria yuccoides

Frost-hardy / Full sun

Magnificent clump-forming succulent perennial growing to a height of 0.9–1.5 m with rosettes of lance-shaped, fleshy, rather floppy, glaucous, greyish green leaves up to 1.5 m long. Thick, arching stems 3 m and more long carry pendulous, vivid red bracts and yellow-tinted, bright green flowers up to 7 cm long in summer. Hardy to −10°C for short periods.

Carpobrotus edulis

Carpobrotus (Aizoaceae)

South Africa, Australia

This genus is related to *Lampranthus*, though distinctive in having fleshy fruit; it comprises some twenty-five species of creeping perennials that form spreading mats with age. They have prostrate, fleshy stems and pairs of fleshy, conspicuously three-angled, opposite, smooth, occasionally spotted leaves. Their very exotic, solitary, daisylike, many-petalled flowers are borne from late spring to early autumn, followed by fleshy fruits. They can be used as ground cover in the mildest temperate climates, preferring exceedingly well-drained, sandy, gritty soils in a position with full sun, taking temperatures down to 0°C for short periods only; otherwise treat them as half-hardy perennials bedded out for the summer months.

Carpobrotus edulis

Hottentot fig

Half-hardy / Full sun

Found growing on coastal sand dunes in South Africa and widely naturalised in other temperate regions. Fleshy three-angled leaves are up to 8 cm long and are often tinted red in hot sun situations. Daisylike flowers are up to 8 cm across, bright yellow fading to pink with age, followed by fleshy fruits, which are edible and used in preserves.

Dasylirion (Nolinaceae)

Desert spoon, sotol
Southern United States, Mexico

Eighteen species belong to this genus of somewhat thin-leaved, yuccalike evergreen shrubs, trees, and perennial succulents, indigenous to arid deserts and mountainous areas in their native habitats. Only in recent years have these amazing hedgehoglike plants been available in the British Isles. They are very distinctive in shape and form, working well in arid Mediterranean-style gardens, where they provide architectural form year-round. There are some good specimens in the Tresco Abbey Garden in southwest England that have taken temperatures down to a chilly −8°c. Fairly large-trunked specimens can now be bought in some specialist nurseries for an awful lot of money, if you are feeling rich! Dasylirions seem quite accommodating in their soil requirements, being less fussy than agaves and probably on a par with most yuccas. As long as the soil drains, they should be okay. Once planted they never need additional water, though the odd deep watering during summer would encourage more rapid growth.

Dasylirion acrotriche

Frost-hardy / Full sun

Evergreen shrub, forming a trunk with age, growing to a height of 3.5–6 m by 2.2 m in its native habitat, though much smaller in maritime climes. Forms a spherical mass of narrowly linear, upright and then arching dark green leaves, margined with hooked yellow spines and fibrous tips. In hot climates, produces a narrow inflorescence up to 4 m tall of densely packed, star-shaped whitish flowers in summer. Grows well in coastal gardens. Hardy to −12°c or lower.

Dasylirion glaucophyllum

Frost-hardy / Full sun

Often encountered in nurseries, similar to *D. acrotrichum*, with wider leaves that have a striking chalky Wedgwood-blue colouration and no frayed leaf tips. Hardiness uncertain, probably to −8°c or maybe lower.

Dasylirion quadrangulatum

syn. *D. longissimum*
Frost-hardy / Full sun

Largest *Dasylirion* species, forming a trunk more than 3 m tall with multiple heads when mature, crown forming a complete almost perfect sphere of extremely narrow, four-angled, fresh green leaves, each 1.2 m long with no marginal teeth and little to no fraying at the tips. These impressive plants make a substantial impact in their native environment. Not widely grown outside of warmer countries, though hardy to −5°c and maybe considerably lower.

*Dasylirion
quadrangulatum*

Dasylirion serratifolium

Sandpaper sotol
Frost-hardy / Full sun

This native of Oaxaca, Mexico, is rather slow growing but nevertheless an awesome plant with narrow

*Dasylirion
serratifolium*

greyish green toothed leaves which arch and curve up to 1.2 m in length. The leaf surface has the texture of fine sandpaper. The whole plant eventually forms a dome shape giving a very architectural feel to the garden. It will take lows down to -8°c on exceedingly well-drained soil.

Dasylirion wheeleri

Desert spoon, sotol
Hardy / Full sun

Found at an elevation of 900–1800 m in its native habitat, where it grows to 3.5–8 m tall and 1.8 m wide with linear, flexible, slightly fleshy, glaucous, silver leaves with fine but vicious hooks along the edges on a trunk 1–1.5 m tall. Insignificant whitish green flowers cluster tightly on a dramatic stalk that emerges from the centre of the clump, 1.8–4.5 m above the foliage, in early summer. By far the hardiest *Dasylirion* species, taking a low of −25°c in its desert habitat, though less hardy in maritime climates.

Echeveria (Crassulaceae)

United States (Texas), Mexico, Central America to
  the Andes

Echeveria, a genus of some 150 species of evergreen succulents and evergreen, occasionally deciduous subshrubs found in dry, often semidesert areas in their native habitats, was named after Athanasio Echeveria Godoy, an eighteenth-century botanical artist. Although they look somewhat similar to sempervivums in form, they are far less hardy and more drought tolerant than their European counterparts. They often used in warmer climates for bedding, but only one is regularly used in cooler climates: *Echeveria secunda* var. *glauca*, with its luscious succulent bluish grey leaves. Many of the hybrid forms are very decorative, with colourful, often large leaves and different growth forms. They prefer full sun, taking temperatures down to freezing or just below for short periods, so they can only be planted out permanently in virtually frost-free gardens, where the soil is very free-draining; otherwise store in dry, frost-free conditions during the winter months. They prefer poor to moderately fertile gritty soil.

Echeveria agavoides

Frost-hardy / Full sun

One of the larger echeverias. Clump-forming species with pale green rosettes up to 20 cm by 25 cm. *Echeveria agavoides* × *E. colorata* has very attractive yellowish green leaves with red tips and edges. Hardy to −5°c without damage, possibly lower.

Echeveria elegans

Frost-hardy / Full sun

Stemless or short-stemmed clump-forming succulent growing to a height of 15–20 cm by 30 cm or more, with rosettes up to 10 cm across with greyish green leaves coated with white powder. When frosted the rosettes take on a very attractive purplish tinge due to cold stress. Hardy to −5°c without damage, possibly lower. Must be kept bone-dry at these temperatures.

Echeveria secunda var. glauca

Blue echeveria
Frost-hardy / Full sun

Popular rosette-forming succulent growing to 38 cm tall when in flower and 30 cm wide or more. Large, glaucous, whitish blue-grey leaves can reach up to

20 cm long. Flower spikes of red and orange flowers in summer. Surprisingly hardy, enduring temperatures down to −5°C without damage; possibly lower for short periods if kept bone-dry outside.

Echeveria hybrid cultivars

Frost-hardy / Full sun

Echeverias hybridise very freely, giving the exotic gardener a wide choice of exciting forms, of which the following is only a small selection. 'Arlie Wright' has large pinkish purple flushed grey leaves, with heavily crimped edges. 'Firelight' has wide bluish green leaves that quickly mature to deep glossy red with frilly edges. 'Perle d'Azur' has lustrous, glaucous, pink leaves. 'Princess Lace' has large rosettes of pale green leaves and crimped edges. 'Wavy Curls' has grey leaves heavily crinkled at the tips.

Furcraea (Agavaceae)

Central and South America

This genus comprises more than twenty species of perennial succulents found growing in desertlike areas in their native habitats. Most furcraeas are large plants when grown under ideal conditions; unfortunately, though, few gardens can meet the minimum frost requirements for them to grow to perfection. Furcraeas grow in semi-arid areas and in cultivation need very well-drained soil in a position with full sun, though they will take dappled shade. Furcraeas produce a handsome rosette of sword-shaped greyish blue leaves up to 1.2 m long, somewhat reminiscent of their relative the yucca, on 1-m trunks.

Furcraea parmentieri

syn. _F. bedinghausii_
Half-hardy / Fun or dappled shade

Produces a trunk up to 4 m high in its native habitat, with bluish sword-shaped leaves, from which rises an enormous pyramidal panicle of bell-shaped, creamy green flowers up to 6 cm across, followed usually by small bulbils rather than seed, on stems that can reach a staggering height of 6–8 m. Being monocarpic, the plants die after flowering, though with all those bulbils, they will have a succession for the foreseeable future. The winters in cool-temperate gardens are too cold for them to grow to any significant size; fortunately, they make excellent large container plants that can spend the summer in the garden and then be brought into frost-free conditions for the winter. I store mine at a minimum temperature of 5°C, keeping them virtually dry during the coldest months to prevent them from going mouldy. They can take dips down to −5°C for short periods only.

The Tresco Abbey Garden in southwest England has the perfect growing conditions for these beauties, which have been in cultivation there since 1894. At least one or two plants flower most summers, with the occasional flush when more than fifty plants have been in flower at the same time, which is amazing since they take fifteen to twenty years to flower!

Echeveria elegans

Echeveria hybrid cultivar

Furcraea foetida 'Mediopicta'

syn. *F. gigantea* 'Mediopicta'
Half-hardy / Sun or dappled shade

Handsome, succulent, rosette-forming perennial, occasionally clump-forming, growing to a height of 1–1.2 m by 2 m, with stems up to 1 m, with terminal rosettes of broadly lance-shaped, bright, glossy, midgreen leaves up to 2.5 m long, with creamy white longitudinal lines and mostly smooth margins with the occasional spine. In summer bears inflorescences 6–12 m high of strongly scented white flowers followed by bulblets. As a container plant, will be much smaller in proportion.

Furcraea selloa

Half-hardy / Sun or dappled shade

Succulent rosette-forming perennial, occasionally clump-forming, with stems up to 1.5 m high, bearing terminal rosettes of narrow, sword-shaped, glossy, bright green leaves up to 1.2 m in length, with sharp-hooked brown spines. Openly branched inflorescence can reach up to 5 m high and bears white flowers flushed with green. As a container plant will be much smaller in proportion. Variety *marginata* is a lovely form with green leaves that can have white or yellow edges.

Hesperaloe (Agavaceae)

Rio Grande area of Texas, United States, to northern Mexico

This genus of about three species of perennial succulents is closely related to *Yucca*, although the flowers are more aloelike in form. They are indigenous to semi-arid and arid regions in their native habitats.

Left

Furcraea selloa

Right

Hesperaloe parviflora and flower

They prefer poor to moderately fertile soil, preferably slightly acidic. Established plants are drought resistant. They make good container plants with a loose, relaxed appearance and look fabulous when in bloom. They also look effective combined with other desert plants.

Hesperaloe parviflora

Hardy / Full sun

Clump-forming, succulent, yuccalike plant growing to a height of up to 1 m by 2 m wide, with arching, very narrow, swordlike, leathery, dark green leaves 60–90 cm long, frequently with curly threads along the edges. Panicle-like inflorescence, 1–2 m long or more, bears tightly packed, pendent, pink to rose red flowers with golden yellow throats in early summer, with repeat blooms in warm climates. Hardy to about −20°C.

Lampranthus (Aizoaceae)

South Africa

This genus of some sixty species of erect to prostrate perennial succulents occupies semidesert and coastal desert areas in its native habitat. Many hybrid forms are available, all having daisylike flowers in abundance from summer to early autumn. Quite often lampranthus species are just sold as red, pink, yellow, and so forth. They provide some of the most spectacular displays of bright flowers (in white, red, orange, yellow, purple, pink, and shades in between) found in the succulent world and are widely used as ground cover in warm countries and in areas of cooler countries that get little frost. They can also be bedded out for the summer months or grown in containers, which should be placed in a hot, full-sun situation and then brought into just frost-free conditions for the winter. Most of the species commonly found will survive a short period at −7°C if dry; otherwise only a few degrees below freezing for short periods only. They prefer poor, well-drained soil in a position with full sun that gets baked in summer, as they thrive in dry conditions.

Lampranthus hybrid

Lampranthus aurantiacus

Frost-hardy / Full sun

Spreading, sparsely branched succulent perennial with upright stems becoming prostrate with age, to a height of 30 cm by 45 cm with semi-cylindrical, tapering, minutely spotted, frosted, bluish green leaves up to 3 cm long. Bright yellow or orange daisylike flowers up to 5 cm across are borne in profusion from summer to autumn, opening in sunshine and closing when it gets cloudy.

Lampranthus deltoides

Frost-hardy / Full sun

Spreading succulent perennial, growing to a height and spread of 30 cm with a profusion of short stems bearing three-sided, bluish grey leaves up to 1 cm long. Bright pink to red, scented flowers up to 2 cm across are borne from summer to early autumn.

Lampranthus roseus

Frost-hardy / Full sun

Short-lived, creeping or semi-erect or mounding succulent perennial growing to a height of 30–50 cm with indefinite spread. Leaves are three-sided, glaucous, greyish green, up to 3 cm long and covered in irregular translucent dots. Rose-pink to reddish daisylike flowers are up to 4 cm across and borne from midspring to early summer.

Lampranthus spectabilis

Frost-hardy / Full sun

Prostrate, spreading, mounding, succulent perennial with branching stems, growing up to 30 cm tall with an indefinite spread, having narrowly cylindrical, three-sided, bright green to greyish green leaves 5–7.5 cm long, slightly flushed red at the tips. Profuse pink to reddish purple, sometimes white, flowers 5–7.5 cm across are borne from summer to early autumn. 'Tresco Apricot' has pure apricot flowers. 'Tresco Brilliant' has magenta flowers. 'Tresco Red' has intense red flowers.

Nolina (Nolinaceae)

Beargrass
Southeastern and southwestern United States
  through Mexico and into Guatemala

This widespread group of plants has representatives growing in the driest deserts through to moist and humid tropical jungles. The plants can be either trunked or stemless, this latter group being the grassy-looking plants seen in images of the "old West" in the cowboy films of the fifties and sixties. Some of the desert species are proving themselves to be surprisingly hardy in northern Europe and the British Isles. A few are being tried out by enthusiasts and appear to take damp conditions well. They prefer well-drained soil but are more tolerant of less-than-perfect conditions than agaves. As with dasylirion, you could never water one and it would be fine but extra water would speed up growth.

Nolina longifolia

syn. *Oaxaca nolina*
Frost-hardy / Full sun

Probably the most likely beargrass to be encountered, from Oaxaca and Puebla, Mexico. Large specimens of this can be seen in many European succulent collections, including a very ancient one

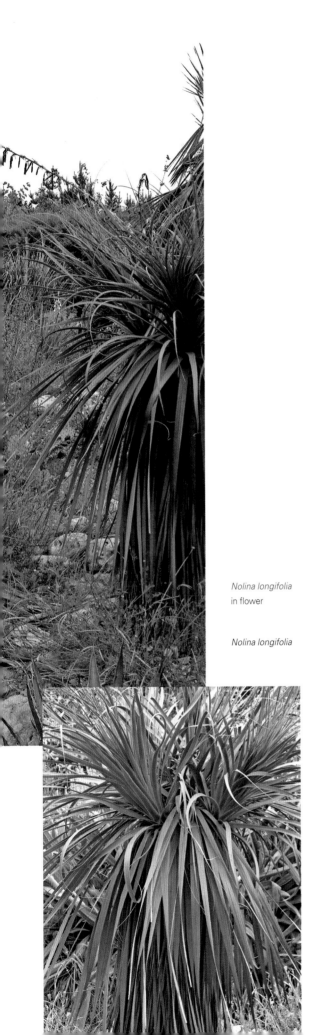

Nolina longifolia
in flower

Nolina longifolia

in the Tresco Abbey Garden (mislabelled *Beaucarnea recurvata*). With age, forms a sparsely branched small tree up to 7 m tall, though usually much smaller, with a slightly swollen trunk base and beautifully fissured bark. Up to a dozen branches each hold a rosette of lax pendulous leaves, up to 2 m long, somewhat reminiscent of *Cordyline australis*. As with other members of the genus, leaves have tiny but wickedly sharp serrations along the margins, like miniature hacksaw blades. Can produce a panicle of hundreds of tiny white flowers up to 2 m high. Can reportedly take −8°c and maybe lower.

Nolina sp.'La Siberica'

Frost-hardy / Full sun

A newly discovered plant from northeastern Tamaulipas, Mexico, with rosettes up to 5 m by 1.5 m across in the wild. It doesn't even have a proper specific name as yet! Though not currently available, it is mentioned here purely because it is going to be the "must-have" plant of the future, according to Paul Spracklin, who has seen it growing wild in Mexico. It grows in the same forests alongside *Agave montana* at an altitude of 3000 m and higher, which means that all the superlatives used to describe that agave apply equally to this. A single-trunked plant, though it does occasionally branch, with a dense head of midgreen linear leaves; highly reminiscent of *Cordyline australis* except that the leaves end in a frayed tuft and the old leaves persist to form a dense petticoat that has a really attractive twist to it. It has style and presence. Hardy to −10°c or lower.

Nolina nelsonii

Blue nolina

Frost-hardy / Full sun

Arguably the most handsome of the genus, and more arguably one of the most attractive succulent plants, hailing from northeastern Tamaulipas, Mexico. Typically forms a single trunk, 30 cm across and 4–5 m tall, rarely branching, topped by a head of stiff, intensely blue leaves up to 80 cm long held in a spherical rosette in the manner of *Yucca rostrata*. Mature plants will infrequently produce a showy inflorescence, densely packed with thousands of

providing cultural information for more than four hundred stonecrop species and varieties, many of them photographed in their native habitats.

Sedum kamtschaticum

Frost-hardy / Sun or dappled shade

Clump-forming, spreading, rhizomatous, semi-evergreen, low-branching perennial indigenous to Siberian Russia, north and central China, and Japan, growing to a height of 13 cm by 40 cm with lance-shaped, glossy, fleshy, toothed, deep green leaves up to 4 cm long. Flattish flower heads up to 5 cm across, containing star-shaped, rich golden yellow flowers, open from pink buds from midsummer to late summer. 'Variegatum' has pink-tinted, midgreen leaves with cream edges and golden yellow flowers.

Sedum morganianum

Semi-tender / Full sun

Hanging evergreen perennial from Mexico (trailing in the wild) growing to 60 cm long or more, with succulent stems and densely crowded, spiralling, cylindrical, pointed, curved, fleshy, glaucous, blue-green leaves up to 2 cm long. Small, long-stemmed heads of pink to deep purple-scarlet star-shaped blooms are borne from spring to summer. Excellent for suspended pots or hanging baskets. Overwinter at a minimum of 5°C.

creamy, starry flowers. Seems amenable to cultivation outside of its dry habitat and, although relatively new to Europe, has endured lows of −12°C in some North American gardens.

Sedum kamtschaticum 'Variegatum'

Sedum (Crassulaceae)

Stonecrop
Mountainous areas of the Northern Hemisphere,
	with a few in arid parts of South America

This genus includes some six hundred species of usually succulent annuals and evergreen, semi-evergreen, or deciduous biennials, perennials, subshrubs, and shrubs, and numerous hybrids. Most gardeners when hearing the name "stonecrop" think of *Sedum acre*, the low-spreading and mat-forming succulent with tiny leaves. Luckily for us, though, there are many more and larger forms, such as the also well known *Sedum spectabile*, with its large leaves and pink autumn flowers. They are all comparatively easy-to-grow plants that give a truly exotic feel to the garden with their succulent leaves. They prefer moderately fertile, well-drained soil in full sun. Some of the more vigorous species will take light dappled shade. All the sedums mentioned here are hardy to at least −10°C unless otherwise stated.

Sedum: Cultivated Stonecrops by Ray Stephenson (1994) is a definitive study by one of the world's authorities

Sedum obtusatum

Hardy / Full sun

Delightful small evergreen succulent perennial from California growing to a height of 5 cm by 20 cm with terminal rosettes of fleshy, spoon-shaped, blunt-tipped, glaucous, midgreen leaves up to 2.5 cm long, flushed purplish red in autumn. Star-shaped bright yellow flowers up to 1 cm across are borne in summer.

Sedum praealtum

Frost-hardy / Full sun

Reminiscent of the large *Crassula ovata* (money tree or jade plant), this is a shrubby, tall-growing sedum from Mexico, to 1.8 m in the wild though more like 25–30 cm tall in cultivation. Grown hard in very dry, freely draining soil, this can look quite astounding; grown soft in richer soil, it is a sprawling mess! Apple-green stems and leaves 3 cm long, slightly incurving, eventually reach about 1 m in good conditions. After a hot summer, it can flower very early the next spring with dense sprays of light yellow stars. Hardy to at least −6°c, probably lower if kept bone dry during the winter months.

Sedum sieboldii
'Mediovariegatum'

Sedum sieboldii

Frost-hardy / Full sun

Attractive, evergreen, succulent, mound-forming perennial from Japan, growing 10–15 cm by 30 cm with arching stems that radiate from the centre forming a circle, covered in thick, fleshy, rounded, bluish green leaves 1.8 cm across, often tinged purplish red on the edges. In autumn dense heads of small pale pink flowers are borne. 'Mediovariegatum' has bluish grey leaves with irregular cream centres. 'Variegatum' has bluish green leaves with cream mottling. Hardy to at least −6°c, probably lower if kept bone dry during the winter months.

Sedum spathulifolium

Hardy / Full sun

Clump-forming evergreen succulent from western North America with long runners growing to a height of 15 cm by 60 cm with thick, spoon-shaped, fleshy leaves, often colouring to purplish red, mainly clustered in rosettes at stem tips. Tiny bright yellow flowers are borne from late spring to early summer. 'Cape Blanco' has thick, rounded,

Sedum spathulifolium 'Cape Blanco'

glaucous, silvery grey leaves. 'Purpureum' has silvery grey new growth and mature leaves heavily tinged purplish red.

Sedum spectabile

Ice plant

Hardy / Full sun

Upright, clump-forming, unbranched deciduous perennial from China and Korea, growing to a height and spread of 46 cm with light green stems and opposite pairs of whorled, thick, ovate, spoon-shaped, slightly scalloped, glaucous, greyish green leaves 5–10 cm long. In late summer produces large heads up to 15 cm across, with small densely packed, star-shaped pink flowers with prominent stamens. Flower heads are often top-heavy if the soil is too fertile, causing the plant to open up. 'Brilliant' has intense pink flowers. 'Iceberg' has pale green leaves and white flowers. 'Septemberglut' has intense rich pink flowers, while 'Indian Chief' has dark pink to purplish red flowers.

Sedum telephium

Hardy / Full sun

Upright, clump-forming, rhizomatous, deciduous perennial from Europe, Siberia, China, and Japan, growing to 60 cm high by 30 cm wide, with thick, light green stems and alternate, pointed, oval, toothed, glaucous, fleshy, greyish green leaves up to 8 cm long. Luxurious heads up to 12 cm across of many star-shaped, purplish red flowers are borne from late summer to early autumn. *Sedum telephium*

subsp. *maximum* 'Atropurpureum' reaches 45–60 cm tall with glaucous, very deep purple-red stems and leaves, topped by small heads of purplish red flowers. *Sedum telephium* 'Munstead Dark Red' grows to 60 cm with purple-tinted, dark green leaves, topped with heads of deep purplish red flowers that darken with age. *Sedum* 'Vera Jameson' is a hybrid with purple stems and foliage, with heads of soft pink flowers.

Sempervivum (Crassulaceae)

Houseleek, hens-and-chickens

Central and southern Europe and Mediterranean
  islands

This is a genus of some fifty species of dense, mat-forming, evergreen succulent perennials. They typically grow in rocks and crevices at 900–2400 m above sea level in the mountainous regions of their native habitat. There are also more than three thousand named cultivars with a wide range of rosette sizes, forms, and colours. They are well known to gardeners as the hardy houseleek, with their rosettes of thick, succulent leaves that range from bright yellow through various shades of green, grey, pink, purple, red, orange, and brown, to almost black in some varieties. Small silvery hairs are commonly found along the leaf margins, and in many varieties the leaf tips bear a tuft of longer hairs that can form a "cobweb" over the surface of the rosettes. In some places they are traditionally grown on roofs between tiles or thatching and even in gutters, thought in ancient times to guard against thunderbolts, storms, and sorcery and to ensure the

prosperity of the occupants. These succulents prefer poor to moderately fertile, sharply drained soil in full sun and do not mind extended drought periods; they easily take −10°C and lower.

Sempervivum arachnoideum

Cobweb houseleek

Frost-hardy / Full sun

Mat-forming succulent growing to 13 cm high by 30 cm or more wide, with rosettes 1–2.5 cm across, with fleshy, midgreen to red leaves. The leaf tips are connected by a white cobweb of hairs. There are many varieties, differing in colour, size, and degree of cobwebbing. Subspecies *tomentosum* has tightly packed leaves with silver cobwebbing.

Sempervivum tectorum

Common houseleek

Frost-hardy / Full sun

Mat-forming succulent growing up to 10 cm high by 30 cm or more wide, with open rosettes up to 10 cm across of very fleshy, thick green leaves with pointed reddish tips. Common houseleek seen in many gardens and often found growing on walls and old rooftops in the British Isles.

Sempervivum hybrid cultivars

Frost-hardy / Full sun

Sempervivums are very promiscuous and hybridise freely, creating myriads of new forms, of which this is only a small collection. 'Booth's Red' has attractive, dense, purplish red rosettes to 8 cm across or more. 'Commander Hay' forms a sizable mound of richly red-tinted rosettes, individually up to 15 cm across. 'Corona' has myriads of small red-tinted rosettes that turn a brighter red in winter. 'Director Jacobs' has flat rosettes of deep red silver-haired, short, wide leaves. 'Hall's Hybrid' forms a flattish rosette up to 8 cm across, with sap green leaves changing to wine red toward the base. 'Red Ace' has long, purplish red pointed leaves with silver hairs on the edges. 'Reginald Malby' forms medium-sized, flattish rosettes in rich mahogany red. 'Virgil' has bluish grey rosettes up to 8 cm across, flushed purple with darker tips. 'White Eyes' is an attractive form with bright green rosettes having a central section in contrasting pale yellowish green.

Above left

Mixed sempervivums

Above

Sempervivum 'Corona'

Sempervivum 'Virgil'

Yuccas

Many yuccas are exceedingly winter-hardy and handsome to boot, with their swordlike, bold foliage, adding an architectural look to the landscape either in the border or as specimens. Several have been used in temperate gardens over the decades, often establishing large clumps with time. Many new forms that are less known in moist temperate cultivation have been introduced in recent years, of which many are proving to be very gardenworthy indeed. Mary and Gary Irish discuss these monstrous plants in great detail in *Agaves, Yuccas, and Related Plants* (2000).

Yucca aloifolia
'Marginata'

Yucca (Agavaceae)

Dry regions of North and Central America, with a few in the Caribbean

Plants in this genus of some forty species of rosette-forming, often woody-based, evergreen perennials, shrubs, and trees are indigenous to dry areas such as deserts, scrub, and plains. They are grown in cultivation for their bold form, with linear to lance-shaped open rosettes, and their erect or occasionally pendent panicles of showy white to cream-white bell-shaped flowers. They work well in the Mediterranean- or desert-style garden, with other viciously spiky plants. Many new species have been introduced in recent years and have proved to be tough plants, surviving well in temperate climates, especially if given exceedingly well-drained, poor to slightly fertile soil in full baking sun. Most are hardy to −15°c or below in a dry position.

Yucca aloifolia

Dagger plant, Spanish bayonet
Hardy / Full sun

Slow-growing shrub or small tree growing to a height of 8 m when in flower by 3–4 m, less in temperate cultivation, with erect single stem or simple branched stems and densely arranged, stiff, narrowly lance-shaped, toothed, dark greyish green leaves up to 50 cm long, each ending with a viciously sharp point. White, bell-shaped, pendent flowers are borne on long spikes from summer to autumn. 'Marginata' has dark greyish green leaves edged yellow. 'Tricolor' has green leaves striped yellow or white in the centre.

Yucca elephantipes

Giant yucca, spineless yucca

Frost-hardy / Full sun

Large, upright shrub or usually small tree growing to a height of 10 m in its native habitat, though usually much less in temperate cultivation, with several to many sparsely branched trunks arising from a markedly swollen wood base near ground level. Narrowly lance-shaped, light to midgreen leaves, 60–100 cm long, are stiffly leathery, with toothed margins. On mature plants pendent creamy white flowers are borne in dense, erect panicles from summer to autumn. Hardy to −7°c for short periods only. 'Variegata' is a showy form with leaves with creamy white edges, hardy to −5°c for short periods only. Plants cut back from these temperatures will regrow from the woody base, but not every year.

Yucca faxoniana

Yucca faxoniana

Hardy / Full sun

Evergreen, single, thick-trunked shrub or tree, producing the fattest trunk of any yucca, reaching 50 cm in diameter, growing to a height of 3–5 m topped with a rosette of stiff, sharply pointed leaves up to 9 cm long, occasionally with black edges and curly filamentous threads. Older leaves become yellowy brown and hang down, forming a thick thatchlike skirt around the trunk. Central erect spike up to 1.2 m tall is borne in summer with creamy white bell-shaped flowers. *Yucca carnerosana* is almost identical.

Yucca filamentosa

Adam's needle

Hardy / Full sun

Clump-forming, usually trunkless shrub growing to a height of 0.9 m by 1.5 m with rigid, dark green leaves up to 75 cm long, margined with curly white filamentous threads. Flowering spikes up to 3 m tall bear myriads of pendulous bell-shaped white flowers, often tinged green or cream, from midsummer to late summer. 'Bright Edge' is a dwarf cultivar with yellow-edged leaves and green-tinged cream flowers. 'Golden Sword' is similar though somewhat larger in stature. 'Ivory Tower' has spikes of green-tinged white flowers.

Yucca filifera

Izote yucca

Hardy / Full sun

One of the largest yuccas, this is the Mexican equivalent of the more familiar North American Joshua tree, being widespread throughout central and northeastern Mexico. Forms a many-branched tree to 10 m in its native habitat, often with contorted limbs twisting in several directions. Typically has dark green rosettes, up to 1 m in diameter, with rigid leaves that have strongly filiferous margins. Large (to 1.8 m) drooping inflorescence densely packed with creamy white bells is produced in spring, followed by 6 cm long fleshy fruits. Unlike the Joshua tree, seems to adapt to cultivation outside of the desert environment and is becoming widely grown by enthusiasts in places like Germany, Holland, and Belgium, where it has proven to be hardy down to −15°C.

Yucca glauca

Spanish bayonet
Hardy / Full sun

Clump-forming yucca growing to 60 cm tall and 90 cm wide with narrow, bluish green lance-shaped leaves with thin straight filaments along the margins. Panicles up to 90 cm tall with off-white, bell-shaped flowers occasionally tinged green or reddish brown are borne in summer.

Yucca gloriosa

Candle yucca, palm lily, Roman candle, Spanish dagger
Hardy / Full sun

Erect evergreen treelike shrub growing 1.8–2.4 m tall, with a stout stem, normally unbranched, with stiff, lance-shaped, pointed, arching leaves up to 60 cm long, bluish green maturing to dark green. From late summer to autumn, pendent, bell-shaped white flowers are borne, occasionally purple-tinged, up to 5 cm long, on upright panicles.

There is a huge amount of confusion between this species and *Yucca recurvifolia*. Most of the plants coming into the British Isles from Italy labelled *Y. gloriosa* are actually *Y. recurvifolia* (except the variegated from, which is the real thing, *Y. gloriosa* 'Variegata'). The main difference is the stiffness of the leaves of this form plus a much later flowering period, often not until November and very often not making it before the first frosts of the winter.

Yucca recurvifolia

Hardy / Full sun

Robust, treelike shrub, sometimes multistemmed, growing to 1.2–2.4 m high and 1.2 m across when in flower, with stiffly leathery, lance-shaped, arching to strongly drooping, bluish to deep green leaves, up to 90 cm long, with slightly toothed margins. Large, pendent, creamy white, bell-shaped flowers, up to 8 cm long, are borne on panicles typically in early summer.

Yucca rostrata

Beaked yucca, Big Bend yucca
Hardy / Full sun

The species name *rostrata* refers to the fruit, which resembles the beak of a bird. Handsome, stout, single-trunked arborescent yucca from the Chihuahuan desert, northern Mexico, that grows to a height of 1.8–4.5 m. Mature plants may branch and become multiheaded. Linear powdery greyish blue leaves 25–60 cm long, margined with short teeth, radiate from the centre and eventually form a tight skirt of dead leaves around the trunk. Spikes of white bell-shaped flowers up to 6 cm long are borne on mature plants in summer.

Yucca whipplei

Our Lord's candle
Frost-hardy / Full sun

Exquisite, clump-forming, stemless, hedgehoglike shrub growing to a height of 1 m by 1.2 m with dense rosettes of rigid, slender, linear, finely toothed bluish green leaves with spiky tips, up to 90 cm long. In summer, panicles up to 3 m tall bear fragrant, pendent, bell-shaped, creamy white, often purple-tinged flowers. Hardy to −10°C. More moisture intolerant than many other yuccas, thus best in a dry, very well-drained situation.

Other Spiky Things

Although aciphyllas are neither cacti nor succulents nor yuccas and are in fact alpine plants, I have included them here because of their amazing spikiness. They look good growing among cacti and succulents, on a scree bed or as potted plants. Beware, though—they bite!

Aciphylla (Apiaceae)

Bayonet plant, spear grass
New Zealand and Australia

This genus comprises some forty species of evergreen perennials found growing in sparse grasslands and mountainous to alpine areas. They belong to the carrot family and some are aromatic. They are known for their fearsomely spiky foliage and are often bizarre-looking plants, more odd than attractive, with flattened, stiff, linear, divided, leathery, sharply spined leaves and a carrotlike taproot. The flowers, though rarely produced in cool-temperate climates, are candelabra-like, with long branching stems of small cream to white blossoms. Some of the more alpine species are difficult to cultivate, though the following are relatively easy. Most prefer cool conditions that are not too wet. All the species mentioned here are hardy to about −10°C and prefer moist, gritty, well-drained, humus-rich soil. Although they can be difficult to find, they are worth growing, but be careful where you site them as they can be vicious to your ankes! I remember one elderly lady visiting my garden and prodding a plant contemptuously with her umbrella.

Aciphylla aurea

Golden Spaniard
Frost-hardy to hardy / Full sun

Evergreen, rosette-forming perennial growing to a height and spread of approximately 1 m, though far less in temperate gardens, with long bayonet-like, rigid, pinnately dissected, brownish yellowish green leaves. Bears spikes of golden flowers up to 2 m tall from late spring to early summer.

Aciphylla glaucescens

Spear grass
Frost-hardy to hardy / Full sun

Rosette-forming perennial growing to 1 m tall and wide with narrow, strap-shaped, three-pinnate, spine-tipped, silvery grey leaves with almost white midribs. Greenish yellow flower spikes up to 2 m tall are borne in summer.

Aciphylla scott-thomsonii

Giant Spaniard
Frost-hardy to hardy / Full sun

As its common name suggests, a truly giant plant. Evergreen, clump-forming perennial growing to the staggering height of 4.6 m (when in flower) with a foliage spread and height of 2–3 m in the wild, though much less in temperate cultivation. Much dissected, viciously spiny foliage is bronze when young and turns silvery grey with maturity.

Aciphylla squarrosa

Frost-hardy to hardy / Full sun

Evergreen, clump-forming perennial growing to a height of 60–90 cm and a spread of 1–1.2 m with tufts of pointed, finely divided, narrow bluish leaves up to 60 cm long. Heads of greenish creamy yellow flowers are held on stiff stems up to 2 m tall from the base.

Climbers and Scramblers

Climbers and scramblers can be some of the most interesting and versatile exotic plants for the garden, as they have many uses apart from being attractive. They can cover fences, garage walls, old tree trunks, veranda posts and railings, pergolas, arbours, gazebos, house walls, oil storage tanks—the list is endless. In fact, if you are like me, you will soon run out of places to grow them! Climbers create wonderful backdrops to other plants and often make the garden feel a lot larger than it actually is as you start to hide the boundaries. I have nearly lost one side of my house to the well-known climber *Parthenocissus quinquefolia*, the common Virginia creeper, which not only climbs the walls but has now also gone up the roof! I remember seeing a house in my youth that was so covered that all you saw were the windows, doors, and a chimney pot. If you have little wall space or have used it up, you can use dividing screens in the garden as climbing supports, or use single posts or wigwams for climbers as you would for runner beans in the vegetable garden. You can even grow climbers up other more established climbers, getting a prolonged flowering season.

There are many climbers and scramblers to chose from, including very hardy plants that have an exotic appearance, such as *Hydrangea anomala* subsp. *petiolaris*, which can be grown on a north- or east-facing wall; those that are borderline, needing to be planted against a south- or west-facing wall; and those that are hopelessly tender but can still be grown in the garden with plenty of protection or used as container plants and brought out for the warmer months of the year. Some climbers are self-supporting, having small suckers, aerial roots, or twining tendrils, while the scrambling climbers like to do just that, scramble! The following are those that fit into the exotic plant category, having unusual flowers or handsome leaves or both.

Left

Vitis vinifera 'Purpurea'

Aconitum (Ranunculaceae)

Northern Hemisphere

Aconitum is a genus of one hundred species of perennials and biennials, found in grassland and scrub areas in the Northern Hemisphere, with mostly tuberous and occasionally fibrous roots and sometimes twining. Here we are dealing only with the twining forms. All are hardy to −15°C and lower. They prefer cool, moist conditions in dappled shade, though they will take full sun and are tolerant of most soils.

Aconitum hemsleyanum

Climbing monkshood
Hardy / Shade

Twining climber from central and western China, growing to a height of up to 3 m, with thin stems and deeply cut three- to five-lobed green leaves. Racemes of large violet-blue "monkshood" flowers are borne from midsummer to early autumn. Best results achieved by planting the tuberous root in shade and moisture-retentive soil. All parts of the plant are highly toxic—simple skin contact has caused numbness in some people.

Aconitum volubile

Hardy / Full sun

Twining climber from eastern Asia, growing to a height of up to 3 m. Similar to *A. hemsleyanum* and often thought of as synonymous, but it has fewer flowers on each stem. Handsome foliage with glossy, small, rounded, three-lobed green leaves. Racemes of flowers have a light blue-lilac colour with green and white. Best grown with tops in the sun and base in the shade of a host shrub.

Actinidia (Actinidiaceae)

Japan, Korea, Manchuria, and Russia

This genus comprises about sixty species of deciduous and evergreen twining, woody, climbing plants. These perennial climbers are native to high grasslands, low scrub, and second-growth forest, or the main forests of China and Russia. They are usually grown for their exotic, sometimes variegated, foliage and often scented flowers, followed on some by edible fruit for which male and female plants are required. Most prefer a rich, well-drained soil.

Actinidia arguta

Tara vine
Hardy / Full sun

Vigorous, deciduous, woody climber growing to a height of up to 7 m, capable of scrambling into trees if desired. Ovate-oblong bristle-toothed dark green leaves up to 12 cm long. Clusters of three scented white flowers, each up to 2 cm across, are borne in early summer. 'Issai' is a self-fertile form that fruits without cross-pollination.

Actinidia deliciosa

syn. *A. chinensis*
Chinese gooseberry, kiwi fruit
Frost-hardy / Full sun

Native to the Yangtze River valley of northern China and Zhejiang Province on the coast of eastern China, the kiwi fruit was introduced to New Zealand in the early twentieth century and became a popular garden vine there before becoming known for its *deliciosa* fruit around the world.

Vigorous, deciduous climber, scrambling to a height of 10 m in its native habitat, though usually less in cool-temperate gardens. From stout shoots

Actinidia deliciosa 'Hayward'

covered with reddish brown hairs, broadly ovate, heart-shaped, midgreen leaves appear, up to 20 cm long. In early summer, clusters of two to three (sometimes more) creamy white flowers appear, turning yellow with age, up to 4 cm across. Well-known hairy, greenish brown fruits are produced in autumn. As *Actinidia* is dioecious, both male and female vines must be planted together for pollination prior to fruiting. Prefer to be grown in well-drained, deep, fertile soil with plenty of water during the summer months. For best fruit production, needs a warm spring and autumn; otherwise grow just for the large and handsome foliage. Hardy to −10°C when fully defoliated. Female cultivars include 'Blake', 'Bruno', and 'Hayward'. Male cultivars include 'Matua' and 'Tomuri'.

Actinidia kolomikta

Hardy / Full sun

Deciduous climber growing to a height of 3–4 m or more. Remarkable on account of the handsome, tricoloured variegation of many of its leaves, up to 15 cm long. Terminal half is creamy white, flushed pink and green. Variegation is not apparent on very young plants; appears in its second or third year after planting, being more prominent on leaves in full sun. Vigorous and ornamental, ideal supported on a sunny wall. Flowers small, white, with yellow stamens and a pistil, slightly lemon scented, in spring. If male and female plants are present, edible fruit is produced.

Actinidia pilosula

Hardy / Sun or dappled shade

Deciduous climber from China, growing to a height of 3–3.5 m, with graceful twining stems and narrow, tapering, pointed deep green leaves that look as though the tips have been dipped in white paint, with a hint of pink on some leaves. More subtle than *A. kolomikta*, with a better habit. Flowers, larger coral pink bells, produced in spring. Grows in any reasonable soil.

Actinidia polygama

Silver vine

Hardy / Sun or dappled shade

Deciduous climber or twining vine, from eastern Asia, growing up to 4.5 m high, with ornamental ovate-oblong dark green leaves with pale silver or gold patches especially at the tips, to 15 cm long. Clusters of three melon-scented, five-petalled flowers 2.5 cm across are produced in early summer. Female plants produce yellowish green fruits in autumn.

Actinidia kolomikta

Agapetes (Ericaceae)

Eastern Asia to the western Pacific, including Australia

Agapetes is a genus of about ninety-five species of spreading to erect shrubs that are occasionally epiphytic in the wild. Here we are dealing with only one species, *A. serpens*, an arching shrub that can be trained as a climber against a wall or fence.

Agapetes serpens

Half-hardy / Dappled sun to shade

Grows to a height of 2 m, with small, shiny, green, tightly packed, lance-shaped leaves up to 2 cm long. Auxiliary, solitary, narrowly urn-shaped red flowers up to 2 cm long with inverted, darker red, V-shaped markings are borne from late winter to spring. Sometimes used as a hanging basket plant. Prefers moderately fertile acid to neutral soil.

Agapetes serpens, flowers

Right

Akebia quinata

Akebia (Lardizabalaceae)

Chocolate vine
Eastern Asia

Akebia is a genus of just four species of deciduous to semi-evergreen twining climbers, which grow in forest margins in their native habitat. In cultivation they are grown for their interesting flowers and foliage. *Akebia quinata* is very exotic looking for trellises and especially on pergolas, where the flowers hang in a purple haze above your head, giving off a delicious, almost intoxicating fragrance, especially when mixed with *Clematis armandii*, which flowers at the same time. These climbers prefer moist humus-rich soil, although they tolerate dry conditions surprisingly well.

Akebia quinata

Hardy / Sun or dappled shade

Semi-evergreen, twining climber growing to a height of 10 m, though usually smaller, especially if pruned regularly. Leaves are in clusters of typically five oblong to ovate green leaflets tinged purple in winter when frosted, up to 7.5 cm long. Highly scented chocolate-purple flowers are borne on delicate pendent racemes up to 12 cm long in early spring. 'Alba' is more refined and attractive when grown in a small ornamental garden. Leaves lanceolate, small, silver below, on red leaf stalks. White flowers accentuated by a purple centre in summer, followed by red fruit in autumn.

Akebia trifoliata

Hardy / Sun or dappled shade

Semi-evergreen climber growing to a height of 10 m, with trifoliate light green leaves on long stalks, 6–15 cm long and 4–14 cm wide. Flowers on auxiliary racemes, with three conspicuous sepals 2 cm across, with smaller pale purple male flowers at the ends of the inflorescences in early spring.

Ampelopsis (Vitaceae)

North America and temperate Asia

This is a genus of about twenty-five species of deciduous shrubs and woody tendril-bearing vines in the grape family, growing to a height and spread of 5 m. They are grown in cultivation for their ornamental grapelike fruit and highly colourful autumn foliage, and are excellent for covering pergolas, fences, old tree stumps, oil tanks, and house walls. They can be invasive, so prune often to keep them in shape; otherwise you will lose your house! They prefer moist, well-drained, humus-rich, fertile soil in full sun to dappled shade, although they tend to flower more profusely in a sunny position.

Ampelopsis brevipedunculata

Porcelain berry

Hardy / Sun or dappled shade

Vigorous woody vine, growing to a height and spread of 5 m, with palmate three- to five-lobed dark green leaves, hairy underneath, 5–15 cm long. Twines with the help of nonadhesive tendrils that occur opposite the leaves; closely resembles grapes in the genus *Vitis*. Branched, auxiliary cymes of small green flowers are produced in summer, followed in autumn by attractive, spherical, pinkish lilac to green and later bright blue fruit, up to 8 mm across. 'Elegans' is a less vigorous form with deeply lobed, variegated dark green leaves, greatly mottled pink and white.

Ampelopsis megalophylla

Pepper vine

Hardy / Sun or dappled shade

Vigorous climber with glaucous shoots growing to a height of 10 m with large pinnate green leaves up to 46 cm across, being the largest in the genus; turning bright crimson in autumn. Small green flowers in summer are soon followed by rose red berries that ripen to black in autumn. Excellent grown over pergolas and arbours.

Ampelopsis thunbergii

Hardy / Sun or dappled shade

Vigorous vine, with deeply divided and lobed leaves, silvery underneath. Establishes itself quickly and produces large bunches of fruits in varying shades of turquoise, blue, and white.

Antigonon (Polygonaceae)

Mexico and Central America

This genus of three species of vigorous, tendril-bearing, climbing plants in the knotweed family hails from moist tropical forests and scrubland areas. The plants form a dense canopy that is covered in racemes of pink flowers all summer and are very useful for covering unsightly structures as they are such rampant growers, especially when in full bloom. They should be planted in a well-drained position that stays moist during the summer.

Antigonon leptopus

Confederate vine, coral vine, Mexican creeper

Half-hardy / Full sun

Vigorous, rampant, tuberous-rooted Mexican climber growing to a height of 4.5 m and a spread of up to 6 m, though usually less in cool-temperate gardens. Heart-shaped, almost triangular, prominently veined bright green leaves with strongly frilled margins are 5–14 cm long. Tiny, coral pink, occasionally white, flowers are borne in airy panicles up to 15 cm long or more in midsummer. Evergreen in mild areas with only light frost. Although

Antigonon
leptopus

not hardy, the tubers will survive lows of −6°c if well mulched; otherwise store the tubers in frost-free conditions during the winter months or grow as a conservatory climber, where it will soon take over!

Apios (Fabaceae)

North America

This genus comprises two species of twining, climbing plants that are grown for their edible roots, though they make excellent ornamental garden plants with their handsome flowers and lush green foliage. Both prefer sandy, fertile, well-drained soil.

Apios americana

American potato bean, bog potato, groundnut,
  Indian potato, potato bean, Virginia potato, wild
  bean, wild potato
Frost-hardy / Sun or dappled shade

With a vinelike growth habit, twines upon and through shrubbery on the forest floor in its native habitat, throughout North Carolina and many other parts of the United States, where it reaches 3–4.5 m high once established. Pinnately compound leaves have five to seven leaflets covered in silvery hairs. From late summer to autumn, striking inflorescences are borne in clusters of brownish red, pea-shaped flowers with long stalks, followed by pods 5–10 cm long. Underground stems 5–7.5 cm beneath the soil, with periodic swellings (the groundnut itself) up to 5 cm in diameter, are

edible but should be boiled or roasted for maximum flavour. Botanically, these swollen stems are tubers and function as storage organs for the plant. Hardier if well mulched.

Aristolochia (Aristolochiaceae)

Dutchman's pipe, birthwort
Temperate and tropical regions throughout the
  world

Members of this genus of about three hundred species of vigorous deciduous and evergreen climbers, sometimes shrubs and perennials, are grown for their interesting leaves and often bizarre flowers, which trap pollinating insects. This may be one of the earliest groups of plants, the paleoherbs. The flowers are composed of sepals fused into a calyx tube shaped like a calabash pipe. The more tender species are better grown as greenhouse or conservatory plants, though several will take lows of −5°c, and thus should be considered only for the mildest parts of cool-temperate regions or gardens with suitable microclimates. All prefer humus-rich, well-drained soil; the hardy forms overwinter most successfully in dry soils.

Aristolochia californica

California Dutchman's pipe, California pipevine
Half-hardy / Sun or dappled shade

Deciduous perennial climber from California, growing to a height of 4.5 m and a spread of 3 m, though usually less in cool-summer climates. Heart-shaped leaves are finely covered in white hairs. Flowers, up to 4 cm long, contorted, tubular, yellow-greenish with a dull reddish purple throat, hang like pendulous pipes along the stems in summer. Only for the warmest gardens as it only takes lows of about 0°c.

Aristolochia fimbriata

Frost-hardy with a thick mulch / Sun or dappled shade

Perennial climber from Brazil, growing to a height of 2–3 m and a spread of 3 m, though usually less in temperate gardens. Also a good ground cover if

there is nothing for it to climb. Due to its tendency to be prostrate, it is useful for scrambling down walls and also makes a very good hanging basket plant. Leaves are dark green, heart-shaped, with prominent pale green-silver veining. Exquisite curving, tubular flowers with fringed edges, greenish brown outside and purplish brown with yellow markings inside, are produced along the stems thoroughout the summer months. Dies back to the ground in winter.

Aristolochia littoralis

Calico flower

Tender / Sun or dappled shade

Vigorous evergreen twining climber, growing to 6 m tall by 4.5 m wide, though usually much less in temperate gardens. Leaves are heart-shaped, glaucous, pale green, 5–10 cm long. Flowers are solitary, rounded, deep purplish brown, with cream markings and veins, up to 10 cm across, appear from summer to autumn. Although usually considered tender, the roots will take lows of −5°C if well mulched during the winter months. Plays an important role in the life of native pipevine swallowtail butterflies: the flowers provide nectar for the butterflies, and the leaves are an important food source for the caterpillars of this butterfly.

Aristolochia macrophylla

syn. *A. durior*

Dutchman's pipe

Frost-hardy / Sun or dappled shade

Vigorous deciduous twining climber, growing up to 9 m tall with a spread of 6 m, with large heart-shaped leaves, dark green above and paler below, 10–30 cm long. Extremely decorative foliage enriches any wall or tree, and stem becomes richly textured and thickened with corky deposits with age. Flowers are solitary, shaped like a curved pipe, rounded, brownish green, mottled yellowish, purple, and ivory, up to 3 cm long, borne in early summer, hidden by the foliage.

Bignonia (Bignoniaceae)

Southeastern United States

Bignonia contains just one species, a beautiful climber that deserves to be grown more often.

Bignonia capreolata

Cross vine, trumpet flower

Frost-hardy / Sun or shade

Vigorous, woody, evergreen or semi-evergreen tendril climber, growing up to a height of 10 m.

Above left

Aristolochia littoralis

Above

Aristolochia macrophylla

In ideal conditions can easily cover the side of a house. Each lustrous dark green leaf consists of two narrowly oblong leaflets and a central branched tendril. Funnel-shaped, deep reddish orange flowers with a darker throat up to 5 cm long are borne in clusters from the leaf axils in summer. Prefers moist, well-drained soil in full sun for the best flowers, although it can be grown in a shadier position with accordingly fewer flowers. Evergreen in mild areas, semi-evergreen in colder areas. Foliage develops a reddish purple cast in cool weather. Can be used as a ground cover. 'Tangerine Beauty' has orange flowers with a red throat. Hardy to −10°C and lower.

Billardiera (Pittosporaceae)

Mostly southwestern Australia

Bomarea caldasii

Named after Jacques-Julien Houton de Labillardière, a French botanist, this genus contains about forty evergreen, woody-stemmed, twining climbers and a few perennials that are herbaceous in temperate climates. They are grown for their delightful little flowers and interesting fruit. Although mostly small in stature, they are nevertheless pleasing plants for well-drained soil against a sunny wall.

Billardiera longiflora

Frost-hardy / Sun or partial shade

Most commonly grown *Billardiera* species, a striking climber that grows to a height of 2 m with narrow dark green leaves. Flowers are pendulous, bell-shaped, greenish yellow, occasionally tinged purple and produced singly in the leaf axils in summer, followed by vibrant purple fruits in autumn. Prefers a south- or west-facing wall or a warm part of the garden in partial shade. Hardy to −5°C for short periods; mulch during the winter months. 'Cherry Berry' is a red-fruited, less vigorous form, with darker green leaves covered by smooth white hairs. *Billardiera longiflora fructu-albo* has pure white berries and is slightly less vigorous than the species but is otherwise identical.

Bomarea (Alstroemeriaceae)

South America

The approximately one hundred evergreen and herbaceous, tuberous-rooted, scrambling and twining climbers belonging to this genus, closely related to *Alstroemeria*, are grown for their exquisite tubular or bell-shaped flowers. Although they are considered tender, it is worth trying them against a warm south-facing wall, or otherwise in a conservatory. Give them moist, humus-rich soil. The edible roots are sometimes boiled as a potato substitute in their native habitat.

Bomarea caldasii

Semi-tender / Full sun

Herbaceous, thin-stemmed, twining climber from Ecuador, 2–4 m tall, covered with oval green leaves with twisted leaf stalks. Clusters of tubular flowers up to 4 cm long are borne in summer at the ends of the shoots, in a shade of orangish red with a yellow throat flecked brown.

Bomarea hirtella

Semi-tender / Sun or dappled shade

Herbaceous twining climber growing to 2 m tall or more, with terminal clusters of narrow tubular flowers that are soft red, with a greenish yellow, darker-spotted throat in summer, followed by triangular seedpods containing bright reddish orange seeds.

Bomarea multiflora

Semi-tender / Full sun

Climbing herbaceous plant collected by Martyn Rix in Mexico, growing to a height of 2–2.5 m, with drooping heads of fifteen to thirty tubular greenish yellow flowers, tinged orange-red inside with brown flecks in the throat. Hardy to 0°C, hence only for the warmest gardens or as a conservatory plant that can be brought out for the summer months.

Bomarea salsilla

Semi-tender / Full sun

Herbaceous twining climber, growing to a height of 2–2.5 m tall, with heads of five to ten slightly pendent, bell-shaped dark pink flowers with blue and black markings in the throat in spring to early summer.

Bougainvillea (Nyctaginaceae)

South America

This is a genus of wonderful sprawling climbers that many adventurous exoticists would love to grow in their gardens. Unfortunately, cool-temperate climates do not suit them. Although they can take temperatures down to 0°C for short periods, they need hot, dry summers to thrive so are best grown as conservatory plants, where they do well. Smaller manageable plants can be brought out in hot, dry weather, into a position with full sun against a south-facing wall. Store at a minimum of 5°C. If kept in a warmer situation during the winter, they will flower continuously.

Campsis (Bignoniaceae)

Japan, China, and the southeastern United States

This genus contains just two species of vigorous, showy climbing plants that use aerial roots to attach their long stems. The flowers are very large and exotic, and the plants are surprisingly hardy given their flamboyance. It takes two or three years to establish a framework of branches before the plants

begin to flower abundantly, but it is well worth the wait. All are hardy to −10°C. In colder areas it is advisable to grow them against a warm south-facing wall; otherwise grow them over walls and fences in well-drained soil in full sun.

Campsis grandiflora

syn. *Bignonia grandiflora*
Chinese trumpet vine, Chinese trumpet creeper
Frost-hardy / Full sun

Vigorous aerial-rooted climber from China and Japan, growing to a height of 8 m and higher, with pinnate leaves consisting of seven or nine oval, pointed, toothed leaflets. Clusters of stunning trumpet-shaped strong orange or red flowers, 5–10 cm

Campsis grandiflora

long, are produced en masse from high summer to autumn.

Campsis radicans

syn. *Bignonia radicans*
Frost-hardy / Full sun

Deciduous, vigorous, woody-stemmed climber with aerial roots, from the southeastern United States, growing up to a height of 12 m, though it can be regularly pruned to a more accommodating size. Pinnate leaves with seven to eleven oval, pointed, toothed leaflets. Terminal clusters of trumpet-shaped orange, red, or yellow flowers, 6–8 cm long, are formed from high summer to autumn. 'Flamenco' has rich orange flowers. Forma *flava* has rich yellow flowers.

Campsis radicans, flowers

Campsis radicans f. *flava*, flowers

Campsis ×tagliabuana 'Indian Summer'

Hybrid between *C. grandiflora* and *C. radicans*. Climber growing to about 4 m with pinnate leaves, dark matte green, lighter on the underside, 25–40 cm long. Flowers clustered in large, often pendent racemes, trumpet-shaped, apricot with darker centre, up to 8 cm long, from late summer to autumn. *Campsis ×tagliabuana* 'Madame Galen' has large salmon-red flowers.

Canarina (Campanulaceae)

Canary Islands and tropical east Africa

This genus encompasses three species of herbaceous, tuberous, scrambling climbers grown for their attractive flowers.

Canarina canariensis

Canarina canariensis

Canary Island bell flower

Tender / Dappled shade

Summer-deciduous climber with fleshy branching stems and arrow-shaped green to grey-green leaves, up to 8 cm long, with finely serrated margins. Grows to a height of 1.5 m in its native habitat in the Canary Islands, though less in temperate climates. Bell-shaped, waxy, pale orange-red flowers with darker crimson veining, up to 6 cm long, are borne singly from the leaf axils from late winter to spring. Being winter flowering, suitable only for conservatory culture in temperate climes. Plants are dormant in summer and need a well-drained, humus-rich compost.

Clematis (Ranunculaceae)

Worldwide, at higher elevations in tropical regions

This is a genus of deciduous or evergreen mostly twining climbers and herbaceous perennials that are grown for their beautiful flowers, often followed by interesting seed heads. Clematis are excellent plants for covering walls, trellises, pergolas, and even old tree stumps, or let them scramble through other shrubs and trees. Plenty of information on clematis is available to the avid gardener. Here I only cover one species, *C. armandii*, because of its very exotic-looking evergreen foliage, which makes an excellent foil for other plants even when not in flower.

Clematis armandii

Frost-hardy / Full sun

From central to western China, this is a vigorous twining climber once established, growing to a height of 3–5 m, with leaves split into three glossy, leathery, evergreen leaflets up to 15 cm long. From spring to early summer, it bears deliciously scented, flattish, single white flowers 4 cm across. Prefers humus-rich, well-drained soil in a south or westerly aspect in full sun with its roots in the shade. Protect from desiccating wind, as it can make the foliage look rather tatty. Prune hard immediately after flowering if required to ensure flowers the following

Clematis armandii 'Snowdrift'

spring. Hardy to −10°c. 'Apple Blossom' has pink flower buds opening white and is much less vigorous than the species. 'Snowdrift' has very fragrant white flowers, very floriferous.

Dregea (Asclepiadaceae)

syn. Wattakaka

Southern Asia, Africa; four species in China

Members of this genus of about twelve species of evergreen, woody-steamed, twining climbers are grown for their delightful hoya-like flowers. An oddity well worth having in the exotic garden.

Dregea sinensis

Frost-hardy / Full sun

Deciduous, woody, scrambling climber from China, growing to a height of 3 m, with soft, oval, midgreen leaves, heart-shaped at the base, greyish underneath, 4–10 cm long. Clusters of ten to twenty-five small,

star-shaped, highly scented, pale white to cream flowers with a pink flush are borne from late summer to early autumn, followed by pairs of slender pods up to 7 cm long. Prefers a warm, sunny wall in rich, well-drained soil, in a sheltered corner protected from wind. Hardy to −10°C for short periods.

Eccremocarpus (Bignoniaceae)

Chile

The five species of evergreen herbaceous or tendril climbers in this genus are grown for their attractive flowers, which are produced over a long period.

Eccremocarpus scaber

Chilean glory flower

Half-hardy / Dappled shade

Fast-growing, evergreen tendril climber, growing to a height of 2–3 m, with deep green, soft compound leaves. Racemes of waxy red, orange, pink, or yellow lopsided tubular flowers are borne from late spring to summer, followed by inflated fruit pods, which contain many winged seeds that self-sow readily. Prefers moist soil. Hardy to 0°C so will only survive in the warmest gardens. Often grown as an annual that will flower the same season from an early sowing.

×*Fatshedera* (Araliaceae)

Aralia ivy

Originating in France, ×*Fatshedera* is the result of an intergeneric cross between *Fatsia japonica* 'Moseri' and *Hedera helix* 'Hibernica'. The plant combines the shrubby shape of *Fatsia* with the five-lobed leaves of *Hedera*.

×*Fatshedera lizei*

Hardy / Dappled or full shade

Very junglelike plant that can be grown as a handsome shrub up to 1.5 m or trained against a wall or support, where it can grow up to a height of 1.5–3 m, with palmate, five- to seven-lobed, bright glossy green leaves with prominent veins, up to 15 cm across. 'Annemeike' has gold-splashed foliage, 'Pia' has wavy-edged leaves, and 'Variegata' has green leaves edged with cream. Prefers free-draining soil. Very tolerant of adverse conditions; good in planters.

Hardenbergia (Fabaceae)

Australia

Named after Franziska Countess von Hardenberg, this is a genus of three species of evergreen, woody-stemmed, twining climbers or subshrubs and trailers, grown for their handsome foliage and abundant racemes of pealike flowers. They flower from late winter to early spring, making a spectacular show. Grow them in well-drained soil in the warmest gardens.

Hardenbergia comptoniana

Half-hardy / Sun or dappled shade

Delightful woody-stemmed, twining climber, growing to a height of 2.5 m, with leaves consisting of three to five lance-shaped, deep green leaflets, up to 6 cm long. Racemes of small, deep purple, pealike flowers are borne in spring. Hardy down to 0°C for short periods, and hence will grow only in the warmest gardens. Excellent as a frost-free conservatory plant.

Hardenbergia violacea

Coral pea, vine lilac

Half-hardy / Sun or dappled shade

Woody-stemmed, twining climber, growing to a height of 3 m in ideal conditions, with narrowly oval, dark green, glossy leaves with prominent veins, 7–10 cm long. Racemes of violet-purple pealike flowers in spring. There are several named cultivars with different coloured flowers and forms. Hardy to −3.8°c for short periods.

Hedera (Araliaceae)

British Isles to the Himalaya, China, Korea, Japan, Canary Islands, Madeira, Azores, and northern Africa

Members of this genus of evergreen, woody-stemmed, trailing and self-clinging climbers have adventitious roots that enable them to attach to walls and trees; otherwise they will grow as a ground cover. Once established, they grow fast, and some can become invasive. Although hardy, they give a subtropical feel to the garden, especially some of the large-leaved forms. Being shade tolerant, they make excellent plants for a north-facing wall or underneath a canopy of trees. All prefer well-drained soil. A large range of interesting spe-

cies and hybrids can be found on the market; here I will only cover a few, as so much information is already available to the avid gardener.

Hardenbergia violacea, flowers

Hedera canariensis

Canary Island ivy

Hardy / Sun or shade

Vigorous evergreen self-clinging climber, growing to a height of 6 m, with large, heart-shaped, unlobed, glossy green leaves with purple stems. 'Gloire de Marengo' has exquisite silver-grey leaves edged with cream. 'Ravensholst' has large, triangular, glossy green leaves.

Hedera colchica

Persian ivy

Hardy / Sun or shade

Grows to a height of 10 m with large, oval, unlobed, leathery green leaves on green stems. 'Dentata' has brownish purple stems and large light green leaves that droop. 'Dentata Variegata' grows to about 5 m high with bold creamy yellow variegation, making it

Hedera colchica 'Dentata'

Hedera colchica
'Dentata
Variegata'

an excellent choice for brightening up a shady corner. 'Sulphur Heart' (syn. 'Paddy's Pride') grows to a similar height, with leaves variegated light green and yellow.

Hedera helix

Common English ivy

Hardy / Sun or shade

Exceedingly well-known climber and ground cover that can reach massive proportions if left unhindered. Has spawned many cultivars in various colour combinations, of which the following are only a few. 'Adam' grows to about 1.2 m high with smallish light green leaves variegated yellow-cream. It is rather prone to frost damage but will soon generate new growth in spring. 'Atropurpurea' grows to about 4 m high, with dark green leaves that turn a delicious deep purple in winter. 'Buttercup' grows to about 2 m high, with light green leaves that turn vivid butter yellow in full sun. 'Goldheart' grows to about 6 m high, with rich dark green leaves with a bright golden yellow splash in the centres.

Holboellia (Lardizabalaceae)

Eastern Asia and western China

Plants in this genus of five species of evergreen twining climbers are grown principally for their handsome dark foliage. Although the flowers are insignificant, they are nevertheless sweetly and heavily scented. All prefer well-drained, moderately fertile, preferably humus-rich soil in full sun to dappled shade, sheltered from cold, dessicating winds.

Holboellia coriacea

China blue vine

Frost-hardy / Sun or dappled shade

Vigorous evergreen twining climber from central China, growing to 7 m tall, though usually less in cool-temperate gardens. Glossy, leathery green leaves consist of three leaflets. Bunches of highly scented, small, purplish white male flowers and, lower down the stem, larger purple-tinged green female flowers are formed in late spring, followed occasionally by purple sausage-shaped fruit in a hot summer. Hardy to −10°C.

Holboellia latifolia

Frost-hardy / Full sun

Vigorous evergreen climber with similar stature and foliage to *H. coriacea*. Flowers from late winter to early spring. Hardy to about −5°C for short periods.

Humulus (Cannabidaceae)

Common hop

Northern temperate regions

This genus contains two vigorous herbaceous climbers that are very useful for covering unsightly buildings or old tree trunks quickly. They are grown in gardens primarily for their attractive foliage, especially the ornamental forms. They naturalise in woodland areas, where they can grow up to a height of 21 m in one season! They can become rather rampant and invasive after a few years, so should be placed wisely. Plant them in well-drained soil. Hops have been used by the brewing industry for many centuries: the dried flowering heads of female plants are used as a flavouring and preservative in beer. The English name "hop" comes from the Anglo-Saxon *hoppan* (to climb). Young leaves and shoots are said to be very delicious if cooked, with a unique flavour; the juvenile leaves can also be used in salads.

Humulus lupulus
'Aureus' with splashes
of colour added by
a hybrid agapanthus
(middle left), a verbena
(lower right), and
Tibouchina urvilleana
(upper right)

Humulus lupulus

Hardy / Sun or light shade

Vigorous, widely suckering, herbaceous climber with rough stems. Leaves green, three- to five-lobed, up to 15 cm long. Female flower spikes become drooping clusters of soft conelike hops in autumn. For garden use, though, 'Aureus' is far more attractive, growing to a height of 6 m with bright, soft yellow leaves that become greener with age. Pale greenish yellow flower spikes are borne in pendent clusters in autumn. 'Golden Tassels' is a dwarf form, less invasive and bushier than the yellow form, growing to a height of 3 m. Good on trellis or support or laced through a shrub. 'Prima Donna' grows to only about 2 m and is therefore not as invasive or hard to control as other varieties. 'Taff's Variegated' grows to a height of 5 m and has dark green leaves with paler markings. 'Wye Challenger' is a handsome red-stemmed form.

Hydrangea (Hydrangeaceae)

Eastern Asia (from Japan to China, the Himalaya, and Indonesia) and North and South America

This genus comprises about one hundred species of evergreen and deciduous shrubs, trees, and climbers, of which we are only interested in the latter here. The following make excellent climbing plants for positions with dappled to full shade, such as a north-facing wall. They prefer moist, humus-rich, well-drained soil.

Hydrangea anomala subsp. petiolaris

syn. *H. petiolaris*
Hardy / Dappled to full shade

Deciduous, woody-stemmed, self-clinging root climber from Russia, Korea, and Japan, growing to 15 m, with handsome, roundish, midgreen, toothed leaves up to 10 cm long. Large lacecap blooms of white flowers in early summer. New plants may take several years to flower.

Hydrangea seemannii

Frost-hardy / Dappled to full shade

Kennedia macrophylla

Evergreen, woody-stemmed, aerial-rooting, climbing hydrangea from Mexico, growing to a height of 7 m, with long, dark, glossy green leaves and 15-cm domed heads of mainly fertile white flowers, surrounded by a few sterile florets, borne in summer. Flower buds are enclosed by conspicuous bracts. Hardy to about −10°C.

Hydrangea serratifolia

syn. *H. integerrima*
Hardy / Sun or shade

Closely related to *H. seemannii*. Evergreen, woody-stemmed, aerial-root climber from Chile, growing to a height of 10 m, with leathery, sometimes toothed, fresh green leaves, with densely set, entirely fertile, creamy white, sometimes tinged pink flowers in columnar panicles, up to 15 cm long in late summer. Will flower best on a sunny wall or up a tree trunk.

Kennedia (Fabaceae)

Australia
Semi-tender / Dappled shade

This genus includes sixteen species of evergreen, woody-stemmed, twining climbers and trailers, grown for their very exotic pealike flowers. Unfortunately, they are suitable for growing only in the mildest gardens or in a conservatory, as they take temperatures down to 0°C for short periods only. If grown outside, they should be protected with horticultural fleece or similar in cold weather. All prefer moist, fertile, well-drained soil.

Kennedia coccinea

Vigorous evergreen twining climber, growing to a height of 2–3 m, with leathery, wedge-shaped green leaflets up to 8 cm long. Bright scarlet pealike flowers with yellow blotching, 18 mm across, are borne all summer.

Kennedia macrophylla

Vigorous evergreen twining climber, growing to a height of 2–3 m or more, with green leaflets up to 8 cm long. Trusses of brownish red pealike flowers with yellow blotching are borne from spring to summer.

Kennedia nigricans

Black bean, black coral pea

Vigorous evergreen twining climber, growing to a height of 2 m or more, with leaves divided into three leaflets with notched tips. Small trusses of pealike, velvety, blackish purple flowers with yellow patches, 35 mm long, are borne in spring.

Kennedia rubicunda

Dusky coral pea

Vigorous evergreen twining climber, growing to a height of 3 m, with leaves divided into three leaflets, up to 12 cm long. Pealike coral-red flowers, 35 mm long, are borne from spring to summer.

Lapageria (Philesiaceae)

Chilean bell flower
Chile

Named after Empress Josephine, Napoleon's first wife, née Josephine de la Pagerie, this genus contains only one species.

Lapageria rosea

Half-hardy / Dappled shade

Thin, woody-stemmed, evergreen twining climber, growing to a height of 5 m in ideal conditions, though usually less. Leaves are dark green, leathery, oblong to oval. Flowers pendent, narrow, bell-shaped, fleshy, waxy, rose-crimson with paler flecking, 7–10 cm long, from summer to late autumn. Variety *albiflora* is a soft white form. 'Nash Court' is soft pink-flecked rose and 'Flesh Pink' has delightful salmon-pink flowers. Prefers moist, well-drained, humus-rich soil. Will take temperatures down to 0°C, and hence should only be planted in the warmest gardens or grown as a conservatory plant.

Muehlenbeckia (Polygonaceae)

New Zealand, Australia, New Guinea, and South America

Plants in this genus of about fifteen species of evergreen and deciduous, thin-stemmed, summer-flowering, scrambling climbers and shrubs are grown for their interesting foliage.

Muehlenbeckia complexa

Maidenhair vine, necklace vine
Frost-hardy / Sun or dappled shade

Vigorous in mild areas, semi-deciduous twining climber, growing to a height of 4.5 m, forming a tangle of black wiry stems with small rounded dark green leaves, 0.5–1.5 cm. Can also be used as a ground cover. Clusters of inconspicuous, greenish white flowers are borne from spring to late autumn, followed by three-lobed whitish fruits. Not the most handsome of plants, but useful for covering oil tanks and other small structures, or larger ones with time. Can also be trimmed and used for topiary, holding its shape well. Prefers well-drained, moist soil but tolerates drought well. Hardy to −5°C and lower.

Mutisia (Asteraceae)

South America

This genus comprises about sixty species of evergreen tendril climbers and shrubs with attractive, long-lasting flowers. The two described here prefer humus-rich, well-drained soil.

Mutisia decurrens

Half-hardy / Sun or dappled shade

Evergreen tendril climber from the temperate forest of the southern Andes, growing to a height of 3 m, though usually less in a temperate climate, with narrow, lanceolate, grey-green leaves, 7–13 cm long, which can become rather tatty if not tidied up regularly. Attractive, large, daisylike, bright orange flowers up to 10 cm across are borne in summer. Hardy down to 0°C, although the roots will take −5°C for short periods if well mulched during the winter, and the plant will return from the base in spring; hence should be grown in a warm location next to a south-facing wall or similar, or as a conservatory plant brought out for the summer months.

Mutisia ilicifolia

Half-hardy / Sun or dappled shade

Shrubby evergreen climber from Chile, growing to a height of 3 m, though usually less in temperate gardens. Leaves are spiny-toothed, stiff, leathery, up to 6 cm long, with the midrib extending beyond the blade, branching and forming a strong twining tendril, covered in fine downy white hairs. Daisylike flower heads of soft pink are up to 35 mm across.

Pandorea (Bignoniaceae)

Bower of beauty, bower vine
Eastern Australia

The genus and specific name of this plant is derived from the Greek legend of Pandora (Pandora's Box), because of the boxlike seed capsules. The evergreen, woody-stemmed, twining climbers belonging to this genus of six species and several cultivars are grown for their striking flowers and attractive leaves. Although on the edge of hardiness, they are worth considering for the warmest gardens in cool-temperate areas, or grown as conservatory plants. All prefer moist, well-drained soil.

Pandorea jasminoides

syn. *Bignonia jasminoides*
Half-hardy / Full sun

Bushy, twining, woody-stemmed vine, growing to a height of 5 m in ideal conditions, though usually less, with evergreen pinnate leaves composed of five to nine lance-shaped leaflets. Clusters of pinkish white flowers with darker pink flushed throats are borne from late winter to summer. Hardy to 0°C, although perennial if the roots are heavily mulched during heavy freezing periods. 'Alba' is a white-flowered form that is reputed to be slightly hardier than the species, with flowers up to 7 cm across. 'Charisma' is a selected form with variegated leaves

that are midgreen, irregularly splashed yellow, otherwise the same as its parent. 'Rosea Superba' is a heavy-flowering cultivar with slightly larger and darker flowers than the species.

Pandorea pandorana

Pandorea pandorana

Half-hardy / Full sun

Bushy, twining, woody-stemmed vine, growing to a height of 5 m in ideal conditions, though usually less, with bright, glossy, evergreen pinnate leaves composed of six pairs of ovate to lance-shaped leaflets. Large flower clusters bear a multitude of small creamy yellow flowers, with deep wine-purple markings inside the throat. 'Golden Showers' is a golden form, producing quantities of orange to red flowers in early spring, not as hardy as the species.

Parthenocissus (Vitaceae)

Eastern Asia and North America

The ten species in this genus of vigorous, deciduous, woody-stemmed, tendril-producing climbers are mostly self-clinging in habit, many having adhesive pads at the ends of their tendrils. With their lush, attractive foliage and stunning autumn colouration, they are very useful for covering ugly walls and

Pandorea pandorana

other structures comparatively quickly. The stems can be quite thick with age. The tiny flowers and fruit are insignificant. All prefer moderately fertile soil in full sun to dappled shade and are fully hardy; they can take dry conditions once established.

Parthenocissus henryana

Chinese Virginia creeper / Silver vein creeper

Hardy / Sun or dappled shade

Deciduous, self-clinging Chinese species growing to a height and spread of 9–10 m, with palmate leaves consisting of five leaflets up to 12 cm long that are dark velvety green, with conspicuous silvery white veining when grown in a shady situation, slightly purple on the underside. In autumn the foliage turns brilliant red with white veins. After a hot summer, dark blue fruits are formed.

Parthenocissus quinquefolia

Virginia creeper

Hardy / Sun or dappled shade

Vigorous, deciduous, woody-stemmed, self-clinging tendril climber native to the eastern United States, growing to a height and spread of 15 m or more, with dark green, five-lobed, toothed leaves up to 12 cm across or more, which turn brilliant flame-crimson in autumn. This rampant climber covers my house up to the chimney pot! Variety *engelmannii* is a more compact form with smaller leaves.

Parthenocissus tricuspidata

Boston ivy, Japanese creeper

Hardy / Sun or dappled shade

Vigorous, woody-stemmed, self-clinging tendril climber, growing to a height and spread of 20 m or more, with variable three-lobed or trifoliate leaves that turn rich crimson in autumn. 'Crûg Compact', growing to 5 m tall, is a compact, small-leaved form with spectacular crimson autumnal leaves and dull blue berries. 'Fenway Park' is a desirable form that was discovered as a sport on the venerable 'Green

Above left

Parthenocissus quinquefolia

Above

Parthenocissus tricuspidata, fall colour

Monster' (the Boston ivy wall at the Fenway Park ball stadium in Boston) in 1988 by Peter Del Tredici of the Arnold Arboretum. Leaves emerge bright golden yellow, retaining their colour when grown in full sun, and in autumn have an attractive red overlay. 'Green Showers' has larger leaves than the species. 'Lowii' grows to similar gargantuan proportions, with handsome, deeply cut, crinkled, three- to seven-lobed leaves that turn crimson in autumn. 'Star Shower' has new foliage dramatically marbled creamy white and green. 'Veitchii' is exceedingly vigorous, growing to a height of 20 m, with spectacular red-purple autumn leaf colouration.

Passiflora (Passifloraceae)

Passionflower

Mostly tropical America, with a few shrubby species in Asia and the Pacific Islands

The genus *Passiflora* includes around five hundred species of predominantly evergreen climbing vines with coiling tendrils, grown for their highly exotic flowers and fruit. Most *Passiflora* species are tender and make excellent conservatory plants, especially when grown in the ground. Many can be grown in containers that can be brought outside during the summer months; thus grown, the plants will be much smaller than if grown in the ground. There are a few relatively hardy species that can be grown outside permanently in cool-temperate climates, provided they are grown in a warm corner of the garden, preferably against a south- or west-facing wall that is sheltered from cold desiccating winds. They prefer deep, moist, humus-rich soils.

The name "passionflower" was bestowed by Christian missionaries who arrived in South America in the sixteenth century and found a plant that to them symbolised the death of Christ. The five sepals and five petals of the flower, which are similar in appearance, represent the disciples without Peter and Judas. The double row of coloured filaments, known as the corona, signifies the halo around Christ's head or the crown of thorns. The five stamens and the three spreading styles with their flattened heads symbolise the wounds and the nails respectively. The vine's tendrils resemble the whips used to scourge Christ. These plants are discussed in great detail in *Passiflora: Passionflowers of the World* by Torsten Ulmer and John M. MacDougal (2004).

Passiflora caerulea

Blue passionflower, common passionflower
Frost-hardy / Sun or dappled shade

Most commonly grown passionflower in temperate gardens, from Argentina and Brazil. Fast-growing, evergreen or semi-evergreen, woody-stemmed, tendril-bearing climber with glossy dark green leaves, usually palmately lobed with five parts, though they can have as few as three lobes or as many as nine. Flowers are white, occasionally flushed pink, with a blue- or purple-banded corona from summer to autumn followed by ochre yellow egg-shaped fruits. 'Constance Elliott' is a beautiful white-flowered cultivar. Hardy to −10°c and lower.

Passiflora incarnata

May apple, maypop, wild passionflower
Frost-hardy / Sun or dappled shade

Vigorous evergreen twining climber from the eastern United States, growing to a height of 2.4–3.7 m, with large, three- to five-lobed, dark green leaves with lightly toothed edges, up to 15 cm in length and width. Flowers are composed of ten lavender-white tepals arranged in a shallow bowl shape, above which is a flattened purple-and-white-banded corona. In the centre the white fleshy stigma is

Pileostegia viburnoides

syn. *Schizophragma viburnoides*
Hardy / Sun or dappled shade

Slow-growing, evergreen, woody-stemmed, self-clinging climber, attaining a height of 6–9 m. Leaves are large, dark green, glossy, leathery, and narrowly oblong to sword-shaped. Wide, loose heads of small creamy white flowers with prominent stamens are borne from late summer to autumn. Prefers moist, rich, well-drained soil in a position with dappled shade, although it flowers more prolifically with some sun. Useful for growing on a north-facing wall.

Passiflora caerulea, flower

Schizophragma (Hydrangeaceae)

China, Korea, Japan

Schizophragma is a genus of two deciduous species of ornamental woody climbers in the hydrangea family that climb by means of short, adhesive aerial roots. They can grow up either a wall or a large tree, and once established can cover large areas. They can be grown up a north-facing wall, though they flower more profusely in a sunnier aspect. Reddish brown stems provide some interest in winter. Like hydrangeas, they have to be established before fully flowering, though it is well worth the wait. They prefer humus-rich, moist, well-drained soil.

Passiflora incarnata, flower

Schizophragma hydrangeoides

Hardy / Sun or dappled shade

Deciduous, woody-stemmed, self-clinging root climber, growing to a height of 10.5 m, with dark green, broadly oval, pointed, toothed leaves up to 15 cm long. Inflorescence of creamy white flowers in flat heads, 20–25 cm across, with small fertile central flowers and teardrop-shaped outer ones, produced on pendent side branches in summer. 'Moonlight' has bluish green leaves with pewter markings and dark green veining. 'Roseum' is a beautiful form with pink-flushed bracts.

surrounded by five stamens in summer, followed by ovoid fruit. Deciduous in frost-prone areas, where it will die down to the ground during the winter months to re-emerge in spring. Although root hardy to −10°c and lower, should be mulched during the coldest months.

Pileostegia (Hydrangeaceae)

Northern Africa and Eurasia

This genus comprises four climbing or prostrate evergreen shrubs in the hydrangea family that grow with the support of aerial roots and are prized for their handsome foliage and flowers. Only one is commercially available.

Schizophragma integrifolium

Hardy / Sun or dappled shade

Deciduous, woody-stemmed, self-clinging root climber, growing to a height of 10.5 m, with very attractive, oval to pointed, heart-shaped silver-green leaves. White flowers are borne in flat heads up to 30 cm across, with marginal sterile flowers each with a conspicuous large white bract in summer.

Smilax (Smilacaceae)

Throughout the world in tropical and temperate regions

This genus of more than two hundred species of deciduous and evergreen, prickly-stemmed, scrambling, tendril-climbing plants is found in tropical and temperate regions throughout the world, though few species are in cultivation. The roots of *S. officinalis* are one of the sources of sarsaparilla, used in herbal medicine and as a flavour for root beer in North America. Male and female flowers are borne on separate plants. These plants are suitable for the warmest gardens only or as cool conservatory plants. They prefer, as does clematis, their roots in the shade in well-drained soil and their upper growth in the sun.

Smilax aspera

Half-hardy / Full sun

Rather tender evergreen climber that grows to a height of 3 m in its native habitat (southern Europe, North Africa, and the Canary Islands), with angular, prickly stems forming a dense canopy. Leaves grey-blotched, leathery, glossy, varying from heart-shaped to lanceolate. Tiny pale green flowers are borne in racemes in late summer, followed in a warm climate by red fruits. 'Maculata' is a lightly variegated form. Prefers well-drained soil against a south-facing wall, in a sheltered position. Hardy to −5°C for short periods so should only be grown in the warmest areas. Cover with fleece in prolonged cold weather. Excellent as a conservatory plant.

Smilax china

Half-hardy / Full sun

Deciduous, woody-based, scrambling climber with straggly, sometimes spiny stems, growing to 5 m tall in a warm, virtually frost-free location. Has rounded green leaves and umbels of yellowish lime green flowers in late spring, followed by small red berries in autumn. Hardy to about 0°C; hence only for the warmest gardens or as a conservatory plant. Prefers its roots in shade and the rest in full sun.

Solanum (Solanaceae)

Mostly tropical America

This is a genus of about fourteen hundred species of annuals, perennials, shrubs, trees, and vines in the nightshade, potato, and tomato family. All have a simple five-petalled structure with a central cone of yellow-orange stamens, followed by fleshy fruits that are invariably poisonous to some extent. Most are tender, though a few species are frost tolerant and work well in cool-temperate climates if grown in a sheltered corner away from desiccating winds. They prefer fertile soil in a sunny aspect.

Solanum crispum 'Glasnevin'

Frost-hardy / Full sun

Vigorous, woody-stemmed, evergreen or semi-evergreen scrambling climber, growing to a height of 6 m, with pointed to oval lance-shaped leaves. Purplish lilac flowers up to 2.5 cm across are borne in clusters at branch tips in summer. Hardy to −10°C for short periods. Will regrow from the ground if badly frosted.

Solanum jasminoides 'Album'

Frost-hardy / Sun or dappled shade

Woody-stemmed, semi-evergreen scrambling climber, growing to a height of 6 m, though often less. Dark green, oval to lance-shaped leaves. Exquisite, pure white, star-shaped flowers up to 2.5 cm across are borne in clusters from summer to autumn.

Tetrastigma (Vitaceae)

Indonesia and Malaysia to northern Australia

This genus of about ninety species of woody-stemmed climbers is allied to *Cissus* and *Vitis* (grape vine). One species, *T. voinierianum*, is grown for its handsome foliage.

Tetrastigma voinierianum

syn. *Cissus voinieriana*

Chestnut vine, tropical lizard vine

Tender / Dappled shade

Evergreen, woody-stemmed, coarse, stout, rampant vine or liana, climbing by tendrils, growing to 10 m tall or more in ideal conditions; will achieve this in a large, heated atrium or greenhouse. Young stems and petioles are often densely tawny, woolly. Thick, leathery, palmate leaves, up to 38 cm across, with leaflets, usually five, up to 20 cm long, weakly serrated and velvety underneath. Prefers moist, rich, well-drained soil. A marvelously exotic climbing plant to try if your garden is virtually frost-free or if you can wrap it in fleece all winter or offer it a cool conservatory.

Trachelospermum
(Apocynaceae)

India to Japan

Trachelospermum comprises about twenty woody-stemmed evergreen twining climbers, grown for their glossy foliage and highly fragrant blossoms, belonging to the periwinkle family. Grow them like jasmine, over a trellis, up a wall, along a fence, or in a container with a trellis behind. Plant them where their sweet summer fragrance can be enjoyed under a window or near a doorway. They also work well as ground covers. They prefer fertile, well-drained soil.

Trachelospermum asiaticum

Frost-hardy / Full sun

Dense, much-branched, leafy climber from Japan and Korea, growing to a height of 6 m in ideal conditions though usually less, with pointed, oval, leathery, glossy dark green leaves up to 5 cm long. Flowers hang in loose clusters and are windmill-shaped, jasminelike, sweetly scented, creamy white with a buff-yellow eye aging to yellow-cream, from early to late summer. Prefers to be grown against a south-facing wall. Minimum temperature −5°c.

Trachelospermum jasminoides

Frost-hardy / Full sun

Hailing from China, this fine evergreen climber grows to a height of 9 m in its native habitat, though usually less. Larger in leaf than *T. asiaticum*, up to 10 cm long and slightly less frost resistant. Flowers are also larger, white aging to creamy white. 'Tricolor' is a variegated form with green leaves splashed red and yellow. 'Variegata' is apparently hardier; leaves are edged and splashed with cream and often tinged pinkish crimson in winter. 'Waterwheel' is a very narrow-leaved form, with fragrant white flowers turning cream, 2.5 cm across, borne in high

Trachelospermum jasminoides

summer, on self-clinging stems to 7 m high, though not particularly fast growing. Grow against a warm, sunny wall. Minimum temperature −5°c.

Tropaeolum (Tropaeolaceae)

Mexico to southern South America

The name of this genus is derived from the Greek word *tropaion* (trophy), a term used for the tree trunk on which were hung the shields and helmets of defeated enemies. In this genus are more than eighty species of annuals, perennials, and occasionally tuberous plants in the nasturtium family, varying greatly in hardiness. All have long-spurred, five-petalled flowers in a wide range of warm colours. Here we are dealing only with the climbing species.

Tropaeolum ciliatum

Frost-hardy / Dappled shade

Vigorous, climbing, herbaceous perennial from Chile, growing to a height of 6 m in its native habitat, though usually less in cooler gardens. Leaves midgreen with five to seven lobes. Dusky, golden yellow trumpet-shaped flowers with deep red centres and veining are borne all summer. Evergreen in a mild winter. Can cover large areas in one season when established.

Tropaeolum majus

Frost-hardy / Sun or dappled shade

Well-known, very common scrambling climber from Colombia to Bolivia, growing up to 3 m high in one season from seed and thus useful for quick coverage. Almost round, matte green leaves are sometimes slightly lobed. Long-spurred flowers, over 5 cm across, in shades of red, orange, and yellow can be used, along with the leaves, in a salad, giving a strong peppery taste. Seeds can be pickled in vinegar and used in place of capers and are very delicious when used in salads or on pizzas.

Tropaeolum tricolor

Tropaeolum peregrinum

Canary creeper

Frost-hardy / Sun or dappled shade

Delightful perennial climber hailing from Ecuador and Peru, grown as an annual in temperate gardens, reaching 2 m tall or more depending on the summer. Leaves are light green and five-lobed. Clusters of bright yellow flowers, 25 mm across, with serrated edged petals, are borne all summer.

Tropaeolum speciosum

Scottish flame flower

Hardy / Shade

Fleshy, rhizomatous, perennial, soft-stemmed climber, growing to 3 m tall or more when growing well. Leaves are bluish green, palmate, five- to seven-lobed. Clusters of spectacular brilliant scarlet red flowers, 25 mm wide, are borne through summer to autumn, followed by shiny deep blue berries. Sometimes called the Scottish flame flower because the growing conditions in Scotland are similar to its native habitat, the temperate forests of Chile. Often grown through yew hedges to show it off to its best. Can be difficult to establish. Prefers dryish shade and is hardy to −15°c.

Tropaeolum tricolor

Semi-tender / Sun or dappled shade

Climbing or trailing perennial with delicate stems, from tuberous roots, growing to 1 m tall, with light bluish green, six-fingered, palmate leaves. Clusters of attractive, small, semi-pendulous, conical orange or yellow flowers with black-tipped red spurs appear from spring to early summer. Grow this little gem from Bolivia and Chile in the warmest gardens or as a container plant.

Tropaeolum tuberosum

Half-hardy / Sun or dappled shade

Herbaceous, tuberous-rooted, soft-stemmed climber, reaching 2–3 m tall, with three- to five-lobed greenish grey leaves. Bears cup-shaped flowers with yellowish orange petals, reddish orange sepals, and a conspicuous long spur. 'Ken Aslet' has showy red-streaked tubers and bluish green leaves, and flowers with red sepals and orange petals from midsummer to autumn. Hardy down to 0°c and will survive a few degrees of frost if well mulched or replanted deeper; otherwise dig up and store the tubers in frost-free conditions during the winter months.

Vitis (Vitaceae)

Grape vine

Northern Hemisphere

In this genus are sixty-five species of woody-stemmed, deciduous, tendril-bearing vines, producing fruit that can be small and unpalatable or large, sweet, and delicious to eat. There are many hundreds of cultivars, especially with *V. vinifera*, the European grape used for eating and making wine. The Asian species are primarily grown for their attractive foliage and brilliant autumn colouring. They prefer deep, well-drained, moderately fertile soils, often preferring alkaline soils. Here we are dealing with the more ornamental species.

Vitis coignetiae

Crimson glory vine

Hardy / Sun or dappled shade

Extremely vigorous, deciduous, woody-stemmed, tendril-producing vine from Korea and Japan, growing to a height of 15 m, with large, green, rounded, toothed, leathery, puckered, three- to five-lobed leaves, hairy underneath. In autumn, they become bronze and then brilliant scarlet red. Best autumn colour is achieved in poor soils. Small, pale green flowers in summer are followed by inedible black fruit. 'Claret Cloak' has handsome, large leaves that remain deep red-purple throughout the growing season, turning dark olive green, then scarlet in autumn.

Vitis pulchra

Hardy / Sun or dappled shade

Extremely vigorous, deciduous, woody-stemmed, tendril-producing vine, growing to a height of 12 m. Similar to *V. coignetiae* but with even bigger leaves, which are textured and tinted red all year. Splendid autumn colours, reputedly the best of all the Asian species.

Vitis coignetiae

Vitis vinifera 'Purpurea'

Hardy / Sun or dappled shade

Vigorous, deciduous, woody-stemmed, tendril-producing vine, growing to a height of 7 m, though usually smaller, with toothed, three- or five-lobed, bronze-purple leaves that are white-haired when young. Young shoots are downy white, soon turning purple. Small pale green flowers are borne in summer, followed by green or purple fruit.

Exotic Annuals and Tender Perennials

One of the pleasures of growing annuals—let alone exotic ones—from seed is the great feeling of satisfaction and fulfillment that results from watching them germinate and start to grow, then planting them out, where they soon give you a marvellous display; and especially if you want to grow a particular plant en masse, annuals from seed are considerably cheaper than ready-grown plants. Many exotics like *Ricinus communis* 'Zanzibarensis' grow from seed to a staggering 3 m tall by the end of summer. If your garden is fairly new and your specimen exotics have a few years to go before reaching a good size, annuals can fill the gaps quickly and cheaply, lending pretty much instant size and colour to your garden.

Tender perennials are those that live for more than one year or are perennial or subshrubs in native habitats that rarely, if ever, see frost. Most will not survive outside in temperate gardens unless you are blessed to live in a virtually frost-free area. Still, a mild winter quite often allows the odd tender perennial to survive, such as the *Cobaea scandens* (cup-and-saucer vine) that has survived a few winters in my Norfolk garden even though most gardeners grow it as an annual. Many of the more tender perennials need only minimal winter protection to keep them at or above 5°c, and some will survive frost-free in a shed or outhouse. For gardeners who prefer hardy exotics, this might seem like a lot of work, as these plants have to be brought in and stored for the winter and then hauled out again in late spring. Some with limited storage space might wish to have only a few plants such as this, but if you don't mind the effort required to make your garden look "over the top," these are the plants for you. The seasonal heights I report here are for plants grown in a cool-summer climate; these plants tend to grow larger in areas with hotter summers.

Left

Amaranthus tricolor

Amaranthus (Amaranthaceae)

Tropical to temperate areas worldwide

Included in this genus are about sixty species of annuals and short-lived perennials, of which some are rather weedy and are often found growing on wasteland in their native habitats. Several forms (especially some of the new hybrids), having a dazzling range of leaf colours and flowers, make spectacular annual plants for bedding, easily raised from seed and planted out when frosts have finished. There are far more worth growing than mentioned here, so start looking in your seed catalogues! These plants prefer fertile soil and full sun; tall varieties should be staked against wind damage.

Amaranthus caudatus

Love-lies-bleeding
Annual / Full sun

Attention-getting, bushy plant from the Andes of South America, growing to 1.2 m tall and 45 cm wide. Soft bright green leaves set off contrasting bright purple-red cascading tassels, which can grow to 30 cm long or more. Sow seed in early spring and plant out after last frost; germination takes ten to fourteen days. 'Viridis' (green tails amaranth) is a green cousin with alluring bright green tassels. 'Fat Spike' is an easy annual, growing up to 1.2 m high, with midgreen leaves with occasional purple markings. It produces attractive spikes of deep purple-red flowers 7.5 cm thick tapering to 2.5 cm at the top.

Amaranthus cruentus

syn. *A. paniculatus*
Prince's feather, purple amaranth, red amaranth
Annual / Full sun

Attractive species indigenous to the Americas, growing to a height of 60 cm or more, with oval to lance-shaped green leaves, often with a purple-red hue, topped by heads of erect or drooping greenish-to-red tassels in summer and early autumn. 'Hot Biscuits' has giant 60-cm-long, cinnamon-coloured plumes on plants up to 1.2 m tall.

Amaranthus tricolor

Chinese spinach, Joseph's coat
Annual / Full sun

Attention-getting, erect, bushy plant from Africa and Asia grown for its brightly variegated, almost psychedelic foliage, reaching 60–92 cm tall or more with elliptic to lance-shaped midgreen and chocolate basal leaves topped with bright yellow leaves splashed from the base to the centre with deep red markings, up to 20 cm long. The inflorescence is in the form of an erect, deep red, brushlike spike 15 cm tall, which can be pinched out if you want only the foliage. 'Flamingo Fountains' has thin, lance-shaped, carmine red leaves. 'Illumination' grows to 45 cm tall, with elliptic to ovate, coppery brown lower leaves, changing to bright rose topped with gold.

Arctotis (Asteraceae)

Zulu daisy
Southern Africa

Arctotis is a genus of some fifty species of erect to spreading annuals and perennials, occasionally subshrubs, found in dry stony soils in their native habitats. They are normally grown in cultivation as jazzy flowered annuals, as they tend to suffer from botrytis if overwintered under cover. The following look showy in the Mediterranean-style garden as either summer bedding or container plants. They prefer light, sharply drained, moist soil in a position with full sun, where they can soak up the heat!

Arctotis fastuosa

Cape daisy, monarch of the veldt
Perennial used as annual / Full sun

Spreading perennial growing to a height and spread of 30 cm or more, with elliptic, coarsely hairy, deeply lobed, silvery white leaves up to 15 cm long. Vivid orange daisylike flower heads up to 10 cm across, with deep purple or black at each petal base, are borne from midsummer to early autumn. 'Zulu Prince' is a beautiful garden form with white petals and orange and black markings at the base, creating a ring effect.

Arctotis × *hybrida*

Below

Arctotis × *hybrida*
'Flame', flower

Arctotis ×*hybrida*

Perennial used as annual / Full sun

Probably hybrids between *A. venusta* and *A. fastuosa*,
growing to a height and spread of 20 cm or more.
'African Sunrise' has rich orange flowers with a dark
centre that is dwarf and compact. 'Apricot' has soft
creamy apricot flowers deepening to an almost
orange centre with a small black halo. 'Bacchus' has
dark wine coloured flowers. 'Flame' is brilliant tangerine with a pewter grey centre. 'Rosita' is upright
and slender with delicious pale pink flowers. 'Torch'

Right

Arctotis ×*hybrida*
'Wine', flower

is an improvement on 'Flame' with a striking black centre. 'White' has white flowers with dark centres. 'Wine' has wine pink flowers. 'Yellow' has brilliant burnished golden yellow flowers.

Asclepias (Asclepiadaceae)

South Africa, tropical North and South America

This genus comprises more than one hundred species of evergreen and deciduous mostly clump-forming and a few shrubby plants. Most are found growing in well-drained scrubby areas or grasslands, with a few species in damp marshy locations. The genus contains a few gardenworthy forms, though *A. curassavica* is the best for exotic effect. The milky sap can cause skin irritation in some people.

*Asclepias
curassavica*

Asclepias curassavica

Blood flower, Indian root
Perennial used as annual / Full sun

Attractive and showy evergreen subshrub growing to 1 m high by 60 cm, though usually less as an annual in cool-temperate gardens. Opposite, midgreen, lance-shaped leaves are up to 15 cm long. Auxiliary cymes of vivid red to orangish red flow-

ers, 5 cm across or more, are formed near the terminal branch ends from early summer to autumn. Hardy to about 5°C; otherwise overwinter in a frost-free greenhouse or grow fresh from seed each year.

Beta (Chenopodiaceae)

Beet
Europe and the Mediterranean region

This genus contains one biennial species and two main forms, one grown for its edible roots (beet) and the other for its edible leaves and stalks (chard). Here we are dealing with the ornamental forms of *B. vulgaris* (Swiss chard). In Victorian times chard was used more as an ornamental than a garden vegetable because of its wide range of colours. Chards are very decorative and tropical looking in the border, with the added benefit that you can eat them! All prefer light, well-drained soil that doesn't dry out.

Beta vulgaris var. *cicla*

Chard
Biennial used as annual / Sun or dappled shade

Edible ornamental growing to a height and spread of 30 cm or more, with clusters of upright then arching, often puckered to a varying degree, glossy midgreen leaves, with a wide leaf stalk. 'Yellow' has exquisite, broad, golden yellow stalks and veins on glossy midgreen leaves. 'Bright Lights' is an exciting mixture offering coloured stems in shades of red, white, pink, violet, green, gold, orange, yellow, and some bicoloured! 'Rhubarb Chard' has rich ruby red leaf stalks and veins, with glossy dark green to purple foliage.

Calceolaria (Scrophulariaceae)

Pouch flower, slipper flower, slipperwort
Temperate to tropical areas of western South
America, Central America, and Mexico

Calceolaria is a large genus of some three hundred species of annuals, biennials, perennials, and shrubs found growing in diverse habitats ranging

Calceolaria
integrifolia hybrid

Calceolaria
'Kentish Hero',
flower detail

from dry scrub to alpine. They are not seen that often in gardens today but were much loved by Victorian gardeners for summer bedding as well as house or conservatory plants. The indoor forms have pouchlike flowers in a range of gaudy colours, often heavily spotted. The forms mentioned here take lows of 0°c for short periods and may survive in virtually frost-free locations. They prefer humus-rich compost added to the soil before planting and kept moist in hot weather.

Calceolaria 'Camden Hero'

Semi-tender to half-hardy / Sun or light shade

Sturdy plant growing to a height of 30 cm with soft greyish green leaves and round burnt-orange-terracotta pouches.

Calceolaria ×clibranii

Semi-tender to half-hardy / Sun or light shade

Grows to 45 cm tall with midgreen leaves and slender stems carrying bunches of large, pendent, bright yellow pouches. May need supporting, as stems break easily.

Calceolaria integrifolia

Frost-hardy / Sun or light shade

Virtually hardy plant that will make a small shrub after a few years, to around 60 cm high, with light green, puckered, slightly sticky leaves. Many large bunches of small bright yellow pouches are borne all summer long.

Calceolaria 'Kentish Hero'

Semi-tender to half-hardy / Sun or light shade

Rather wiry plant growing to about 30 cm with green leaves smothered with clusters of vivid orange pouches that deepen to a rusty colour with age. Plant is very brittle so should be handled carefully.

Cleome (Capparidaceae)

Spider flower
Subtropical and tropical areas worldwide

Members of this genus of some 150 species of annuals, perennials, and evergreen shrubs are found growing in free-draining sandy soils on plains and in mountainous valleys in their native habitats. The most commonly grown are *Cleome hassleriana* hybrids, which look gorgeous planted en masse. The common name is derived from the spidery flowers with long, waving stamens that are held on tall, strong, leafy stems.

Cleome hassleriana

syn. *C. hasslerana, C. spinosa*
Spider flower
Annual / Full sun

Upright plant from Argentina, southern Brazil, Paraguay, and Uruguay, with hairy stems growing to 1.5 m tall by 45 cm wide. Stems bear five- to seven-palmate, finely toothed, hairy, scented leaflets up to 12 cm long, with spines at the base of each leaf stalk and sometimes on the stems. Scented flowers with prominent stamens up to 7.5 cm long

Cleome hassleriana

are clustered in terminal heads up to 3 cm across, in shades of white, pink, and purple. Each flower head continues to grow over a period of several months, gradually getting longer. 'Cherry Queen' has bright rose flowers, 'Helen Campbell' has the purest white flowers, 'Pink Queen' has vivid pink flowers, and 'Violet Queen' has rich violet flowers. Prefers light, sandy, well-drained soil. For bushy plants, pinch out the main stem at 10 cm tall.

Cobaea (Polemoniaceae)

Tropical South America to Mexico

This genus encompasses some twenty species of evergreen and herbaceous climbers found growing in forests and thickets in their native habitats. *Cobaea scandens*, a wonderful plant for covering a trellis, fence, or wall in one season, is the only form generally available.

Cobaea scandens

Cobaea scandens

Cathedral bell, cup-and-saucer vine
Perennial used as annual / Full sun

Vigorous, upright, dense, evergreen (though usually deciduous in cool-temperate gardens), semi-woody climber usually grown as an annual, reaching 6–8 m tall or more. Midgreen, alternate-pinnate leaves each have a terminal branching tendril for climbing. Large bell-shaped flowers are borne singly from the upper leaf axils and start very pale greenish white, then turn a rosy purple, gradually darkening until they fall off after about four days. Distinctive flowers of *C. scandens* f. *alba* are creamy, greenish white and less commonly grown than the purple form, though equally attractive and vigorous. Plants look good scrambling through shrubs and trees. Usually grown as a fast-growing annual but will survive mild winters, creating even larger plants the following season. Prefers moderately fertile, moist, well-drained soil.

Cuphea (Lythraceae)

Southeastern United States, Mexico, and
subtropical to tropical Central and South America

Cuphea is a genus of some 250 species of annuals, evergreen perennials, and low-growing subshrubs found in pastures and woodland clearings in their native habitats. Grown in cultivation for their colourful tubular flowers borne en masse throughout the summer, they were widely used by Victorian gardeners, but many have been almost lost to cultivation in recent years. They look good planted in pots and containers as well as used as summer bedding in the exotic border. All prefer moderately fertile, well-drained soil.

Cuphea cyanea

Tender perennial / Sun or dappled shade

Soft-stemmed, branching subshrub growing to a height and spread of 30–46 cm with deep green ovate leaves 5–8 cm long. Masses of terminal racemes of yellow-tipped, orangish red flowers up to 3 cm long with two tiny violet-blue petals are carried all summer into late autumn.

Cuphea ignea

Cigar plant
Perennial used as annual / Sun or dappled shade

Delightful, freely branching, spreading, soft-stemmed subshrub (usually grown as an annual), growing to a height and spread of 30–60 cm with bright green, narrow, lance-shaped leaves up to 8 cm long. Bears tiny, deep red, tubular flowers with a whitish ash-coloured tip 3 cm long, from which it derives its common name. 'Variegata' is a vivid form with bold yellow blotches on the leaves.

Cuphea micropetala

Tender perennial / Sun or dappled shade

Magnificent upright, aristocratic plant growing to a height and spread of 76 cm with midgreen lanceolate leaves up to 15 cm long. From summer to late autumn, bears terminal leafy racemes of fat tubular creamy yellow flowers, orange at the base and frilly at the mouth, up to 4 cm long.

Cuphea ×purpurea

Firefly
Tender perennial / Sun or dappled shade

Short, bushy, occasionally lax subshrub with sticky, hairy stems, growing to a height and spread of

30–45 cm, with midgreen lanceolate leaves up to 7.5 cm long. From summer to late autumn produces attractive, narrow, tubular cerise pink to purplish red flowers flaring at the tips.

Dicliptera (Acanthaceae)

Tropical and warm-temperate regions worldwide

This genus comprises about 150 annual and perennial soft- and woody-stemmed shrubs. Only one species is generally available for cultivation: *Dicliptera suberecta*, which is very useful for containers and summer bedding.

Dicliptera suberecta

syn. *Justicia suberecta*

Hummingbird plant, king's crown, Uruguayan
   firecracker plant

Tender perennial / Sun or dappled shade

Perennial subshrub from Uruguay with slender stems growing to a height of 60 cm and a width of 45 cm. Leaves are midgreen to greyish green, up to 4 cm long or more, covered in fine, velvety grey hairs. All summer into autumn, bears auxiliary and terminal clusters of very showy orangey brick red, tubular, upright flowers up to 4 cm long that attract hummingbirds. Roots will survive some winters if heavily mulched; otherwise overwinter in a frost-free location and plant out in later spring. Old clumps divide easily.

Impatiens (Balsaminaceae)

Warm-temperate regions worldwide

This large genus contains some 850 species of upright annuals and evergreen perennials and subshrubs found growing in a diverse range of habitats, from moist woodlands to areas near streams and lakes. All have succulent, brittle stems with luxuriant fleshy foliage that gives a very exotic effect. Best known in cultivation are the popular bedding and houseplant *I. walleriana* (busy lizzie) and the popular New Guinea hybrids. Several others will also grow in cool summers. They prefer moist, well-drained, humus-rich soil.

Impatiens niamniamensis 'Congo Cockatoo'

Tender perennial / Dappled shade

Upright, succulent, continuously flowering evergreen perennial, growing to 76 cm tall and 38 cm across with spirally arranged, ovate to elliptic, dark green leaves up to 25 cm long. Flowers are tubular, curved, shaped like a parrot's beak, long-spurred, deep red with a yellow upper petal. Another *I. niamniamensis* cultivar, 'Variegata', has leaves with prominent, wide, creamy yellow edges surrounding various shades of green in the middle.

Impatiens sodenii

Tender perennial / Dappled shade

Upright, succulent, evergreen perennial growing to a height of 1–1.2 m with leaves formed in whorls around the stem. Finely toothed, elliptic to lance-shaped midgreen leaves up to 15 cm long have a prominent pale greenish yellow midrib. Flowers are long-stemmed, pale lavender to white, up to 5 cm across, from summer to autumn.

Impatiens tinctoria

Tender perennial / Dappled shade

Upright, vigorous, tuberous perennial growing to a height of 76 cm by 38 cm with spirally arranged, oblong to lance-shaped, toothed, midgreen leaves up to 23 cm long. From summer to autumn, bears exquisite racemes of long-stalked, spurred, orchid-like white flowers with throats marked magenta and scented, up to 6 cm across.

Ipomoea (Convolvulaceae)

Morning glory

North America, West Indies, South Africa, and Asia

Ipomoea is a genus of some five hundred species of annuals and perennials, often climbing, trailing, or scrambling, and a few trees and shrubs, found growing in diverse habitats in warm regions from scrub to woodland and cliffs to seashores. They are grown in cultivation for their handsome flowers, which are often produced in profusion over a long period. They prefer a sunny sheltered location in moder-ately fertile soil, where they will flower for months. Use them to cover walls, pergolas, and wigwams.

Ipomoea alba

Belle de nuit, moonflower

Perennial used as annual / Full sun

Perennial, twining climber grown as an annual to 5 m with rounded, ovate, occasionally three-lobed, long-stalked, midgreen leaves up to 20 cm long. Loose heads of up to eight wide, saucer-shaped, fragrant white flowers up to 15 cm across open at

Ipomoea batatas 'Blackie'

Ipomoea batatas 'Marguerite'

Ipomoea batatas 'Tricolor'

sweet potato is a vigorous grower in a warm summer, trailing as long as 60–90 cm, though only half that length in a cool summer. It looks fabulous trailing over walls and in containers and hanging baskets. Plant it in moist, humus-rich, free-draining soil in full sun for the best colour and overwinter at a minimum temperature of 7°C on the dry side.

'Blackie' has dramatic deep purple-black foliage and deeply cut, lobed leaves. 'Black Heart' is virtually black with heart-shaped leaves. 'Marguerite' has chartreuse, lime green foliage with heart-shaped leaves. 'Tricolor' (syn. 'Pink Frost') is a multicoloured cultivar with green, pink, and white foliage, not quite as vigorous as the preceding. Two more recently introduced compact forms are 'Sweet Caroline Light Green' and 'Sweet Caroline Purple'.

Ipomoea coccinea

syn. *Quamoclit coccinea*
Red morning glory, red star, small red morning
 glory / Star glory / Star morning glory
Annual / Full sun

Twining climber growing to 1–3 m tall or more, with alternate, heart-shaped, ovate, entire or coarsely toothed deep green leaves 7.5–10 cm long. Racemes of three to eight small, carmine red, tubular flowers, up to 2 cm across, with yellow throats, are borne in summer.

Ipomoea indica

syn. *I. learii*
Blue dawn flower, oceanblue morning glory
Tender perennial / Full sun

Vigorous climber growing to 9 m tall in a warm climate or conservatory. As a container plant or planted out for the summer months, more like 2.5–3.5 m, with evergreen, broadly heart-shaped or three-lobed, pointed midgreen leaves, 7.5–15 cm long. From late spring to early autumn bears a profusion of funnel-shaped, intense dark blue to purplish blue flowers up to 9 cm across, in bunches of three to five, fading during the day to purplish red.

dusk and stay open all night. A must for those warm tropical summer evenings in the garden!

Ipomoea batatas

Sweet potato
Perennial used as annual / Full sun

Use of the sweet potato for ornamental purposes rather than as a vegetable crop has become increasingly common in the southeastern United States in the past few years. 'Blackie' was the first ornamental sweet potato cultivar to make its way into the nursery trade, and several forms are now becoming increasingly available in the British Isles. The ornamental

Ipomoea lobata

syn. *Mina lobata*
Spanish flag
Perennial used as annual / Full sun

Climber to 2–3.5 m tall, with crimson-flushed stems and stalks. Bears toothed midgreen to deep green leaves to 10 cm long, with dense one-sided racemes of small tubular scarlet flowers that fade to yellow, then white, giving a very exotic effect all summer to autumn.

Ipomoea tricolor

Morning glory
Annual / Full sun

Fast-growing, twining climber to a height of 2–3.5 m with midgreen, ovate, heart-shaped, pointed leaves, up to 10 cm long. All summer to autumn bears showy, wide funnel-shaped, clear sky blue flowers with central white tube and yellow interior base, up to 8 cm across. Some of the many forms of this popular ornamental climber available include 'Black Knight', very dark purple flowers with a cerise throat and white at the base; 'Candy Pink', large pink flowers; 'Crimson Rambler', white-throated red flowers; 'Heavenly Blue', intense blue flowers with a prominent white throat; 'Minibar Rose', variegated foliage with green leaves irregularly splashed white and rosy crimson flowers with white throats.

Iresine (Amaranthaceae)

South America and Australia

*Ipomoea lobata,
flowers*

The approximately eighty species of annuals, upright perennials, and evergreen subshrubs in this genus are found growing in dry, open areas in their native habitats. The few species grown in cultivation are valued for their richly coloured leaves; the flowers are insignificant. The two described here are very eye-catching, especially when planted in groups in subtropical beds. They prefer to be over-wintered at a minimum of 10°c, slightly higher than many other tender perennials. They are quite happy being grown as windowsill plants for the winter. In spring, they grow readily from tip cuttings. They work well in pots and containers and can be kept bushy by occasionally pinching out the growing tips.

Iresine herbstii

Beefsteak plant, blood leaf
Perennial used as annual / Full sun

Upright, bushy, short-lived perennial growing to 1.5 m tall in its native habitat, though more like 46–60 cm in cool-summer gardens as an annual, with waxy, ovate to rounded, pointed, variegated leaves, varying in colour from green-yellow to very

Iresine herbstii

deep purple-red, with prominent veining, up to 8 cm long. 'Aureoreticulata' has midgreen leaves with striking, prominent yellow veins. 'Brilliantissima' has vivid magenta leaves and stems with lighter veining. 'Wallisii' has bronzy red-black leaves.

Iresine lindenii

Perennial used as annual / Full sun

Handsome, upright, bushy, compact plant growing to 60 cm tall with dusky-purple stems and narrow, very dark beetroot-purple, ovate, pointed leaves 10–18 cm long.

Iresine herbstii
'Brilliantissima'

Iresine lindenii

Nicotiana (Solanaceae)

Tobacco plant
Australia, North America, tropical South America, South Pacific, and western Africa

Nicotiana encompasses some sixty-seven species of erect annuals, biennials, perennials, and a few shrubby forms, found growing in mountain areas and valleys, often in moist soils, in their native habitats. The genus includes tobacco (*N. tabacum*), which contains the toxic alkaloid nicotine, which besides being addictive to people is used as an insecticide. Here, though, we are interested in those with interesting flowers and sometimes big leaves. The cultivated garden forms, much used by Victorian gardeners for mass bedding, include some delightful plants that can be used to soften harder plantings with their delicate flowers. They prefer well-drained, fertile, moist soil. Taller forms may need staking in exposed situations.

Nicotiana glauca

Half-hardy perennial often used as annual / Sun or light shade

Vigorous, semi-evergreen, many-branched shrub or small tree with long, arching, glaucous shoots, reaching 7.5 m tall in the wild, though more like 1.2–2.5 m tall as an annual in temperate gardens. Leaves are ovate, bluish grey, thickish, and rubbery, 10–25 cm long. Bears tubular rich yellow flowers up to 4 cm long in summer and autumn.

of large ovate-elliptic midgreen leaves, beautifully and architecturally arranged around a robust central stem. In summer bears terminal inflorescences of small greenish white to greenish red flowers. 'Variegata' has leaves heavily variegated with splashes of cream and white with pink flowers in summer.

Nicotiana sylvestris, flowers

Pseudogynoxys (Asteraceae)

Mexico

From this genus of about thirteen species of perennial climbers and shrubs, only one is generally available: *Pseudogynoxys chenopodioides*, formerly known as *Senecio confusa*. This very exotic-looking climber deserves to be grown more often.

Pseudogynoxys chenopodioides, flowers

Nicotiana langsdorffii

Annual / Sun or light shade

Upright, branched, sticky-leaved plant growing to 1.5 m tall by 38 cm with basal rosettes of ovate leaves up to 25 cm long. Bears drooping, slender-branching, tubular, pale lime green flower clusters up to 5 cm long, with spreading, five-lobed mouths.

Nicotiana sylvestris

Biennial or perennial used as annual / Sun or light shade

Handsome, fast-growing, sticky-leaved plant growing to 1.5 m tall by 60 cm with basal rosettes of dark green elliptic-ovate leaves up to 35 cm long. Terminal panicles of deliciously scented, sticky, tubular, skinny flowers with five-spreading lobes, up to 10 cm long, are borne from summer often to early autumn.

Nicotiana tabacum

Tobacco

Annual or biennial / Sun or light shade

Basal rosetted, fibrous-rooted plant occasionally grown in the ornamental garden for its large, coarse leaves. Grows 0.9–1.5 m tall, makes broad columns

Pseudogynoxys chenopodioides

syn. *Senecio confusa*

Mexican flame vine, orange-glow vine

Tender perennial / Full sun

Twining, sprawling climber growing to a height of 6 m or more, though more like 1–3 m in temperate gardens. Thick, lance-shaped, toothed midgreen leaves are up to 8 cm long. Bright orange blossoms borne in small clusters 2.5–5 cm across cover the vine in summer. Flowers change from orange to almost red as they age. Prefers well-drained, moderately fertile soil in a warm situation, so best planted against a south-facing wall or as a container plant trained up bamboo canes in a sunny corner. Minimum temperature 7°c, kept on the dryish side during the winter as it is prone to botrytis.

Rhodochiton (Scrophulariaceae)

Mexico

One species of perennial vine, found growing in wooded areas in its native habitat, is the sole member of this genus. In cultivation, it is grown for its exquisite tubular, pendent flowers. This very attractive climber deserves to be grown more often.

Rhodochiton atrosanguineus

Perennial used as annual / Full sun

Thin-stemmed climber, short-lived perennial generally used as a fast-growing annual, growing to

Right

Ricinus communis 'Carmencita', seed head

Far right

Ricinus communis 'New Zealand Purple'

a height of 1–3 m with heart-shaped, rich green leaves up to 8 cm long. Single, tubular, rich purplish black flowers with star-cup-shaped, rosy pink calyces are borne on long pendent stalks from summer to autumn. Prefers fertile, humus-rich, moist, well-drained soil.

Ricinus (Euphorbiaceae)

Eastern and northeastern Africa to the Middle East

The one species belonging to this genus is an erect, exceedingly fast-growing, often mound-forming, suckering, evergreen shrub found on wastelands, building sites, roadsides, and rough stony areas in its native habitat. It is grown in cultivation for its dramatic glossy green or maroon-purple foliage. This is a fantastic instant foliage plant for the exotic garden, quickly filling gaps between other plants and looking especially good when planted as a thicket. The plant contains the toxin ricin, used in 1978 to assassinate Georgi Markov, a Bulgarian journalist who spoke out against the Bulgarian government. While waiting at a bus stop near Waterloo Station in London, he was stabbed in the leg with the point of an umbrella, embedding a perforated metallic pellet that contained the toxin. It was also found in powder form in the U.S. mail just after 9/11. So don't eat the plant!

Ricinus communis

Castor-bean plant, castor-oil plant

Perennial used as annual / Sun or dappled shade

Upright, branching shrub that grows to a stagger-ing height of up to 12 m in its native habitat, though in cool-temperate gardens it reaches a height of 1.8 m or more as an annual. Some will grow up to 3 m by September from a sowing in April. The leaves are alternate and broadly ovate, five to ten lobed and toothed, glossy midgreen, 15–46 cm across.

'Carmencita' is tall and well branched, growing 2–3 m tall, with brownish dark bronze-red foliage and bright red female flower buds and seed heads.

'Carmencita Pink' grows to 1.5 m tall with eye-catching red stems, dark greenish purple foliage, and from summer to autumn, flowers that are fol-lowed by conspicuous, highly ornamental, deep pink seedpods.

'Crimson Spire' is a tall variety growing up to 3.6 m with red stems, coppery foliage, and reddish brown flowers, getting even bigger than 'Zanziba-rensis', with more colour!

'Gibsonii' is a compact form growing to a height of 1.2–1.8 m with metallic dark red foliage.

'Impala' is a compact plant that grows to around 1.2–1.8 m with carmine red young shoots and leaves, followed by handsome leaves of a rich bronze-green colour carried on dark red stems. From summer to autumn, produces clusters of creamy yellow flow-ers that are followed by spikes of brilliant scarlet-coloured pods.

'New Zealand Purple' is a recent introduction growing to around 1.8 m with metallic rich coppery bronze-purple foliage stems and leaves.

'Red Spire' grows to a height of 1.8–3 m with red stems and bronze-flushed leaves.

'Zanzibarensis' grows to a height of 1.8–3 m with white-veined, midgreen leaves, up to 60 cm across. Chiltern Seeds in Cumbria, England, sells a form, with some plain green-stemmed and some with a hint of pink similar to a giant form of 'Carmencita Pink' but without the flowers.

'Zanzi Palm' is another form from Chiltern Seeds that is fast growing, to a staggering 3.6 m. A very architectural palmlike plant, with large green leaves, good for the back of the border.

Salvia (Lamiaceae)

Sage

Tropical to temperate areas worldwide

Members of this large genus of some nine hundred species of annuals, biennials, herbaceous perenni-als, and soft-wood evergreen shrubs are invariably found in sunny situations in such diverse habitats as light woodland, moist grasslands, and rocky slopes to scrub. They are quite often aromatic and hairy. Probably the best known are the summer bedding plant *S. splendens* or salvia, the bright red annual used en masse in parks and gardens, and also the common culinary herb sage. Many species and cultivars that have become more popular in recent years fit in well with the exotic/Mediterranean-style garden. All prefer full sun and moderately fertile, well-drained soil. Most have to be treated as tender perennials, surviving mild winters or re-emerging from the ground if cut down by frost, especially if well mulched. In warm gardens some may remain semi-evergreen. All will take lows of down to about 0°C unless otherwise marked. The hardier forms respond well to mulching.

Salvia coccinea

Tender perennial / Full sun

Upright, bushy perennial, often grown as an annual, 60–75 cm tall, with heart-shaped, toothed, hairy, dark green leaves up to 6 cm long. Small flowers, only 2 cm long, are soft red, borne on slender open ter-minal spikes. 'Coral Nymph' has exquisite, delicate coral pink flowers. 'Lady in Red' has intense scarlet red flowers. 'Snow Nymph' has white flowers.

Salvia confertiflora

Tender perennial / Full sun

Upright, woody-based perennial growing 1.2–1.5 m by 60 cm with ovate, scalloped, yellowy green leaves, up to 20 cm long, covered with reddish brown hairs, especially on the underside, and an unpleasant scent if crushed. Unbranched stems have thin terminal spikes up to 30 cm long carrying orangey brownish red flowers, 1 cm long, from late summer to midautumn.

Salvia discolor

Tender perennial / Full sun

Upright plant with branched, white-woolly, square stems up to 50 cm tall and wide with oblong to ovate midgreen leaves up to 6 cm long, densely white and woolly on the underside, less so above. Handsome long terminal racemes carry deepest indigo-black flowers up to 2.5 cm long with green calyces and silvery bracts. Leaves and stems are very sticky and scented.

Salvia 'Indigo Spires'

Tender perennial / Full sun

Cross between *S. farinacea* and *S. longispicata*. Upright perennial with a somewhat sprawling habit, growing to 1.5 m tall, with green coarsely toothed leaves to 7.5 cm long. From summer to midautumn, distinctive elongate inflorescences up to 30 cm long, with whorls of blue-violet flowers and purplish calyces, 1.3 cm long, are borne. Will regrow from the roots if cut down by frost.

Salvia involucrata

Tender perennial / Full sun

Shrubby, somewhat woody-based perennial, with sparsely branched stems up to 1.5 m long, with ovate, tapering, purplish green leaves to 12 cm long. Bears dense terminal racemes of exquisite rosy magenta flowers, up to 5 cm long, from late summer to midautumn. 'Bethellii' has slightly bigger, velvety leaves, with showy, bright sugary pink, furry flowers. Will regrow from the roots if cut down by frost.

Salvia leucantha

Tender perennial / Full sun

Spreading evergreen subshrub with very white woolly stems, especially when young, growing to 60–100 cm tall, with handsome, narrow, lance-shaped, midgreen leaves up to 15 cm long, thickly felted on the underneath. Terminal racemes of white or purple flowers up to 2 cm long, extending from bell-shaped, velvety, purplish lavender-blue calyces, appear late summer to autumn. 'Midnight' is a stunning form with dark velvety purple flowers and calyces.

Salvia leucantha, flower spike

Senecio (Asteraceae)

Worldwide

This is a huge, diverse genus of some 1250 species of annuals, biennials, perennials, lianas, and shrubs, some of them succulent, found growing in varied locations, from mountainous areas to the sea, and in dry-arid to moist habitats. Included are many exciting plants that look spectacular in the exotic garden; those mentioned here are only a small selection. All of these plants are very different in habit and form.

Senecio cineraria

syn. *Cineraria maritima*
Perennial used as annual / Full sun

Mound-forming evergreen subshrub usually grown as an annual though perennial in mild winters, growing up to 60 cm tall and wide, with ovate to lance-shaped, deeply dissected and lobed, soft-felted silvery white leaves up to 15 cm long. Mustard-yellow flowers are produced in subsequent summers, though these can be removed. Dwarf cultivars grow to a height and spread of about 30 cm and include 'Alice', with deeply dissected, felted silvery white foliage; 'Cirrus', with elliptic, finely lobed, silvery greyish green leaves; 'Silver Dust', with very deeply dissected, velvety, light grey to almost white leaves; and 'White Diamond', a compact form with deeply cut greyish, almost white, leaves. All prefer well-drained, fairly poor soil.

Senecio grandifolius

syn. *Telanthophora grandifolia*
Tender perennial / Full sun

Evergreen, upright shrub with thick, sparsely branched, purple velvet stems, 2–3 m tall, with enormous, shiny, lobed midgreen to deep green leaves up to 46 cm long, velvety orangish brown beneath. Large, domed, dense flower heads of small bright yellow daisylike flowers, 1 cm across, are borne mostly in winter. Best grown as a container or conservatory plant, brought out for the summer months. Prefers fertile, well-drained soil and a minimum temperature of 5°C.

Senecio macroglossus

Cape ivy, Natal ivy
Tender perennial / Full sun

Evergreen, twining climber with semi-succulent growth, becoming woody with age, to 3 m tall or more in its native habitat, though more like 1–1.5 m as a container-grown plant. 'Variegatus' is the preferred form, with thick, succulent, triangular, dark green with variable creamy yellow leaves, up to 7.5 cm long, edged with pale veins. Flowers are white to pale creamy yellow, daisylike, and up to 5 cm across. Prefers moderately fertile soil. Best grown as a container plant brought out for the summer months. Minimum winter temp 5°C.

Thunbergia (Acanthaceae)

Tropical and southern Africa, Madagascar, and subtropical to tropical parts of Asia

This is a genus of about one hundred species of annuals, evergreen perennials, climbers, and a few shrubs, found growing in woodland or rocky areas, climbing through trees and shrubs in their native habitats. They are grown in cultivation for their often very showy flowers. Best known and most commonly used is *Thunbergia alata*. Some of the other species are highly attractive but unfortunately cannot be grown outside in cool-temperate gardens. Nevertheless, they are worth trying in a conservatory that doesn't drop below 15°C in winter. In this category are *T. grandiflora*, with ridiculously attractive lavender to violet-blue flowers, and the even more ridiculously beautiful *Thunbergia mysorensis*, with hooded, two-lipped bright yellow flowers borne on pendent racemes up to 60 cm long.

Thunbergia alata

Black-eyed Susan
Perennial used as annual / Full sun

Evergreen, fast-growing, perennial, thin-stemmed, twining climber grown as an annual to 1.5–2 m in temperate climates. Triangular, pointed, toothed midgreen leaves are up to 8 cm long. From summer to autumn, bears numerous auxiliary, solitary, long

*Thunbergia
mysorensis,*
flowers

Thunbergia alata

tubed, five-lobed flowers, normally bright orange
or yellow, occasionally white, either with or without
a dark blackish brown centre, up to 4 cm across.
Suzie hybrids have orange-yellow or white flowers with dark centres. Prefers moisture retentive,
humus-rich, well-drained soil in a sheltered position. Looks good in containers climbing a wigwam
of bamboo canes.

*Tithonia
rotundifolia
'Torch', flower*

Tithonia (Asteraceae)

Mexico and Central America

Tithonia encompasses ten species of upright, stout-stemmed, multibranched, occasionally woody-based, sometimes hairy annuals, perennials, and shrubs, found in thickets and wastelands and on roadsides. *Tithonia rotundifolia* is the most commonly grown for its glorious bright orange daisylike flowers, which give spots of intense orange colour in late summer into autumn, making the plant a handsome addition to the late-season border. All prefer moderately fertile, well-drained soil.

Tithonia rotundifolia

Mexican sunflower
Annual / Sun to light shade

Vigorous, branching plant growing to 1.8 m tall with coarse, three-lobed or entire, hairy midgreen leaves 10–30 cm long. Bright orange to orangish red daisylike or zinnia-like flowers up to 7.5 cm across with yellowy orange tufted centres are borne on long, hollow, tapering flower stalks up to 18 cm long from late summer through autumn to first frost. 'Aztec Sun' grows up to 1.2 m tall with bright golden yellow flowers. 'Fiesta del Sol' is a dwarf form, about 90 cm tall, with brilliant orange flowers. The bushy 'Goldfinger' reaches 0.9 m tall with rich deep orange flowers. 'Torch' grows 0.9–1.5 m tall and has reddish orange flowers.

Tweedia (Asclepiadaceae)

syn. *Oxypetalum*
Southern Brazil and Uruguay

Belonging to this genus is only one species of evergreen twining or scrambling shrub found growing in scrub and rocky locations in its native habitats.

Tweedia caerulea

Perennial used as annual / Full sun

Attractive, erect shrub with whitish hairy stems 30–60 cm tall or more, with oblong to lance-shaped, velvety, light greyish green leaves, 5 cm long or more. The five-petalled powder blue flowers, up to 2.5 cm across, are borne in bunches of three to four from summer to early autumn. Although a perennial, it can be grown as an annual in cool-temperate gardens, flowering well in the first year; otherwise overwinter at a minimum of 5°c. Save the seeds in autumn. Can be grown as a border plant but works better as a container plant, where the delicate flowers can be more easily admired.

Zea mays
var. *japonica*
'Quadricolor'

Zea (Poaceae)

Central America

Only four annual grasses indigenous to rough, disturbed ground and field edges belong to this genus. One of these is the well-known edible *Z. mays*. There are some exquisite coloured forms that work well bedded out during the summer months in the exotic garden. They prefer a warm location in fertile, moist, well-drained soil.

Zea mays

Maize, sweet corn
Annual / Full sun

Edible corn with colourful cultivars available for ornamental purposes. 'Harlequin' grows to a height of 1.2 m with striped green, red, and white foliage and cobs with deep red grains. 'Variegata' has green leaves boldly striped with creamy white.

Zea mays var. *japonica*

Japonica striped maize corn, striped-leaf Japanese maize
Annual / Full sun

Extremely beautiful ornamental corn from Japan, reaching 1.5–2 m tall with variegated leaves striped with green, white, yellow, and pink. Corn tassels are dark purple and kernels are rich burgundy. 'Quadricolor' is similar.

Ferns

There are at least twelve thousand species of ferns, many of which can be found in tropical and subtropical regions of the world on virtually every continent. Unlike those fern relatives the cryptogams, which are a relic group of nonflowering seedless vascular plants that have roots and stems and reproduce by spores, the ferns are highly successful and found in virtually every habitat where flowering plants grow, from sea level to high mountains. Ferns are an extremely ancient group of plants, with early fern fossils predating the beginning of the Mesozoic era some 360 million years ago. Ferns are older than land animals and far older than the dinosaurs, having thrived on Earth for 200 million years before the flowering plants appeared.

Most ferns are luxuriant and predominantly green. The majority are indigenous to tropical, subtropical, and temperate rain forests, with some surviving on salt-sprayed cliffs or in seasonally dry areas. Most prefer shade from a canopy of larger trees or grow in shady, moist habitats by rivers, streams, humid gullies, ravines, and waterfalls—in fact, anywhere that stays permanently moist. Ferns differ from flowering plants in that they are relatively delicate and grow only in suitably moist conditions. Hence, creating conditions that suit them is very important. If you live in a dry area, you can create a microclimate with irrigation systems and misting. Adding leaf mould and other forms of organic matter to your soil will make it more lush and verdant as well as holding in moisture. Some ferns will even grow in cracks and crevices in rocky areas if you add organic matter and moisture.

Ferns are a very diverse group, ranging from climbers, aquatic forms, and palm-like tree ferns to the extraordinary filmy ferns with leaves just one cell thick. There are also many epiphytic ferns, as well as more traditional herbaceous forms. In ferns of all varieties, the stems are called rhizomes and grow below, at, or slightly above ground level. The leaves of ferns are called fronds, growing up from the rhizome each year in spring.

Fern collections became extremely popular in the Victorian period, to the point of being a craze. Passionate enthusiasts kept them in garden ferneries and specially designed glasshouses, also known as ferneries. Many of the stately homes had ferneries, but truly the fad went through all of society, with many people having at least a small collection. A vast number of ferns were collected by families on Sunday outings, as well as by avid collectors who went into the wilds and discovered many new

Left

Asplenium scolopendrium

cultivars. Today ferns are coming back into fashion, from those that are indigenous to those that hail from around the world, including the currently popular tree ferns from the Southern Hemisphere.

Unlike in the Victorian era, it is now illegal to take ferns from the wild, though luckily for us, most garden centres have at least a small collection for sale, with several nurseries specialising in this verdant group. Many of the original Victorian ferneries have been reconstructed in recent years, and fern collections are now more common in larger gardens. Ferns are also fabulous plants for the exotic garden, adding extra lushness to shady corners where few other plants will grow.

A more in-depth look at this alluring group of plants can be found in *The Plantfinder's Guide to Garden Ferns* (2003) by Martin Rickard and *Fern Grower's Manual* (2001) by Barbara Joe Hoshizaki and Robbin C. Moran.

Adiantum (Adiantaceae)

Maidenhair fern

North and South America, with a few from
  temperate parts of Europe, Asia, and Australia

This large genus includes some two hundred species of terrestrial evergreen to semi-evergreen and deciduous ferns, many from tropical and subtropical areas, especially in North and South America. They can be found growing on woodland margins, in shady crevices and cracks on rock faces, and by streams and watercourses; some prefer deep shade and all require moist conditions. They are some of the most beautiful ferns, with their lush and delicate appearance. Unfortunately, only a few are hardy or half-hardy, but if a niche microclimate can be found for them in the garden, they are highly rewarding to grow. They prefer humus-rich, moist soil, preferably in a humid location.

Adiantum aleuticum

Aleutian maidenhair fern, northern maidenhair fern
Hardy / Dappled shade

*Adiantum
capillus-veneris*

Deciduous or semi-evergreen fern from coastal northwestern America and Japan, with short creeping rhizomes, growing to a height and spread of 30–60 cm, with deeply dissected triangular pale to midgreen blades 20–30 cm long, giving a delightful lacy appearance. Thin circular stalks and midribs are black. New growth is often tinged pinkish bronze. Give it a secluded, moist corner out of the wind. 'Japonicum' (Japanese maidenhair) is slightly

smaller, with rosy-pink new fronds, maturing to green. 'Miss Sharples' has a height and spread of 45 cm and is a very pretty fern with a stout, creeping rootstock, bearing dainty, divided fingerlike midgreen fronds, emerging pale green in spring and deepening in colour with age; stalks glossy dark brown to black. Lime tolerant.

Adiantum capillus-veneris

Southern maidenhair fern, true maidenhair fern
Frost-hardy / Dappled shade

The only British native maidenhair, usually as a maritime species found mostly along the south coast and inland on sheltered walls. Mine is growing on a vertical waterfall over flints, where it seems happy through most winters even when wet. Evergreen, though deciduous at temperatures much below −2°c, with short creeping rhizomes and fronds to a height of 30–38 cm, more in warm situations. Triangular, bipinnate light green fronds up to 70 cm long with fan-shaped pinnae are produced on wiry,

glossy black stalks. Distinguished from other bi- or tripinnate maidenhairs by the linear or oblong, rather than round, spore-bearing area under the distal edges of the pinnae. There are several cultivated forms. Hardy to −5°c and lower if mulched.

Adiantum pedatum

American maidenhair fern, eastern maidenhair fern,
   five-fingered maidenhair
Hardy / Dappled shade

Deciduous (evergreen in warmer climates) fern from eastern North America and eastern Asia, with strong creeping rhizomes, growing to a height and spread of 30–45 cm. Bears bright green, broadly ovate, pinnate fronds up to 35 cm long, with leaflets up to 30 cm across with oblong or triangular pinnules. Stalks thin and wiry, glossy dark brown to black. A graceful and delicate fern that forms small colonies with age. To the gardener virtually indistinguishable from *A. aleuticum*.

Adiantum venustum

Evergreen maidenhair, Himalayan maidenhair
Hardy / Dappled shade

Deciduous (evergreen in mild winters) fern from the Himalaya and China, with creeping rhizomes, growing to a height and spread of 22–38 cm. Fronds narrowly triangular, tripinnate, 15–30 cm long, with narrowly fan-shaped dull-green segments on black stalks. Juvenile fronds emerge vivid pinkish bronze from late winter to early spring. Prefers a position that is not too damp.

Asplenium (Aspleniaceae)

Spleenwort
All continents except Antarctica

Asplenium is a large genus of more than six hundred species of evergreen or semi-evergreen terrestrial and

Asplenium nidus

Asplenium scolopendrium

epiphytic ferns found in a diverse range of habitats. They prefer humus-rich, moist but well-drained soil in dappled shade. They often have leathery fronds, usually from a single crown, forming a somewhat fountainlike structure arising from rhizomes covered with masses of roots, hairs, and scales. Like all members of the family Aspleniaceae, spleenworts have their sori (clusters of spores) and indusia (flaps that serve to protect the sori) along the veins on the underside of the fronds.

Asplenium nidus

Bird's-nest fern
Tender / Dappled shade

Fairly slow-growing, evergreen epiphytic fern with very glossy, brightest green, oval to lance-shaped, entire fronds, often with undulating margins, up to 1.5 m long, forming an open shuttlecock shape up to 1 m wide. Can be placed outside during the summer months, either in a container or planted out, in a shady moist corner or tied to the side of a tree fern. Must be kept moist at all times for best growth. Slugs love it! Overwinter at a minimum of 5°C.

Asplenium scolopendrium

Hart's-tongue fern
Hardy / Shade

Robust evergreen terrestrial native of Europe, North America, and western Asia, with short creeping rhizomes, growing to a height of 45–70 cm by 60 cm. Irregular shuttlecock-like crown is composed of entire, straplike, leathery, glossy, bright green fronds up to 60 cm long, heart-shaped at the base, often with wavy margins on short stems. There are various cultivars. 'Angustifolium' has fronds much narrower than the species. 'Crispum' has midgreen fronds with strongly wavy margins and is usually sterile. 'Crispum Bolton's Nobile' has broad fronds up to 45 cm long. 'Crispum Speciosum' has sharply tapering fronds, occasionally with yellowish stripes. 'Cristatum' has much more divided fronds, each ending in a spreading crest. 'Furcatum' has lance-shaped fronds with a variable degree of undulation to the margins, with tips much divided and subdivided. 'Muricatum' has fronds distinctly wrinkled, puckered, and pleated. They prefer humus-rich, moist, well-drained alkali to neutral soils but will take slightly acidic soils. Most will take dry conditions for short periods only.

Athyrium (Dryopteridaceae)

Lady fern

Temperate to tropical regions worldwide

Members of this large genus of about 180 species of widely variable, deciduous, terrestrial ferns have short creeping rhizomes and soft textured fronds that are often brittle. All of the following prefer fertile, humus-rich, well-drained, neutral to acidic soils, preferably moist, although some take dryish conditions in their stride.

Athyrium filix-femina

Lady fern

Hardy / Sun or dappled shade

Graceful, variable, deciduous (in cold regions), clumping fern with erect rhizomes, found mostly in the Northern Hemisphere, including the British Isles. Fronds grow to 1.2 m tall by 60–90 cm wide or more, usually lance-shaped, two- to three-pinnate, spreading, arching, light green, occasionally with reddish brown stalks borne like upright shuttlecocks and arching outward with age. Pinnae are variable in size but usually elliptical with long, pointed tips.

Prefers dappled shade but will take full sun if given plenty of water in hot weather. More luxuriant on acidic soil but tolerates alkaline conditions.

The more than three hundred cultivars include many very gardenworthy plants, with some rather fancy forms like 'Frizelliae' (Mrs. Frizell's lady fern, tatting fern), growing to a height of 20 cm by 30 cm, with fronds 10–20 cm long and pinnae reduced to small circular lobes along each side of the midrib resembling tatting (homemade lace). 'Frizelliae Cristatum' has longer fronds crested at the tips. Both tolerate dry conditions well. 'Victoriae' grows to about 90 cm tall and is very rare; plants sold under this name are usually in fact members of the Cruciatum Group.

Athyrium niponicum

Hardy / Dappled to full shade

Deciduous fern from eastern Asia, growing to 30–35 cm tall by 50–60 cm wide, with short creeping reddish brown rhizomes. Fronds pinnate to pinnatifid, lance-shaped, arching, silvery grey-green or midgreen, up to 35 cm long with red-purple midribs and yellowish stems. Variety *pictum* (Japanese painted fern) is truly stunning, one of the showiest ferns for the exotic garden, electrifying shady areas with its fronds 30–38 cm long in a soft shade of metallic silver-grey with hints of red and blue. Variety *pictum* 'Ursula's Red'

Athyrium filix-femina

has superb red-pink and silver fronds developing a blackish red central stripe as they mature. 'Pictum Crested' (painted lady fern) has purplish red midribs suffusing into silvery grey with bluish green lamina and crested pinnae—another excellent form.

Athyrium otophorum

Eared lady fern

Hardy / Dappled to full shade

Attractive fern hailing from China and Japan, growing to a height of 30–46 cm with bipinnate, triangular, lance-shaped, pewter-green fronds with dark reddish stems and veining. New foliage unfurls reddish, contrasting well with older foliage. Retains its fronds well into autumn. Excellent as a specimen plant.

Blechnum (Blechnaceae)

Hard fern

Australasia, southeastern Asia, and Mexico to
southern South America

This genus comprises some two hundred species of usually evergreen, rhizomatous, terrestrial and epiphytic ferns with erect or running fleshy stems covered in glossy brown scales. Most blechnums, except the special crested forms, have simple fronds that are divided only once. In most species, the pinnae are fairly wide with little space in between, giving the fronds the appearance of large, coarse, textured leaves. There are many forms worth trying. They prefer woodland conditions or shady herbaceous borders in acidic, or at least neutral, moisture-retentive, humus-rich soil.

Left

Athyrium niponicum var. *pictum*

Blechnum chilense

Cyrtomium falcatum, fronds

Blechnum chilense

Hardy / Dappled to full shade

Exotic-looking evergreen fern hailing from Chile and Argentina, with creeping rhizomes, clump-forming with outlying clumps, sometimes becoming erect and trunklike with age; growing to a height of 90–150 cm, though much less in dry climates, with an indefinite spread. Ovate, lance-shaped, dark green, pinnate foliage is up to 1 m long by 22 cm across, with long brown scaly stalks. Sterile fronds have oblong toothed pinnae, while fertile ones have linear lance-shaped pinnae.

Blechnum discolor

Crown fern, New Zealand water fern
Frost-hardy / Dappled to full shade

Very attractive evergreen fern from New Zealand, with erect rhizomatous trunk, growing to a height of 30–50 cm, producing shuttlecock-like crowns of narrowly lance-shaped, pinnate, shiny, dark green fronds, up to 90 cm long by 5–15 cm wide, tapering at both ends in branching clusters. Juvenile fronds are covered in light brown hairs. Sterile fronds have oblong pinnae, whitish green underneath.

Blechnum spicant

Deer fern, hardy fern, ladder fern
Hardy / Dappled to full shade

Very attractive, fairly low-growing, evergreen fern native to Europe, northern Asia, and North America, with short creeping rhizomes. Reaches 30–45 cm tall and 60 cm wide. Produces tufts of narrowly lance-shaped, pinnate, leathery, glossy green, sterile fronds. Fertile fronds are taller. 'Cristatum' is a more compact form with crested frond tips, reaching only 10–20 cm tall. Prefers neutral to acid soil.

Cyrtomium (Dryopteridaceae)

Central and eastern Asia, South Africa, Central and South America, Hawaii

Members of this genus of some fifteen to twenty species of fast-growing evergreen or deciduous ferns are found growing in moist, rocky areas of woodland in their native habitat. Most species have distinctive fronds, providing a strong contrast to the lacier ferns. They prefer moderately fertile, humus-rich, sandy, moist, well-drained soil in dappled to full shade. They tolerate drier air than most ferns.

Cyrtomium falcatum

Japanese holly fern
Frost-hardy / Dappled to full shade

Evergreen (often deciduous in cold climates) fern from Japan and eastern Asia, growing up to 60 cm by 1.1 m. Foliage arching, with glossy, rich dark green pinnate fronds, 20–60 cm long, with short-stalked, oval to pointed, leathery leaflets, covered with reddish brown scales when juvenile, the whole creating a very attractive hollylike appearance. 'Butterfieldii' has coarsely serrated margins. 'Cristatum' (syn. 'Mayi') has heavily crested frond tips. 'Rochfordianum' is an attractive form with deeply cut leaflet margins. Often sold as houseplants. In cold winters, mulch with straw or something similar. Hardy to about −5°c for short periods.

Cyrtomium fortunei

Hardy / Dappled to full shade

Striking evergreen fern from eastern China, Japan, and Korea, growing to a height of 60 cm by 40 cm with upright, dull, pale green to grey-green, broadly sword-shaped fronds 30–60 cm long, with fairly narrow pointed leaflets up to 5 cm long with serrated edges. Variety *clivicola* has more spreading fronds with lobed leaflets.

Cyrtomium macrophyllum

Large-leaved holly fern
Hardy / Dappled to full shade

Very attractive evergreen fern from eastern Asia and Japan, growing to 45 cm tall by 60 cm wide, with spreading, broad fronds 20–50 cm long, with ovate to oblong leaflets 10–20 cm long, forming a very luxuriant plant.

Dryopteris (Dryopteridaceae)

Buckler fern, shield fern, wood fern
Worldwide, though mainly temperate regions of the Northern Hemisphere

Dryopteris is a genus of some two hundred species of terrestrial ferns (and numerous hybrids); this genus contains the largest number of ornamental ferns for the garden, and most are easy to grow. In their native habitats, they grow in woodlands, by lakes and streams, and in rocky mountainous areas. Many associate well with other herbaceous plants. Although mostly deciduous, many retain their foliage during the winter months in mild areas; this foliage should be removed in spring to make way for the attractive new growth. All of the following prefer moist humus-rich soil in a sheltered location in dappled shade. *Dryopteris affinis* and its cultivars tolerate sun and wind more than the other species.

Dryopteris affinis

Dryopteris affinis

Golden male fern
Hardy / Sun or dappled shade

Handsome evergreen (though deciduous in cold winters), very upright fern growing to 90 cm high by 70–90 cm wide, producing a shuttlecock of lance-shaped, bipinnate fronds from an erect rhizome, arising pale green as they unfurl in spring, contrasting well with the light brown scaly midribs, maturing to dark green. 'Crispa Gracilis', with a height and spread of 30 cm, is a dwarf evergreen form with congested leaflets twisted at the tips. 'Cristata Angustata', 45–60 cm tall and wide, is a handsome fern with long, narrow, arching, crested fronds, 5 cm wide. 'Cristata' (syn. 'Cristata the King'), 60–90 cm tall and wide, is a magnificent fern with arching fronds with crested tips and pinnae.

Dryopteris erythrosora

Autumn fern
Hardy / Dappled shade

Hailing from China and Japan, this bold and beautiful, usually deciduous fern with a slowly creeping rhizome grows to 60 cm tall by 40 cm wide. Juvenile papery fronds display a coppery red colouration, maturing to deep green and deeply cut. Variety *prolifica* has fronds narrower than the species, giving a lighter, finer appearance. Bulbils are sometimes produced on the fronds. Tolerant of dry conditions.

Dryopteris filix-mas

Male fern

Hardy / Dappled shade

Deciduous fern (evergreen in mild winters) forming a large clump of lance-shaped, pinnate-pinnatifid, midgreen fronds, 1–1.2 m tall by 1 m wide, with green midribs. Fronds arise from a crown of large rhizomes, often developing many crowns over the years. Along with bracken, this is the commonest British fern, found in most wooded areas of the country. 'Barnesii', with a height and spread of 1.2 m, is an attractive form with narrow fronds and pinnae with serrated edges. 'Crispa', 30–38 cm tall and wide, is a fine dwarf form with compact fronds and crisped pinnae. 'Grandiceps Wills', with a height and spread of 90 cm, is an outstanding fern with neatly crested pinnae and large terminal crests producing many crowns. 'Revolvens', 60–90 cm tall and wide, has broad fronds gracefully swept backward and slightly twisted, giving a very elegant appearance.

Dryopteris wallichiana

Wallich's wood fern

Hardy / Dappled shade

Very attractive deciduous fern with erect rhizomes and lance-shaped, pinnate-pinnatifid, dark green

fronds in a loose shuttlecock shape, to 90 cm high and 0.75 m across or more. The frond midribs are covered with usually dark brown or black scales, providing a magnificent contrast with the new yellowish green fronds in spring.

Matteuccia (Dryopteridaceae)

Ostrich-feather fern, ostrich fern

Europe, eastern Asia, and North America

Just three species of hardy terrestrial ferns, usually found in deciduous woodlands in their native habitats, belong to this genus. They are very exotic-looking ferns that grow well in permanently moist, lime-free to neutral areas of the garden. The genus is named in honour of Carlo Matteucci (1800–1868), an Italian physicist.

Matteuccia orientalis

Hardy / Dappled to full shade

Deciduous, rhizomatous fern from Asia, growing to a height of 60–90 cm, with distinctive midgreen, spreading, broadly pinnate to pinnatifid, arching fronds. Fertile fronds 15–22 cm long are initially green and soon turn brown. Chunkier than *M. struthiopteris*, it is an attractive fern that deserves to be grown more widely. Prefers moist soils but takes dry conditions as well.

*Matteuccia
struthiopteris*

Matteuccia struthiopteris

Ostrich fern, shuttlecock fern
Hardy / Dappled to full shade

Deciduous, rhizomatous fern eventually forming a small trunk with age. Erect, broadly lance-shaped, pinnate, pale green sterile fronds, up to 1.2 m long, are borne in swirls reminiscent of a shuttlecock. Fertile fronds, narrowly lance-shaped and dark brown, to 30 cm long or more with linear pinnae, appear in late summer. Spreads slowly by horizontal rhizomes or stolons, producing separate "shuttlecocks," forming attractive colonies with time.

Osmunda (Osmundaceae)

All continents except Australia

This genus comprises about ten species of perennial, deciduous, clump-forming, deep-rooted, terrestrial ferns found in moist to wet locations in woodlands and waterside areas. They need plenty of moisture for best results and are rugged, adaptable, and long-lived, whether grown in sun or shade. They can be used effectively in the landscape planted singly or en masse, giving a lush appearance to a moist border or pond margin.

Osmunda regalis

Flowering fern, royal fern
Hardy / Sun or shade

Stately deciduous fern, producing clumps of dense, massive, branched rhizomes, becoming erect with age, with foliage up to 2 m by 4 m. Broadly ovate to oblong, fresh green fronds up to 1 m tall are formed from bronzy brown crosiers in spring. With autumn's first frost, foliage turns into an explosion of rich golden colour for a week or so. 'Cristata' has pinnae with crested tips. 'Purpurascens' bears eye-catching coppery fronds in spring, turning green in early summer. Both forms grow to a height and spread of up to 1.2 m.

Osmunda regalis

Platycerium (Polypodiaceae)

Staghorn fern
Africa, Asia, and Australia, with a few in South America

Belonging to this genus are about eighteen species of evergreen epiphytic ferns with short creeping rhizomes that normally clasp tree trunks and branches in their native habitats in temperate and tropical rainforests. They are grown for their amazing, often antlerlike foliage, bearing both sterile and fertile fronds. Although not hardy, they are spectacular ferns that are often grown on blocks of wood or cork that can be hung in a moist shady corner. They can also be temporarily attached to the side of a tree fern for the summer months, then brought in when frost threatens and stored at about 5°C, keeping on the dry side. During the summer months they should be kept moist at all times for best growth, preferring full to dappled shade. They make wonderful conservatory

*Platycerium
bifurcatum*

plants, often attaining great size with age. They are usually found in the houseplant section of garden centres or specialist nurseries.

Platycerium alcicorne

Antelope ears, elkhorn fern, staghorn fern
Tender / Dappled to full shade

Evergreen epiphytic fern hailing from eastern Africa, Madagascar, Seychelles, and Mauritius, reaching a height and spread of 80 cm with rounded, entire or slightly lobed, sterile fronds up to 38 cm long that lie flat and are midgreen to deep green, then papery brown when mature. Leathery, grey-green, fertile fronds, 60 cm long, are normally erect, dividing several times. An excellent conservatory plant for a dank shaded corner or even a bathroom!

Platycerium bifurcatum

Common staghorn fern, elkhorn fern
Tender / Dappled to full shade

From Java to eastern Australia, somewhat variable evergreen epiphytic fern with erect or horizontal, rounded, entire, wavy, sterile fronds up to 45 cm long or more, midgreen to deep green, then papery brown. Greyish green fertile fronds are 25–80 cm long or more, protruding from the root ball. Each frond divides into two segments a number of times along its length. Usually the most commonly available species, easy to grow.

Polystichum (Dryopteridaceae)

Holly fern, shield fern, sword fern
Worldwide

Plants in this genus of about two hundred species and countless cultivars of usually evergreen, terrestrial ferns are found in a range of habitats from alpine regions to tropical rainforests worldwide. The species described here are hardy, preferring humus-rich, well-drained conditions in dappled to full shade, taking fairly dry conditions well once established, though on moister soils they are correspondingly larger. It is advisable to remove the old fronds each year before the new ones unfurl, so you can enjoy the new growth. Though many in this genus are very gardenworthy and easily obtained, only a few can be listed here. Most garden centres usually have a selection, and the less common forms can be obtained from specialist nurseries.

Polystichum proliferum

Mother shield fern
Hardy / Dappled to full shade

Very beautiful fern, indigenous to moist, wet mountain forests in southeastern Australia, growing to 45 cm tall and 90 cm across, even larger in the wild, often forming an erect, thick, trunklike base up to 10 cm tall. Fronds are lance-shaped, arching, bi- or tripinnate, and dark green. Can produce a rather large rootstock with age. The name *proliferum* refers to the prolific buds that grow into small plants at the tips of the fronds.

Polystichum setiferum

Soft shield fern
Hardy / Dappled to full shade

Evergreen or semi-evergreen fern indigenous to the British Isles and western, southern, and central Europe, growing to a height of 1 m by 90 cm, with drooping, soft, lance-shaped, bipinnate, light green to midgreen fronds, 30–100 cm long, with up to forty leaflets on each side of stalks covered in brownish orange scales. Plantlets often form on frond midribs. Besides the plain species, there are more than a dozen distinct groups of *P. setiferum*, two of which are described here.

Polystichum setiferum

Polystichum setiferum Divisilobum Group

Hardy / Sun or shade

Some very architecturally interesting evergreen ferns both for the woodland and the garden, having light green, graceful, finely dissected, three-pinnate fronds, creating attractive mounds of foliage that swirl around the plants, 5–75 cm high, creating a very desirable appearance that looks good throughout the season, whether planted singly or en masse. Plantlets often form along the midribs. They prefer full to dappled shade, though they take dry conditions well once established and will also grow in full sun if moist. 'Dahlem', 0.75 m by 45 cm, has narrow, lance-shaped, fairly stiff, almost erect fronds becoming tripinate, whereas 'Herrenhausen', 50–60 cm tall and wide, is a fairly recent cultivar from Germany with a broader spreading habit, having dark green fronds with pointed leaflets. Plantlets are borne profusely on older fronds. 'Iveryanum', 50 cm by 60 cm, has flat fronds finely divided with uniform crests; it also has a terminal crest crested at the tips. 'Plumosum' is an upright form, 45–75 cm tall and wide, with tri- or rarely quadripinnate fronds, finely divided with extremely overlapping pinnae.

Polystichum setiferum Plumosodivisilobum Group

Hardy / Sun or shade

Ferns with compact, soft fronds with overlapping pinnae. Group includes 'Plumosodivi silobum',

Woodwardia radicans

face, which readily root when they touch the ground. They excel at covering moist shady banks and as an understorey in woodland gardens, preferring dappled to full shade, although some will take full sun if regularly watered. All prefer humus-rich soil. They give a very tropical feel to the garden, especially when well established, forming colonies with time, especially in gardens that have few frosts.

Woodwardia fimbriata

Giant chain fern

Frost-hardy / Dappled to full shade

Evergreen fern with graceful arching fronds, reaching 0.9–2 m tall and wide or more in its native habitats in the northwestern United States, usually smaller in the British Isles. Elegant lance-shaped, pinnate, luscious bright green fronds are up to 1.8 m long or more in ideal conditions. Minimum temperature −8°c for short periods.

Woodwardia radicans

European chain fern

Frost-hardy / Dappled to full shade

Spectacular evergreen chain fern that can reach 1.8 m by 3 m or more in favourable conditions, with arching, broadly lance-shaped, pinnate, midgreen to dark green fronds up to 2 m long, with conspicuous bulbils on the frond tips. Hails from southwestern Europe, Madeira, and the Canaries. Hardy to about −5°c, defoliating at lower temperatures, though it will usually regrow from the ground if mulched with straw around the base.

Woodwardia unigemmata

Walking fern, Asian chain fern

Frost-hardy / Dappled to full shade

Collected by Roy Lancaster from Mount Omei in western China, a spectacular species growing to about 1 m by 3 m or more, with huge, elegant, arching, pinnate, midgreen fronds that emerge red and fade through brown to green, up to 1.5 m long. Bulbils are produced at the frond tips and propagate easily. Minimum temperature −8°c for short periods.

with leafy, very overlapping pinnae, giving a somewhat mosslike appearance; 'Plumosum Densum', a slightly smaller form with a loose shuttlecock shape to 40 cm with frilly lacelike fronds tending to lie more horizontal than vertical, in a characteristic spiral shape; and 'Plumosum Bevis', growing to a height and spread of 60–80 cm, with elongated pinnae with segments that sweep elegantly toward the tips at the ends of the fronds.

Woodwardia (Blechnaceae)

Chain fern

Eurasia and North America

This genus of about ten species of evergreen or deciduous terrestrial ferns is indigenous to damp, sheltered places in warm-temperate regions of Eurasia and North America. The ferns are mostly large with a spreading and arching habit, often with plantlets (bulbils) at the frond tips on the upper sur-

Cyathea australis

Tree Ferns

Tree ferns are usually grouped into two families, Cyatheaceae and Dicksoniaceae, which include more than five hundred known species. They are native to the tropics and subtropical parts of the Southern Hemisphere, though several grow well in cool-summer climates if sited well. Until the latter part of the twentieth century they were rare in the British Isles, apart from some of the well-known stands in Cornwall and other southerly parts of England and at Inverewe Gardens in Scotland, where they are bathed in warmth from the Gulf Stream in winter. Now species like *Dicksonia antarctica* are readily available at most of the larger garden centres, with several other species available from specialist nurseries.

These giants of the fern world add a truly exotic feel to the garden with their superficially palmlike fronds, giving strong shape and stately form to tranquil areas in dappled shade. Having been around at the time of the dinosaurs, they have a very alluring primitive appearance. Their vertical trunklike rhizome (often reaching a great height), from which the fronds emerge, varies in size and proportion from species to species. These trunks are not dead, as I have heard them described by some British gardening TV personalities—they are very much alive, transporting moisture and nutrients from the ground to the fronds.

The fronds are held at the trunk tops in a radiating or spreading fashion, unfurling over many weeks from the crown, where all the new growth arises. These new fronds are often called croziers. Unlike trees, tree ferns will not regrow from the trunk if the crown is removed or destroyed, and will subsequently die. Many species, such as *Dicksonia antarctica*, have trunks that are covered in a thick mass of roots, while other species like cyatheas have trunks that are more solid, almost woody, forming fewer roots above ground level, though they are often covered in fine hairs and old frond bases. All tree ferns have small roots that do not thicken like those of other plants.

Most of the tree ferns obtained in the British Isles are produced from land clearance in the Southern Hemisphere. They can be anywhere from 30 cm to 4.5 m tall

and from 12 cm to 45 cm wide. They are shipped as sawed-off trunks (or large cuttings) with the crowns intact; the trunks will produce new fibrous roots from the base when planted, which stay quite thin and wiry. Sometimes they have already been planted in containers where they have subsequently rooted, a more expensive way to buy them. They can also be obtained fairly cheaply as young trunkless plants.

Because tree ferns are slow growers, it is advisable to purchase them at a size to suit your garden. Planting them in groups of different sizes gives a more natural appearance. As they are imported fairly dry to make them considerably lighter during transportation, they need to be rehydrated by soaking the trunk. Always look into the crown to see if there are new frond buds ready to emerge, especially if they as yet have no fronds. All prefer a humid atmosphere, benefiting from regular misting in hot or windy weather, or from using a timed watering system that very slowly dribbles onto the side of the trunk, just below the crown. If left to become bone dry, they will produce inferior fronds in subsequent years and may even die. For the price you have paid for your new acquisition, it would be a rather expensive loss! They deserve to be treated well and will subsequently reward you handsomely with lush growth and years of pleasure and great majesty.

Cyathea brownii

Cyathea (Cyatheaceae)

Subtropical and tropical regions worldwide

This genus of some six hundred species of tree ferns is distributed widely in the subtropics and tropics, producing some of the tallest tree ferns in the family Cyatheaceae, reaching a staggering 15 m. Most have a rather graceful habit with arching, soft fronds on fairly slender trunks. The older fronds remain for some time before falling and leave smooth scars on the trunk at the frond bases. The forms from the most southerly regions or highest elevations have the greatest hardiness. They prefer being constantly moist in humus-rich, preferably fertile soil in a shady, humid position.

Cyathea australis

Rough tree fern
Frost-hardy / Sun or shade

Truly spectacular fern hailing from moist areas of eastern Australia and Tasmania, growing up to a height and spread of 6 m or more in its native habitat, though less in our cool-temperate gardens. Trunk stocky and black with prominent frond scars. Fronds are dark green on the upper surface and a lighter shade of green on the reverse, bi- or tripin-

nate, attaining a length of 3.5 m with a rough textured surface to the frond bases, with each frond leaflet up to 1 m in length. Will take temperatures down to about −10°C for short periods, though it is advisable to insulate the trunk and crown when nighttime temperatures stay below freezing for any period of time. Can be planted in a somewhat sunny situation as long as the soil is moist, although it dislikes desiccating winds.

Cyathea brownii

Norfolk Island tree fern
Half-hardy / Dappled shade

Largest of all tree ferns, with an erect trunk a staggering 5–16 m tall or more, with tripinnate fronds 3–5 m in length. Common in rain forests, near streams and gullies, hence prefers well-drained, moist, humus-rich soil in dappled shade. Tolerates only a small amount of frost, so unless you have frost-free conditions, must be overwintered as a containerised plant, at least a few degrees above freezing, the fronds being hardy to about −3°C. Or if you want to be experimental, try wrapping the fern in position with a ludicrous amount of protection. Now becoming available in the British Isles but only as relatively small plants.

Cyathea cunninghamii

Slender tree fern

Half-hardy (?) / Part to full shade

Tall, uncommon tree fern from New Zealand, Tasmania, and eastern Australia, slowly growing to 6 m tall or more in its native habitats, with a slender, dark brown trunk usually 6–15 and occasionally 20 cm in diameter. Midgreen fronds are bipinnate-pinnatifid, lance-shaped, up to 3 m long or more in the wild, where the plant is often found growing in cool, humid, fairly dark gullies and on stream banks, hence requires a position protected from wind that is moist and humid. As yet its hardiness has not been proven, though it should be at least as hardy as *C. medullaris* with similar winter protection.

Cyathea dealbata

Ponga, silver tree fern

Frost-hardy / Part to full shade

The ponga (pronounced punga) is one of the national symbols of New Zealand, a magnificent tree fern with an erect trunk that can reach up to 10 m tall or more, with tripinnate midgreen to deep green fronds, whitish silver on the underside as well as on the stems and frond bases, up to 4 m long in its native habitat. Retains its frond stems on the trunk. Will resist some frost, taking lows of −5°c or more for short periods, in a sheltered position away from prevailing winds as fronds are rather brittle. In colder areas, trunk and crown should be protected. Tolerates drier conditions than some other ferns as long as the base is well mulched, though it will be lusher in moist conditions.

Cyathea dregei

Frost-hardy / Sun or shade

Large, erect, stout-trunked tree fern found growing in grasslands and on stream banks in its native habitats in South Africa, Madagascar, and parts of eastern Africa, most frequently at 900–1800 m high, where it grows up to 5 m tall, with large, arching, bi- or tripinnate fronds up to 3 m long, green above and paler underneath, with brown rough-surfaced stems. Usually grows in fairly open situations, hence

is used to hot sun and equally cold freezing nights, and should have reasonable hardiness down to at least −5°c, and probably lower when mature, with adequate frost protection.

Cyathea medullaris

Black tree fern, mamaku, sago fern

Half-hardy / Dappled shade

Absolutely beautiful, very exotic-looking, rapid-growing, black-trunked tree fern hailing from New Zealand, 10–15 m tall by 3–6 m wide, with a rosette of bipinnate-pinnatifid to tripinnate, broad, lance-shaped, very long (up to 6 m) fronds, deep green above and paler beneath, with narrowly oblong, finely tapering segments. Frond stem bases are black and hairy. Paul Spracklin on the Essex Riviera has been growing an imposing specimen in his garden since 2000, producing fronds 3 m long, with the trunk growing 30 cm and sometimes more in one season when fed weekly with dilute seaweed extract and kept moist during the growing season; he suggests a mulch of well-rotted manure to really boost its growth. In winter he wraps it with a layer of fleece, then a layer of roofing insulation, leaving the fronds sticking out; the fronds are subsequently browned by frost, which is not a problem as new ones are produced the following year. During this period it has taken lows of −5°C without any ill effects.

Cyathea smithii

Katote, soft tree fern

Frost-hardy / Dappled shade

Most southerly-occurring tree fern in the world, found in New Zealand and on surrounding islands, including the sub-Antarctic Aucklands. Upright and stout, tapering toward the top, growing to 8 m tall or more, with a rosette of narrowly lance-shaped fronds (somewhat reminiscent of *Dicksonia antarctica*) 1.2–1.8 m long, with yellow green midribs and pale to dark brown stems. Midribs of dead fronds are retained as a prominent skirt around the trunk in the wild. When the plant is exported to the Northern Hemisphere, the dead fronds are removed for transportation. Should take lows of about −5°c for short periods; otherwise wrap for the winter months.

Dicksonia (Dicksoniaceae)

Southeastern Asia, Australia, New Zealand, the
South Pacific, Central and South America

The genus *Dicksonia* encompasses about twenty to twenty-five species of evergreen or semi-evergreen ferns, normally with upright, trunklike rhizomes but occasionally creeping in habit. They are found growing in places as diverse as New Guinea and the isolated Juan Fernandez Islands in the Pacific. They grow on the fringes of rain forests or in protected parts of more open forest, as well as in high-elevation forests in the tropics and mountain forests in subtropical regions and southern temperate regions. Although related to *Cyathea*, *Dicksonia* is considerably more primitive, with fossil records dating back as far as the Jurassic and Cretaceous periods. The trunks of dicksonias as well as the basal portions of the frond stems can be covered with long hairs instead of scales as with those in the family Cyatheaceae. In the wild they are usually clothed in their old leaf bases and fibrous roots. They prefer moist, humus-rich soil in the dappled shade of taller trees. The trunks should not be allowed to dry out. They are very useful plants for growing either permanently in the garden, where they look spectacular, or in tubs and containers. Several take some degree of frost and are excellent specimen plants for the garden.

Dicksonia antarctica

Soft tree fern, woolly tree fern
Frost-hardy / Part to full shade

The most famous tree fern in Northern Hemisphere cultivation, and truly majestic to boot! Dense, dark brown trunk (rhizome) grows to 6 m and higher in its native habitat, cool mountain forests of Tasmania and north to Queensland. Masses of dense fibrous roots adorn the lower parts, and overlapping frond stalk bases persist after the fronds are shed on the upper section. Bipinnate-pinnatifid lance-shaped fronds grow to 3 m long in the wild, though usually half this in cool-summer gardens. When juvenile, fronds are tightly packed in the crown, emerging in spring, unfurling into an attractive hairy crozier over a week or so, transforming into bright pale green fronds maturing to darker green.

Imported trunks are usually between 15 and 30 cm in diameter, though sometimes larger ones can be found. Occasionally the plants are multitrunked or bent, making interesting features in the exotic garden. Prefers humus-rich soil with added organic matter. Trunk should be kept moist at all times; otherwise the fronds will become small and inferior in future years. This can be done with a timed misting system or with spaghetti tubing pinned to the trunk several centimeters below the crown, slowly dripping onto the trunk, especially in hot weather. An occasional liquid seaweed feed during the growing season is desirable for the biggest fronds.

My oldest *D. antarctica* has been in the ground since 1990 with no protection, taking lows of at least −10°c. In Martin Rickard's garden in central England, it has survived a similar period with protection down to a chilly −15°c. Tucking a handful of straw into the crown will protect your valuable plant from the worst frosts.

Dicksonia fibrosa

Golden tree fern, wheki-ponga
Frost-hardy / Part to full shade

Relatively small and slow-growing species of *Dicksonia* with a thick gold-brown fibrous trunk made up of matted roots (the reason for the name *fibrosa*), found in fairly cold areas at elevations up to 823 m in its native New Zealand, where its reaches a height of up to 6 m, though much smaller in cultivation. Fronds closely resemble *D. antarctica*, though shorter at 1–2 m, dark green, bipinnate-pinnatifid, lance-shaped, with hairy leaf stalks that are brown when mature. Upper surface of the frond has a rough texture caused by the upturned edges of the pinnules. Prefers a cool, moist, shaded environment in humus-rich soil. Almost as hardy as *D. antarctica*, taking lows down to about −8°c for short periods, and maybe lower with protection.

Dicksonia squarrosa

Hard tree fern, rough tree fern, wheki
Frost-hardy / Part or full shade

Suckering tree fern with a delicate appearance. Upright stem produces side crowns up the trunk, as

*Dicksonia
antarctica*

*Dicksonia
antarctica,*
new fronds

well as underground runners producing side shoots,
when mature. Faster growing than other dicksonias,
up to a height of 8 m in the wild in its native New
Zealand, though much smaller in cultivation. Trunk
is covered in brown hairs and persistent frond bases.
Fronds are 1–3 m long, lance-shaped, bipinnate to
pinnatifid, dark green and glaucous green underneath, with frond stalks covered in dense brown to
black hairs. Prefers humus-rich, well-drained, moist
soil in a humid, sheltered location, with plenty of
water in the growing season. Never let the trunk dry
out. Hardy to about −5°c for short periods, lower
with protection. Excellent in containers or as a conservatory plant.

Houseplants Outside

Many visitors to my garden are surprised to see so many so-called houseplants, thinking for some reason that they will live only in a house! Many houseplants are no different from, say, petunias and pelargoniums, which we do plant outside during the summer months although they are not hardy. In fact, many houseplants are hardier than you might think. Aspidistras, for instance, will take many degrees of frost in their stride, living permanently in the garden in a shady corner. Several have been living happily in my garden for more than a decade, not just surviving but thriving. *Chlorophytum comosum* (spider plant) grows very well in the garden and makes a good hanging-basket plant or edging for a border. It takes cold nights well and has survived for many winters in my garden, dying back like a typical herbaceous perennial, only to return in spring. Even *Tradescantia* is a returning perennial in my garden, re-emerging in midspring. I am lucky to have sandy soil, which it prefers, and a microclimate that keeps it warm enough during the winter months.

The more tender houseplants can be bedded out after the last frosts have passed. *Solenostemon* (syn. *Coleus*), for instance, is regaining popularity as a summer bedding plant, as it was in Victorian times. Coleus, in fact, prefers being in the garden rather than collecting dust on a window ledge in the house. The intrepid Victorians bedded out many houseplants on the grounds of stately homes and in well-known public places like Regents Park in London. These plants were then tucked in a greenhouse before autumn frosts returned.

Houseplants, because of their fantastic flowers and leaf colouration, create impact in the garden, giving the place a strong feeling of being in the tropics. One thing to remember is that if you bring out plants that have been used to fairly low levels of light, they will need to be acclimatised to outdoor conditions. Even plants that naturally grow in full sun will scorch, so they should be brought out to a shady corner of the garden to begin with and then slowly acclimatised for a week or so to stronger light. A single layer of horticultural fleece will protect them while they are acclimatising. Many houseplants prefer dappled shade, as they grow naturally as understorey plants in tropical and subtropical forests.

The following selections have been grown in my garden in Norfolk and by other intrepid exoticists in England. Most of them can be found in the houseplant section in garden centres. These also need acclimating to cooler nights, as they will all have been grown in warm greenhouses. Experimentation is part of the fun when it comes to this kind of gardening, and although not always successful, it invariably does work. Obviously, plants from hot, moist tropical forests will not survive our temperate summers, though I think you will be pleasantly surprised at how many will! They can either be planted out in a sheltered corner with dappled shade or as a collection of potted plants near the house, where they can easily be watered in hot weather. There are many more to experiment with than are listed here.

Aphelandra squarrosa (bottom) with Dahlia 'Bishop of Llandaff'

Aphelandra squarrosa

Saffron spike, zebra plant
Semi-tender / Dappled shade

Usually available 30 cm high, though growing much taller in the wild. Leaves are 15–25 cm long, ovate, deep glossy green, with strikingly contrasting creamy white veins and a pronounced midrib. Flowers and bracts are bright yellow, sometimes edged in red. Several hybrids are available. Works well in groups as ground cover, preferring dappled shade in humus-rich soil. Overwinter indoors or under glass at a minimum temperature of 5°C.

Aspidistra (Lilaceae)

Eastern Asia

This is a genus of eight species and several cultivars. Aspidistras are emblematic of the English Victorian period, as plants for the house and very tough ones at that, withstanding dark areas in hallways and rooms, taking low light levels and neglect in their stride. They grow equally well as garden plants for very shady corners that are on the dry side in winter, easily taking lows of −10°C with little leaf damage. They eventually form dense thickets and respond well to a high-nitrogen feed in spring. The rhizomes are prone to vole damage in winter and the leaves to slug damage, which can make them look tatty. *Aspidistra elatior* is the most commonly available.

Aspidistra elatior

Cast-iron plant
Frost-hardy / Full shade

Hails from China. Tough, parallel-veined, oblong-lanceolate, leathery dark green leaves reach

Aphelandra (Acanthaceae)

Tropical North, Central, and South America

This genus contains about 170 species of shrubs and subshrubs in the acanthus family that usually flower year-round. *Aphelandra squarrosa* is the most commonly available species.

45–75 cm long and 7.5–10 cm wide on stiff, upright stalks, directly from their tufted rhizomatous roots. Inconspicuous, four-segmented, solitary cream to purple flowers appear at ground level and are more of an oddity than attractive. 'China Sun' has long, wide leaves speckled with pale yellow spots. 'Okame' has unusually broad foliage, deep green leaves with small, very random, creamy ochre dots. 'Variegata' has leaves longitudinally striped white. *Aspidistra lurida* 'Ginga' (syn. *A. elatior* 'Milky Way') has leaves with stripes and spots.

Begonia (Begoniaceae)

Tropical and subtropical regions worldwide

This genus of about nine hundred species of perennials, shrubs, and climbers includes a great diversity of plants with root systems that can be fibrous, rhizomatous, or tuberous, grown for their foliage and/or flowers. Hardy forms are discussed in the earlier section "Bulbs and Tubers." Our focus here is the so-called houseplant (tender) forms. These make very alluring and highly decorative houseplants, grown for their interestingly shaped or highly coloured foliage that arises from the rootstock or from canelike stems. Many of the tropical forms make excellent summer bedding or specimens to be used in arrangements of containers and pots in a moist, shady area of the garden, where their distinctive textures shimmer in the play of light and shadow that makes shade gardening so compelling. They work in the garden just as well as the more common *Begonia semperflorens* group and the large-flowered tuberous forms that have been popular over the decades.

Rex begonias, which grow from a rhizome, are aptly named the "kings" of the begonia world, because they have exceptionally beautiful and wildly varied leaves. These can be long and pointed or rounded and even spiralling; they can be streaked, bordered, spotted, splotched, wrinkled, or hairy, or they can have undulating margins. They can be every colour of the rainbow or metallic, while the undersides are often burgundy to pink. They usually have panicles of pink flowers held above the foliage.

There are many tender begonias worth trying in the garden; the ones described here are only a small selection of the many now available, especially the United States. *Begonia rex* hybrids are particularly popular in the United States and are among the top ten favourite houseplants in the United Kingdom. Begonias were much vaunted by the late Christopher Lloyd, who bedded them out annually in his subtropical garden at Great Dixter in East Sussex, England. He reportedly once said, "If I had to choose only one group of plants to be stuck on a desert island with, I would choose foliage begonias." All begonias prefer fertile, well-drained, moist organic soil. For more information, see *Begonias: Cultivation, Identification, and Natural History* by Mark C. Tebbitt (2005).

Begonia aconitifolia

syn. *B. sceptrum*
Tender / Dappled shade

Cane-stemmed begonia from Brazil growing up to 3 m high, though more like 1 m in general cultivation. Bears glossy, velvety green leaves with dull reddish veining and few to several silvery white stripes between the veins. Leaf is ovate, fan-shaped, with four to six fine-toothed lobes up 20 cm long. In autumn bears pendulous white or pale pink flowers up to 5 cm across. 'Metallica' produces bronzy leaves with pronounced silver markings.

Begonia bowerae

Semi-tender / Dappled shade

Rhizomatous begonia to 25 cm high by 20 cm wide, with ovate to entire, undulating-surfaced green leaves 5 cm or more long, marked with chocolate-brown patches and fringed with hairs. Upright sprays of 2-cm-wide pink or white flowers are borne from winter to early spring. Excellent begonia for growing en masse as ground cover or in containers with other exotics.

Begonia 'Burle Marx'

Semi-tender / Dappled shade

Named after the famous Brazilian landscape architect, a beautiful plant growing to more than 1 m tall. Ovate to oblong leaves up to 25 cm or more across are heavily textured, dark green, with a reddish bronze overlay strengthening toward the margins and maroon–purplish red undersides. Large puckered leaves are held more horizontally and are less lopsided than those of other begonias, giving a unique appearance. Prefers to dry out between waterings.

are held on long red petioles. Leaves can reach up to 50 cm across, giving a very tropical effect. Small creamy white flowers are borne in branched clusters from winter to spring.

Above

Begonia carolineifolia

Above right

Begonia ×hybrida 'Dragon Wing'

Begonia carolineifolia

Palm leaf begonia

Semi-tender / Dappled shade

Rhizomatous, exotic-looking begonia from Mexico and Guatemala, growing up to 60 cm or more tall with succulent upright stems. Huge, palmate, glossy green leaves, with six to ten arching, toothed leaflets up to 25 cm long, with burgundy undersides,

Begonia ×hybrida 'Dragon Wing'

Semi-tender / Sun or dappled to full shade

Not a houseplant but nonhardy and included here because of its popularity. Grows to about 38 cm high by 45 cm wide, with winglike, deep, exceedingly glossy green leaves 10–15 cm long. Because the hybrid is sterile, flowers all summer until frost, with bold drooping clusters of red or pink flowers. Often sold as a canelike begonia but really a cross between a shrublike begonia and a semperflorens and should be considered shrublike. Often thought of as rather gaudy and brash but nevertheless fits in well with cannas, bananas, and other lush plantings. Needs plenty of room and is undaunted by hot summers, which just make it grow even bigger! Prefers a shady position for the lushest growth but is equally happy in full sun, where the leaves become bronzed and slightly smaller. Also makes an excellent container, window-box, or hanging-basket plant.

Begonia 'Little Brother Montgomery'

Semi-tender / Dappled shade

Very attractive cane-type begonia growing to about 40 cm tall. Maple-shaped, somewhat rexlike leaves up to 25 cm long have a dark green background and veining with silver speckles that merge in the leaf margins. Young leaves have a pink tinge. One parent thought to be *B. palmata*. A favourite of the late Christopher Lloyd.

Begonia luxurians

Semi-tender / Dappled shade

Exceptionally handsome Brazilian shrublike begonia, growing to a height of 4 m in its native habitat, though more like 75 cm tall by 60 cm wide in cultivation. Dark green, umbrella-like, palmate leaves with ten to twenty leaflets, to 25 cm long by 3 cm wide, are borne at the top of mostly unbranched stems, giving a very junglelike effect. Clusters up to 10 cm across of fragrant creamy white flowers appear from spring to summer.

Begonia popenoei

Tender / Dappled to full shade

Rhizomatous begonia that can grow to 60 cm–1.2 m tall, with huge, round, glossy green leaves that can reach a staggering 45 cm long and wide. Large, loose panicles of fragrant white flowers are held well above the foliage in spring to early summer. Handsome specimen plant for a shady, moist but well-drained corner. Also an excellent container plant.

Begonia rex

Semi-tender / Dappled shade

Creeping rhizomatous perennial native to the remote monsoon-drenched mountainous regions of Assam in northeastern India and rare in cultivation, though it has played a very important role in the development of the Rex Cultorum Group, which contains those hybrids with *B. rex* parentage with showy foliage, now the most commercially important of all the begonia species available. Like the species, these have an aversion to direct sunlight, preferring light shade for best leaf colouration. Most will take cool temperatures down to 5°C, though 7°C or higher is preferable. A window ledge in a cool room in your house is the perfect place to keep them during the winter months, where they will look good no matter what the weather outside is doing.

Begonia 'Escargot'

Unfortunately, many, or should I say most, of the rex begonias on sale at garden centres and other outlets are labelled simply as "rex begonia" or just "begonia"! For a more comprehensive list, you have to go to a specialist grower. The following is just a small selection of rex hybrids. 'Emerald Giant' has

Right

*Chlorophytum
comosum*
'Variegatum'

Far right

*Chlorophytum
orchidastrum*
'Orange and
Green', foliage

large mostly silver leaves with dark green central veining and red edges. 'Escargot' is one of the most stunning begonias available, with large swirled leaves in shades of silvery pistachio green with dark green centres and margins, and reddish green leaf stalks with dense reddish hairs. 'Red Robin' is very compact, with alluring, smallish heart-shaped leaves with contrasting matte black centres and edges and a wide band of blood red between. 'Sal's Moondust' has swirled leaves with dark purplish grey edges and centres interspersed with silver and randomly spotted with purple. 'Vesuvius' has medium-sized deep red leaves with almost black edges and centres.

Calathea (Marantaceae)

Peacock plant
Mexico to northern Argentina

Calathea includes about three hundred herbaceous perennials, known for their handsome, attractively patterned, ovate to lanceolate leaves. They are used extensively in tropical gardens. Surprisingly, some of the smaller calatheas are happy in cool-summer gardens, as long as the nighttime temperatures do not drop much below 10°C, in which case they make good plants for a moist, shady corner of the garden. They are readily available in the houseplant section of garden centres, though there is usually little choice, as they are normally just labelled *Calathea*. One of the most commonly available is *C. makoyana*, a lovely plant with translucent light green leaves, patterned with fine lines and alternate large and small ovals in dark green. The underside has a similar patterning in purple.

Chlorophytum (Lilaceae)

Subtropical regions of Africa and Asia

All members of this genus of about 215 species of fleshy-stemmed perennials have linear to lance-shaped leaves that arise from the rootstock. Chlorophytums look very attractive planted en masse and thus make good ground covers. They take low temperatures well and in a mild winter will

usually come back from the rootstock. Containers and hanging baskets, where the offsets hang gracefully, are good settings for them. Although they take drought well, they produce lush foliage with plenty of water. High-nitrogen feed in spring and summer is beneficial.

Chlorophytum comosum

Spider plant
Frost-hardy / Sun or dappled shade

Most readily available chlorophytum, with linear leaves to 38 cm long, green or striped white. Flowering stems produce panicles of small white starlike flowers. Attractive plantlets are formed at the flowering nodes, which hang down as they mature. 'Variegatum' has white and cream margins. 'Vittatum' has recurved leaves with a central white stripe.

Chlorophytum orchidastrum 'Orange and Green'

Tender / Dappled shade

New form now being distributed in Europe grows to about 35 cm tall. Looks nothing like a chlorophytum—in fact, more like a hosta! Leaves are broad,

elliptic, glossy, and dark green, up to 12 cm across, with brilliant orange stems and midribs, giving its common name. Very tropical-looking plant that is attractive planted in groups; also works well in containers.

Clivia (Amaryllidaceae)

South Africa

Clivia miniata, flowers

This genus consists of four species of perennials and many hybrids, all clump-forming plants with stocky rhizomes and straplike leaves at various times depending on the species. The funnel-shaped flowers are produced on long, thick stems in shades of red, orange, and yellow, followed by red berries. They are tolerant of only light frost but grow well in temperate gardens during the summer months, preferring a shady corner away from wind in moist, well-drained soil. Unless you live in an area with only very light frost, grow them in containers, where they tend to flower more profusely when potbound, often with their roots protruding from the surface. *C. miniata* is the most commonly available.

Clivia miniata

Half-hardy / Part or full shade

Clivia miniata 'Kirstenbosch Yellow', flowers

Spring-flowering species with leaves up to 60 cm long and quite broad, though usually less. Flowers are wide open, funnel-shaped, yellow-throated, and deep orange. Variety *citrina* has primrose yellow blooms; 'Kirstenbosch Yellow', soft yellow with a darker strip down the middle; 'Striata', rarely offered, has orange flowers with white- or cream-variegated foliage.

Codiaeum (Euphorbiaceae)

Asia and the western Pacific

Plants in this genus of fifteen species of evergreen perennials, shrubs, and small trees are grown for their fantastically marked and variegated, almost unreal-looking foliage. Although they are considered desperately tender, I have been growing them as summer bedding for more than a decade, and as long as the nighttime temperatures don't fall much below 10°C they seem to be quite happy. As they are greenhouse grown, they will need at least a week to acclimate to cooler growing conditions and may drop a few leaves in the process. They prefer dappled shade in a windfree corner of the garden, in humus-rich, moist soil. They look best grown

in groups, having the appearance of stained glass windows when the sun shines through their leaves. They make excellent container plants for the conservatory, brought out during the warmer months, or dig them up before the nights become cold and use as a house or heated conservatory plant for the winter. The most commonly available species is *C. variegatum* and its many hybrid forms.

Cyperus (Cyperaceae)

Bulrush, paper plant, papyrus
Northern and tropical Africa

The best-known member of this genus of about six hundred species of annual and perennial sedges must be papyrus, the raw material for the writing paper of ancient Egypt, made from thin strips of stem pith pressed together while still wet. *Cyperus papyrus* is the bulrush of the Old Testament.

Codiaeum
variegatum

Cyperus involucratus

syn. *C. alternifolius*
Umbrella plant
Semi-tender / Full sun

Clump-forming aquatic plant with leafless stems growing to 1.2 m tall, topped by numerous, thin, leaflike bracts, 15–25 cm long, that radiate from the centre. Prefers a rich, peaty, moist soil. Roots should never be allowed to dry out and will flourish in up to 10 cm of water. Overwinter at 5°C. 'Nanus' (dwarf umbrella plant) is a dwarf variety that grows to about 60 cm tall. 'Variegata' is variegated green and white.

Cyperus papyrus

Papyrus
Tender / Full sun

Vigorous, clump-forming, aquatic marginal. Many three-sided, leafless stems, growing up to 5 m tall in ideal conditions but as summer bedding more

Above left

Cyperus involucratus

Left

Cyperus papyrus

like 1.5–2 m tall, are topped by dense umbels of one hundred or more soft, thin, drooping spikes, 20–30 cm long. Can be grown as a pond marginal, in a large container as a bog plant, or in humus-rich soil that is kept moist in full sun. During the winter keep on the dry side at a minimum temperature of 7°c.

Ficus (Moraceae)

Tropical and subtropical regions worldwide

Members of this genus of more than eight hundred species of mainly evergreen trees, shrubs, and woody climbers are usually found in moist forests in tropical and subtropical regions. They are grown for their ornamental foliage, as with the common rubber plant, *Ficus elastica*, and for their edible fruit, as with the common fig tree, *F. carica*, whose "fruit" is actually an inverted flower. Both fit in well with the exotic garden style, though rubber plants can only be bedded out for the warmest months of the year. In this section we are only dealing with types more commonly referred to as houseplants. Do remember that they must be acclimated to outdoor conditions as discussed at the beginning of this section . . . be forewarned!

Ficus elastica

Ficus elastica 'Belize'

Ficus elastica

Rubber plant
Tender / Sun or shade

Hailing from the eastern Himalaya through India to Java, this well-known evergreen, much-branched tree can reach massive proportions, up to 30 m in warm climates. Our houseplants are basically large cuttings! The large elliptic leaves are 30 cm or more long and are glossy, thick, and leathery, rich dark green often flushed red, especially in full sun. There are many hybrids worth trying, though only a few are generally available at your local garden centre. 'Belize' has variegated green and cream leaves with an overlay of pinkish red and red terminal buds. 'Decora' has broad, very dark green, slightly bronzed leaves, with large red terminal buds. 'Doescheri' has leaves mottled greyish green, irregularly edged in pale cream. 'Variegata' has leaves irregularly variegated in cream and green. Smaller plants can be grouped together as bedding, while specimens can either be bedded out in the warmest months or kept as large container plants for a sheltered corner of the garden.

Ficus pumila

Creeping fig
Half-hardy / Dappled shade

Perennial, self-clinging, branching climber from China and Japan that can grow to a height of 3 m and more in the wild, with unlimited spread. Flat, thin, and leathery heart-shaped green leaves grow up to 5 cm across, though usually smaller on juvenile plants. 'Dorte' has cream-centred green leaves. 'Minima' has thin stems and small juvenile leaves 1 cm long. 'Sonny' has green leaves with creamy white margins. Makes an excellent summer ground cover for a moist position in dappled shade, where it will spread quite rapidly. Will take temperatures down to freezing for short periods only; hence should be stored in frost-free conditions over the winter months and kept on the dry side.

Gerbera (Asteraceae)

Transvaal daisy
Mostly South Africa, Madagascar, Asia, and
 Indonesia

Gerbera hybrid,
flower detail

The forty or more species of herbaceous perennials in this genus have leaves in rosettes and solitary flowers on long, stiff, green stalks. Although normally considered as houseplants, they take cool temperatures well and hence do well in the garden. They flower continuously all summer and look good planted in groups. They prefer full sun in light sandy soil and do not like wet conditions.

Gerbera jamesonii

Barberton daisy
Frost-hardy / Full sun

Evergreen perennial with large, daisylike, variably coloured flowers, intermittently flowering on long stems, with soft, jagged-edged leaves in rosettes. Make excellent, long-lasting cut flowers. Can take lows of −5°c for short periods. Most cultivars are derived through a cross between *G. jamesonii* and *G. viridiflora* and although attractive are not as hardy in the garden, though they work well in containers in full sun.

Hypoestes (Acanthaceae)

Polka-dot plant
Tropical Africa and Asia

A few of the more decorative forms of this genus of forty or more perennial subshrubs are used as houseplants. *Hypoestes phyllostachya* is the most commonly available.

Hypoestes phyllostachya

Tender / Dappled shade

Perennial subshrub to 60 cm, though usually less in the garden. Leaves are up to 6 cm long, ovate, deep bronze-green, freckled, with small irregular pink spots. Small, long, lavender flowers are borne from the leaf axils. 'Splash' has larger, brighter spotting. Tip pruning makes for a bushier plant. Can be purchased as quite small plants that will rapidly grow during the summer. Make good ground cover in dappled shade, brightening up a dark corner. I treat them as an annual, although they can be brought into frost-free conditions for the winter if pruned to a manageable size.

Justicia brandegeeana

Tolerates cool conditions well but must be lifted when the first frosts arrive and stored at a minimum of 5°c. Good in containers.

Justicia candicans

syn. *Jacobinia ovata, Justicia ovata*
Red justicia
Frost-hardy / Sun or dappled shade

Compact branching semi-evergreen shrub with a spreading habit. Hailing from Arizona, it will grow to about 1 m in a hot summer, though less when cool. Leaves are bright green and heart-shaped. Inflorescence is in the form of a bright red tube that attracts hummingbirds in the wild. Flowers profusely from summer to autumn. Can be planted out permanently in areas that have minimal frost; otherwise dig up and store in a frost-free location for the winter, keeping on the dry side. Takes −5°c for short periods.

Justicia carnea

Brazilian plume
Semi-tender / Sun or dappled shade

Evergreen shrub growing to about 1 m in a warm location in the garden, though taller in a conservatory. Leaves velvety and conspicuously veined. Inflorescence is a plumelike spike of deep pink flowers, borne at the branch tips from summer to autumn. Pinch out the tips when young to make bushier plants. Bring in before the first frost and store at a minimum of 5°c, where it will mostly defoliate.

Justicia rizzinii

syn. *Jacobinia pauciflora*
Semi-tender / Sun or dappled shade

Dense, twiggy shrub 25–55 cm high with a similar spread, with small oval leathery leaves and tubular red flowers. 'Firefly' is a more heavily flowering form, with tubular bright red flowers with a golden yellow tip. Tolerates cool conditions well but must be lifted when the first frosts arrive and stored at a minimum of 5°c. If kept warmer, will continue flowering into the winter.

Justicia (Acanthaceae)

Tropical and subtropical America

This large genus comprises more than four hundred species of perennial subshrubs and shrubs, including several popular houseplants that grow well in the garden provided they are protected from desiccating winds in a sheltered corner. They prefer moist, well-drained soil in sun to dappled shade. If they become straggly they can be tip pruned.

Justicia brandegeeana

syn. *Beloperona guttata*
Shrimp plant
Semi-tender / Sun or dappled shade

Small evergreen shrub with small elliptical green leaves, distinguished by its inflorescence, a curved array of soft overlapping pink and yellow bracts that enclose small insignificant white flowers, blooming continuously through summer into autumn.

returned to frost-free conditions before the frosts appear and stored at 5°c on the dry side, where it will usually defoliate. Many cultivars are available, with names like 'Patriot Rainbow' and 'Orange Carpet', though often sold just as *L. camara* or plain *Lantana*.

Maranta (Marantaceae)

Prayer plant

Central and South America and the West Indies

Maranta is a genus of about thirty-two species of evergreen tropical perennials with elliptical leaves that are flat during the day and closed at night, hence the common name. Although commonly grown as houseplants, they work well as a ground cover in a shady, humid corner of the garden during the summer months.

Maranta leuconeura

Tender / Part to full shade

Growing to a height and spread of 25–30 cm and often much wider, spreading across the ground almost prostrate. Leaves are dark green, oval, marked grey or maroon and veined silver, red, or purple; greyish green or maroon on the underside. 'Tricolour' is one of the most commonly available cultivars, though there are many other forms to look out for.

Lantana (Verbenaceae)

Tropical South, Central, and North America, and South Africa

Members of this genus of about 150 species of evergreen perennials and shrubs have attractive small flowers grouped into dense, flat-rounded heads, with the youngest flowers in the centre. *Lantana camara* is the most commonly available form.

Lantana camara

Semi-tender / Full sun

Evergreen perennial with scrambling stems, growing to a height of 1.2–3.5 m in the wild but more like 30–60 cm in the temperate garden. Works well as a standard. Green leaves are quite small and rough to the touch. Flowers appear in shades from red, orange, pink, and yellow to creamy white and often bicoloured due to the florets aging to another colour, giving a very attractive appearance. Prefers light, sandy, free-draining soil in full sun and takes drought well once established. Takes cool temperatures but prefers a hot, sunny corner of the garden for the best flowers. Works well as a container plant,

Nepenthes (Nepenthaceae)

Pitcher plant

Tropical southeastern Asia, Australia, and Madagascar

Plants in this genus of about seventy highland and lowland species are grown for their bizarre flowers, which can be male or female. From the stems arise leaflike expanded petioles, ending in a tendril, which in some species aid in climbing and at the end of which forms a pitcher, considered the true leaf. The pitcher starts as a small bud and gradually expands to form a globe- or tube-shaped trap. In the wild, insects are attracted by their bright

colours and the sweet nectar around the rim of the pitcher. Once inside, the insects and sometimes small rodents slip down the waxy walls and drown in liquid at the bottom of the pitcher, where they are slowly ingested into the plant. Although these plants are from warm, moist areas of the world, I have found that the highland species do well in a cool-temperate climate during the warmest summer months, when nighttime temperatures are above 13°c. They should be hung in a shady area that can be kept moist most of the time and sprayed with water daily to keep the humidity up. In winter they should be kept somewhere warm and humid, such as a bathroom in the house.

Pelargonium (Geraniaceae)

Mostly South Africa and a few from the Middle East
  and Australia

This very well known genus contains 250 species of annuals, perennials, and subshrubs, and countless hybrids, used as houseplants and summer bedding plants since the Victorian period. The foliage is variable though usually light green, rounded or palmate with conspicuous rounded lobes, often covered in fine hairs and darker blotches; some have succulent leaves. The flowers are simple, five-petalled. Most species are semi-tender, taking a minimum of 1°c. For best flowering they need to be sited in a position with full sun and deadheaded frequently. There are four groups:

Zonal: The traditional pelargonium used as a houseplant and for bedding/containers and often referred to as a geranium, which it is not. These plants have rounded leaves, distinctively marked with darker zones, and typical single-petalled, semi-double, or fully double flowers. A good range of interesting hybrids with multicoloured leaves, some quite dazzling, is available.

Regal: Shrubby plants with oval, rounded leaves that are deeply serrated and broadly trumpet- to fan-shaped. The flowers are very exotic looking. These are attractive as specimen container plants if grown well.

Pelargonium tomentosum

Ivy-leaved: Trailing forms, with rounded, often roundly pointed, lobed, succulent, leathery leaves. Good for trailing over the sides of large containers and hanging baskets.

Scented-leaved: Plants with irregular star-shaped flowers and often strongly scented leaves. Very useful in the exotic garden, especially forms like *P. tomentosum* and the large-leaved *P. papilionaceum*.

Pentas (Rubiaceae)

Tropical areas in Arabia, Africa, and Madagascar

Shrubs in this genus of about forty species have green leaves 8–20 cm long and flowers in shades of red, mauve, purple, pink, and white. Many are widely used in the tropics and subtropics as ornamental plants as well as hedging.

Pentas lanceolata

Tender / Full sun

Grows to 1.8 m by 1 m, less in cultivation, with lance-shaped midgreen velvety leaves and large terminal heads of diversely coloured flowers. Prefers well-drained, moist soil. Removing the spent flowers lengthens the flowering season. Usually found as small to medium plants and occasionally as attractive standard plants. I find it best to keep them as container plants brought out into the garden for the summer months. Store at a minimum of 7°C during the winter, when they may partially defoliate.

Peperomia (Piperaceae)

South America and South Africa

This genus encompasses at least one thousand species of evergreen herbs in the pepper family, grown for their ornamental foliage and elongated flower stalks. In warm climates they can be grown as ground covers or as epiphytes.

Peperomia
caperata

Peperomia caperata

Tender / Full shade

Exotic houseplant, growing 15–25 cm high and 15–22 cm wide in a temperate climate. Dark bluish green, heavily veined, puckered, heart-shaped leaves are borne on pinkish red stems. Inflorescence is in the form of bizarre, creamy white, erect, slender spikes of minute, bisexual flowers, giving a solid appearance. As with other houseplants, they must be acclimated to outdoor conditions before planting. They prefer a shady position in humus-rich soil that does not dry out. They can also be tied or pinned to the side of a tree fern. Bring them in before the weather becomes too cold in autumn and store at a minimum of 10°c. Watch out for leaves going mouldy in winter and keep on the dry side; otherwise treat as an annual.

Plectranthus (Lamiaceae)

Africa, Madagascar, Asia, Australia, and the Pacific islands

This genus comprises about 350 species of annuals, perennials, and shrubby herbaceous, semi-succulent, or succulent plants, only a few of which are found in cultivation. Often aromatic, they are generally grown for their handsome evergreen foliage. Several forms make excellent exotic garden plants that also work well in containers and the more spreading forms in hanging baskets. All respond well to tip pruning as they can become somewhat straggly. They prefer moderately fertile soil and must be brought in before frosts appear; alternatively, take cuttings in late summer and overwinter at a minimum of 5°c.

Plectranthus ambiguus

Half-hardy / Sun or dappled shade

Evergreen perennial growing to a height of 60 cm and a spread of 46 cm with light green hairy leaves and stems that root freely as they touch the ground.

Plectranthus argentatus in bloom

Plectranthus argentatus with other plants in a container

Makes a good ground cover and also looks good spilling over the edges of containers and hanging baskets. Erect heads of small, narrow, dark purple flowers appear in late spring.

Plectranthus argentatus

Silvery plectranthus, silver spurflower
Half-hardy / Sun or dappled shade

Handsome, lavish, upright, spreading evergreen shrub from Australia, growing to a height and spread of 60 cm, with silvery-haired square stems and velvety, ovate, silvery grey leaves, up to 11 cm long, with scalloped edges. Terminal candelabras up to 30 cm long bear whorled, tubular, pale lilac-blue flowers up to 1.2 cm long from summer to early autumn. Makes a great foil for dark-leaved plants.

Plectranthus ciliatus

Half-hardy / Sun or dappled shade

Straggly, soft evergreen shrub, spreading by runners and growing to about 20 cm high by 90 cm wide, with square dark purple stems and ovate, pointed, shiny leaves with prominent purple veining and midrib and lightly scalloped margins, with dark purple on the underside. 'Easy Gold' is a recent introduction with deep burgundy stems and golden yellow leaves, irregularly splashed from the centre with green and prominent purple veining, followed by spikes of lavender flowers in autumn. 'Sasha' is a compact plant with variegated foliage, including greens, yellows, gold, and bronze.

Plectranthus madagascariensis 'Variegated Mintleaf'

Plectranthus forsteri

syn. *P. coleoides*
Semi-tender / Sun or dappled shade

Trailing and hanging evergreen perennial to 90 cm long with ovate, hairy, light green leaves, 6–10 cm long, with sharply scalloped edges. 'Marginatus' (syn. *P. coleoides* 'Variegatus') is the best and most commonly available form, with light green leaves and prominent creamy white edges. Looks fabulous in hanging baskets and trailing down the sides of large containers. 'Aureus Variegatus', with beautiful, bold leaves, is irregularly variegated green with chartreuse to yellow margins. Some leaves are without any green colouring.

Plectranthus madagascariensis

Mintleaf
Semi-tender / Sun or dappled shade

Trailing, semi-succulent shrubby perennial from Madagascar, Mozambique, and South Africa, with square stems, growing to a height and spread of 30 cm or more. Leaves up to 4 cm long are fleshy green, occasionally crinkled, coated with white hairs. Terminal spikes of whorled, tubular pale lavender-blue or white flowers up to 1.2 cm across are borne in early summer. Excellent for ground cover or in pots. 'Variegated Mintleaf' (syn. *P.* 'Variegatus') has scented leaves with attractive white variegation. Hybrids include 'Cuban Oregano', a robust plant that forms a compact mound of thick, slightly felted foliage with a fragrant scent when rubbed.

Plectranthus oertendahlii

Candle plant
Tender perennial / Sun or dappled shade

Attractive, trailing, semi-succulent, freely branching, stem-rooting perennial from South Africa, growing to 20 cm tall, then trailing to 1 m, with square reddish purple stems and oval to almost rounded, scalloped, bronzy green leaves up to 4 cm long, with whitish grey veins above and soft velvet purple on the undersides. Open terminal racemes up to 20 cm long of whorled white or light mauve-blue flowers are borne intermittently all year. Looks handsome trailing over the edges of large containers or hanging baskets.

Plumbago (Plumbaginaceae)

Tropical and subtropical regions worldwide

Plumbago includes about fifteen species of tropical semi-evergreen or deciduous shrubs, small trees, perennials, annuals, and woody-stemmed scrambling climbers. Here we are dealing with the latter.

Plumbago auriculata

syn. *P. capensis*
Cape leadwort
Semi-tender / Full sun

Fast growing, vigorous, woody, straggly climber from South Africa, growing to about 6 m tall and 3 m wide, though much less in cool-summer gardens unless grown in a conservatory, where it can become rather rampant! Leaves are simple, light green, and can be rather sparse if the plant is not pruned every year to keep it a more manageable shape. Covered in summer with pale blue five-petalled flowers. Smaller plants can be grown in containers and brought out during the warmer summer months and placed near a south-facing wall. Overwinter at a minimum temperature of 5°c; it will mostly defoliate.

Schefflera (Araliaceae)

Tropical and subtropical regions worldwide

Members of this genus of about nine hundred species are commonly grown as houseplants just about everywhere. Luckily, though, there are scheffleras that can grow outside in the cool-temperate garden. Several of the following were collected by intrepid plant hunters Bleddyn and Sue Wynne-Jones of Crûg Farm Plants in Wales, who are constantly introducing new plants to our gardens.

Schefflera arboricola

Half-hardy / Sun or dappled shade

Delightful evergreen, scandent shrub growing to 4 m tall, though less in the garden, with leaves comprised of seven to eleven ovate, dark green leaflets on wiry stalks. Bears long panicles of pale flowers followed by orange fruit.

Plumbago auriculata, flowers

Schefflera arboricola

Schefflera delavayi

Half-hardy / Sun or dappled shade

Exciting new introduction with fantastic divided leaves on large multistemmed shrub. Should be hardier than other scheffleras, to at least −4°c and maybe lower for short periods.

Schefflera elegantissima

syn. *Dizygotheca elegantissima*
Tender / Sun or dappled shade

Forms an erect branched shrub to 2 m tall. Leaves are long-stalked, palmate, cannabis-like, with seven to ten linear-lanceolate, deeply toothed, shiny dark purple-bronze leaves, up to 15 cm long, that turn dark green with age. Prefers moist, well-drained soil with added humus. Must be overwintered in frost-free conditions at a minimum of 5°c but preferably warmer.

Schefflera gracilis

Half-hardy / Sun or dappled shade

Elegant small shrub growing to only 1.5 m tall in the mountains of northern Vietnam, with leaves comprised of seven to eleven ovate, dark green leaflets, held in two false whorls on wiry purple-tinted stems. Loose panicles of pale flowers in rounded, clustered heads are followed by purple-blue fruit. Protect from cold winds and severe frost when young. Hardiness not yet known but very promising.

Schefflera hoi var. fantsipanensis

Half-hardy / Sun or dappled shade

From the mountains of Phan Si Pan in Taiwan, where it forms an elegant small tree or shrub to 5 m tall, though probably less in the garden. Leaves composed of seven to eleven narrowly ovate to lanceolate, dark green leaflets on wiry purple stems. Terminal racemes of yellow pubescent flowers are held on rounded heads, followed by blue-black fruit. Prefers fertile soil in full sun and dislikes cold wind. Hardiness as yet unknown, though it will probably be as hardy as the others.

Schefflera taiwaniana

Frost-hardy / Sun or dappled shade

An exquisite shrub, eventually forming a small tree 3–4 m tall, with a spreading canopy, though much smaller in the garden. Leaf stems are long and reddish purple, 45–50 cm long, with seven to eight leaflets that taper to a broadly tipped apex. Terminal inflorescence appears in midsummer. Pinch the tips out to keep it bushy. Hardy to at least −5°c and probably lower in a sheltered corner.

Solenostemon (Lamiaceae)

syn. Coleus
Coleus, flame nettle, painted nettle
Tropical and subtropical areas in Africa and Asia

Members of this genus of about sixty species of shrubby plants and countless hybrids are grown for their highly colourful foliage, often variegated and blotched in rainbow colours. These tender perennials, some of which are prostrate or trailing, are traditionally grown as house or conservatory plants but also make excellent annual bedding plants for the garden. The flowers have little importance so should be pinched out as they appear, which also prolongs the plant's life and keeps it bushy. Solenostemons grow well in moist, well-drained soil with added organic matter and look good grouped in clay pots. They are still generally referred to by their old name, *Coleus*, in the trade and by gardeners.

Solenostemon scutellarioides

syn. *Coleus blumei*
Tender / Light shade

This species and its cultivars are the most widely available solenostemons. They have square, semi-succulent stems and nettlelike leaves, and train well as standards. The many cultivars include 'Display', orangish brown leaves with purple veining and yellow edges; 'Juliet Quartermain', soft, toothed, nettlelike leaves coloured rich ruby; 'Mission Gem', rose pink leaves edged with yellow, maroon, and green; 'Peter's Wonder', stunningly marked leaves, deep violet, green, and bright yellow; and 'Pineapple

Beauty', dark maroon leaves tipped golden yellow-green.

Sparmannia (Tiliaceae)

Tropical Africa, South Africa, and Madagascar

This genus includes three to seven species of evergreen shrubs and small trees found growing in open woodlands in their native habitats. They are usually grown in temperate cultivation for their foliage and winter flowers. All prefer moist, fertile, well-drained soil with added organic matter.

Sparmannia africana

Semi-tender / Sun or dappled shade

Large, vigorous, many-branched shrub from South Africa, with hairy stems and leaves, growing to a height of 2–4 m. Leaf stalks are up to 23 cm long, with broadly ovate to rounded and shallowly lobed pale green leaves up to a staggering 46 cm across, somewhat reminiscent of *Paulownia tomentosa* leaves when pollarded. Despite its tropical ancestry, I find *S. africana* grows astoundingly well planted out for the summer months. Even a small cutting taken in spring will reach up to 2 m tall or more by autumn, with huge leaves. Takes temperatures down to freezing for short periods only so should be stored over winter at a minimum of 5°c. Will make an even larger plant the following summer and seems not to mind the root disturbance! 'Variegata' has pale green leaves irregularly marked white and is not quite so vigorous; tends to revert to green so should have these sections pruned out, and is best grown in dappled shade as the white markings tend to burn in full sun.

Top

Sparmannia africana

Above

Sparmannia africana 'Variegata'

Tradescantia (Commelinaceae)

Spiderwort

North, Central, and South America

Plants in this genus of about seventy species of deciduous or evergreen annuals and perennials are grown for their flowers or foliage and range from semi-tender to fully hardy. They are tuberous or fibrous rooted and have fleshy, succulent stems and leaves that can be narrow, pointed, elliptical, or lance-shaped. The three-petalled flowers are held within leaflike or spathelike bracts and have bearded stamens. Many of the forms commonly known as wandering Jew make attractive, fast-growing ground covers for the summer months, most taking temperatures down to 0°C. I have had various forms as returning perennials in my garden for many years, being killed to the ground and returning in mid-to-late spring from their roots, forming a luscious carpet. For the greatest hardiness they need to be grown in a fairly dry situation during the winter months; otherwise dig up and store at a minimum of 5°C on the dry side, watching out for mould on the leaves and stems during the winter.

Tradescantia cerinthoides

Tradescantia fluminensis 'Maiden's Blush'

Tradescantia cerinthoides

syn. *T. blossfeldiana*

Flowering inch plant, moss inch plant

Half-hardy / Dappled shade

Lush, evergreen creeping perennial to about 15cm tall with a sprawling nature and indefinite spread. From southeastern Brazil and northern Argentina, commonly found individually or in clumps in wooded areas and fields in the wild. It has pointedly oval stem-clasping leaves up to 7cm long with shiny dark green upper surfaces and rich purple on the undersides with white hairs. The intermittent blooms are formed in clusters of three-petalled, pink flowers with white centres, surrounded by two leaf bracts. 'Variegata' has lengthwise creamy stipes. Drought- and cold-tolerant once established. Can tolerate heavy shade and full sun.

Tradescantia fluminensis

syn. *T. albiflora*

Wandering Jew

Half-hardy / Sun or dappled shade

Popular evergreen perennial with trailing, rooting stems to 60 cm or more, with oval, pointed, fleshy leaves up to 5 cm long, glossy green above and sometimes tinged purple underneath, that clasp the stem. 'Albovittata' has bluish green leaves with variable, broad white stripes. 'Maiden's Blush' has green foliage with brilliant cerise to white irregular bands at the leaf nodes. 'Variegata' has green leaves irregularly striped creamy white.

Tradescantia pallida

syn. *Setcreasea purpurea*

Purple heart, purple heart tradescantia, purple queen

Half-hardy / Sun or light shade

Popular ground cover in subtropical parts of the world, hailing from eastern Mexico. Evergreen, sprawling perennial, growing up to 30 cm high by 60 cm or more wide, though usually less in cool-summer climates. Has dark purple stems and fleshy leaves about 2.5 cm wide by 7.6–12.7 cm long.

Pinkish white flowers appear in summer. Prefers well-drained soil. Dig up before first frost and store at a minimum of 5°c on the dry side, keeping an eye out for mould during the winter months. Will also take freezing temperatures in the garden if grown in a dry situation.

Tradescantia spathacea

syn. *Rhoeo discolor*

Boat lily, Moses-in-his-cradle

Tender / Dappled shade

Short-stemmed, clump-forming perennial hailing from Mexico, Guatemala, and Belize, having rosettes of fleshy, erect leaves up to 35 cm long in warm conditions, less in cool-summer climates. Leaves are broadly spear-shaped, dark green and purple underneath. Small creamy white flowers appear in bracts at the leaf bases all year. 'Vittata' (syn. 'Variegata') has handsome cream and pink, vertically striped leaves. Prefers moist, organically rich soil and looks good planted en masse. Prone to slug damage. Takes cool summers well but must be brought in before first frost and kept on the dry side during the winter months and checked regularly for mould.

*Tradescantia
pallida*

Tradescantia zebrina

syn. *Zebrina pendula*

Wandering Jew, inch plant

Semi-tender / Sun or dappled shade

Popular houseplant from Mexico, prostate with trailing, rooting stems to 60 cm and more. Leaves, 4–8 cm
long, longitudinally striped dark green with two silver bands, purple on the underside. Many forms are
available with striations in different colours.

*Tradescantia
zebrina*

Palms and Palmlike Plants

Palms are the most evocative of all plants that can be grown in the exotic garden, redolent of the long, hot days and blue skies of Mediterranean and tropical climates. Their distinctive silhouette epitomises the exotic look and creates great impact in the garden. Botanically speaking, palms belong to the Arecaceae (previously Palmae), a family of monocotyledonous plants. Their characteristic shape usually makes them easy to recognise, although they are sometimes confused with palm look-alikes such as cordylines, yuccas, and even bananas! Cordylines and cycads are included later in this section under their own family names to avoid confusion. Yuccas are included in the earlier section with cacti, succulents, and other spiky plants.

Left

Cycas revoluta, new growth

Palms

Interest in growing palms in temperate climates has expanded dramatically since the late 1980s as avid and experimental gardeners have realised that palms are not restricted to subtropical and tropical countries. The most cold-hardy palms are usually found growing at high elevations or in cold inland areas that do not benefit from a maritime influence, or they grow at the cooler edges of their natural distribution.

Many specialist nurseries now retail at least a dozen different species and forms of palms, from nonhardy to very hardy. Even borderline palms can be grown in cool-temperate gardens if you are prepared to either wrap them during the winter months or bring them into frost-free conditions, giving them just enough water to keep them going. According to palm pundit and pioneer Martin Gibbons of the Palm Centre in London, more than one hundred species will survive outside in the British Isles and warmer areas in southern England. Some like *Trachycarpus fortunei* (windmill palm) will take biting lows of −17°C, although most are far less hardy. There will always be a range of palms that would be suitable for your location, especially if they are sited well and you have an awareness of your local climate and/or garden microclimate.

Many factors affect the ability of palms to grow in temperate gardens. The age of the palm is important: the more mature the plant, the better its ability to take cold. It is advisable to grow small palms for a few years in a container, improving their hardiness, before planting them out permanently. Soil makeup also matters: palms can take colder

Brahea armata

conditions if their roots are not sitting in water, hence free-draining soils are preferable to clay or boggy soils. With the latter, grit and sand should be added to aid drainage. Organic matter in the form of compost and well-rotted manure are beneficial to both.

The health of the palm you purchase is important, too. Plants with yellowing leaves or stunted growth, as well as plants that are severely pot-bound, will be harder to establish once in the ground. Choose plants that look as though they are growing well and have been kept in good condition by the retailer. Palms in pots full of weeds usually have not been fed so should be avoided, unless you know they are a bargain!

The length of a cold spell also has a big impact on palms. For instance, an occasional quick dip down to −8°c for a few hours will have little effect apart from some browning of the frond tips, whereas a prolonged period of say −3°c will do far more damage as it will get into the heart of the palm.

Your garden microclimate and the amount of time you are prepared to spend on protecting your palms in cold weather will also have a great impact on the type of palm you can grow. If you have a south-facing slope with good protection from cold, biting winds, and are blessed with very free-draining soil, you will have several degrees advantage over a garden on flat ground without a shelter belt and with clay soil. Palms sheltered by other trees and shrubs are more likely to fare better than those that are exposed to the full brunt of cold, desiccating winds.

Palms growing in a container are more susceptible to frost, as the root-ball is not protected by the ground, so should be brought into a shed, where they can tolerate being without light during the winter months when they are dormant. Container plants that are too large to move should be wrapped with burlap and straw or something similar during freezing periods. Small palms in the ground are best completely covered during the winter months, which also protects them from cold, desiccating winds. The cover can be removed during warm spells.

Most palms are rather slow growing; luckily, though, many specialist nurseries carry large specimens of all sizes, imported from warmer growing regions like Italy and Florida or diverse places like Chile and Morocco, in enormous containers for those who have a big crane to lift them!

Brahea (Arecaceae)

Baja California, Mexico, and Central America

This genus of eleven species of small-to-medium-sized palms, normally single stemmed, is named after Tycho Brahe, a Danish astronomer. Members are found growing on dry, open slopes and rocky canyons in their native habitat. All love dry heat, hence must be grown in a full sun position in exceedingly well-drained soil.

Brahea armata

Blue hesper palm, Mexican blue palm
Frost-hardy / Full sun

Slow-growing, solitary-trunked palm, up to 12 m tall with a crown of up to thirty leaves in its native habitat, much less in temperate climates. Handsome, stiff, palmate leaves, up to 1 m in diameter, are an alluring pale greyish blue colour; often considered to be the bluest of all the palms. Hardy to around −10°c when larger. Works well as a container plant that should be kept next to the house in winter. Prefers a position that is dry in winter but moist in summer.

Brahea edulis

Guadalupe palm, palma de Guadalupe
Frost-hardy / Full sun

Solitary, bare trunk 45 cm in diameter, slow growing, up to 12 m tall in its native habitat, much shorter in a temperate climate. Shiny green palmate leaves are 90–180 cm long and 90 cm wide, divided into seventy to eighty segments. Similar conditions to above. Suited to pot culture.

Butia (Arecaceae)

Jelly palm, Pindo palm, wine palm
Northern Argentina, southern Brazil, Paraguay, and
  Uruguay

All members of the genus *Butia* are native to grasslands, dry woodlands, and savannahs of South America.

Butia capitata

Butia capitata

Jelly palm
Frost-hardy to hardy / Sun or shade

Very tropical looking and handsome palm instantly recognisable by its thick, stout trunk and long pinnate leaves, which range from light green to bluish grey, growing to 1.5–3.5 m long (especially when grown in the shade) and strongly recurved toward the ground. Grows up to about 7.5 m tall in ideal conditions, though usually much less in cool-summer climates. Leaf stems are 0.6–1.2 m long, with spines along both edges. Plants grown on poor, dry

soil will have much smaller leaves, and plants grown in full sun are often more compact. Prefers fertile, moist soil and grows well in high-rainfall regions, although drought and wind tolerant. Most cold tolerant of all the butias, taking lows of −10°C to −12°C for short periods when mature. Makes an excellent container plant as it is rather slow growing. Fruits from this palm are used to make jam (jelly in the United States), hence the common name.

The apparent variability in specimens of *B. capitata* is also due to the fact that there are several other species in this genus that are very similar in appearance. *Butia yatay* resembles *B. capitata* but grows taller with a thicker trunk; some experts assert that *B. eriospatha* and *B. paraguayensis* are subspecies of *B. yatay*. All of these hybridise readily and it is suspected that many of the plants offered as *B. capitata* may be hybrids.

Chamaedorea (Arecaceae)

Mexico, Central and South America

This genus contains some one hundred species of mostly small understorey palms that are indigenous to rain forests. Both single-stemmed and clumping palms with either pinnate fronds (feather palms) or undivided fronds are included. Many are highly sought after and are grown throughout the tropics and subtropics for landscape ornamentation. The following will take cool-temperate cultivation if given optimum growing conditions.

Chamaedorea microspadix

Cold-hardy bamboo palm
Frost-hardy / Dappled to full shade

Graceful, suckering, multitrunked palm with clean slender trunks, to a height of 2.5 m in ideal conditions. Pinnate leaves are up to 60 cm long with papery matte leaflets 20 cm long and 2.5 cm wide arranged sparsely on the stems. Drooping inflorescence appears in summer. Prefers rich, moist, well-drained soil. Hardy to −9°C for short periods, though it is advisable to wrap with fleece below −3°C. Grows well as a container plant and is often used as a houseplant.

Chamaedorea radicalis

Frost-hardy / Dappled to full shade

Chamaedorea growing up to 3 m high in its native habitat, though usually under 1.2 m in cultivation, with thick and leathery leaves. One of the most notable things about this attractive palm is that the inflorescence arises from near or below ground level. Appears to grow well in cool climates. Hardy to about −6°C or −8°C when larger.

Chamaerops (Arecaceae)

European fan palm

Western Mediterranean region, southwestern
Europe, and northwestern Africa

Chamaerops is a genus of just one species of shrubby palm, the northernmost naturally occurring palm in the world. Its fronds look as though they spring straight out of the ground, although trunks can form in temperate cultivation; in fact, I have one with a rather stately single 1.75-m trunk!

Chamaerops humilis

Frost-hardy to hardy / Full sun

One of only two indigenous palms growing in Europe (*Phoenix theophrastii* is native to Turkey and Crete), native to the hot, dry hills and mountains facing the Mediterranean. Clump-forming, rarely single-stemmed palm growing 2–3 m or taller, though often less in cool-summer climates. Palmate leaves are triangular fan-shaped to 60 cm in width

and length and are deeply divided into multiple segments that are themselves split at the tips on spiny stems. Small clusters of ochre yellow flowers appear close to the trunk hidden by the leaves in summer. Prefers sandy, well-drained soil. Very drought and wind tolerant once established. Will take lows of −10°C for short periods with little damage if grown in a sheltered location on exceedingly well-drained soil. A blue narrow-leaved form, 'Cerifera', is native to the Atlas Mountains in Morocco. 'Vulcano' is a bushy form from the Aeolian Islands in Italy with short, very stiff, palmate leaves that are sometimes silvery green on the underside.

*Chamaerops
humilis*

Jubaea (Arecaceae)

Chile

This genus encompasses just one species of palm native to the warm-temperate coastal regions of Chile. In the wild, populations have been significantly reduced by overharvesting. This species has the thickest trunk of any palm known, able to reach a staggering 1.5 m in diameter! The largest indoor palm in the world, in the centre of the temperate house at the Royal Botanic Gardens, Kew, is a member of this species, 16 m high and still growing.

Left

Jubaea chilensis

Below

Livistona australis

Jubaea chilensis

Chilean wine palm, coquito palm

Frost-hardy / Full sun

Solitary, slow-growing, bare, massive-trunked palm up to 25 m high with a crown 5 m across in ideal conditions. Pinnate, stiff, feathery leaves are dull green with grey-green underneath and up to 1.5 m wide and 3.6 m long. Overall stature is considerably less in cool-temperate cultivation. Smaller specimens, 2–3 m tall, can be purchased, though most enthusiasts begin with even smaller plants. Hardy to at least −10°c for short periods when mature. Protect small plants with fleece in cold weather. Prefers a south-facing position on well-drained soil. Has the most southerly distribution of all the American palms.

Livistona (Arecaceae)

Australia and southeastern Asia

Members of this genus of some thirty species of medium to tall palms are found in tropical and subtropical areas and are indigenous to locations as diverse as streambanks, swamps in woodlands, rain forests, and inland gorges, where they often form extensive colonies.

Livistona australis

Australian cabbage palm
Frost-hardy / Full sun

Growing to 30 m high with a grey trunk up to 30 cm wide in its native Australian habitat. Palmate, deeply split leaves are 1.5 m long. Considerably smaller in cool-temperate climates. Hardy to around −5°C for short periods. For most areas it is advisable to grow it as a container plant that can be moved close to a house in freezing periods or kept in a cold greenhouse or shed. *Livistona chinensis* (Chinese fan palm) is less hardy, taking lows of around −3°C, so it is advisable to grow it as a container plant.

Nannorrhops (Arecaceae)

Afghanistan, Saudi Arabia, Iran to Pakistan

The one species belonging to this genus is extremely common in its native habitats but extremely rare in cultivation, though it is now becoming more readily available. It must have a hot, dry situation in full sun to thrive.

Nannorrhops ritchieana

Mazari palm
Frost-hardy / Full sun

Slow-growing palm, only recently brought into cultivation, with a usually subterranean trunk that occasionally reaches 1–2 m high. Leaves palmate, deeply split, greyish blue-green. Best grown as a container plant for several years before planting out, to improve its hardiness. Prefers a south-facing position near a building or wall with well-drained soil. Takes −10°C for short periods when mature and much lower when dry; otherwise protect with fleece below −4°C or overwinter in a cold greenhouse or outhouse.

Nannorrhops ritchieana

Phoenix (Arecaceae)

Tropical and subtropical Africa, Canary Islands, Crete, and western Asia

Members of this genus of about seventeen species of feather-leaved palms can be either solitary or clustered.

Phoenix canariensis

Canary Island date palm
Frost-hardy / Full sun

Very large palm hailing from the Canary Islands, growing to about 20 m tall, with a crown spreading to 9 m across in its native habitat. Crown is composed of a large number of graceful arching green fronds up to 6 m long, sharply spined at the base. Many years ago on Grand Canary I got two 5-cm-long spines in my leg; the spines had to be surgically removed, leaving me with twelve stitches. Be warned! Although a

Above

*Phoenix
canariensis*

Right

*Phoenix
dactylifera*

much smaller palm in cool-temperate cultivation, they are well worth growing. Purchase one with as large a base plate (where the leaves appear from) as you can find, as older plants are much hardier than small juvenile ones. Prefers good well-drained soil and takes cold well once established, although regular watering in summer will produce a bigger plant. The most famous—and probably the most mature—Canary Island date palms are growing in the Tresco Abbey Garden. Hardy to −8°c when established. In very cold weather tie the fronds together to protect the growing point.

Phoenix dactylifera

Date palm

Half-hardy / Full sun

Growing up to around 21 m high, with a graceful spreading crown up to 9 m across, in its native habitat in the Middle East, though much less in temperate cultivation. Trunk is slender, often suckering. Grey-green fronds have sharply pointed stiff leaflets reduced to spines near the trunk. Hardy to −5°c for short periods in a very sheltered location; otherwise grow as a container plant.

Rhapidophyllum (Arecaceae)

Southeastern United States

The sole member of this genus is very popular among palm enthusiasts in cold climates for its extraordinary ability to tolerate cold.

Rhapidophyllum hystrix

Needle palm, porcupine palm

Hard / Sun or dappled shade

Very slow-growing, small, suckering, shrubby fan palm that is virtually trunkless, with an overall height of about 2 m. Over time will form an impenetrable thicket. Green palmate leaves, deeply indented with blunt tips, grow up to 1 m across on mature plants, otherwise less. Prefers well-drained, moist soil with added organic matter, though tolerant of dry conditions. One of the world's hardiest palms, taking lows of −20°c. Protect from frost when young.

*Rhapidophyllum
hystrix*

Phoenix roebelenii

Dwarf date palm, pygmy date palm

Semi-tender / Sun or shade

Graceful, small palm from Southeast Asia, growing to 3 m high by 2.4 m wide, very popular as a houseplant. Solitary or multiple trunks are covered with the remains of old leaf bases. Arching green fronds have lower leaflets reduced to sharp spines. Responds well to a high-nitrogen feed in early summer. Takes lows of down to 0°c for very short periods only, hence is best grown as a container plant that is brought in for the winter months. Can be purchased as small trunkless plant or as specimen.

Phoenix theophrastii

Frost-hardy / Full sun

Slow-growing palm from Crete and Turkey, with solitary or multiple bare trunks to 20 m in its native habitat. Attractive silver-grey-green fronds are 3–3.5 m long, with vicious spikes at the base. Requires free-draining soil. Hardy to −8°c for short periods when mature.

Rhapis (Arecaceae)

Southeastern Asia

Right

Rhapis humilis

This genus contains about eight species of small palms native to southeastern Asia from southern Japan and southern China south to Thailand. The Japanese first began collecting *Rhapis* from China in the seventeenth century, exclusively for the highest levels of nobility and the imperial palaces, where they were grown as indoor palms. As with many other palms, *Rhapis* are dioecious, having male and female plants.

by frost, usually regrows from the roots. Also excellent as an indoor plant as it takes low light and grows slowly into a magnificent specimen over the years.

Rhapis humilis

Slender lady palm

Semi-tender / Dappled shade

Slow-growing, clump-forming palm with slender stems wrapped in tightly woven light brown fibres, up to 4.5 m high and 3 m wide in its native environment, though much less in temperate cultivation. Green palmate fronds are 60–90 cm across and divided into many drooping segments. Hardy to 0°C for short periods. Prefers well-drained soil in dappled shade near a wall or building. Works well as a container plant that can be brought in during cold spells. All the plants grown for cultivation come from root suckers as female plants are not known.

Rhapis excelsa 'Variegata'

Rhapis excelsa

Lady palm

Half-hardy / Dappled to full shade

Palm with multiple slim stems wrapped in tightly woven light brown fibres, growing to 3 m tall by 2.4–4.5 m wide in its native habitat, though much less in temperate cultivation. Palmate, shiny green fronds are constructed of five to eight stiff segments with blunt tips. 'Variegata' has fronds with white stripes and is not hardy. Prefers well-drained soil. Will tolerate temperatures of −5°C for short periods, especially if protected with fleece in a sheltered corner. Grows well under trees. Keep roots on the dry side in winter. In cold areas grow as a container plant that can be brought in during cold spells. If killed to the ground

Sabal (Arecaceae)

Southeastern United States, South America, West
 Indies, and Bermuda

This is a genus of about sixteen species of single-stemmed or stemless palms, indigenous to low-lying regions and swampy areas in subtropical and tropical forests.

Sabal minor

Blue palmetto, dwarf palmetto, scrub palmetto
Frost-hardy / Full sun

Slow-growing, trunkless palm to 3 m high by 3.5 m wide in its native environment in the southern United States, much less in cool-summer areas. Fronds form at ground level or just above the crown and are stiff, glaucous, greenish blue, split into many narrow segments, up to 1.5 m in length and width. Prefers moist, well-drained soil but is drought tolerant when mature. Cold-hardy down to −15°c for short periods. Protect with fleece below −5°c and keep roots dry during the winter months.

Sabal palmetto

Cabbage palmetto, palmetto palm
Frost-hardy / Full sun

Single-trunked, slow-growing palm to 15 m or taller, with a crown 3.7–5 m across in its native environment, though much less in cool-temperate cultivation. Pinnate green fronds are up to 3.7 m long including the stem and up to 1.8 m across, with drooping leaf segments that are split to half the width of the frond. Prefers well-drained soil in a sunny position. Hardy to about −8°c for short periods; protect with fleece below −4°c and keep the roots dry in winter. Tolerant of salt-laden air, hence works well in coastal areas. State tree of South Carolina and Florida. Common name "cabbage palmetto" comes from the fact that the growing heart of the new fronds, or terminal bud, superficially resembles a cabbage and is extracted as a food.

Serenoa repens,
blue form

Serenoa (Arecaceae)

Southeastern United States

Serenoa repens is the sole species currently classified in the genus *Serenoa*. It forms large colonies in its native habitat, particularly in coastal areas, hence is very tolerant of salt-laden winds. Humans have known the benefits of saw palmetto for centuries; the indigenous peoples of Florida used the berries as a staple food, and the plant was included in the medicine man's arsenal of healing herbs.

Serenoa repens

Saw palmetto
Frost-hardy / Full sun

Multistemmed, branching or subterranean-trunked palm from the southeastern United States, 90 cm to 4.5 m high by 2 m wide, that forms dense clumps and creates large colonies in its native habitat, especially in coastal areas. Grows to smaller proportions in cool-summer areas. Fronds are fan-shaped, divided into multiple stiff segments with rather spiny stalks, and different forms can be yellowish green to bluish green and silver-green. Best to grow as a container plant for some years before planting out. Mature plants will take lows of −7°c for short periods but should have protection below −3°c. Prefers well-drained soil.

Trachycarpus (Arecaceae)

Fan palm
Northern India through Nepal, northeastern India, Burma, China, northern Thailand, and Vietnam

Members of this genus of nine species of solitary small to medium-sized palms grow in the wild in an approximate band along the lower Himalaya, often on terrain above 2000 m, and are the most popular of all palms for temperate gardens. Their chief attraction for growers and palm enthusiasts is their cold hardiness and ease and speed of growth. They have been grown for more than a hundred years in the British Isles, and though they were first introduced into Holland in 1830, the best-known introduction was by the intrepid English plant collector Robert Fortune, who acquired his first windmill palm (*Trachycarpus fortunei*) in 1894 on the island of Zhoushan (formerly Chusan) off the coast of eastern China. He sent some seeds to the Royal Botanic Gardens, Kew, where they grew successfully as tropical palms in the palm house. These early palms fetched high prices, but as more seeds were introduced from China, the price fell, igniting a passion for palms and exotic plants in general, creating the exotics boom of the British Victorian period.

The fan palm's cold hardiness is legendary and well tested, and as it is readily available it is usually the first hardy palm that gardeners purchase. It grows as far north as Scotland in the British Isles and Vancouver in southwestern Canada. Although it takes cold well, its main enemy is cold desiccating winds, which damage the leaves, so this palm should be grown in a sheltered position, where it prefers being moist during the growing season.

Martin Gibbons has been one of the main collectors of little-known species of *Trachycarpus* on various expeditions he has made in recent years, and is introducing them to the marketplace. These species appear to have a cold tolerance similar to *T. fortunei*, making them potentially excellent additions to the temperate garden. Other species to look out for in the future, aside from the ones mentioned below, are *T. oreophilus* and *T. princeps*, found on a difficult and hair-raising expedition by Gibbons and Tobias W. Spanner; no seed has yet been brought out of China.

Trachycarpus fortunei, flowers

Trachycarpus fortunei

syn. *Chamaerops excelsa*
Chusan palm, windmill palm
Hardy / Sun or part shade

Solitary, fibrous leaf-base-covered trunk grows to 15 m, producing up to 30 cm of trunk in a year once established. Fan-shaped leaf is palmate, dark green, up to 1 m across, with forty to fifty segments, forming a compact crown of thirty to forty palmate leaves on long stalks. Leaves on juvenile plants have five or six deep green leaves up to 30 cm across. Both male and female are required to set fruit. Flowers are yellow and on female trees after flowering produce hundreds of blue-black kidney-shaped seeds with a white bloom that hang down like small grapes. Prefers moist, well-drained soil when young. Hardy to −17°C for short periods.

Trachycarpus latisectus

syn. *T. sikkimensis*
Windermere palm
Hardy / Partial shade

Named after the Windermere Hotel in Darjeeling by Martin Gibbons and Tobias W. Spanner, this species was only recently described and brought into cultivation; it is threatened in its native environment in the Sikkim Himalaya. Trunk is bare; very large, leathery, palmate leaves have up to seventy distinctive leaflets that are glossy, broad, up to 5 cm wide. Requires rich, loamy soil.

Trachycarpus nanus

Hardy / Full sun

Only member of the genus that rarely produces a trunk and then only to 30 m or so, with a maximum overall height of 60–90 cm. Pretty species with very deeply cut, sometimes green or blue, palmate leaves, with up to thirty segments. Growing at 1800–2300 m, it is very cold-hardy, although it is slow growing and initially somewhat more difficult than most other members of the genus. Requires a very well-drained soil. Native to Yunnan Province in China, though now rare through predation by goats, which eat the inflorescence and thus destroy its ability to reproduce. First reported by Abbé Delavey in 1887 and subsequently rediscovered by Martin Gibbons and Tobias W. Spanner on a small expedition in 1992; now starting to appear in cultivation in Europe and the United States.

Trachycarpus takil

Kumaon fan palm

Hardy / Full sun

Close relative of *T. fortunei* only recently brought into cultivation and nearly extinct in its native habitat in the province of Uttranchal Pradesh (Kumaon) in central northern India, where the species grows at an altitude of 2400 m. *Trachycarpus takil* is a big palm, broadly similar in appearance to *T. fortunei* but larger in all its parts and probably a good few degrees hardier, thus making it the hardiest in the genus. Trunk fibres sometimes fall naturally, leaving a bare trunk. *T. takil* has more numerous leaf segments than *T. fortunei* (up to sixty); these are rigid and split the blade to a fairly regular depth. Area where the leaf stalks join the top of the trunk is much tidier in *T. takil* than in *T. fortunei*, which is ragged and messy.

Trachycarpus wagnerianus

Miniature Chusan palm

Hardy / Full sun

Grows to a height of 3–7 m, slowly at first but then after three to four years explodes into growth, especially in moist, rich soil. Small, stiff, pinnate leaves are up to 0.75 m long on a mature plant, more like 30 cm long when juvenile. Leaf segments are edged with white woolly fibres. Leaves are so stiff that they are unaffected by windy conditions.

Trithrinax (Arecaceae)

South America

Members of this small genus of only three species are native to the subtropical regions of Brazil, Bolivia, Paraguay, Argentina, and Uruguay. In their native habitats they often endure cold and severe drought, except for *T. schizophylla*, which inhabits moist forest. The name derives from the Greek *tri*, three, and *thrinax*, trident, a reference to the stiff, spine-tipped leaves.

Trithrinax acanthocoma

Brazilian needle palm, spiny fibre palm

Frost-hardy / Full sun

From a distance, somewhat similar to *T. fortunei* but with stiffer leaves. Very attractive palm growing to a height of 6 m in its native habitat in Argentina and southern Brazil. Trunk consists of fibres covered with thorny old leaf bases. Leaves are green, stiff, palmate, and multisegmented. Prefers moist, well-drained soil; keep roots dry in winter. Hardy to about −8°c for short periods when mature but should be protected below −3°c, especially when young.

Trithrinax campestris

Caranday palm

Frost-hardy / Full sun

Clump-forming, occasionally single-trunked, with a spined and fibrous burlaplike covering, growing to a height of 2 m and taller in semi-arid areas of northern Argentina and Uruguay that get very cold.

Fronds are up to 46 cm across, palmate, glaucous, blue-green, very stiff, ending in sharp, weaponlike spines. Prefers moist, very well-drained soil; keep roots dry in winter. Hardy to −10°c when mature, less for juvenile plants.

Washingtonia (Arecaceae)

Southwestern United States and northwestern Mexico

The two species of fan palms in this genus have trunks that are clothed in their old leaf bases, which hang like a petticoat.

Washingtonia filifera

Cotton palm, petticoat palm, Washingtonia palm
Half-hardy to frost-hardy / Full sun

Named after the American president George Washington, grows to a height of 18 m and a crown spread of up to 8 m, though considerably smaller in cool-temperate cultivation. Leaves pinnate, grey-green, with threadlike filaments along the edge of each segment. When mature can take lows of −6°c for short periods; juvenile plants will only take lows of around −3°c and should be surrounded with fleece filled with straw during the winter, unless you live in a mild area. Works well as a large container plant that can be brought into a cold greenhouse or outhouse for the winter months; also makes a good conservatory palm.

Washingtonia robusta

Cotton palm, Mexican Washingtonia palm, thread palm
Half-hardy to frost-hardy / Full sun

Often used as street planting in southern United States. Grows to a height of 25 m or more in its native habitat in Sonora and Baja California and the southern United States, with a trunk that bulges at the ground and becomes more slender as it approaches the crown. Leaves are palmate, gently drooping at the leaf tips, rich shiny green, to about 1.5 m long by 1.2 m across, borne on leaf stems with vicious sawtooth spines.

Washingtonia filifera

Washingtonia robusta

Cordylines

Cordylines are distinguished by their tough, colourful leaves, used by native peoples throughout the Pacific region to wrap food before cooking in a pit, and also used as clothing and building material, and in medicine. These plants look best grouped together at varying heights in the shelter of other plants' foliage.

Cordyline (Dracaenaceae/ Agavaceae)

Australia, India, the Pacific region, and tropical America

This genus encompasses fifteen species of evergreen trees and shrubs that are grown for their foliage, especially the tropical forms such as *Cordyline terminalis*, which come in almost every colour imaginable. Unfortunately, we cannot grow these in our temperate gardens other than in a container placed outside for the summer months or as summer bedding. Luckily for us, many colourful varieties of *C. australis* are now available to rival the tropical forms. All prefer organically rich soil.

Cordyline australis

Cabbage tree
Frost-hardy / Full sun

Striking tree that can reach 6–12 m tall (much less in cooler areas), with multiple trunks topped with dense, arching leaves 1–2 m long and up to 5 cm

Cordyline indivisa

leaves to protect the crown. Fleece can be wrapped around as well for extra protection.

Cordyline banksii

Forest cabbage tree
Frost-hardy / Dappled shade

A smaller cordyline, 3–4 m tall, with somewhat lax, drooping leaves. Flower spikes, tinged with pink, are not as dense nor as abundant as those of *C. australis*. Requires moist, deep soil in dappled shade to replicate its forest habitat. Hardy to −9°c.

Cordyline indivisa

Broad-leaved cabbage tree, mountain cabbage tree
Frost-hardy / Dappled shade

Cordyline indivisa, another New Zealand native, has much thicker leaves and is much more exotic than *C. australis*. Species name, meaning "undivided," refers to the unbranching trunk. Tends to be shorter than *C. australis*, up to 1.5 m tall, with very large leaves up to 1.5 m long and 10–15 cm wide that are soft to the touch and that when older tend to have a broad yellow stripe down the middle, with a central vein that is predominately red or yellow. Large inflorescence is white and pendulous. When young is slightly more tender than *C. australis* and more difficult to grow, but once established is probably hardier. Does not like being grown in a pot. There are some good examples in the Tresco Abbey Garden. Hardy to −10°c for short periods when mature. Prefers high rainfall to grow well.

Cordyline kaspar

Three Kings cabbage tree
Frost-hardy / Sun or dappled shade

This cordyline has a short, stout trunk compared to the others and is widely branching, to a height of 2–3 m. Stiff leaves appear on the branches in dense clusters 50–90 cm long and 5–8 cm across. Highly scented flowers are followed by berries, which are white streaked with blue. 'Bronze' has bronze foliage, as its name suggests, and is slightly less hardy than the plain version, probably to −6°c and lower. Grows well in a container.

wide or more. Huge inflorescences are creamy white and highly scented, with a divine fragrance of lilies in late spring, followed by tiny white fruit in autumn. Early settlers in New Zealand ate the crowns of this plant as a vegetable, giving it its common name. Young plants grow as a single stem until they flower, which causes them to branch. This happens many times to form very large heads when mature. Hardy to −10°c. If main shoot is killed by heavy frost, will reshoot from the base.

Many cultivars are now available: 'Purpurea' (purple Torbay palm) has bronze-purple evergreen leaves (darker on some forms than others) on a graceful palmlike plant growing 1–3 m tall. 'Purple Tower' is a vigorous, glossy, more deeply red form of 'Purpurea'. 'Sundance' has swordlike green leaves with an attractive pink base and midrib. 'Torbay Dazzler' has leaves that are brightly variegated green, yellow, and red. As a rule the coloured forms are less hardy. In cold weather tie and wrap up the

Cycads

Cycas circinalis

Cycads are an ancient group of seed-producing plants that have existed since the Jurassic period more than 200 million years ago, a period often referred to as "the age of the cycads," when they would have been a common sight in the more equitable regions of Earth. Unfortunately, there are relatively few left, and many of these face the possibility of extinction in the wild. Because of their overall appearance cycads are often mistaken for palms and tree ferns, but they are not related in any way.

In warmer climates cycads make excellent specimen plants and often attain great size. In cooler climates they are interesting plants for the conservatory that can either live there permanently or be taken outside for the summer months. There are a few intrepid cycad enthusiasts in the British Isles who have risked growing them permanently outside, taking the vagaries of our cold, wet winters. One of them is exotics enthusiast Peter Reid, who gardens in Lymington, Hampshire, a mere 500 yards from the sea on the south coast of England. He has conducted trials with several species of cycads since 2000 with some interesting and promising results.

His cycads are grown in a raised bed some 60 cm high filled with an exceedingly well-draining mix, consisting of 45 per cent 20-mm gravel, 45 per cent sharp sand, and 10 per cent garden compost. This amount of drainage is absolutely essential, allowing rain to drain away quickly in winter. During the summer months from May onward and before the new leaves emerge, he starts a regular feeding regimen, making up for the lack of organic matter in the raised bed.

His garden has experienced overnight lows of around −6°c; the cycads have shown some leaf damage at temperatures lower than −3°c to −4°c, with almost total defoliation at −6°C. He believes that covering the leaves with horticultural fleece or a large cloche would dramatically reduce the amount of leaf damage by preventing water freezing on the leaves. However, even with total defoliation, all the *Cycas* species he is growing push up a new flush of leaves during the following summer. It is too early to say whether the two *Macrozamia* species he is growing outside will recover in the same way after total defoliation. Where cycads typically produce a flush of leaves, macrozamias push up one leaf at a time, inevitably making the process of recovery slower. I have a *Cycas revoluta* and an *Encephalartos lehmannii*, which I overwinter in an unheated polytunnel; both have taken −6°C with no leaf loss at all.

Like so many exotic borderline plants that have recently been introduced, only experimentation and time will tell those that are happy in cool-temperate cultivation. I'm sure over the next few years more cycads will come onto the market, adding to the range of weird and wonderful plants that can be grown in cool-temperate climates.

Cycas (Cycadaceae)

Madagascar to southern and southeastern Asia

Cycas comprises about fifteen species of cycads, found mainly on dry, often stony or rocky slopes in arid or semidesert areas as well as in dry, open woodland habitats. All have whorls of stiff, leathery leaves with linear to lance-shaped leaflets issuing from trunks of varying sizes. They are generally cultivated for their palmlike appearance. In warmer climates, they make excellent specimen plants. In cool climates, they are interesting plants for the conservatory, overwintered frost-free and brought out for the summer months. Or you can experiment with permanent planting in the garden on exceedingly well-drained soil.

Cycas circinalis

False sago, fern palm, queen sago, sago palm
Half-hardy / Full sun

Like other cycads, resembles a palm tree. In its native habitats in southern Asia, India, and on some Pacific Islands, can be found along the seashore or inland in open grasslands, dense forests, and occasionally mountainous areas. Solitary, cylindrical, grey-brown trunk can grow to 6 m in the wild. Mature specimens often branch, producing handsome plants with multiple crowns consisting of bright green, glossy fronds up to 3 m long that darken with age, with narrow leaflets 30 cm long, though much less in temperate cultivation.

Cycas panzhihuaensis

Frost-hardy / Sun or dappled shade

Hailing from the Panzhihua Prefecture of southern Sichuan Province, China, this cycad is similar to *C. revoluta* but with longer fronds that are more upright and elegant. Grows in fairly dry, closed, low woodland or shrubland thickets on moderately to steeply sloping sites. Stout trunk has a thick coat of orange-brown wool, reaching 1–3 m tall in the wild, with thirty to eighty fronds in the crown, which are narrow, 70–150 cm long, with dull to semiglossy, bluish to greyish green leaflets. Among the most cold tolerant of all the Chinese cycads. In its native China, withstands severe frosts and often damp at the same time. Peter Reid grows two specimens outside, one with a caudex the size of a large grapefruit, the other the size of a golf ball. About 50 per cent leaf burn occurs at −6°C. A new flush of leaves is typically produced in late June.

Cycas revoluta

Japanese sago palm
Frost-hardy / Sun or dappled shade

Slow-growing, robustly trunked cycad from Japan, often suckering and branching with age in the wild, where it grows to a height and spread of 1–2 m or more. Whorled leaves are fairly soft and upright when young, gradually reclining as they mature, with narrow, glossy, dark green leaflets. Peter Reid has been growing two outside for several years, one

with a caudex 90 cm tall, the other the size of a honeydew melon. Both have endured overnight lows of −6°C. With spring and summer feeding, a new flush of leaves is produced about the end of July.

Cycas taitungensis

Emperor sago, prince sago
Frost-hardy / Full sun

Large plant in the wild, found growing on rocky exposed hillsides in Taitung Prefecture, southeastern Taiwan, to 3–4.5 m tall by 1.5–3 m wide. Fronds are up to 1.5 m long with leathery, narrow leaflets, looking similar to *C. revoluta*. Peter Reid has two juvenile plants outside, both with caudexes the size of a golf ball. They survive a few degrees of frost, but the fronds are severely burnt below −6°C unless protected. New flush of leaves is typically produced at the end of May.

Dioon (Zamiaceae)

Mexico, Honduras, and Nicaragua

Dioon is a genus of eleven described species of dioecious, arborescent, very slow-growing, palm-like shrubs with cylindrical stems, often with many leaves. The leaf bases are persistent or shedding, thus leaving smooth bark. The genus name is derived from the Greek *dis*, two, and *oon*, eggs, in reference to the paired seeds.

Dioon edule

Chestnut dioon, Mexican cycad, palma de la virgen, virgin palm
Frost-hardy / Sun or dappled shade

Very slow-growing cycad with a short, stocky trunk up to 1.9 m tall, averaging 1 mm of growth a year. Found growing in tropical deciduous oak forests in Mexico and Central America in harsh, dry conditions. Leaves are up to 1.9 m in length, with dark

Cycas revoluta

Dioon edule

Bluish brown caudex is topped with a rosette of rigidly stiff bluish grey leaves with viciously pointed leaflets. Found growing on semi-arid sandstone slopes in its native habitat in eastern Cape Province, South Africa, where the summers are hot and dry and the winters are cold and wet, with frosts being common. Probably hardy to at least −5°C and possibly lower for short periods, especially if kept dry and protected from the severest frosts. Prefers exceedingly well-drained soil. Wild populations are threatened by habitat destruction and collection of plants for horticultural and medicinal uses.

Macrozamia (Zamiaceae)

Australia

The dioecious cycads in this genus of some thirty-eight species are usually found growing in eucalyptus forests on poor soil. The genus name is derived from the Greek *makros*, large, and *zamia*, a genus of cycads. As a genus they are not as prickly as other cycads. The large red-orange seeds were a traditional food source for the indigenous Australians, who had to carefully prepare them as the seeds are toxic.

Macrozamia communis

Frost-hardy / Sun or shade

Large cycad from New South Wales, Australia, with either a subterranean caudex or a short columnar trunk. Forms extensive colonies as an understorey plant in eucalyptus forests and woodlands, on poor sandy soil near the coast, where rain falls throughout the year, hence should enjoy a maritime climate. Fronds can reach up to 2 m above ground level and are green, elegant, and arching, with sharply tipped leaflets. Produces leaves one at a time, unlike most cycads, which produce all their new leaves in one flush. Very fast growing and prolific in cool-summer climates, producing a lush crown. Hardy to at least −5°C and lower for short periods, especially if kept dry and protected from the severest frosts. Some frond damage is sustained at −4°C, and severe damage at −6°C. Damaged fronds are gradually replaced during the summer.

blue-green to grey-green, very stiff, leathery leaflets, tapering to a viciously pointed tip. Peter Reid has a plant with a small 2.5 cm caudex; covered with a cloche through the winter, it suffers no apparent leaf damage at −6°C.

Encephalartos (Zamiaceae)

Tropical and southern Africa

This genus includes some forty-six species of cycad, all of which are endangered. The genus name is derived from the Greek words *en*, within, *cephali*, head, and *artos*, bread, referring to the use of the center of the stem to make a breadlike, starchy food.

Encephalartos lehmannii

Karoo cycad
Frost-hardy / Full sun

Clump-forming medium-sized plant with a height and spread of 2 m or more, less in cool cultivation.

Encephalartos lehmannii

Macrozamia moorei

Frost-hardy / Full sun

This one gets big! A palmlike cycad in the wild, growing up to 4 m high at the apex of the trunk, topped with a rosette of up-curving, blue-green leaves that can reach up to 1.8 m in length. Extremely stout caudex can reach a staggering 80 cm in diameter. Peter Reid's plant arrived as a caudex some 60 cm tall, with no leaves and little root. After several years it has not completely leafed out yet but is nevertheless doing well, having taken −6°C with some leaf damage, though with protection this should be minimal. Paul Spracklin in Essex has a specimen producing leaves up to 1.2 m in length that has been through a few winters with little damage, permanently planted out.

Macrozamia communis

Macrozamia moorei

Perennials and Ground Covers

Exotic gardening is all about creating an illusion of being somewhere other than in a temperate garden. With this style of gardening, many of the more commonly grown herbaceous perennials can be used in conjunction with less traditional, more flamboyant plants, or bedded out with tender perennials and annuals, to create an illusion that they are all exotic. For instance, when perennials such as hostas and ajugas are planted next to gingers, they take on a completely different feel. Alternatively, a selection of those mentioned in this section planted with phormiums and hardy palms would give a Mediterranean feel. Some of these perennials, such as gunnera, rheum, and rodgersia, on their own also give a really tropical, lush feel to the garden.

Many of the following plants are readily available at your local garden centre; the more unusual plants can be obtained from speciality nurseries. At the end of the day, it is a purely personal choice—there are no rules, so create your own style!

Left

Gunnera manicata,
flower spike detail

Acanthus (Acanthaceae)

Bear's breech

Temperate and tropical regions of the Old World

Above

Acanthus mollis

Right

Acanthus spinosus

Many of the approximately thirty species of perennials and subshrubs in this genus are indigenous to dry areas, especially the Mediterranean region. They are grown in cultivation for their dramatic, bold architectural foliage and handsome upright flower spikes. The species described here have several hybrid forms that are worth searching for. They are cold tolerant, taking lows of $-15°c$ in their stride, though they prefer milder winters. All prefer full sun to dappled shade in moist, well-drained, humus-rich soil, though they stand drought well once established. The acanthus leaf is a motif often used at the tops of columns and pillars and in architectural ornamentation on many classical Roman and Greek buildings.

Acanthus mollis

Hardy / Sun or dappled shade

Stately, semi-evergreen perennial growing to a height of 1.2 m or more with long, deeply toothed, soft-spined, glossy bright green leaves up to 60 cm long by 30 cm across. Handsome spikes of funnel-shaped white flowers flushed with light purple are borne in toothed mauve bracts in summer.

Acanthus spinosus

Hardy / Sun or dappled shade

Bold, stately perennial growing to a height of 1.2 m, with dark, glossy green, large, broad, arching, deeply cut, spiny-pointed, architectural leaves. Imposing spires of funnel-shaped, white, often mauve-tinted flowers in spiny bracts are borne freely in summer.

Agapanthus (Agapanthaceae)

African lily, blue lily, lily of the Nile
Southern Africa

Agapanthus comprises ten species of fleshy-rooted, clump-forming perennials, of which some are evergreen. These strong-growing plants are popular for their fine foliage and striking heads of tubular flowers, which are usually held well above the foliage on upright stalks in late summer. Once established, they flower for years. The genus name is derived from the Greek *agapé*, love, and *anthos*, flower. They enjoy full sun in moist, well-drained soil but will tolerate shade, just about any soil, and periods of drought once established. They naturalise readily in the garden and also make excellent container plants, where they tend to flower more profusely when congested. The narrow-leaved forms tend to be hardier than those

Agapanthus
'Ellamae'

Agapanthus
'Snow Cloud'
with *Verbena*
bonariensis
(behind to left)

with wider leaves. In cold areas, mulch in winter to protect the roots from severe frost.

Until the Headbourne hybrids became freely available in the horticultural trade in the 1950s and 1960s, the most commonly encountered agapanthus were forms of the large-flowered *A. africanus* or *A. praecox* (previously known as *A. umbellatus*). Only a few agapanthus species and cultivars are covered here, as they are dealt with in great detail in two Timber Press books, *Agapanthus for Gardeners* by Hanneke van Dijk (2004) and *Agapanthus: A Revision of the Genus* by Wim Snoeijer (2004).

Agapanthus africanus 'Albus'

Frost-hardy / Full sun

Bluish green leaves give rise to stems up to 76 cm tall with very large heads of the purest white flowers from midsummer to early autumn. Frost-hardy if grown in dry soils.

Agapanthus cultivars and hybrids

Frost-hardy / Full sun

Most of the following cultivars and hybrids are frost-hardy if grown in dry soils; mulch in cold

Below

Agapanthus
'Tinkerbell'

Below right

Agapanthus
inapertus, flower
head

weather. *Agapanthus* Ardernei hybrid has green leaves that give rise to 70-cm stems with heads of pure white flowers in summer. 'Blue Giant' has rich green, straplike leaves that give rise to stems up to 1.2 m tall with rounded umbels of open bell-shaped, luxuriant, rich blue flowers from middle to late summer. 'Buckingham Palace' is stately, one of the last to flower. Green leaves give rise to stems 1.5 m tall with rounded flower heads of delicious deep blue flowers. 'Ellamae' is a deciduous to semi-deciduous vigorous perennial that makes a large clump of gracefully arching green strap-like leaves with dark bluish violet flowers in umbels to 1 m and taller, in high summer. Water moderately during the summer months. 'Jack's Blue' is a recent hybrid introduction from New Zealand with large heads of intense deep purple-blue flowers on upright stems 1.2–1.5 m tall from midsummer to autumn. 'Snow Cloud' is evergreen, with stems 92 cm–1.2 m tall and large, extremely floriferous heads of pure white flowers in summer. Not as hardy as some of the others, taking lows of −5°c, which will cause it to defoliate, hence should be grown in the warmest gardens with a winter mulch or as a container plant brought into frost-free conditions for the winter. 'Tinkerbell' is a small agapanthus with greyish green leaves edged with cream, and pale blue flowers carried on 35-cm stems. Delightful plant for a prominent position. Works well in raised well-drained beds or as a container plant where it can be appreciated more closely.

Agapanthus inapertus

Drakensberg agapanthus
Frost-hardy / Full sun

Dense, clump-forming, deciduous perennial with erect, blue-green, strap-shaped leaves up to 70 cm long. From late summer to early autumn, stiff upright stems bear pendent umbels, 10–15 cm across, of heavily drooping tubular flowers, intense purple-blue, occasionally white, up to 4.5 cm long, on stiff upright stems up to 1.5 m tall. Hardy to about −5°c for short periods, hence should be mulched well and grown in the warmest areas of the garden. My clump was given to me by Mike Nelhams of the Tresco Abbey Garden, where frost

is virtually unheard of. I grow this gem as a container plant that is brought into an unheated polytunnel for the coldest months of the year.

Ajuga (Lamiaceae)

Bugle
Europe, Asia, Africa, and Australia

Members of this genus of about forty species of perennials and annuals from the mint family (Lamiaceae) spread quickly by fleshy stems and self-layering. They make excellent ground covers but can become invasive in some areas. The most commonly grown is *A. reptans* and its many cultivars, an excellent plant for a lush exotic effect, especially the dark purple forms that mimic more tropical ground covers. They prefer moist, well-drained soil in full sun to dappled shade and can take drought for short periods. All are hardy but prone to mildew. *Ajuga reptans* and its cultivars are the most commonly grown, forming dense mats.

Ajuga reptans

Hardy / Sun or dappled shade

Vigorous, semi-evergreen, low, creeping, carpet-forming perennial from Eurasia, growing to a height of 10–20 cm and a spread of 30–90 cm or more. Foliage is spoon-shaped, green, often purple

Ajuga reptans

tinted, especially in sun. Short spikes of attractive blue flowers are borne in spring. There are many cultivars. 'Atropurpurea' has small rosettes of gloss, deep purple-bronze foliage. 'Braunherz' has exceedingly gloss, dark purple-bronze foliage. 'Burgundy Glow' has grey leaves with reddish markings. 'Burgundy Lace' has foliage variegated with bronze-purple, cream, and green. 'Catlin's Giant' is very exotic looking, with large bronze-green foliage and tall attractive flower spikes. 'Jungle Beauty' is another luscious form with large green-bronze leaves with red margins. 'Jungle Bronze' has an upright habit with big, undulating-edged, lustrous bronze leaves. 'Multicolor' (syn. 'Rainbow') has foliage marked green, cream, pink, and purple. 'Purple Brocade' has leaves variegated with purple. 'Variegata' has leaves variegated with cream.

Amicia (Fabaceae)

Andes to Mexico

Amicia is a genus of seven perennial herbs or shrubs with tuberous roots in the pea family. The most commonly available is *Amicia zygomeris*, which is a fine plant for the back of the exotic border or as a specimen on its own and well worth hunting out.

Amicia zygomeris

Frost-hardy / Full sun

Handsome if not striking perennial herb always admired by visitors to my Norfolk garden, growing to a height of 1.2–2.1 m on hollow stems. Groups of four-pinnate leaves up to 8 cm long, heart shaped, which miraculously close up at night, are held on downy stalks up to 10 cm long. Greenish yellow pea-like flowers with maroon markings, up to 30 mm wide, are borne from late summer to autumn. Prefers humus-rich, moist, well-drained soil. Hardy to −10°C for short periods; mulch in prolonged cold spells.

Amicia zygomeris and flower detail

Astelia (Lilaceae)

New Zealand, islands in the Southern Hemisphere, and Australia

The twenty-five species of clump-forming, evergreen perennials in this genus are grown for their stunning sword-shaped, somewhat phormium-like leaves with a silvery sheen. The flowers are insignificant. They grow in alpine to lowland forest areas, where many are epiphytic. All prefer moist, free-draining soils in dappled shade.

Astelia chathamica

Half-hardy to frost-hardy / Dappled shade

Evergreen, clump-forming perennial hailing from the Chatham Islands (New Zealand), growing to a height and spread of 80 cm–1.6 m, with broad, arching, swordlike, deeply furrowed leaves, with a

Astelia chathamica 'Silver Spear'

striking silvery sheen, up to 1.6 m long and 7.6 cm wide. 'Silver Spear' is even more silvery. Although often considered to be on the borderline of hardiness, one growing in my Norfolk garden has not just survived but thrived for more than a decade, easily taking lows of −5°c and short periods down to −10°c.

Astelia nervosa

Half-hardy to frost-hardy / Dappled shade

Evergreen, clump-forming perennial growing to 60 cm tall, up to 2 m when in flower, and 1.5 m wide. Long, gracefully arching, silvery greenish grey leaves. 'Red Devil' is a striking red form. 'Westland' is an outstanding form with reddish bronze and silver foliage.

Bergenia (Saxifragaceae)

Afghanistan to southeastern Tibet and the Himalaya

Bergenia, named after the eighteenth-century botanist Karl August von Bergen, is a genus of eight
species of evergreen perennials and many cultivars.
They usually have large, rounded, spoon-shaped,
leathery leaves with indented veins that sprout from
tough, woody, fleshy, terrestrial rhizomes. They are
essential plants for ground cover in situations with
part to full shade, giving a very lush, tropical look
to the garden with their large leaves, and the added
benefit of handsome spikes of five-petalled, mostly
pink flowers in spring when little else is in flower.
The hybrids come in shades from white through
pink to mauve and red. Bergenia are tolerant of a
wide range of soils but prefer humus-rich, moist,
well-drained soil in partial to full shade. Remove
all damaged foliage in late winter to early spring.
Promptly remove spent flowering stems.

Bergenia 'Ballawley'

Hardy / Part to full shade

Evergreen, clump-forming perennial growing up
to 60 cm tall, with glossy, broadly ovate, midgreen
leaves up to 30 cm long that turn a very handsome
purple reddish bronze in winter, especially when
frosted. Red flower stems are borne from mid to
late spring topped with bright crimson bell-shaped
flowers.

Bergenia ciliata

Hardy / Part to full shade

Evergreen, clump-forming perennial growing to a
height of 30 cm and a spread of 50 cm with rounded, dark green leaves up to 30 cm long, densely
covered in short hairs. Erect spikes of pinkish white
flowers are borne in spring. In frost-prone areas the
foliage dies back to the ground, so it is advisable to
lightly mulch around them.

Bergenia cordifolia

Hardy / Part to full shade

Evergreen, clump-forming perennial growing to a
height of 45 cm with somewhat puckered, rounded
to heart-shaped midgreen to dark green leaves up
to 30 cm long, with a purple blush in winter. Pale
to dark pink flowers are borne on fleshy stems up
to 60 cm tall. 'Purpurea' is a form with leaves that
are a richer purple-red and with bell-shaped flowers that are magenta-purple. Most frequently found
bergenia, and probably hardiest, coming as it does
from Siberia!

Crambe (Brassicaceae)

Eurasia

Crambe, whose name is derived from the Greek word for cabbage, is a genus of twenty species of annuals and perennials in the cabbage family. All are vigorous plants with large leaves on fleshy stems. One in particular, the most commonly available species, *C. cordifolia*, is a spectacular architectural plant, giving a strong Mediterranean effect in summer with its enormous, cloudy sprays of delicate gypsophila-like flowers, especially when looked at with a blue sky behind.

Crambe cordifolia

Giant gypsophila, heartleaf crambe, ornamental sea
  kale
Hardy / Full sun

Perennial growing to a height of 1.2–2.2 m, with huge, greyish green, glossy, puckered, tooth-edged, lance- to heart-shaped leaves up to 35 cm long. In spring, enormous, billowing heads of small white flowers are borne. Prefers humus-rich, well-drained soil but will tolerate poor soil. Hardy to −15°C.

Cynara (Asteraceae)

Canary Islands, northwestern Africa, and the
  Mediterranean

The genus *Cynara* contains ten species of perennials and herbs that resemble giant thistles. With their large, often spiny leaves and tall heads of thistlelike flowers, they are imposing ornamental plants for the exotic garden. The stems and immature flower heads of some species, the best known of which is *C. scolymus* (globe artichoke), can be eaten. The most commonly grown is *C. cardunculus*.

Cynara cardunculus

Cardoon
Hardy / Full sun

Statuesque, perennial, clump-forming plant growing to a height of 2.4 m with enormous, thick,

*Cynara
cardunculus*

architectural, pointed, lobed, greyish silver-green leaves up to 1.2 m long by 60 cm across. The flower heads, borne in summer, are thistlelike, purple, held well above the foliage and much loved by bees. May need staking, as it can become rather top-heavy when in flower. Prefers well-drained soil in a position with protection from high winds. Hardy to −15°C.

Darmera (Saxifragaceae)

syn. *Peltiphyllum*
Western United States

Darmera contains just one species, found growing on mountainous streamsides in its native habitat.

Darmera peltata

syn. *Peltiphyllum peltatum*
Hardy / Sun or dappled shade

Rhizomatous, slowly spreading herbaceous perennial, growing to a height and spread of 90 cm–2 m, larger in its natural habitat. A very tropical-looking plant that is dead hardy! Flowering stem is

Darmera peltata

produced before foliage in late spring, topped with rounded heads of small, usually pink, occasionally white flowers. Long leaf stalks are topped by large, dark green, rounded, deeply lobed, coarsely toothed, veined, parasol-like leaves up to 60 cm across. Prefers a moist to boggy location but will take drier situations, in which case it will be smaller. Well worth growing if you have the room.

Echium (Boraginaceae)

Canary Islands and Madeira, the Mediterranean, Africa, and western Asia

This is a genus of about sixty species of rosette-forming, hairy, annuals, evergreen biennials, perennials, and shrubs, native to stony hillsides, cliffs, open woodland, and grassy areas. They are grown for their often one-sided panicles or spikes of roughly funnel- or bell-shaped flowers in shades of blue, purple, white, yellow, or red. They are imposing, statuesque plants for the exotic garden. Unfortunately, the larger forms from the Canary Islands are less frost-hardy than the more commonly grown European species, hence can be grown only in warmer areas or gardens with a microclimate with little frost, or they can be grown with protection against a south-facing wall. Echiums are a good choice for sheltered seaside gardens, preferring dry, well-drained, poor soils and only needing watering in the driest spells. They are among the top ten plants grown in the Tresco Abbey Garden in southwest England, where *E. pininana* flowers within fifteen months from seed, occasionally reaching a height of 6 m.

Echium candicans

syn. *E. fastuosum*
Pride of Madeira
Half-hardy / Full sun

Large, showy, open, often rounded, woody-based biennial reaching 1.5–2.5 m tall and 1.5–3.5 m wide on coarse, heavy branches. Leaves are grey-green, rosetted, lance-shaped, prominently veined, 15–25 cm long. Spikelike clusters of bluish purple flowers are borne above the foliage from spring to summer. Hardy to −5°C for short periods with protection.

Echium pininana

syn. *E. pinnifolium*

Frost-hardy / Full sun

Giant, imposing plant hailing from La Palma laurel forests in the Canary Islands. Rosette-forming biennial or occasionally short-lived perennial growing to 4 m tall and 90 cm wide on a single, tough, woody stem. Leaves are elliptical to lance-shaped and covered in rough, silvery hairs. In summer tall spires of funnel-shaped blue flowers appear, much loved by bees. This is the echium often seen growing in gardens of southwestern England. Frost-hardy in dry soils.

Echium pininana × E. wildpretii

Frost-hardy / Full sun

Hybrid between *E. wildpretii* and *E. pininana* that is lower growing than either parent, growing to a height of about 2 m with a low rosette of silver, hairy, spear-shaped leaves. 'Pink Fountain' is topped with a flower spike covered with small pink funnel-shaped flowers. 'Snow Tower' is a spectacular white-flowered form originating in a Guernsey garden. Hardy to −5°c for short periods with protection.

Echium wildpretii

Frost-hardy / Full sun

Another spectacular plant from the Canary Islands growing to a height of 2 m by 60 cm on a single woody stem, surrounded with a dense rosette of narrow, lance-shaped, light green silver-haired leaves up to 20 cm long. From late spring to summer, topped with a dramatic, dense column of funnel-shaped crimson-red flowers. Hardy to −5°c for short periods with protection.

Echium wildpretii,
flower spike

Epimedium (Berberidaceae)

Barrenwort, bishop's hat, bishop's mitre, horny goat
weed

Asia (particularly China) and the Mediterranean
region

The approximately forty species of evergreen and deciduous, clump-forming, rhizomatous perennials belonging to the genus *Epimedium* are grown in cultivation for their attractive foliage and small spring flowers. By virtue of their rhizomatous roots and sturdy constitution, epimediums are tough ground covers that can compete with tree roots and withstand dry shade, though they still give a very lush, exotic look to an otherwise difficult area of the garden and are a good alternative to ivy. All prefer cool dappled shade under deciduous trees in humus-rich, well-drained soil and can tolerate drought once established, though they do require moisture to produce the lushest foliage. All are fully hardy, although frost may damage the young flowers and foliage. This fascinating family of ground covers is described in detail in *The Genus Epimedium and Other Herbaceous Berberidaceae* by William T. Stearn (2002).

Epimedium acuminatum

Hardy / Dappled shade

Evergreen, clump-forming, spreading, rhizomatous perennial growing to 30–40 cm high by 90–100 cm wide or more, with leaves divided into three lance-shaped to narrowly ovate, serrated leaflets, 5–18 cm long. Young leaves midgreen, with reddish brown markings, turning green with age. Long, spurred flowers with white sepals and purple petals, 3–4 cm across, are borne on wiry stems above foliage from midspring to early summer.

Epimedium ×*versicolor*

Hardy / Dappled shade

Evergreen, clump-forming, rhizomatous perennial growing to a height and spread of 30 cm, with leaves normally divided into five to fifteen midgreen, heart-shaped, spiny-edged leaves up to 9 cm long, bronzy red when young. From late spring produces pink to yellow flowers with orange-red tinted spurs

up to 2 cm across. 'Neosulphureum' has pale yellow flowers. 'Sulphureum' has slightly darker yellow flowers with longer spurs.

*Epimedium
×versicolor*

Epimedium ×*warleyense*

Hardy / Dappled shade

Evergreen, clump-forming, spreading, rhizomatous perennial growing to 40–50 cm high by 0.75 m or more wide, with leaves divided into five to nine ovate, sparsely spiny, midgreen leaflets, bronzy when young, 7–12 cm long. Flowers spurless, yellow with stunning coppery orange-red sepals, 1.5 cm across from mid to late spring. A most delightful ground cover, bred by Miss Ellen Willmott in the early twentieth century.

Equisetum (Equisetaceae)

Horsetail

Worldwide except Australia and New Zealand

The curious plants in this genus of about thirty species of somewhat rushlike, flowerless perennial herbs are the relics of an ancient family known through fossils from as early as 325 million years ago, the Upper Carboniferous era, the geological period when the remains of plants were laid down that became the vast coal deposits in use worldwide today. All species consist of erect, cylindrical, segmented, somewhat bamboolike stems, which have a very architectural and unmistakable appearance. Equisetums are found growing in wet places, such as standing water, shallow ponds, ditches, marshy areas, wet meadows, and moist woodlands, as well as drier areas. They are grown more as a curiosity than as gardenworthy plants, as they can become invasive; hence they should be grown only as containerised pond marginals or in terra-cotta pots standing in a dish of water, where they will look rather imposing and statuesque with their upright habit.

Equisetum hyemale

Equisetum hyemale

Hardy / Sun or dappled shade

Decorative, evergreen, colony-forming horsetail reaching 90 cm–1.5 m tall with rigid, rough, rounded, unbranched, dark green, leafless stems ringed with black bands. Small, pointed cones are borne at stem ends. Variety *robustum* is an impressive form growing up to 3 m tall. Both forms travel far and wide and so should be carefully sited; otherwise they make excellent container plants. Grow in any soil except the driest.

Eryngium (Umbelliferae)

European coastal regions, Turkey, North Africa, China, Korea, and central Asia

Some of the 230 or so species of hairless annuals, biennials, and deciduous and evergreen perennials in this genus make excellent Mediterranean-style garden plants with their stunningly architectural, somewhat spiny, thistlelike appearance in foliage and form. They make good cut flowers and dry well. Most prefer moist, well-drained soil in full sun and will tolerate drought once established.

Eryngium agavifolium

Frost-hardy / Full sun

Agavelike, evergreen, rosette-forming perennial from Argentina, growing to a height of 1–1.5 m or more by 60 cm, with sword-shaped, prominently and sharply toothed, olive green basal leaves up to 0.75 m long. Flowering stems are lightly branched, bare and cylindrical, topped from summer to early autumn with umbels of tightly packed greenish white flowers with entire to spiny-toothed bracts. Looks dramatic growing through gravel. Hardy to at least −10°C.

Eryngium giganteum

Miss Willmott's ghost
Hardy / Full sun

Taprooted, rosette-forming, fairly short-lived herbaceous perennial hailing from the Caucasus to Iran,

growing to 90 cm or more tall by 36 cm wide, with long-stemmed, heart-shaped to triangular, deeply toothed, spiny, midgreen to dark green basal leaves up to 15 cm long. Greenish silvery mauve-blue flower heads are surrounded by up to ten large silvery white bracts. Very imposing, statuesque plant.

Eryngium pandanifolium

Frost-hardy / Full sun

Tufted, clump-forming evergreen perennial indigenous to Argentina, Brazil, Uruguay, and Paraguay, growing to a height of 2–3 m, with linear, narrow, serrated-edged, silvery green leaves, 1–1.5 m long. From summer to midautumn, many upright stems bear cylindrical umbels, 1 cm long, of short-bracted purplish brown flowers. Hardy to −5°c although it will take lower temperatures; foliage will become damaged but will regrow in spring.

Eryngium planum

Hardy / Full sun

A clump-forming plant growing from 50 to 90 cm tall, featuring basal rosettes of elliptic to oblong, cordate-based, serrate, dark green leaves up to 10 cm long, with smaller, spiny-lobed, blue-tinted stem leaves. The small, stemless, greyish blue flowers are tightly packed heads surrounded by narrow, spiky, bluish green bracts up to 2.5 cm long. This is a tap-rooted plant which transplants poorly, and is therefore best left undisturbed once established. It prefers dry sandy soils in full sun.

Eryngium proteiflorum

Frost-hardy / Full sun

Taprooted, rosette-forming, evergreen perennial from Mexico, growing to 90 cm or more tall by 45 cm wide, with narrow, linear, spiny-edged, silvery green basal leaves with a white midrib, 13–30 cm long. In autumn multibranched stems are produced bearing cylindrical umbels of bluish grey flowers with lance-shaped, spiny-edged, lustrous, silver-white, protea-like bracts up to 10 cm long. Prefers well-drained, dry and poor to moderately fertile soil. Dislikes wet winter conditions. Hardy to about −5°c. Works well as a container plant that can be brought into a drier situation for the winter months.

Above left

Eryngium planum

Above

Eryngium agavifolium

Euphorbia (Euphorbiaceae)

Tropical to temperate areas worldwide

This large and diverse genus contains around two thousand species of annuals, perennials, biennials, shrubs, and trees, both evergreen and deciduous. They come in many diverse forms and shapes according to their habitat, ranging from succulent cactuslike species to leafy cool-temperate forms. Here a few of the most gardenworthy forms that fit well with a Mediterranean style of exotic gardening are described. Many of the more tender forms can either be grown in containers brought out for the summer months or bedded out in the garden for the summer season. All species contain a poisonous milky sap that can cause severe irritation if it comes into contact with skin or eyes.

Euphorbia amygdaloides

Wood spurge
Hardy / Dappled shade

Hailing from temperate Eurasia, rhizomatous, bushy, spreading, soft, leafy, evergreen perennial with reddish green stems, growing to a height of 60–80 cm, with dark green, matte, long spoon-shaped to ovate leaves, red underneath, 2.5–8 cm long. Terminal sprays of yellowish green flowers are borne from spring to summer. Variety *robbiae* has more robust, larger, darker green foliage, while 'Purpurea' has thicker leaves that are dark green strongly tinted purplish red, and new growth in a lighter red-purple-wine colour. Makes a good ground cover. After it flowers, remove the stems to encourage new growth. Prefers moist, humus-rich soil, though it can take drought for short periods. Hardy to −15°C.

Euphorbia characias

Hardy / Dappled shade

Upright, evergreen subshrub from southern Europe and the Mediterranean, with erect, densely woolly, purplish green stems, woody at the base, growing to a height and spread of 1.2 m. Linear to ovate, bluish grey-green leaves up to 13 cm long are arranged spirally along stems and densely crowded near tips

but sparse at base. Dense heads of cupped, pale yellow-green whorled bracts contain dark purple-brown nectar glands from late winter to early summer. Subspecies *wulfenii* and its cultivars are generally used more in cultivation, with heads of bright yellow-green bracts containing yellow-green nectar glands. 'John Tomlinson' has large, bright green, almost spherical heads. 'Lambrook Gold' has cylindrical, bright golden green heads.

Euphorbia dulcis

Frost-hardy / Dappled shade

Rhizomatous, herbaceous perennial hailing from temperate Europe, with erect stems, growing to a height and spread of 30 cm with narrow, lance-shaped, downy, often dark purple-bronze-tinted leaves up to 8 cm long, with yellow-green, sometimes red-tinted, inflorescences. By far the more exotic gardenworthy form is 'Chameleon', a stunning plant. Oblong leaves emerge dusky purple in spring, mature to a rich burgundy-purple and acquire a reddish tinge in autumn. Showy bracts appear in late spring and are usually tinged reddish purple with greenish yellow centres. Hardy to −10°C and lower.

Euphorbia griffithii

Frost-hardy / Sun or dappled shade

Vigorous, rhizomatous, herbaceous perennial from Bhutan, Tibet, and Yunnan Province, China, with erect stems that are reddish green when young and grow to a height and spread of 90 cm. Leaves are linear, lance-shaped, dark green with a prominent red midrib, and 9–15 cm long. In autumn the foliage turns yellow. 'Dixter' is a marvellous form with dark foliage, with a strong coppery tint and dusky orange heads in summer. Selected by the well-known garden writer Christopher Lloyd at his garden at Great Dixter, it grows to a height and spread of 80 cm. The inflorescence has vivid orange-red bracts in summer, which become more copper toned with age. 'Fireglow' is a stunning form with vivid orange-red bracts in summer, growing to a height of 75 cm. Prefers moist, free-draining, humus-rich soil. Hardy to −10°C.

Euphorbia mellifera

Honey spurge
Frost-hardy / Full sun

Handsome, imposing, rounded evergreen shrub with stout shoots, growing to a height and spread of 2 m or more, with oblong to narrowly lance-shaped midgreen leaves with a prominent cream midrib, to 20 cm long. Richly honey-scented heads of golden yellow–terra-cotta flowers with small bronze-green floral bracts are produced in terminal clusters up to 10 cm across from late spring to early summer. (The name *mellifera* is derived from the Latin name for honey bee, *Apis mellifera*.) Prefers light, free-draining soil. Hardy to −5°C and lower for short periods.

Euphorbia myrsinites

Creeping spurge, donkey tail
Frost-hardy / Full sun

Clump-forming, evergreen perennial hailing from southern and eastern Europe to Turkey, growing to a height of 25 cm and a spread of 50 cm with semi-prostrate stems clothed in spirally arranged, round-ed, pointed, finely toothed, succulent, fleshy, bluish grey-green leaves, up to 6 cm long. Terminal heads of bright yellow flowers 5–8 cm across in spring. Prefers light, free-draining soil. Hardy to −10°C.

Euphorbia stygiana

Wolf milk plant
Frost-hardy / Full sun

Handsome, imposing, clump-forming, domed, woody-based perennial, strongly branched, with stout shoots, often forming a small tree in its native habitat in the Azores, growing to a height of 2.5 m. Leaves are oblong, narrowly lance-shaped, dark bluish green, 10–15 cm long, with a prominent cream midrib. Pale yellow flowers are borne spring to summer. Prefers moist, well-drained soil. Hardy to −5°C for short periods.

Farfugium (Asteraceae)

Green leopard plant, leopard plant
Eastern Asia

This genus contains just two species of rhizoma-tous, evergreen perennials in the daisy family that grow near streams and waterways and near the seashore in their native habitat. In cultivation, they are grown for their handsome, often striking foliage, which has a luxuriant tropical appearance, especially some of the variegated forms. In warm climates they produce orange-yellow daisy flowers from autumn to winter or when grown in a con-servatory or as a houseplant. They prefer moist, humus-rich soil in dappled shade for the lushest foliage, though they will survive in full sun if kept well watered in hot weather.

Farfugium japonicum

syn. *F. tussilagineum*, *Ligularia japonicum*
Frost-hardy / Sun or dappled shade

Loosely clump-forming, evergreen herbaceous per-ennial from Japan, growing to a height and spread of 60 cm, with long-stalked, kidney-shaped, rounded,

Farfugium
japonicum
'Argenteum'

Farfugium japonicum

glossy rich green leaves, 15–30 cm across. The Japanese eat its boiled stems with soy sauce as a side dish (called *kyarabuki*). 'Argenteum' (syn. 'Albovariegatum') has green and grey leaves irregularly edged in white. 'Aureomaculatum' has attractive random acid-burn-like yellow spots. 'Crispatum' (syn. 'Cristata') has green leaves with crumpled, crimped, and crested edges. 'Ryuto' is a Japanese selection that looks as though it were suffering from nuclear fallout, with heavily contorted and twisted green leaves, a true oddity for admirers of very bizarre plants. 'Lunar Landing' is a form of 'Ryuto' that is even more incredible, with heavily pockmarked and cratered leaves, fantastic!

Farfugium japonicum 'Aureomaculatum'

Geranium
maderense

Geranium (Geraniaceae)

Cranesbill

Temperate areas worldwide

This genus of some three hundred species of annuals, biennials, and herbaceous evergreen to semi-evergreen plants is often incorrectly confused with the genus *Pelargonium*. Geraniums are one of the mainstays of the cottage garden style, but the two described here work well in the exotic garden. They are the rather tender *G. maderense*, which grows to perfection in the Tresco Abbey Garden in south-west England, and the hardier though somewhat similar *G. palmatum*, which grows well in my Norfolk garden. Both prefer humus-rich, very well-drained soil.

Geranium maderense

Semi-tender / Sun or dappled shade

Robust, highly attractive, evergreen, though usually short-lived, perennial hailing from Madeira, growing to a height and spread of up to 150 cm. Short, erect stems bear rosettes of five- to seven-lobed, deeply toothed, exotic-looking bright green leaves, up to 30 cm across, on long reddish brown stalks. Once the plant begins to produce an inflorescence, leaves arch downward and support the plant like buttresses. From early spring to late summer, produces masses of almost flat, five-petalled, vivid pinkish magenta flowers up to 4 cm across, with purple-pink veins, becoming darker toward their magenta centres, borne in impressive clusters up to 60 cm across. Upper parts of flower stalks are densely covered with sticky purple glandular hairs.

Will take temperatures down to almost freezing for short periods only; makes a good container plant for colder areas, brought into frost-free conditions for the winter months.

Geranium palmatum

Semi-tender / Sun or dappled shade

Similar in appearance to *G. maderense* and also hailing from Madeira, this taprooted, rosetted evergreen biennial or short-lived perennial is often self-seeding. Grows to a height and spread of 1.2 m. Rosettes of long-stemmed, lobed, finely divided midgreen leaves are up to 35 cm across. Flowers are flattish to saucer-shaped, five-petalled, pinkish purple, up to 4 cm across, on large terminal heads up to 60 cm across or more. Flowering stems are covered in purple glandular hairs. Hardy to about −5°c for short periods.

Gunnera (Gunneraceae)

South America, South Africa, Australia, and the Pacific

The approximately forty-five species of fleshy-stemmed perennials in this genus, grown for their foliage, range from minuscule ground-hugging species to spectacular giants. All prefer moisture-retentive soil or growing as a waterside plant in full sun. If you want to grow a plant with the largest leaves possible, it has to be *G. manicata*, an absolute essential for the exotic garden—that is, if you have enough room. There is a valley with swaths of them growing to perfection at Abbotsbury Gardens in Dorset, a sight to behold.

Left

Geranium palmatum

Gunnera manicata

Gunnera manicata

Hardy / Full sun

Extremely large and dramatic clump-forming herbaceous perennial, indigenous to regions from Colombia to Brazil, growing to 1.8–3 m high and 3–4 m wide, with enormous rhubarblike, rounded, palmately lobed, prominently veined, sharply toothed deep green leaves, spiny underneath, 2–2.5 m

wide, on prickly stalks 2.5 m long. In early summer tiny red flowers are formed on wide, erect spikes 1–1.8 m tall. Hardy to −15°C. When cut down by frost, place the old leaves over the crowns to protect from prolonged freezing periods. Can be grown in very large containers.

Gunnera tinctoria

Hardy / Full sun

Herbaceous perennial from Chile, similar to *G. manicata* but smaller, slower spreading, and more compact, growing to a height of 1.8 m with a spread of 2.4 m. Heart-shaped, rounded, deeply lobed, toothed, deep green leaves up to 1.5 m across are borne on prickly stems up to 1.5 m long. Inflorescence similar to *G. manicata* but shorter, to about 60 cm tall, with redder flowers and fruit. Hardy to −15°C. When cut down by frost, place the old leaves over the crowns to protect from prolonged freezing periods.

Hemerocallis
(Hemerocallidaceae)

Daylily
China, Korea, Japan, and Eurasia

Hemerocallis is a genus of some fifteen species of rhizomatous perennials, and countless hybrids, grown for their fabulous flowers. As their common name suggests, they open for only one day, but because they flower in succession over many weeks, often with dozens of blooms out at once, they create strong splashes of intense colour in the garden. In their native habitats they can be found growing on woodland margins and in mountainous areas. Much breeding has been carried out in recent years, especially in the United States. Since the early 1930s, hybridisers in the United States and England have made great improvements in daylilies.

Originally the only colours available were yellow, orange, and tawny red. Today, though, colours range from pastels and near whites to yellows, oranges, pinks, vivid reds, crimson, purple, nearly true blue, and fabulous blends. Numerous forms can be obtained from your local garden centre, but for a wider choice there are many nurseries that specialise in this voluptuous group of plants. More than thirty thousand hybrids have been bred over the years, and many work really well in the exotic garden. 'Burning Daylight' is a particularly good choice for adding a splash of colour. They are hardy and prefer fertile, moist, well-drained soil in full sun to light shade.

Heuchera (Saxifragaceae)

Alum root, coral bells, rock geranium
Rocky Mountains of the United States and a few in Mexico

This genus encompasses some fifty-five species of semi-evergreen and evergreen perennials indigenous to woodlands and rocky sites in their native habitats. They are grown in the exotic garden for their luscious foliage as much as for their airy sprays of flowers. *Heuchera*—named after Johan Heinrich

Heuchera
'Fireworks'

von Heucher (1677–1741), professor of medicine at Wittenburg University—has been much hybridised in recent years, producing a handsome range of sumptuous leaf colours, from green to amber, yellow, purple, silvery, and variegated. My favourites include 'Amber Waves', a handsome form with golden yellow-bronze foliage; 'Chocolate Ruffles', with strong bronzy green leaves with brownish overtones and white flowers; 'Fireworks', with profuse bronzed, lightly ruffled foliage; 'Palace Purple', with metallic bronze-red foliage; 'Pewter Moon', with silver-veined, deep purple-red foliage; 'Pewter Veil', with greenish purple-red foliage with overlaid silver-grey between the veins; and 'Plum Pudding', with rich purple-magenta leaves overlaid with silver and a red underside. All form dense clumps of basal foliage with kidney-shaped to rounded, toothed leaves on thin, wiry leaf stalks. Fine, branching flower stems carry sprays of small flowers, usually five-petalled but sometimes petalless, from late spring to autumn. They are hardy and prefer moist, humus-rich, well-drained soil in full sun to light shade. This wonderful group of plants is discussed in great detail in *Heucheras and Heucherellas: Coral Bells and Foamy Bells* by Dan Heims and Grahame Ware (2005).

Hosta (Agavaceae/Hostaceae)

China, Korea, Japan, and Eastern Russia
Hardy / Sun or shade

This genus of about seventy species of mostly clump-forming, occasionally rhizomatous or stoloniferous perennials was named for Dr. Nicholaus Host (1761–1834), physician to the emperor of Austria. Countless hybrids have been raised, mainly in the United States. Hostas are grown primarily for their fabulously exotic, dense, luxuriant foliage. The leaves can be different shades of green, yellow, greyish blue, or variegated; they range from small to very large and are often glaucous. Hostas bear one-sided racemes of funnel-shaped flowers, mostly in summer. All are hardy, and all prefer fertile,

moist, well-drained soil in full to partial shade, making a good ground cover under deep-rooted deciduous trees, although they will take full sun if watered regularly. Their only drawback is that slugs and snails absolutely adore them! There are far too many forms to mention, and they are discussed in great detail in *The Color Encyclopaedia of Hostas* by Diana Grenfell and Mike Shadrack (2004), so I will cover only a few of the largest, all of them clump-forming, here.

Hosta 'Big Daddy'

Grows to 60 cm high and 1 m wide with rounded to heart-shaped, cupped, deeply puckered, glaucous grey-blue leaves 28 cm long. Bell-shaped, greyish white flowers appear on leafy, glaucous stems, up to 80 cm tall in summer.

Hosta 'Francee'

Grows to 50 cm high and 1 m wide with ovate to heart-shaped, puckered light green leaves with irregular white margins. Stems up to 65 cm high are topped with lavender-blue funnel-shaped flowers in summer.

Hosta 'Frances Williams'

Grows to 60 cm high and 1 m wide. Well-known hosta with large, heart-shaped, puckered, glaucous bluish green leaves with irregular, wide, yellowy green margins. Bell-shaped, off-white flowers are held above foliage in early summer. Magnificent once established.

Hosta sieboldiana

Grows to 1 m high and 1.2 m or more wide, with handsome, thick, ovate to heart-shaped, heavily puckered and veined, bluish grey-green leaves, paler beneath, 25–50 cm long. In summer, pale greyish lilac, bell-shaped flowers appear on 1-m leafy stems, fading to white with age.

Above

Hosta 'Francee'

Below

Hosta 'Frances Williams'

leaves. They are grown in cultivation for their erect, usually dense spikes of flowers, which look very majestic and stately as they gently nod in the summer breeze. The common name refers to the supposed resemblance of the flower spike to a red-hot poker. Countless hybrids are available to the avid gardener. I have included here a few of my favourite forms that work well in the exotic garden, especially those that resemble aloes when in flower. All prefer moist, sandy soil in full sun to light shade.

Hosta sieboldiana

Hosta 'Sum and Substance'

Kniphofia caulescens

Hardy / Sun to light shade

Robust, stout, evergreen perennial, alpine species indigenous to the high grassy slopes of South Africa's Drakensberg Mountains, growing to 1.2 m high by 60 cm wide with narrow, thick, arching, blue-green, finely toothed, glaucous leaves up to 1 m long, tinted purple at the base. Stiff, tall,

Kniphofia caulescens, flower heads

Hosta 'Sum and Substance'

Grows to 75 cm high and 1.2 m wide, with ovate to heart-shaped, pointed, midgreen leaves up to 50 cm long, puckering with age. From late summer racemes of pale lilac, bell-shaped flowers are borne on stems 1 m long.

Kniphofia (Liliaceae)

Red-hot poker
Southern and tropical Africa

Kniphophia comprises about seventy species of evergreen or deciduous rhizomatous perennials, found growing in mountainous areas, often in moist places in rough grass and along streamsides. They are mostly clump-forming in habit, with usually arching, linear to strap-shaped, light green to blue

coppery stems up to 30 cm high on mature plants bear flowers in short oblong-cylindrical racemes of soft orange-red, fading to pale yellow, from late summer to midautumn.

Kniphofia northiae

Hardy / Sun to light shade

Evergreen perennial forming solitary plants up to 1.5 m tall and 1 m wide with broad, linear, arching, glaucous, bluish green leaves with a deep central keel, tapering up to 1.2 m long. Tall stems are topped by very large, dense racemes of pale yellow flowers opening from red buds from early to late summer.

Kniphofia 'Prince Igor'

Hardy / Sun to light shade

Deciduous perennial growing to 1.5 m or more tall by 90 cm wide with straplike, linear grey-green foliage. Tall coppery green stems are topped with racemes of seductive deep orange-red flowers from early to midautumn. Very useful for the back of the border.

Kniphofia 'Royal Standard'

Hardy / Sun to light shade

Upright, clump-forming, rhizomatous perennial growing to a height of 90–100 cm with basal tuft of coarse, sword-shaped, bluish green, linear leaves up to 90 cm long, from which arises a succession of thick, naked flower stalks with dense terminal racemes of drooping tubular flowers 15–25 cm long. Emerging flowers are red, maturing to lemon yellow. Each raceme acquires a two-toned appearance since the lower flowers open first and show yellow while the upper buds and emerging flowers show a bright vermilion red.

Leonotis (Lamiaceae)

Wild dagga

Southern and southeastern Africa

The name of this genus of about thirty species of aromatic annuals, perennials, and evergreen and semi-evergreen subshrubs and shrubs is derived from the Greek *leon* (lion) and *otis* (ear), alluding to the resemblance of the corolla to a lion's ear. The stems are velvety and woody at the base and square in section. The leaves are long, narrow, rough above and velvety below, with serrate edges. They are grown for their characteristic bright orange flowers carried in compact whorls along the flower stalk. Apricot and creamy white flowered forms are also found. The two species described here add impact in the exotic garden with their fabulously soft and furry orange flowers, borne profusely from late summer into autumn. They are easy to grow but do best in full sun, in well-drained loamy soil with plenty of organic matter added; they are drought resistant once established. Plants should be cut back at the end of winter. Wild dagga is widely used in traditional medicine to treat fevers, headaches, coughs, dysentery, and many other conditions. It is also used as a remedy for snakebite as well as other bites and stings, and as a charm to keep snakes away.

Leonotis leonurus

Wild dagga

Half-hardy / Full sun

Upright, semiwoody perennial, up to 2 m tall and 1 m across, though usually smaller in cool summers, as they thrive on heat. Leaves are midgreen to dark green, narrow, lace-shaped, tapering, and softly hairy up to 12 cm long. Tactile, velvety, tubular, two-lipped bright orange flowers up to 6 cm long are carried in whorls toward the top of the stem. Water well in summer but keep almost dry in winter. As it only takes lows of 0°c, can be grown outside only in the warmest areas, though it works exceedingly well as a container plant brought into frost-free conditions for the winter, or planted out as summer bedding. This plant is smoked or made into a medicinal tea by the Hottentot tribe of South Africa because of its euphoric effects; it is often referred to as a mild cannabis substitute, with its active component being leonurine.

Leonotis ocymifolia

Half-hardy / Full sun

Woody-based herbaceous subshrub (evergreen in warm climates) growing to 3 m tall in its native

Leonotis leonurus
and flower detail

habitat, though more like 1.5–2.5 m tall in cool-temperate gardens in a sunny position. Leaves ovate, toothed, midgreen, and hairy on the underside, up to 8 cm long. Dense whorls of two-lipped, tubular, velvety orange flowers up to 4 cm long are borne from late summer into autumn. 'Harrismith White' is a form with equally velvety white flowers.

Ligularia (Asteraceae)

Central and eastern Asia and a few from Europe

Although *Ligularia* has been reclassified, there are still some 125 species in the genus. They are large, robust, often coarse perennials, found in moist grasslands and woodlands and by streams and rivers in their natural habitats. They are grown in cultivation for their often large, alluring leaves and their daisylike yellow to orange flowers borne from summer to autumn. They look perfectly placed in the exotic garden with their delicious leaves and glowing flowers. Unfortunately, like hostas they are much loved by slugs and snails! When grown well they form large clumps. Most species and hybrids are hardy, preferring continuously moist, deep, fertile, humus-rich soil in full sun to dappled shade.

Ligularia dentata

Hardy / Sun or dappled shade

Vigorous, clump-forming perennial from China and Japan, growing to 1–1.5 m high by 1 m wide. Leaves are midgreen, rounded to kidney-shaped, and deeply toothed, often red tinted on the underside, with red basal leaf stalks up to 30 cm long or more, especially if well fed! 'Desdemona' is slightly

Ligularia dentata
'Desdemona'

Lobelia cardinalis

smaller at 1 m with rounded dark brownish green leaves that are a deliciously dark purplish maroon on the underside. Flowers are a voluptuous deep orange. 'Othello' is similar, with leaves coloured deep rich purple, purple-red on the underside.

Ligularia przewalskii

Hardy / Sun or dappled shade

Clump-forming perennial growing to 2 m high by 1 m wide with midgreen, deeply cut, palmately lobed, toothed leaves. Dark bronze-purple-green stems bear dense racemes of bright yellow flowers up to 2 cm across. Very imposing plant for moist situations.

Ligularia hybrids

Hardy / Sun or dappled shade

Hybrids have been bred for both fine foliage and flowers and include such gems as 'Gregynog Gold', with large coarsely toothed green leaves and towering pyramids of golden orange flowers; 'The Rocket', with tall, almost black stems that show off the bright yellow flowers to perfection; 'Weihenstephan', with large flowers of deep gold; and 'Zepter', which is slightly shorter, with densely packed flowers of rich golden yellow.

Lobelia (Campanulaceae)

North, Central, and South America, and other tropical and temperate areas worldwide

Lobelia is a genus of some 370 species of annuals, perennials, and shrubs found growing in habitats ranging from marshes and riverbanks to woodlands, mountain slopes, and deserts. They are grown in cultivation for their often brightly coloured flowers and sometimes interesting foliage. Although diverse in nature, all have similarly distinctive flowers, consisting of two-lipped tubular flowers, each with five lobes. Many gardeners think immediately of *Lobelia erinus*, especially the blue forms like 'Crystal Palace', traditionally used as an edging plant or in hanging baskets. The most interesting forms, though, are the larger ones that have become more widely available in recent years, of which several fit the exotic bill

well. The forms mentioned here prefer deep, fertile, moist soil in sun or dappled shade.

Lobelia 'Bees' Balm'

Hardy / Sun or dappled shade

Short-lived, upright, clump-forming perennial growing to 76 cm high by 30 cm wide with bronzy reddish purple stems and leaves to 15 cm long. Tubular bright crimson flowers, 3.5–4.5 cm across, are formed on racemes up to 46 cm long from mid to late summer.

Lobelia cardinalis

Cardinal flower

Hardy / Sun or dappled shade

Short-lived, upright, clump-forming perennial growing to a height of 100 cm, often with green reddish stems. Leaves are sometimes glossy, bronze-tinted light green, oblong, narrowly pointed, up to 10 cm long. From summer to early autumn bears terminal racemes up to 35 cm long of bright red flowers up to 25 mm across.

Lobelia laxiflora

Torch lobelia

Frost-hardy / Sun or dappled shade

Hairy, spreading, shrubby plant from Mexico, growing to a height of 90 cm with lance-shaped, pointed, linear, finely toothed, light green leaves up to 8 cm long. Scarlet, yellow-tipped, tubular flowers appear in summer. Hardy to −5°C, hence best grown in the warmest gardens or bedded out for the summer months.

indigenous to meadows, scrubland, and woodland areas in their native habitats. They are cultivated for their handsome glaucous foliage and elegant flower, which fit in well with the exotic garden style. They can form quite large clumps or thickets with age, preferring moderately fertile, humus-rich soil and full sun, although they will take some shade. On poorer soils the leaves will be correspondingly smaller. They will need staking in windy areas. Although they are hardy, early growth can be cut back by late frosts.

Macleaya cordata

syn. *Bocconia cordata*
Hardy / Full sun

Creeping, rhizomatous perennial growing to 2.5 m high by 1 m wide. Lower stems have large leaves with five to seven deep lobes, grey-green above and

Left
Lobelia tupa

Lobelia tupa

Frost-hardy / Sun or dappled shade

Vigorous, upright, clump-forming perennial growing to 2 m tall by 90 cm wide, with reddish purple stems and ovate to lance-shaped, velvety, pale greyish green leaves up to 30 cm long. Flowers narrowly tubular, two-lipped, brick red to orange-red, up to 6 cm long, with prominent maroon calyces, borne on racemes up to 40 cm long. Very exotic looking. Hardy to −5°C and lower if mulched well during colder periods.

Macleaya (Papaveraceae)

Plume poppy, tree celandine
China and Japan

This genus in the poppy family consists of just two species of hardy herbaceous perennials that are

Macleaya cordata
and in bloom

grey-white beneath, up to 25 cm wide. From mid to late summer, bears large panicles of creamy white feathery plumes up to 76 cm tall. Can be grown successfully in large containers if considered too invasive for the garden. 'Spetchley Ruby' is a form with ruby red seed heads and ruby tones to the leaves.

Macleaya ×kewensis

Hardy / Full sun

Cross between *M. cordata* and *M. microcarpa*. Rhizomatous perennial growing to 2.5 m tall by 1 m wide or more with five- to nine-lobed greyish green leaves, topped with loose panicles of creamy beige flowers all summer. 'Flamingo' has pink buds and buff pink flowers.

Macleaya microcarpa

syn. *Bocconia microcarpa*
Hardy / Full sun

Somewhat similar to *M. cordata*. Rhizomatous perennial growing to 2.5 m tall by 1 m wide or more. Leaves are five- to seven-lobed, greyish olive green, and soft white on the underside. Flowers are pinkish bronze in summer. 'Coral Plume' has pinker flowers. 'Kelway's Coral Plume' has showy deep beige–coral pink flowers opening from pink buds in summer.

Myosotidium (Boraginaceae)

Chatham Island daisy, Chatham Island forget-me-not
New Zealand (Chatham Island)

This genus consists of just one species of evergreen perennial found growing on sandy to rocky, windswept, wet parts of coastal areas in its native habitat. Its thick, fleshy leaves are somewhat reminiscent of a hosta or small rhubarb, with showy forget-me-not–like flowers. The whole plant has a very exotic appearance and is well worth having in the garden even though it is not the easiest of plants to grow, preferring mild climates with cool summers and disliking extremes of weather.

Myosotidium hortensia

Half-hardy / Sun or dappled shade

Clump-forming evergreen perennial growing to a height and spread of 60 cm with highly glossy, bright green, almost succulent, ovate to heart-shaped, deeply ribbed and veined leaves with undulating margins, up to 30 cm long on fleshy stalks. Dense rounded heads of bell-shaped pale to dark blue, five-petalled flowers up to 1 cm across are borne from late spring to summer. Prefers moderately fertile, humus-rich soil and a sunny location with slight shade at midday or dappled shade. Benefits from a seaweed-based fertiliser during the growing season. Will take lows of 0°c for short periods only, hence is only suitable for the warmest gardens or in coastal areas that do not freeze in winter; otherwise grow as a container plant brought into frost-free conditions for the winter.

Persicaria (Polygonaceae)

Worldwide, mostly India and Japan

This somewhat confused genus includes fifty to eighty species in the knotweed family. There are many fascinating forms that make excellent exotic garden plants as they mimic more tropical-looking plants. They prefer moist soil and full sun or dappled shade, although many will take drought for short periods once established.

Persicaria microcephala

Hardy / Sun or dappled shade

Vigorous, spreading, semi-evergreen perennial, found in the Himalaya to China, with an open habit

and woody basal growth to a height of 1–1.5 m with lance-shaped, strongly veined green leaves with bronze and pewter markings, up to 20 cm long. Heads of small pinkish red flowers are borne from summer to autumn. 'Red Dragon' is a fantastic form and vigorous grower boasting spring leaves that are deep burgundy with a pewter chevron and a metallic sheen; underside is plum-pewter with magenta veins. Older foliage becomes greener, although new growth is always stunning. Terminal bunches of tiny white flowers are borne from summer to autumn. Plants can become rather floppy, hence should be staked early on.

Persicaria virginiana

syn. *Tovara virginiana*
Hardy / Sun or dappled shade

Mounding herbaceous perennial found in the Himalaya to Japan and in parts of the northeastern United States, growing to a height of 50–120 cm with ovate, tapering to fine point, midgreen leaves with dark green markings, 10–23 cm long. From late summer to early autumn, bears slender, very loose, terminal and auxiliary spikes 10–30 cm long, of cup-shaped green flowers turning red. 'Compton's Form' has bold chevrons on large lime green leaves that fade from dark red ochre to tan depending

on the age of the leaf. 'Filiformis' has red-flushed, chevron-marked leaves and long spikes of small deep red flowers from midsummer to autumn. The smaller 'Painter's Palette' is a veritable explosion of coloured foliage with its irregularly marked soft yellow and green leaves, with a pronounced central chevron of reddish brown. 'Variegata' is another outstanding form, with rounder and broader leaves that are boldly splashed with cream.

Petasites (Asteraceae)

North America, Europe, and Asia

This genus—whose name derives from the Greek word *petasos*, a type of hat with a wide brim—comprises about fifteen species of rhizomatous, herbaceous perennials that can be found in mountainous meadows, in damp or boggy woodland areas, and on streamsides in their native habitats. They are grown in the exotic garden for their handsome leaves, although some can be rather invasive. They prefer moist to wet, humus-rich soil in a sheltered location in sun or dappled shade. They tend to go floppy in hot weather, especially if grown in a drier situation.

Petasites hybridus

Butterbur

Hardy / Sun or dappled shade

Erect, stout, rhizomatous perennial growing to a height of 90 cm or more. Flowers appear before leaves, often as early in the year as midwinter. Pink emerging flower stalks, pushing their way through the earth, are similar in appearance to button mushrooms. Huge, rhubarblike leaves up to 90 cm across are roundish, heart-shaped at the base, scalloped at the edges, with the portion between the projections finely toothed. Leaves are white and cobwebby with down both above and below when young, but when mature, most of the covering disappears from the upper surface. Common name is derived from the fact that the huge leaves were used to wrap around butter in the days before refrigeration. Really only for larger gardens, or just enjoy them growing in the wild!

Petasites japonicus

Hardy / Sun or dappled shade

Stout, rhizomatous perennial hailing from China, Japan, and Korea, growing to 100 cm tall and 3 m or more wide. Enormous, kidney-shaped, irregularly toothed basal leaves up to 80 cm across, hairy beneath, are borne on stalks up to 1 m long. Variety *giganteus* grows up to 1.6 m or more tall, with leaves up to a staggering 1 m across, creating a devastatingly tropical look. 'Nishiki-buki', occasionally

named 'Variegatus', has green leaves irregularly variegated with paler green and creamy yellow.

Phormium (Agavaceae)

Coastal flax, flax lily, New Zealand flax
New Zealand and Australia (Norfolk Island)

This small genus includes just two species, *P. tenax* and *P. cookianum*, the latter split into two subspecies, *hookeri* and *cookianum*. Many hybrids have arisen from these species, making phormium a very widely cultivated plant in New Zealand and the rest of the world, much loved because of its hardiness and very architectural habit. These large evergreen perennials are found in scrubby areas, as well as on hillsides and riverbanks, in areas ranging from coastal to mountainous habitats in New Zealand. They form big clumps of large, linear, keeled leaves, each folded into a V shape at the base, in a very diverse range of colours, from yellowish green to dark green, and many are vertically striped.

Phormium tenax is the tallest, with foliage up to 3 m tall, and even higher flower spikes that produce upright, curved, tubular orangish red flowers in erect

panicles in summer. *Phormium cookianum* is smaller, with thinner leaves that are arching rather than erect, up to 2 m long in its native habitat. The flowers are greenish yellow, followed by twisted seedpods that hang down from the flowering stalks. There is now an amazing array of superb cultivars that have attractive coloured or variegated foliage and often have much smaller leaves, making them more usable in smaller gardens; in fact, there are some small forms that grow to only 30 cm high! All are good plants for coastal areas. They are hardy to about −12°C for short periods but should be mulched in frost-prone areas. In very cold periods, they can be tied together and wrapped with fleece. They prefer deep, well-drained, fertile soil in full sun to light shade.

Phormium cookianum subsp. hookeri

Mountain flax

Frost-hardy / Sun or light shade

Clump-forming perennial growing to a height of 2 m when in flower, by 3 m wide, with broad, arching, linear, light to yellowish green leaves up to 1.5 m long. Tubular yellow-green flowers up to 5 cm long

Phormium tenax 'Variegata'

are borne in upright panicles to 2 m long in summer. 'Cream Delight' has leaves with broad bands of creamy yellow in the centre and narrow bands toward the margins. 'Dark Delight' reaches 1–1.2 m tall, with slightly arching leaves that are a dark reddish brown. Subspecies *hookeri* 'Tricolor' has leaves with irregular bands of cream-yellow and thin red edges. 'Maori Chief' has pink-and-red-striped bronze leaves. 'Maori Sunrise' has slender apricot-and-pink-striped leaves with a bronze margin. 'Sundowner' is a large, upright form, 2–2.7 m tall with bronze-green leaves 6.5 cm wide with rose pink margins that fade to cream in summer.

Phormium tenax

New Zealand flax

Frost-hardy / Sun or light shade

Clump-forming perennial growing to 4 m tall by 2 m wide with rigid, upright, linear leaves up to 3 m long that are dark green above and blue-green beneath. Stout red-purple panicles, to 4 m long, of tubular dull red flowers, 5 cm long, are borne in midsummer. 'Atropurpureum' grows to a height of 2.5 m with upright reddish purple leaves, 7.5–10 cm wide. 'Dazzler' grows to 1 m tall by 1.2 m wide with arching bronze leaves striped with red, orange, and pink. 'Platt's Black' is an exquisite phormium growing to a height of about 1 m tall, with darkest

Phormium cookianum subsp. *hookeri* 'Cream Delight'

purple-black foliage. 'Purpureum' grows to a height of 1.8 m with rich, dark, blackish purple leaves. 'Variegata' is a large upright plant growing up to 2.5 m tall, with green and cream bands on broad leaves 7.5 cm wide.

Phygelius aequalis 'Yellow Trumpet', flowers

Phygelius × rectus 'Salmon Leap', flowers

Phygelius (Scrophulariaceae)

South Africa

Just two species of evergreen subshrubs, found growing on moist to wet slopes and stream banks in their native habitat, belong to this genus. Both species have been crossed, producing numerous hybrids. I have included them here instead of in "Trees and Shrubs" because they are so often used in herbaceous borders, especially as they usually defoliate when temperatures drop below 0°c, and are a good alternative to fuchsias. They are grown for their heads of very attractive tubular flowers that have five recurved lobes with conspicuously protruding anther and stamens. They flower over a long period from summer quite often into the autumn. When grown as a perennial, they have a

suckering rootstock, forming clumps 1 m across. They prefer moist, humus-rich soil and a position with full sun, preferably against a south-facing wall in areas that have cold winters or frost pockets. They will take temperatures of −6°c and lower if well mulched during freezing spells.

Phygelius aequalis

Frost-hardy / Full sun

Suckering, upright subshrub, growing to a height and spread of 1 m, with pointed, ovate, lustrous dark green leaves up to 11 cm long. Semi-upright panicles of 25 cm or more hold tiered, nodding, dusky pink tubular flowers, up to 6 cm long, in summer. 'Yellow Trumpet' is a very attractive form with light green leaves and bright creamy yellow flowers.

Phygelius × rectus

Frost-hardy / Full sun

Cross between *P. aequalis* and *P. capensis*. Suckering, upright shrub growing to a height and spread of

1.5 m, with pointed, ovate dark green leaves up to 10 cm long. Pale red flowers 6 cm long are produced in summer on panicles up to 30 cm long. 'African Queen' has striking, pendent, light red flowers with yellow throats. 'Moonraker' has light creamy yellow flowers. 'Salmon Leap' has open panicles of dainty, deeply lobed, salmon orangish red tubular flowers with yellow throats. 'Winchester Fanfare' has coral pink tubular flowers with yellow throats.

Phytolacca (Phytolaccaceae)

Pokeweed

North America to South America and eastern Asia

This is a genus of some thirty species of herbaceous perennials, subshrubs, and deciduous or evergreen shrubs and trees that are usually upright in habit, with often large leaves that can be brilliantly coloured in autumn. They can be found in open fields or woodlands in tropical, subtropical, and temperate areas in their native habitats. They are grown in cultivation for their attractive autumn colour and decorative flowers and fruits, which look good in wilder parts of the exotic garden. Most species are easily grown in semifertile, moist, well-drained soil in sun or dappled shade.

Phytolacca americana

Hardy / Sun or dappled shade

Erect, fleshy-rooted perennial hailing from North and Central America, herbaceous in cold winters, growing to a height of 4 m by 90 cm–1.8 m wide. From a stout reddish trunk, widely branching, reddish stems hold midgreen, smooth, ovate to lance-shaped leaves, 15–30 cm long, that give off an unpleasant odour when bruised and are coloured with attractive hues of purple-red to pink in autumn. From midsummer to early autumn, elongated, erect clusters of white to pink flowers are held in racemes 20 cm long, giving way to drooping clusters of very dark purple-maroon, juicy berries that taper at both ends. All parts will cause discomfort if eaten raw, and ingesting the fruit of *P. americana* can be lethal. Native Americans introduced the first colonists to this plant, who in turn delivered it

Phytolacca americana

back to Europe where it became a popular culinary vegetable. In spring, young shoots with their leafy tips, 15–20 cm long, are gathered before they take on their reddish tint and boiled for twenty to thirty minutes in two or more changes of water (which removes the poisonous toxins), then eaten like spinach; the taste is said to be a little like asparagus.

Rheum (Polygonaceae)

Rhubarb

Eastern Europe, the Himalaya, and central Asia to China

Rheum is a genus of some fifty species of robust, rhizomatous perennials, growing in temperate regions in wet meadows and on streamsides as well as in scrubby areas and on rocky slopes in their native habitats. It includes the well-known edible rhubarb, *Rheum ×hybridum*. The decorative rheums are grown for their impressive, junglelike, architectural, often wavy-edged, large basal leaves and tall spikes of frothy flowers, making a good alternative for those who haven't got room in their gardens for *Gunnera*. Rhubarbs prefer free-draining, humus-rich, moist to wet locations in full sun to dappled shade.

Rheum 'Ace of Hearts'

Hardy / Sun or dappled shade

Rhizomatous, basal-clumped perennial growing to 1.2 m tall by 90 cm wide with stiffly upright, extended, heart-shaped, deep-veined, crinkly, wavy-edged dark green leaves, with a striking burgundy colouration on the underside, up to 35 cm long. Tiny pale pink flowers are borne on tall panicles held above the foliage.

Rheum palmatum

Hardy / Sun or dappled shade

Rhizomatous perennial with a very large root system growing to 2.5 m tall and 1.8 m wide when in flower, with broad, rounded, palmate, deeply lobed, three- to nine-lobed dark green leaves that are velvety, purplish red on the underside, up to a staggering 100 cm across on thick stalks. Many tiny star-shaped flowers, creamy green to deep red, are borne in fluffy panicles on tall stems above the foliage. 'Atrosanguineum' has emerging bright red buds, turning purple-red when juvenile and fading to dark green in maturity, and carries tall panicles of warm pink flowers in summer. 'Bowles' Crimson' has large green leaves, crimson underneath, and dark red flowers. Variety *tanguticum* has jagged leaflets that emerge reddish green and become dark green with a purple tint when mature, and enormous flowering stems with erect panicles of abundant white, pink, and crimson flowers.

Rodgersia (Saxifragaceae)

Burma, China, Korea, and Japan

This is a genus of six species of large, vigorous, clump-forming, rhizomatous perennials occurring in moist woodlands and scrublands and by streamsides in temperate mountainous areas in their native habitats. They are grown primarily for their dramatic leaves, reminiscent of more tropical plants, though they do produce short-lived astilbe-like plumes of small flowers. They prefer cool conditions in humus-rich, moist soil in dappled to full shade and are fully hardy, though young foliage can be damaged by late frost.

Rodgersia aesculifolia

Hardy / Dappled to full shade

Hailing from China, bold, clump-forming, rhizomatous perennial growing up to 1.8 m high with palmate, heavily crinkled, midgreen leaves that look surprisingly horse-chestnut-like (hence the specific name), up to 25 cm long, with red veining and stems. Heads of creamy white or pink flowers are borne in summer on stems to 1.2 m tall.

Rodgersia podophylla

Rodgersia aesculifolia

Rodgersia pinnata

Hardy / Dappled to full shade

Bold, clump-forming, rhizomatous perennial from southwestern China, growing to 1.2 m tall by 76 cm wide, eventually forming a clump 1.2–1.5 m wide. Leaves dark green, glossy, partly pinnate or palmate, with five to nine leaflets, crinkled, deeply veined, to 20 cm long. Inflorescence is borne on reddish green stalks with heads of star-shaped yellowish white, pink, or red flowers 30–60 cm long from early to midsummer. 'Superba' has purplish bronze tinted young leaves that turn green with age and large panicles of bright pink flowers.

Rodgersia 'Parasol'

Hardy / Dappled to full shade

Outstanding foliage plant for moist soil, like an oversized *R. podophylla* with huge umbrellas of foliage up to 80 cm across and tall plumes of creamy white flowers in summer.

Rodgersia podophylla

Hardy / Dappled to full shade

Handsome, bold, clump-forming, rhizomatous perennial from Korea and Japan, growing to 1.5 m tall by 1.8 m wide. Palmate leaves are normally three- to five-lobed, jagged, midgreen, glossy, bronze when young and bronze-red in autumn, up to 40 cm long. Star-shaped cream-green flowers are borne in panicles from mid to late summer.

Romneya (Papaveraceae)

Matilija poppy, tree poppy
Western United States, Mexico

Just one species of suckering, woody-based sub-shrub in the poppy family belongs to this genus, found growing in scrubby areas in Southern California and northern Mexico. They are grown in cultivation for their lustrous light grey-green, somewhat aquilegia-like foliage and decadently showy white flowers with intense yellow centres. A clump of these is a joy to behold, fitting the Mediterranean-style garden well. They prefer fertile, well-drained soil in a position with full sun or against a wall in cold areas, taking lows of around −6°C for short periods. They are often slow and difficult to establish, but once happy they spread quickly by runners, hence should be given plenty of space to grow into a substantial thicket.

Romneya coulteri

Frost-hardy / Full sun

Deciduous subshrub with upright, glaucous stems, growing 1.2–2.5 m high, with extremely glaucous, greyish green leaves deeply cut, with a small fringe of hairs at the margin, up to 13 cm long. Showy, scented, solitary flowers have large, crumpled, pure white petals, surrounding many prominent yellow-orange stamens all summer. 'White Cloud' is a form with pure snow white petals and distinctive grey-green leaves on a more vigorous and rapidly spreading plant.

Rudbeckia (Asteraceae)

Black-eyed Susan, coneflower
North America

Rudbeckia is a genus of some fifteen species of annuals, biennials, and perennials found in moist meadows and light woodlands. They are very popular plants in temperate gardens because of their ease of cultivation and late-season flowering, adding colour when many other herbaceous plants have long finished. Although not at all exotic on their own, when planted with exotics like cannas they take on an exotic air, with their bright, vivid yellow daisylike flowers. They are much admired by visitors to my Norwich garden from late summer to early autumn.

Rudbeckia
'Herbstonne'

I have mentioned only two of the tallest forms here, though many more are available. They prefer light to heavy, well-drained, moderately fertile soil that does not dry out during the summer months.

Rudbeckia 'Herbstonne'

Hardy / Full sun

Hybrid of *R. nitida;* vigorous, erect, rhizomatous, clump-forming perennial growing to 1.8 m tall and 90 cm wide with oval, pointed, prominently veined, lustrous midgreen leaves up to 15 cm long. From midsummer to midautumn, branching stems bear daisylike flowers 10–12 cm across with bright yellow petals and a yellowish green, conical central cone.

Rudbeckia laciniata

Hardy / Full sun

Vigorous, rhizomatous perennial, forming loose clumps, with branching stems toward the top, growing to a height of 1.5–3 m with pinnate leaves, with up to five lobed, toothed, prominently veined leaflets. Daisylike flowers with yellow petals and greenish yellow central cone, up to 13 cm across, are borne from midsummer to midautumn.

Smilacina (Convallariaceae)

False Solomon's seal
North and Central America and Asia

Members of this genus of some twenty-five species of mostly rhizomatous perennials are found in woodland areas in their native habitats. Looking somewhat similar to Solomon's seal (*Polygonatum*), they have rather exotic-looking foliage and flowers that work well in woodland gardens or in the border. They prefer moist, well-drained, moderately fertile soil in dappled to deep shade, hence are rather useful for some of those difficult corners of the garden.

Smilacina racemosa

Hardy / Dappled to full shade

Clump-forming rhizomatous perennial growing to 90 cm high by 60 cm wide with narrowly ovate or elliptic, pointed, prominently veined midgreen leaves to 15 cm long, downy beneath and yellow in autumn. Terminal panicles of many white to creamy white flowers, 6 mm across, densely clustered, strongly perfumed, are produced in mid and late spring, occasionally followed by small green berries turning red with age.

Soleirolia (Urticaceae)

Western Mediterranean islands

This genus contains just one species of vigorous, carpet-forming, evergreen perennial that is very useful for moist, shady corners of the garden, where it can be used as a foil for other plants. The masses of tiny leaves clothe slender, spreading stems that root as they run, forming a dense, deep pile carpet. As it covers the ground it will run over rocks, fallen logs, and so on, clinging to their shape so the features of the landscape are picked out. It will even grow on damp, shaded garden and house walls and can be used as a moist lawn under the shade of trees. Quick to establish, it survives periodic dry spells and recovers quickly afterward. It is a superb substitute for moss in a Japanese-style garden, or where the area is too small to have a real lawn. It grows to lawnlike perfection in Cornwall, at St. Just in the graveyard at Roseland Church, under magnificent stands of *Trachycarpus fortunei*.

Soleirolia soleirolii

syn. *Helxine soleirolii*

Baby's tears, mind-your-own-business

Half-hardy / Shade or sun

Soft, mat-forming perennial with translucent, branching, pale green, rounded, short-stalked leaves up to 6 mm long. Bears minuscule pinkish white flowers from its leaf axils in summer. Forms sold as 'Aurea' or 'Golden Queen' have brilliant golden yellow-green leaves, while 'Silver Queen' (syn. 'Variegata') has bluish grey-green leaves. Will grow anywhere—in heavy clay or sand, dry or moist soils, well-drained or boggy situations. Prefers shade but will grow in full sun if moist. Becomes deciduous when the temperature drops below 0°C but soon recovers in spring.

Tricyrtis (Lilaceae)

Toad lily

The eastern Himalaya to the Philippines, Japan, and Taiwan

Tricyrtis is a genus of sixteen elegant, rhizomatous perennials in the lily family that can be found growing in moist woodlands, on cliffs, and in mountainous areas in their indigenous habitats. Although hardy, they have a very exotic appearance with their succulent stems and leaves, and their exquisite flowers. Being late flowering, they can prove invaluable as autumn approaches when there is a distinct lack of floral colour, but they should not be planted in cold spots or their flowering will be cut short by early winter frosts. They prefer moist, humus-rich, well-drained soil in a position with dappled shade (in warmer districts) to sun. I mention only two species here, but many hybrid forms are available that are well worth hunting out.

Tricyrtis formosana

syn. *T. stolonifera*

Formosa toad lily

Hardy / Sun or dappled shade

Rhizomatous perennial from Taiwan, spreading by stolons with zigzagging softly haired stems, growing to a height of 80 cm, with ovate to lance-shaped green leaves mottled with shades of darker purplish green, up to 12 cm long. Branched terminal clusters of upright, star-shaped flowers open from brown or maroon buds into white, pale lilac, or pinkish purple petals with purple spotting and a tinge of yellow, from midsummer to autumn. Several stunning forms are available.

Tricyrtis hirta

syn. *T. japonica*
Hairy toad lily
Hardy / Sun or dappled shade

Upright, arching, clump-forming, rhizomatous perennial from Japan, growing to 80 cm high by 60 cm wide, with hairy stems and lance-shaped, veined, softly hairy, pale green leaves up to 15 cm long. Funnel-shaped, erect white flowers, up to 3 cm long, spotted with dark purple, are produced singly or in clusters from the leaf axils along the stems, or in terminal clusters, from late summer to midautumn. Variety *alba* has green-flushed white flowers with pink-tinged anthers. 'Miyazaki' is a smaller plant with an arching habit, with white or pink flowers with larger lilac-purple spotting. 'Miyazaki Gold' is similar, with golden-edged leaves. 'White Towers' has erect stems with flowers in most of the axils that are white with pink-tinged stamens.

subtropical garden at Great Dixter. Easily grown from seed. Prefers well-drained, preferably moist, moderately fertile soil in full sun. Will take drought once established. Hardy to at least −8°C. Hybrids in a large range of colours can be used to create splashes of vivid colour in the border, usually with a fairly low-growing, sprawling habit. Useful for hanging baskets and spilling over the edge of large containers.

Tricyrtis hirta,
flowers

Verbena
bonariensis
mixed with
orange
Crocosmia
×crocosmiiflora
(Montbretia)

Verbena (Verbenaceae)

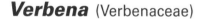

Vervain
North, Central, and South America, with a few
  occurring in Europe

This genus encompasses some 250 species of annuals, perennials, and subshrubs usually found in scrubby wasteland areas and also along roadsides in their native habitats, mostly in temperate to tropical regions. They can be sprawling or erect in habit. There are many gardenworthy forms and countless hybrids, which are often very showy with brightly coloured flowers.

Verbena bonariensis

Frost-hardy / Full sun

Open, clump-forming perennial with a stiffly upright habit and branching square stems growing to 2 m tall. Leaves are dark bluish green, roughly textured, oblong to lance-shaped, up to 15 cm long, with serrated margins. Lilac-purple flowers are borne at the terminal ends in cymes up to 5 cm across from midsummer to autumn. A beautiful plant for any part of the border or for growing at random in gravel. Much used by the late Christopher Lloyd in his

Grasses, Grasslike Plants, and Restios

Grasses are not normally associated with exotic gardens, which is a shame because they add movement and verticality and are a good substitute for plants that we can't grow in our temperate climates such as the more tropical sugarcane, *Saccharum officinarum*. With their current worldwide popularity, many are readily available that fit in seamlessly with this style of gardening. Restios—evergreen, reedlike plants in a wide range of heights—are of considerable architectural merit as well, valued for their sculptural form and attractive, long-lasting seed heads. They are fairly recent introductions to the British Isles, but trials through many winters are producing an ever-growing list of gardenworthy forms, as their hardiness is being established to the point that at least some can be grown in most parts of the British Isles. For more information, see the several books on grasses and similar plants published by Timber Press, including Rick Darke's impressive *The Encyclopedia of Grasses for Livable Landscapes* (2007).

Grasses and Grasslike Plants

Whether short or exceedingly tall, grasses give height, stature, and form, many with a very architectural appearance, with the added attraction that the foliage catches the wind, adding motion to the landscape. If space is limited, you can use some of the smaller species and cultivars, which look especially good weeping over the sides of pots and containers. I have also included a few other plants here that have a similar spiky or grassy feel to them.

Arundo donax

Arundo (Poaceae)

Warm-temperate regions of the Northern
 Hemisphere

Arundo is a genus of three species of evergreen, rhizomatous, perennial grasses found growing on lakes, riversides, and streams. *Arundo donax* is grown in cultivation for its enormous, impressive bamboo-like stems and foliage, which can dominate your garden if let loose! The variegated cultivars are very attractive though less hardy, hence only survive winters in the warmest areas or microclimates or else need to be overwintered in a frost-free environment. They are not particularly fussy about soil type, as long as they are moist and grown in full sun in a sheltered location. For the best foliage, it is advisable to cut growth back to the base annually. If you desire an absolutely enormous plant, leave the old stems on, and they will form an impenetrable thicket. Feed them a high-nitrogen fertiliser and they will probably explode!

Arundo donax

Spanish reed
Hardy / Full sun

*Arundo donax
var. versicolor*

Clump-forming, nobly rhizomatous perennial (fleshy, creeping rootstocks form compact masses from which tough, fibrous roots emerge that penetrate deeply into the soil) growing to a height of 5 m in my garden, with stout stems and arching, broadly linear, grey-green, glaucous leaves up to 60 cm long and 7.5 cm across arranged conspicuously in two opposing ranks on the canes. In warm climates, produces panicles of light green to purple spikelets to 60 cm long from mid to late autumn, though rarely flowers in cool-summer areas. Foliage dries to light brown in winter and rattles in the wind. Variety *versicolor* (striped giant reed, syn. 'Variegata') grows to about 2.4 m tall, with leaves variegated with white stripes. 'Variegata Superba' has leaves with creamy white stripes and margins. The variegated forms tend to be less hardy, taking lows of −5°c and lower with a good mulch.

Has a variety of uses, ranging from music to medicine. Primitive pipe organs were made from it and the reeds for woodwind instruments are still made from its culms, for which no satisfactory substitutes are known. Also used in basketry and for fishing rods, livestock fodder, medicine, and soil erosion control. Has become a pernicious weed in some countries, blocking waterways, especially in the southern United States.

Carex (Cyperaceae)

Sedge
Worldwide, especially northern temperate regions

This enormous genus contains more than 1500 species of deciduous and evergreen, rhizomatous, grasslike perennials, found growing in diverse habitats from temperate to arctic and from high elevations on mountains to tropical lowlands. They range from low-growing forms to tall tussock forms, usually with insignificant flowers. They are grown in cultivation for their interesting range of shapes, sizes, and sometimes coloured foliage. They can add impact to the exotic-Mediterranean garden and look good growing through gravel or used in groups in shady corners or for setting off taller plants. These very versatile, tough plants look good in containers as well.

Carex buchananii

Frost-hardy / Sun or dappled shade

Densely tufted evergreen perennial with short rhizomes and a symmetrical arching habit, growing to a height of 50–76 cm, with upright, linear, reddish brown leaves to 45 cm long or more, curling gracefully at the tips. Prefers moist soil. Hardy to −10°c.

Carex hachijoensis 'Evergold'

Variegated Japanese sedge grass
Hardy / Sun or dappled shade

Handsome tufted, evergreen perennial with short rhizomes, growing to 30 cm by 35 cm, forming low compact mounds of dark green leaves, each with a broad creamy yellow central stripe, up to 30 cm long. Brown flower spikes on 15 cm stems are borne in late spring. Prefers fertile, moist, well-drained soil. Hardy to −15°c.

Carex buchananii

Carex phyllocephala

Palm sedge
Hardy / Sun or dappled shade

Clump-forming evergreen perennial with purple canelike stems growing to a height of 30–60 cm, each stem ending in a whorl of spreading, narrow green leaflets. 'Sparkler' is the most common form in cultivation, with striking leaves having a dark green central band and broad creamy white margins. Prefers moisture-retentive soils though will tolerate dry conditions in dappled shade. Makes an excellent subtropical-looking ground cover.

Carex siderosticha 'Variegata'

Hardy / Sun or dappled shade

Clump-forming, slow-spreading, deciduous, rhizomatous perennial, growing to a height of 30 cm, with fairly broad, linear, lance-shaped pale green leaves up to 25 cm long, edged and finely striped white and slightly pinkish toward the base. Thin, pale brown flower spikes are borne in late spring. 'Shima-nishiki' has pale green leaves with broad yellow borders and cream central stripes. Grows up to 25 cm high and spreads slowly from central stem by contact rooting.

Cortaderia (Poaceae)

South America, New Guinea, and New Zealand

The approximately twenty-five species of evergreen perennial grasses in this genus are usually found growing on grassy plains or in mountainous areas, often near water. They are grown in cultivation for their stunning plumelike flowers (kept throughout the winter) rising above attractive grassy hummocks, the whole giving a very architectural feel whether planted as single specimens or in groups. In the 1970s they were used so often that they received a bad name and subsequently went out of fashion. Luckily, times have changed and this majestic family of plants can be grown to perfection in the exotic garden. They prefer fertile, free-draining soil in full sun and are hardy to at least −10°c. Leave plenty of room for their ultimate growth. They also look good in large containers.

Cortaderia richardii

Toetoe grass, toitoi
Frost-hardy / Full sun

Handsome, clump-forming, densely tufted, evergreen perennial from New Zealand, growing to a height of up to 3 m with arching, linear, tough, pale olive green leaves up to 2 m long. From midsummer, towering upright stems bear nodding golden yellow plumes that stay on into the winter.

Cortaderia selloana

Pampas grass
Frost-hardy / Full sun

Very architectural, clump-forming, tufted, evergreen perennial indigenous to South America, growing to 2.5–3 m tall with arching, linear, rough-surfaced, glaucous, midgreen leaves up to 2.5 m long or more, forming dense, impenetrable clumps. From late summer onward, silvery white, feathery, pyramidal to oblong panicles arise. 'Albolineata' (syn. 'Silver Stripe') is a compact form with white-edged leaves and silver-white plumes, to 2 m tall. 'Aureolineata' (syn. 'Gold Band') is a compact form with rich yellow-edged leaves maturing to deep golden yellow, to 2.2 m tall. 'Pumila' (dwarf pampas grass) grows to 1–1.2 m or more tall, with linear bluish green leaves and masses of upright silvery yellow plumes. 'Roseum' has long plumes tinged pink. 'Sunningdale Silver' is a large plant topped with dense weather-resistant white plumes up to 3 m tall.

Hakonechloa (Poaceae)

Japan

Just one species belongs to the genus—a slowly spreading, rhizomatous perennial, found growing on wet, rocky cliffs in the mountainous district of Tokaido in southeast Honshu. There are also several cultivars of this alluring grass. All have a wonderful flowing form that looks very exotic hanging over small walls and the edges of containers, and by pathways; they are also useful for brightening dull corners of the garden. They prefer fertile, humus-rich, moist, well-drained soil in sun to dappled shade and are hardy.

Hakonechloa macra 'Aureola'

Hakonechloa macra

Hardy / Sun or dappled shade

Very handsome, slowly spreading, rhizomatous perennial forming loose, cascading mounds to 30 cm high by 50 cm wide. 'Aureola' has narrow leaves that are bright yellow with narrow green stripes, gaining a glorious pinkish red tint in autumn that persists through the winter months. 'Albo Striata' is rare and hard to find but more sun tolerant than the golden form, with pendulous green foliage adorned with thick and thin creamy white stripes.

Imperata (Poaceae)

Japan

This genus comprises just six species of slender-stemmed, rhizomatous perennial grasses from tropical and warm-temperate grasslands in their native habitat, of which one, *Imperata cylindrica* 'Red Baron', looks very exotic and delicate.

Imperata cylindrica 'Red Baron'

Japanese blood grass

Frost-hardy / Sun or dappled shade

Slowly spreading perennial grass growing to 40 cm high and 30 cm wide, forming loose clumps of flat, linear, midgreen leaves to 50 cm long that quickly turn an intense blood red from the tips almost to the base. Prefers well-drained, moist soil. Hardy to about −10°c but may need mulch during the winter, especially when plants are young.

Liriope (Ruscaceae)

China, Vietnam, Taiwan, and Japan

This genus of five or six species of evergreen and semi-evergreen perennials is closely related to *Ophiopogon*. They are indigenous to acid woodlands in their native habitats, with tufted, rhizomatous, evergreen and semi-evergreen foliage. They are tough and have a dense root system giving rise to arching, linear, grasslike leaves, forming dense clumps or mats

and sending up exquisite flower spikes. They are very useful for difficult corners of the garden with dappled to full shade. They prefer light, free-draining, moist, acid soil, although they also grow well on neutral soils and take drought well once established.

Liriope muscari

Lilyturf

Hardy / Dappled to full shade

Tufted evergreen perennial forming dense clumps or mats to 30 cm tall and 46 cm wide with glossy, strap-shaped, narrow dark green leaves 25–38 cm long. Purplish green flower stems carry dense spikes of small vivid purplish violet flowers from early to late autumn, followed by black berries. 'Big Blue' has intense violet-blue flowers. 'John Burch' has golden yellow variegated foliage. 'Majestic' has narrow, linear leaves and tall, often flattened spikes of rich lavender-blue flowers. 'Monroe White' has green-stalked racemes of white flowers and prefers deep shade. 'Variegata' has handsome green leaves boldly edged in yellow.

Luzula (Juncaceae)

Woodrush

Mostly cool-temperate regions of the Northern Hemisphere

Plants in this genus of about eighty species of mostly evergreen, tufted, clump-forming, grasslike perennials are found growing in heaths, moors, bogs, scrubland, woodland, and mountainous grassland and on streamsides throughout the temperate regions of the world. Some have a very exotic appearance with wide, short leaves, making them excellent in groups or as ground cover in dryish to moist shaded woodland areas. They will also take sun in moist locations. Most are hardy to at least −10°c.

Luzula sylvatica

Greater woodrush

Frost-hardy / Sun or shade

Tussock-forming, spreading, rhizomatous evergreen perennial with basal, shiny, linear dark green

Miscanthus sinensis 'Zebrinus'

leaves up to 30 cm long by 2 cm across and hairy, especially on the edges. In late spring, groups of tiny, dark brown, open panicles up to 8 cm long are borne on stems 60 cm tall. 'Aurea' has broad leaves that are yellowy green in summer and shiny bright yellow in winter; good for brightening up dull corners of the garden. 'Marginata' has a rather dense habit, with shiny, rich dark green leaves with prominent cream edges and pendent golden brown spikelets in late spring.

Miscanthus sinensis 'Cabaret'

Miscanthus (Poaceae)

Africa to Asia

Miscanthus encompasses some twenty species of deciduous to evergreen, tufted or rhizomatous perennial grasses with reedlike stems occurring in moist meadows and marshlands in their native habitats. Considered the showiest group of warm-season, clump-forming grasses, they are grown in cultivation for their often striking foliage and their panicles of flowers in late summer and autumn, very useful for adding height and backbone and movement to the exotic garden. Although not fussy, they prefer moderately fertile, well-drained, moist soil in full sun and are hardy to at least −10°C.

Miscanthus sacchariflorus

Frost-hardy / Full sun

Deciduous, robust, upright, tufted, clump-forming perennial grass growing to a height of 3 m with flat, linear, arching bluish green leaves up to 90 cm long, with pale silver-green midribs. Takes on warm orangish brownish tones in autumn. Rarely flowers in cool-summer gardens.

Miscanthus sinensis

Japanese silver grass
Frost-hardy / Full sun

Tall, clump-forming grass from Japan with erect stems growing to a height of 4 m with mostly basal, erect to arching, linear bluish green leaves up to 1.2 m long and panicles of silky, pale grey spikelets, tinted purplish brown. 'Cabaret' has broad midgreen leaves with conspicuous white stripes, up to 1.8 m

tall. 'Strictus' (banded miscanthus, porcupine grass) has stiff, upright, gold-banded leaves and stems. 'Variegatus' (variegated Japanese silver grass) has pendulous leaves 1.8 m long with creamy white and pale green stripes. 'Zebrinus' (zebra grass) has long, arching leaves 1.2 m long with pale yellow to almost white horizontal banding. Variety *condensatus* 'Cosmopolitan' has green-centred leaves with wide cream-white margins and grows to 2.5 m tall.

Ophiopogon (Lilaceae)

Lilyturf, mondo grass
Eastern Asia, especially China and Japan

Ophiopogon is a genus of some twenty species of evergreen, rhizomatous, often swollen, sometimes stoloniferous plants found in shady scrub and woodland areas of their native habitats. They are mainly grown for their dense tufts of short grasslike leaves. They are excellent, fairly slow-growing ground covers that make a good foil for other plantings, especially the popular dark form *O. planiscapus* 'Nigrescens'. They prefer slightly acid, moist, well-drained, humus-rich soil in full sun to dappled shade. Once established they can take periods of drought.

Ophiopogon planiscapus

Black mondo grass
Hardy / Sun or dappled shade

Clump-forming, rhizomatous, spreading perennial growing to 20 cm tall by 30 cm wide or more, with dark green, curved, straplike leaves 10–35 cm long. Racemes of lilac-white flowers appear in summer. 'Nigrescens' is a stunning form with almost black foliage, a wonderful foil to exotics with lighter leaves.

Pennisetum (Scrophulariaceae)

Tropical, subtropical, and warm-temperate areas
  worldwide

Pennisetum is a genus of about eighty species of rhizomatous, clump- or mat-forming, annual and perennial grasses found growing in wooded and savannah areas. Many species and hybrids work well in exotic Mediterranean, gravel, and desert gardens, often looking especially good in containers. They prefer moist, well-drained, light, moderately fertile soil in full sun. There are many exciting forms of gardenworthy *Pennisetum* to experiment with; I have included only those with colourful foliage and flowers.

Pennisetum setaceum

Fountain grass
Semi-tender, full sun

Domed, densely tufted, deciduous perennial hailing from tropical Africa, Arabia, and southwestern Asia, often grown as an annual in cooler climates. Grows to a height of 90 cm with upright, slender stems and narrow, linear, rough-textured, rigid midgreen leaves 30–60 cm long. Bears purplish

*Ophiopogon
planiscapus
'Nigrescens'*

*Pennisetum
setaceum*

pink, plumed, bristled, upright then nodding, narrow spikelets up to 30 cm long in summer. 'Atrosanguineum' has delicious burgundy foliage that is green at the base, with nodding plumes of soft reddish purple in summer. 'Burgundy Giant' (syn. *P. macrostachyum* 'Burgundy Giant') is a stunning form with shiny, broad bronze-burgundy leaves up to 25 mm across, with stalks up to 1.2 m topped with whitish pink plumes. 'Rubrum' (purple fountain grass) is rich reddish burgundy, with leaves up to 2 cm across, blooming from late summer to first frost, with racemes up to 30 cm long. Unfortunately *P. setaceum* is rather tender, requiring a minimum of 5°C during the winter months, so must be overwintered or purchased annually as it rarely sets seed. Looks marvellous in containers.

Saccharum (Poaceae)

Warm temperate and tropical areas worldwide

This genus contains some forty species of clump-forming or rhizomatous perennials, found growing in fertile river valleys and by rivers and streams in their native habitats. It includes the well-known edible sugarcane, *S. officinarum*, which is widely cultivated in warm regions of the world. Luckily, though, there are a few that will survive the vagaries of a cool-temperate winter! They prefer moist, well-drained, fertile soil in full sun to dappled shade. The following are hardy down to −15°C and lower.

Saccharum arundinaceum

Hardy sugarcane

Hardy / Sun or dappled shade

Hardiest and most spectacular of the sugarcanes, from India and southern Asia, growing to a height and spread of 2.7 m and more. Handsome foliage provides a wonderful tropical feel and vertical accent to the garden. Clump-forming perennial with long, broad grey-green leaves and white midribs. From late summer to early autumn, produces large panicles of light pink fading to silver, held well above the foliage. Looks imposing throughout the winter with its conspicuously red-tinted and orange-toned foliage.

Saccharum ravennae

Hardy / Sun or dappled shade

Upright, clump-forming perennial from northern Africa and the Mediterranean region, growing to 4.2 m tall with large basal mounds of grey-green leaves to 1.2 m tall and 25 mm across. Large plumes are borne on stout stems that are slightly pink-tinted when first opening, turning a lustrous silver with age, looking good all winter.

Setaria (Poaceae)

Tropical and subtropical regions, especially South America, Africa, and Australia

Members of this genus of more than one hundred annual and perennial species are found growing in woodlands and open grasslands in their native habitats. The only one that suits the exotic garden is *S. palmifolia* with its handsome, somewhat palm-like foliage. Unfortunately, it is not hardy unless you live in a warm, almost frost-free location. Although it gets big, it should be dug up before the first frost and stored at a minimum temperature of 5°C.

Setaria palmifolia

Palm grass

Semi-tender / Full sun

Very attractive, clump-forming, course-textured perennial growing up to 3 m tall in tropical climates and more like 1.5 m planted out annually. Leaves arch from slender stems, changing to linear, tapering, shiny, rich green and conspicuously pleated or corrugated, 7.5 cm across, up to 1.2 m in length. Makes an excellent container plant with its sumptuous pleated leaves hanging gracefully over the sides.

Uncinia (Cyperaceae)

Southern Hemisphere, though mostly Australia to New Guinea and South and Central America

Uncinia is a genus of some fifty rhizomatous or tufted, low-growing perennial species closely related to *Carex*. The form *U. rubra* is much praised by

Setaria palmifolia

gardeners for its exotic-looking reddish brown foliage, which thrives in warmer gardens.

Uncinia rubra

Frost-hardy / Full sun

Loosely tufted evergreen perennial with small rhizomes, growing to 30 cm high by 35 cm wide, with linear, shiny, abruptly pointed red-brown to bronze leaves. Spikes of brown flowers are borne above foliage in summer. Hardy to about −10°C.

Xanthorrhoea

(Xanthorrhoeaceae)

Balga grass, black boy, grass tree
Australia

Xanthorrhoea is a genus of fifteen species of grass trees indigenous to most parts of Australia. They are exceedingly slow-growing, long-lived (to more than 350 years) woody perennials with long, linear leaves and blackened trunks. In temperate climates they are best grown as container plants put out for the summer months and then overwintered at a minimum of 5°C, although they can take temperatures down to almost freezing for short periods. They prefer light, sandy, free-draining soil in full sun. Plants in this family are known as balga (black boy) grass to the Australian aborigines, probably because after a wildfire, the bottom leaves have burned away and reveal a singed black trunk with long green reedlike leaves extending from its top, giving the appearance of a black figure. If you are lucky enough to own one, look after it well, as they are now virtually impossible to obtain! Grass trees have been classified by the Australian government as rare and endangered species; their harvest and subsequent export was prohibited after December 2005.

Xanthorrhoea johnsonii

Xanthorrhoea glauca

Narrow-leaved grass tree
Semi-tender / Full sun

Exceedingly slow-growing and rare form of grass tree with branched, blackened trunk, growing to a height of 6 m in the wild, with very thin, linear, glaucous bluish green leaves.

Xanthorrhoea johnsonii

Black boy, grass tree
Semi-tender / Full sun

With a blackened trunk, this exceedingly slow-growing species grows to 2 m tall by 90 cm wide with clusters of upright, bright green to bluish green, very narrow, grasslike leaves.

Restios

The restios are a family of plants from South Africa, Australia, and New Zealand, related to the sedges and often known as restioids. These plants are reedlike and vary from those a few centimetres tall to the big giants like *Rhodocoma gigantea*. There are believed to be around 38 genera and 400 species in this diverse family. Being cool-season plants, they are most active in spring and autumn, with an evergreen presence all year. There are many beautiful species with few yet in cultivation. They are attractive in pots and can be planted singly or in groups.

Restios are part of the fynbos biotic community of southern coastal South Africa, characterised by natural burning and relatively poor soil. At the National Botanical Gardens in Cape Town, South Africa, researchers have found that smoke treatment of the seeds greatly increases germination. This method is also used at Trevena Cross Nurseries in Cornwall, England. Most restios prefer well-drained acid soil that retains moisture in summer, although some will tolerate soils with higher lime content. A mulch of bark or straw will help retain moisture in summer and protect the roots from frost damage in winter; most will tolerate some degree of frost, although the hardiness of these plants need more research.

John Eddy of Trevena Cross Nurseries has supplied much of the following information. He grows around twenty varieties of restios in his own garden and has found that most of them seem to be very happy in neutral soils. The main consideration to bear in mind is that they do not like very rich soils and they really do need an open, sunny site. Young plants can look rather insignificant but once planted out and established, they transform into amazingly handsome plants worthy of any garden. If space allows, planting in blocks can create a truly tremendous effect.

Chondropetalum tectorum, flowers

Calopsis (Restionaceae)

South Africa

This genus encompasses some twenty-four species, mostly occurring in the southwestern Cape Province of South Africa. They are attractive waterside plants, normally found growing in waterlogged soils on river or stream banks.

Calopsis paniculata

Frost-hardy / Full sun

Tall, exotic-looking, tussock-forming species with rhizomatous roots, growing to 2–3 m high by 2 m wide, spreading to form large groups of finely branched stems much like bamboo culms. Bright green cylindrical stems are topped in autumn by hundreds of light brown spikelets, much used in South Africa as cut foliage. Prefers neutral to acid, well-drained, moist soil, as it occurs naturally in marshy areas. Hardy to −7°C and maybe lower.

Chondropetalum

(Restionaceae)

South Africa

This genus of about fifteen species of rushlike plants is native to the Cape Province of South Africa, forming tussocks up to 2 m tall once used for thatching. They are cool-season plants that are most active in spring and autumn but have a good evergreen presence all year. There are many attractive forms with only a few known in cultivation.

Chondropetalum mucronatum

Frost-hardy / Full sun

Magnificent structural restio forming erect tussocks up to 2 m tall and 1 m wide from rhizomatous roots. In summer, light brown bractlike flowers occur at the terminal ends of each stem. Like *C. tectorum*, it has sheaths at the nodes along the culms, which drop off and leave small, distinct, dark abscission rings. In its native habitat *C. mucronatum* forms extensive stands often much taller than the surrounding vegetation. Prefers acid, well-drained soil in winter that holds some moisture in summer. Makes a fine accent plant for sunny beds and borders. Its true hardiness is unknown but it has survived −5°C at Trevena Cross Nurseries in Cornwall, England.

Chondropetalum tectorum

Frost-hardy / Full sun

Rhizomatous perennial forming an erect tussock up to 1.5 m tall, looking somewhat like the common rush *Juncus effuses* though more relaxed, forming an arc that touches the ground. This is more pronounced in the male form, with the female form usually being more upright. Makes a very attractive, fast-growing, tufted clump with cylindrical, rich dark green stems without any leaves, radiating in an arc up to 2 m wide. Male and female flowers, which are dark brown and narrowly clustered at the stem tips, are borne on separate plants. A very attractive sculptural plant for the garden and also for growing in large pots and containers. Prefers any well-drained, preferably moist soil, as it occurs naturally in marshy areas, but tolerates limey soils. Probably one of the hardiest, reaching the danger zone somewhere between −8°C and −10°C.

Elegia (Restionaceae)

South Africa

Some members of this genus of some thirty species native to the Cape Province of South Africa are rushlike, while others resemble the horsetails. They are cool-season plants mostly active in spring. They tend to be slow growers when juvenile, speeding up with maturity. They prefer moist, fairly poor, well-drained soil in full sun.

Elegia capensis

Frost-hardy / Full sun

Rhizomatous, clump-forming, rigidly upright perennial growing to 2.1 m high by 1.5 m wide, looking strikingly similar to a giant horsetail. Green, well-spaced, dense whorls of threadlike branchelets appear at the nodes up the cylindrical stems.

Produces golden brown flowers in spring followed by dark brown seed heads in autumn at the shoot tips. Highly conspicuous papery leaf bracts are held close to the stems before flowering, giving the whole a very ornamental appearance. As long as it is planted in free-draining soil, it should be hardy to around −8°C.

Elegia grandis

Frost-hardy / Full sun

Clump-forming, rhizomatous perennial, growing to a height and spread of about 1 m, with erect, cylindrical, greyish green stems topped by large showy seed heads with attractive grey bracts all year, widely used as dried foliage in South Africa. This beautiful structural plant will bring an exotic feel to any garden, whether in a pot or in the border, especially when associated with large-leaved plants. Prefers moisture-retentive acid to neutral soil. Has survived −5°C at Trevena Cross Nurseries in Cornwall, England, without showing any signs of damage.

Ischyrolepis (Restionaceae)

South Africa

Ischyrolepis is a genus of forty-nine species of restio, of which only the following two are presently available.

Ischyrolepis ocreata

Frost-hardy / Full sun

Clump-forming, fine-textured restio from South Africa with decorative seed heads in late summer and autumn. Grows like a rush to 1 m high and wide. Prefers well-drained acidic soil. Alternatively can be grown in large tubs and containers in free-draining low phosphate ericaceous compost. Protect from severe frost.

Ischyrolepis subverticillata

Frost-hardy / Sun or dappled shade

Architectural, tufted, clump-forming perennial growing to 1.5 m tall by 1 m wide with long, dark green, arching stems, with whorls of modified branches at each node, with a feathery fernlike appearance. Widely used in the cut flower industry as foliage. Small greenish yellow flowers turn into shiny speckled grey nutlets when mature. In its native habitat it grows naturally as close as 50 m from the sea. Prefers acid soil that drains well in winter but does not dry out too much in summer. Looks stunning when planted in large pots and containers. Has proven hardy to −8°C at Trevena Cross Nurseries.

Restio (Restionaceae)

South Africa, Australia

This genus of almost one hundred rushlike species is found mostly in the Cape Province of South Africa, with a few species in Australia.

Restio bifarius

Frost-hardy / Full sun

Architectural, tufted, clump-forming perennial growing to 1 m high by 60 cm wide with an erect tussock of rushlike foliage with decorative chestnut brown seed heads in summer and attractive deep brown bracts all year. Makes a stunning accent or feature plant in the exotic garden. Prefers well-drained acidic soil, or grow in large containers in very well-drained ericaceous compost. Mulch well with bark. Hardy to about −5°C.

Restio quadratus

Frost-hardy / Full sun

Rhizomatous, clump-forming perennial growing with a reedlike habit to about 2 m high by up to 1.5 m wide in a warm location. Young culms look very attractive, with dark green, soft, fluffy-looking foliage. Mature stems are thick and square with clusters of sterile branches at the nodes giving a feathery appearance. Makes a great specimen plant for the exotic garden. Water very freely for the first summer. Prefers free-draining acid to neutral soil. Probably hardy to about −5°C.

Restio tetraphyllus

Frost-hardy / Full sun

Rhizomatous, creeping, densely clump-forming perennial with a weeping habit, somewhat reminiscent of a miniature bamboo with its smooth, slender, cylindrical green stems to a height and spread of about 1 m. Thin, bright green, thread-like foliage is carried from about halfway up each stem. An Australian variety introduced to Trevena Cross Nurseries in Cornwall, England, many years ago by a specialist grower of Australian plants in northern England, who told them that he had been growing it in his garden for years and that it had survived many harsh winters. In Australia plumes are used commercially as cut foliage in florist shops and flower stalls. Works exceedingly well in pots and containers as long as adequate water is provided at all times—it will not tolerate drying out. Prefers well-drained neutral to acid soil. Hardy to about −10°C.

Rhodocoma (Restionaceae)

South Africa

Rhodocoma is one of the smaller genera of the restio family, with six described species, of which two are mentioned here.

Rhodocoma capensis

Frost-hardy / Full sun

Extremely elegant, clump-forming, tufted perennial, with slightly arching cylindrical stems to 1.5 m tall by 1 m wide, with sturdy and distinct nodes like a bamboo. At each node there is a thick whorl of finely divided, fertile branchlets, giving the whole plant a feathery appearance. Branchlets are covered in tiny brown spikelets when mature, somewhat resembling a large-flowered pampas grass. Very exotic looking for the border and also looks good planted in large pots or containers. Prefers acid soil that is fairly poor in nutrients. Hardy to about −10°C.

Rhodocoma gigantea

Frost-hardy / Full sun

Very attractive, tufted, erect, clump-forming perennial, forming a dense green feathery mass up to 1.2 m high by 1–1.2 m wide, with fast-growing, long, arching plumes to a height of 3 m in one season, similar to a bamboo, topped with chestnut brown seed heads from autumn onward. Prefers very moisture-retentive acid soil, drier in winter. Stunning as an accent plant. Works well as a container plant, especially if your soil is chalky.

Rhodocoma capensis

Trees and Shrubs

An exotic garden without trees and shrubs would be a rather dull place, as they give height and structure to the garden. Though we cannot grow truly tropical or subtropical species and varieties, we can grow plants that are hardy to borderline but have a truly exotic feel. Not only their tropical-looking foliage, flowers, or general habit but also their sheer stature gives backbone and lends interest to the garden. And the fact is that many common or garden trees and shrubs when surrounded by the more tender exotics of the summer add a lush feel to the garden and seem to take on tropical tones of their own.

Although some of the trees mentioned here are fast growing, others will take their time. The urge these days is to purchase plants big, to give instant effect. Unfortunately, large trees and shrubs are very expensive and are often slow to get going again once planted. Young plants, on the other hand, have not had their root growth restricted by being in a pot for many years so tend to grow at a much faster rate, usually overtaking larger plants within a few years. Patience is a virtue and the journey of creating a garden is made all the more enjoyable by seeing the plants mature naturally.

If your garden is a blank canvas, these are the first ornamentals to plant. From here you can then work out where the shadier parts of the garden will be for those plants less tolerant of sun and wind. When purchasing new trees and shrubs always ascertain their eventual height and spread so you can give them plenty of room to grow.

Some of the plants mentioned here might seem rather tender for your location. I look at it this way: if you can have something mature to the point of flowering and you lose it in, say, the seventh winter, you will have enjoyed it for that amount of time rather than not at all, and besides, many trees and shrubs will reshoot from the base after a cold winter. The other thing to consider is that as they mature, many plants tend to become hardier, especially if grown in a warm microclimate or sheltered corner of the garden, or if you are prepared to give them minimal winter protection.

Abutilon (Malvaceae)

Chinese lantern tree
Subtropical areas worldwide

Members of this genus of about 150 species of evergreen and deciduous shrubs, perennials, and annuals are known as Chinese lantern trees because of their hanging flower bells. The flowers have developed to enable fertilisation by hummingbirds. The bright bells are carried from spring to autumn. Abutilons have heart-shaped or slightly lobed leaves. Although mainly tropical to subtropical, several can be planted outside permanently, preferably against the wall of a house or a garden wall facing south or west, where they will derive some winter protection. Horticultural fleece will give a few degrees of frost protection in cold weather. If they are cut down by frost, many will reshoot from the ground. Some are not at all hardy so should either be bedded out for the summer months or used as container plants that can be stored in frost-free conditions over the winter. Most prefer moderately fertile, well-drained soil.

Abutilon megapotamicum 'Variegatum'

Abutilon thompsonii, leaf detail

Abutilon ×suntense

Frost-hardy / Full sun

Fast-growing hybrid capable of withstanding −12°C that makes a fantastic display in spring with large lilac-blue flowers. With an upright habit, grows to 3.5 m tall and 2.4 m across, becoming lanky if not gently pruned each year. 'Violetta' has somewhat vinelike, dark green leaves and large, papery, deep violet flowers that appear in abundance in late spring and early summer. Unfortunately not long-lived but nevertheless a superb plant for the garden.

Abutilon thompsonii

Semi-tender / Full sun

Very upright shrub with bright green leaves, heavily mottled yellow. Pendulous flowers are creamy orange with maroon veining. Although not hardy (well, not in my garden anyway), a must for the exotic border bedded out during the summer months.

Abutilon megapotamicum

Frost-hardy / Full sun

Delightful evergreen to semi-evergreen shrub from Brazil, with scarlet and gold pendulous flowers throughout the summer months, attaining a height and spread of 2.5 m. Prefers being planted against a sunny wall in well-drained soil; excellent for a large container. Habit is quite lax so may need some support or can be tied onto a trellis or wall. Flowers are fairly small but produced in abundance. Hardy to about −7°C with protection. If cut down by frost, will normally reshoot from the base by late spring.

Used in this way the height is really dictated by the size you can store during the winter. Plants grown from cuttings taken in spring will reach a height of 1–1.5 m by the end of the season. I let mine grow to around 3.5 m, then cut them down to 2 m before the first frost arrives and pot in well-drained garden soil. Overwinter at a minimum of 5°C.

Abutilon vitifolium

Frost-hardy / Full sun

Fast-growing, rather weakly branched shrub from Chile that wants to be a tree if not pruned after flowering! Grows to 4.5 m tall and 2.4 m across. Large, saucer-shaped, five-petalled flowers range from violet-purple to pure white with a golden centre and are carried in bunches all over in late spring and early summer. White form *A. vitifolium* var. *album* looks stunning against blue sky with its petticoat-like flowers. Sharply toothed, maplelike grey-green leaves make a good foil for the flowers. Although only considered hardy to around −5°C, has easily taken −8°C for short periods in my garden and would probably take lower temperatures if grown in well-drained soil.

Abutilon hybrids

Semi-tender to frost-hardy / Full sun

Many hybrids are available now in dark maroons to bright yellows and pinks. I find that these work best as container plants for the summer. Most will become substantial plants with time so should be pruned after flowering to keep in shape.

Acacia (Fabaceae)

Mimosa, wattle
Mostly Australia

This genus contains about twelve hundred species of handsome trees and shrubs that tend to flower early in the year and are used widely in the cut flower market. The common name "wattle" derives from the fact that early settlers in Australia used them for simple wattle-and-daub dwellings—the walls were constructed of interwoven acacia branches and then daubed with mud. In Europe and the United States they are more commonly known as mimosa. The flowers are usually highly scented and yellow, in crowded globose heads or cylindrical spikes, set against green to greyish green or silver finely cut foliage. An acacia tree in full bloom is an amazing sight. Give it moderately fertile, well-drained soil, and shelter it from wind.

Acacia baileyana 'Purpurea'

Cootamundra wattle
Frost-hardy / Full sun

Large shrub or small tree to 7.5 m tall if planted in a sheltered, sunny position. Leaves are bluish purple with clusters of ten to twenty-five deep yellow, globular flower heads in spring and sometimes into summer. New foliage has a purplish tint. Hardy to around −5°C.

Acacia dealbata

Silver wattle mimosa
Frost-hardy / Full sun

Fast-growing medium-sized tree to approximately 8 m tall, probably even taller in a sheltered location. Produces the classic florist cut flower in the form of bright yellow sprays composed of twenty-five to thirty-five flowers in globular heads, and feathery leaves that are silvery green to dark green. Takes −7°C in its stride and probably colder for short periods. Grows well on poor soil and is extremely drought tolerant once established. In mild winters will flower from the middle of January, giving a very welcome spot of colour and heralding the spring to come. *Acacia dealbata* subsp. *subalpina* is the hardiest form of mimosa, collected at high altitudes; has endured −11°C in Norwich without any damage and might go even lower. Vigorous evergreen small tree covered in clouds of bright yellow, highly scented flowers in late winter to early spring. Can be hard pruned, coppiced, or pollarded.

Acacia pravissima

Oven's wattle, wedge-leaf wattle
Frost-hardy / Full sun

Acacia pravissima

Evergreen shrub with arching growth, covered in bright yellow mimosa flowers in racemes of six to nine globular heads in spring, aging to orange-yellow to coppery-brown. Phyllodes (flat leaflike stalks that look like tiny flattened triangles) run the length of each stem. New growth is often very bronzy or reddish, especially in the cooler weather of winter. Good acacia for small gardens, with a maximum height of about 6 m in cool-temperate climates. Lower branches can be removed to make it look more like a small tree with pendulous branches.

Acacia rubida

Acacia melanoxylon

Blackwood
Frost-hardy / Full sun

Small to large spreading tree, 8 m tall or more; in northwest Tasmania, reaches 45 m tall with a trunk more than 1 m wide. Phyllodes are greyish, turning dark dull green, and bark is grey. Inflorescence is made up of thirty to fifty pale yellow-cream flowers in globular heads on pubescent to hoary peduncles that appear from January to April. Good in coastal areas. Will take temperatures of −5°C and probably lower in a sheltered position. Hard wood is used for making spears and boomerangs.

Acacia obliquinervia

Mountain hickory wattle
Frost-hardy / Full sun

Shrub to small tree up to 15 m tall in the wild and 5–8 m in cool-temperate cultivation. Twiggy branches are reddish to purple and often glaucous. Inflorescence is bright yellow and globular in shape and consists of twenty to twenty-four flowers per head in March through May. Will take temperatures of −5°C and probably lower in a sheltered position.

Acacia rubida

Red-stemmed wattle
Frost-hardy / Full sun

Medium shrub or small tree up to 5 m tall. All red-stemmed wattles have straight or curved phyllodes up to 20 cm long. Most (even mature plants) carry some juvenile bipinnate leaves. In winter, leaves and stems often have a distinctive red colour. Inflorescence has ten to twenty bright yellow flowers in globular heads in spring.

Albizia julibrissin

Albizia (Fabaceae)

Pink serus, silk tree

Iran to Japan

This interesting genus encompasses about 118 species of deciduous and semi-evergreen subtropical trees and shrubs that will grow in temperate gardens in a very sheltered position on well-drained soil. Albizias are grown for their feathery, bipinnate foliage and unusual flower heads, which are composed of multiple stamens looking like a cross between a shaving brush and a bottlebrush. Most prefer poor, well-drained soil.

Albizia julibrissin

Frost-hardy / Full sun

Very exotic and fast-growing deciduous tree with feathery foliage and pink flowers borne in abundance during the summer months. Capable of growing 1 m a year (slower in cooler climates) and reaching up to 7.5–9 m with a similar spread, though probably only 4.5 m in cool-summer areas. 'Rosea' has sprays of light pink, fine, brushlike, fragrant flowers in late summer on a large shrub or small tree with spreading, layered branches. Hardy to at least −6°c and probably lower in a warm corner of the garden. Can also be grown successfully as a container plant.

Aralia (Araliaceae)

North America, Asia, and Australia

Members of this genus of forty species of hardy shrubs, trees, and herbaceous plants in the ivy family are grown for their architectural foliage and profuse small flowers. The houseplant known as false aralia belongs to the related genus *Schefflera*. Here we are dealing only with *Aralia elata* and its variegated forms. In Japan the young shoots are cooked in tempura batter. Most are deciduous and all have very dramatic compound leaves.

Aralia elata

Japanese angelica tree

Hardy / Sun to part shade

Upright deciduous tree hailing from Japan that can reach 10 m in ideal conditions, growing as a suckering shrub to around 3.5 m in cool-temperate gardens. Stout stems are covered in sharp spines, so avoid planting next to a path! Huge bipinnate leaves reach 90 cm in length and are divided into numerous leaflets, each about 13 cm long. Two variegated varieties are available, 'Aureovariegata', which has leaflets edged in yellow, and 'Variegata', with creamy white margins to the leaflets. Billowing heads of tiny white flowers are produced in late summer on panicles up to 60 cm long. Aralias appreciate shelter, as cold winds can injure their large leaves, but otherwise the plants are very hardy. Foliage tends to appear at the tops of stems; if it becomes too leggy, can be cut to the ground and will reshoot readily. Prefers well-drained soil that doesn't get waterlogged in winter.

Araucaria (Araucariaceae)

Australia, New Caledonia, and other South Pacific
   islands, Chile and Argentina

There are nineteen species in this ancient genus of conifers. Here we deal only with the monkey puzzle, which grows on volcanic slopes in the Andes Mountains in southern Chile and southwestern Argentina. Being among the world's oldest trees, it is very odd looking and is really only suitable for

a large garden. It prefers moist, moderately fertile, well-drained soil in an open position protected from cold winds.

Araucaria araucana

Chile pine, monkey puzzle
Hardy / Full sun

Very popular in the Victorian period, imposing and majestic, looking prehistoric, and not for the timid gardener as it can be difficult to place. A common mistake is to plant near a house, which will cause problems later on, so plant young specimens at the end of the garden. Grows relatively slowly to a height of about 18 m. In Argentina, where some are thought to be a thousand years old, can reach 50 m. Overall appearance is rather open, with widely spaced whorls of stiff, spreading branches that droop on older specimens. Dark green, hard, sharp, overlapping leaves densely cover branches. Received its name because its leaves would supposedly make it difficult for monkeys to climb! Hardy to about −17°C.

Arbutus (Ericaceae)

Ireland, Mediterranean region to western Europe, and western United States

Arbutus is a small genus of fourteen species of evergreen shrubs and trees grown mainly for their leaves, pendulous scented flowers, and interesting bark. They make good garden plants as they grow fairly slowly. They also flower in the depths of winter when not much else is in bloom. All prefer fertile, humus-rich soil in a sheltered position. The following two will tolerate alkaline soils.

Arbutus ×andrachnoides

Red-barked strawberry tree
Hardy / Full sun

Delightful small evergreen tree that flowers in winter, has very tactile bark, and will grow in almost any soil condition to boot! Lustrous dark green leaves are finely serrated and form a dense canopy. Trunk and branches are covered in peeling bark, changing from cinnamon red to sandy yellow. Clusters of small, creamy white, delicately scented flowers are produced from autumn to spring, making it a welcome sight on cold winter days. There are several named forms, some no more than 2–3 m tall. Young plants should be staked for the first few years but they are surprisingly tolerant of strong winds and can succeed in fairly exposed positions near the coast. Very good tree to grow in towns as it tolerates pollution well. Hardy to around −15°C.

Arbutus unedo

Strawberry tree
Hardy / Full sun

Bushy shrub 2–3 m tall in its native Mediterranean region and Ireland, reaching up to 8 m in more northerly areas. Brownish red bark is rough and peeling, with leathery dark green leaves and drooping panicles of white flowers tinged with pink and green. Latin name *unedo* means "I eat one," a reference to the bitter fruit, which is reminiscent of a strawberry. Hardy to around −15°C.

Araucaria araucana

Asimina (Annonaceae)

Southern Europe and eastern North America

This is a genus of eight species of evergreen and deciduous trees and shrubs grown for their interesting flowers and foliage. All are hardy and prefer a position with full sun in moist, well-drained soil.

Asimina triloba

Hoosier banana, Indiana banana, pawpaw (not to be
  confused with the tropical fruit, though it is related
  to the custard apple), poor man's banana
Hardy / Full sun

Deciduous, large-leaved, medium-to-large shrub 2.5–3.5 m tall from the southeastern United States, the only temperate member of a tropical family. Strangely attractive, six-petalled, lurid liver-purple flowers grow directly from the branches in early summer. If grown in a warm location will produce bottle-shaped edible yellow fruits, 7.5–15 cm long. Leaves change to an attractive soft butter-yellow colour in autumn. Will grow in most soils and is best grown against a sunny wall in cooler areas. Two or more plants are needed to produce fruit. Being of a small size, works well in small gardens. Hardy to −15°c and lower.

Aucuba (Cornaceae)

Himalaya to Japan

Members of this genus of three or four species of tough, hardy, evergreen shrubs, much loved by Victorians, are somewhat like laurel in appearance with plain to spotted leaves. Aucubas are not fussy about growing conditions and take drought well. They can be grown in sun or dense shade and are useful for brightening up dark corners of the garden, especially the variegated forms, which resemble the more tropical croton (*Codiaeum*). They produce red fruits if male and female plants are grown close together. Aucubas can be pruned back hard in spring if required. All are hardy to around −15°c and tolerate both dry, sandy soils and very alkaline conditions.

Aucuba japonica

Japanese aucuba, Japanese laurel
Hardy / Sun or shade

Dense evergreen shrub 2–3.5 m high and wide with green shoots and glossy dark green leaves. Small, insignificant clusters of exquisite purple-brown flowers in spring are followed by red berries. Ironically, this shrub is not seen as often as the variegated relatives, which is a shame as it is stunningly magnificent if grown well. There are many cultivars now available on the market. 'Crassifolia' grows to 2.5 m tall and wide, has green leaves up to 25 cm long, and bears small purple-red flowers with yellow anthers in spring. 'Crotonifolia' (male) has glossy dark green leaves that are heavily mottled creamy yellow, spattered with specks and splashes of yellowish cream, like a Jackson Pollock painting in 3D. 'Gold Dust' (female) has glossy dark green leaves that are speckled with gold. 'Longifolia' has narrow, arching, immaculate, plain green leaves, very

similar in appearance to the more tropical croton (*Codiaeum*). 'Picturata' (male) has glossy bright green leaves that are speckled yellow with a predominant central gold blotch. Because this cultivated sport is known to have a higher tendency to revert back to plain green leaves, may require more controlled pruning to retain its effect. 'Variegata', the original variegated introduction of *A. japonica* dating from 1783, has dark green leaves heavily spotted yellow and grows well in deep shade.

Brachyglottis (Asteraceae)

New Zealand and Tasmania

This genus contains about thirty species of ever-green trees and shrubs, herbaceous perennials, and climbers, found growing in scrub, rocky grassland, and forests. Many are excellent plants for a Medi-terranean-style garden. I have included only two here, with delectable, large, exotic leaves. Both pre-fer fertile, well-drained soil, with an annual feeding to make those leaves even bigger!

Brachyglottis repanda

Brachyglottis greyi × *B. repanda*

Half-hardy / Full sun

Shrub growing to 1.8 m tall and 1.2 m wide in gar-dens with little or no frost. Terminal velvety white stems hold large oval to elliptic, floppy, velvety grey-ish green leaves, silvery white on the underside, up to 25 cm long. Hardy to 0°C, hence best either bedded out for the summer months or as a conservatory plant up to about 1 m that can be placed on a sunny patio for the summer months.

Brachyglottis repanda

Semi-tender to half-hardy / Full sun

Spreading shrub growing to a height and spread of 3 m in its native habitat, though usually less in cool-temperate cultivation. Ovate to oblong, wavy margined, glossy dark green leaves are up to 20 cm long, velvety white on the underside. Arching panicles up to 30 cm long of creamy white flower heads are borne in summer. Tolerates only perhaps a light frost, so should only be considered for the warmest gardens. Makes a good container plant that can be brought under cover in winter. Prune yearly to keep in shape. 'Purpurea' has deep purple leaves that are velvety white underneath.

Brugmansia (Solanaceae)

Angel's trumpet
South America

The fabulous plants in this genus of seven species of small trees and shrubs, some of which are nevertheless capable of reaching a staggering 9 m tall or more in their native habitats (scrubby areas and along streamsides in South America, especially along the Andes range), are cultivated for their large, dramatic, extremely exotic, and often ridiculously scented flowers. Many brugmansias flower in bursts with resting periods in between, while others flower continuously. The common name "angel's trumpet" is shared with the closely related genus *Datura*, also known as thorn apple, which is a herbaceous perennial with upright flowers, while *Brugmansia* is a woody perennial often forming a small shrub or tree with pendulous flowers. In the horticultural trade, brugmansias are often mislabelled as *Datura*, much confusing the general public.

Many hybrids and numerous cultivars have been produced, especially in recent years. *Brugmansia* ×*candida*, for instance, is a hybrid between *B. aurea* and *B. versicolor*. Cultivars of *B.* ×*candida* can produce single and double flowers in shades of pink,

yellow, orange, or white. *Brugmansia* ×*insignis* produces flowers in shades of peach to white. *Brugmansia versicolor* has flowers that progress from white to varying shades of salmon pink.

Brugmansias are very easy to grow, requiring humus-rich, moist, well-drained soil, and most are fairly rapid growers. Most prefer cool summers, though some like it hot! They prefer sun to light shade and a position that is protected from prevailing winds, which can desiccate the flowers and foliage. Some species like *B. sanguinea* and *B. vulcanicola* are native to high elevations, hence require moderate temperatures and cool nights to flower and are best grown in shaded positions. Variegated forms, especially with pale to white patches on their foliage, prefer a shady spot because the lighter parts easily burn in full sun, though some will tolerate sun.

Although not considered hardy, *B. sanguinea* and *B. arborea* will take a few degrees of frost. The root system is hardier and will often overwinter outside if heavily mulched around the base, especially if grown against a south-facing wall in a well-drained position. Some of the other forms will also survive outside in a similar position in warmer areas or through mild winters. It is certainly worth trying if you don't have a storage facility; otherwise dig up when freezing nights are predicted and store frost-free for the winter months, leaving them on the dry side, watering occasionally if the soil dries out too much. During the winter they will mostly defoliate. Brugmansias can be stored at any height, as long as you have enough headroom! Watch out for red spider mite, which is prevalent under glass. Return to the outside once the threat of frost has passed. Brugmansias take well to container culture, providing containers are of a good size, where they will need plenty of water and regular applications of fertiliser as they are gross feeders.

Most brugmansias are easily propagated by taking cuttings 15–30 cm long (or longer) from branch ends or intersections from spring to early autumn (autumn is preferable as there is much more cutting material then) and placing them in water, with only about 3 cm of the stem submerged, to grow roots. Shorten the leaves on these cuttings by at least 50 per cent to reduce water loss while the plant is producing a new root system. Change the water every

few weeks as you watch the small white markings on the stems, called lenticels, turn into new roots. As soon as a root system appears, pot the cuttings in gritty, well-drained compost and keep at 7–15°C. Larger cuttings can be taken, even of considerable length. I have rooted branches the size of a person without any problems. This is a good system if you wish to grow a standard brugmansia quickly.

A small number of species and cultivars are available from local garden centres, often only labelled by their colour. Some nurseries produce a few named brugmansias. For the best choice, though, seek out specialist nurseries. One of the most influential growers and hybridisers in Europe, if not the world, is Monika Gottschalk in Herbstein, Germany. There are also some excellent nurseries that hybridise in the United States, listed at the back of this book.

Brugmansia, like *Datura*, is highly toxic in all parts, containing a strong consciousness-changing hallucinogen traditionally used by South American Indians to make contact with the gods and spirits of their ancestors. Without the guidance of a shaman, ingesting *Brugmansia* can be fatal.

Brugmansia arborea

syn. *B. cornigera*
Tender / Sun or light shade

Fairly small, open, evergreen shrub or tree that reaches 2–4 m tall, indigenous to the region from Ecuador to northern Chile and Bolivia. Young stems softly hairy with ovate, entire to coarsely toothed leaves 15–30 cm long. Flowers, developed continuously from late spring to autumn, are shortest of all the species, 12–17 cm long, nodding, trumpet-shaped, scented, and white to creamy.

Brugmansia ×candida 'Grand Marnier'

'Engelsgloeckchen' has small creamy white blooms. 'Sternchen' has small cream to yellowish blooms.

Brugmansia aurea

syn. *B. pittieri*
Tender / Sun or light shade

Open shrub or tree growing to a height of 5–10 m with ovate green leaves, coarsely toothed on young plants and smooth-edged on older ones, 15–24 cm long and sometimes longer. Hails from the Andes of Colombia to Ecuador. Flowers, borne mainly from summer to autumn, are 15–30 cm long, nodding to pendulous, trumpet-shaped, and deliciously scented, in shades of sulphur yellow, golden yellow, and apricot yellow (occasionally white to pink). Flower edges are very distinctive, twisting backward in spirals. 'Culebra' has fascinating if not rather odd white flowers deeply split along their length, looking almost as though they haven't developed properly, with long, thin leaves.

Brugmansia ×candida

Tender / Sun or light shade

Hybrid between *B. aurea* and *B. versicolor*, forming shrub or tree to 3–5 m tall. Young leaves and stems are fuzzy. Leaves ovate to elliptic, entire to coarsely toothed, with wavy margins, 30–60 cm long. From summer to autumn bears trumpet-shaped, strongly scented, pendulous flowers, 23–30 cm long, that can be white, yellow to apricot, or—rarely—pink. 'Grand Marnier' is an old variety with a colour range from pale brownish to apricot. New hybrids like 'Rubirosa', 'Ruby Lady', or 'Swingtime' have large dark pink single flowers, while 'Barcarole', 'Meadow Princess', 'Rosenwalzer', and 'Fascination' have large pink double blooms. 'Luise' has large cream-apricot double flowers. 'Maya' (syn. 'Sunset') has green-grey leaves with irregular white margins and soft creamy yellow-apricot blooms. This beautiful hybrid can be grown in full sun. 'Grazie Variegata' has light green/grey leaves with irregular yellow-green margins. 'Shredded White Fantasy' has unusual mutated flowers.

Brugmansia ×insignis

Tender / Sun or light shade

Open shrub or small tree reaching 2.4–3 m tall or more with green leaves. Nodding to horizontal, stiff, funnel-shaped flowers varying from white to cream and shades of pink are 25–40 cm long and have attractive, wispy, thin petal extensions from the rim that are often twisted or spiralled. Requires more summer warmth than the other species and flowers in bursts. 'Pink Favorite' has salmon pink blooms with darker edges.

Brugmansia sanguinea

Tender / Sun or light shade

Small, robust tree 3–5 m tall. Leaves on young plants are coarsely toothed while those on mature plants are nearly smooth-edged. Nodding flowers are very distinctive and spectacular, generally 15–25 cm long, tube-shaped and usually red at the mouth, becoming yellow, then yellowish green toward the base. Other colour forms are common. Hot summers inhibit flower development, as they prefer

*Brugmansia
sanguinea
'Feuerwerk'*

Brugmansia
suaveolens

cooler conditions; they also tolerate slight frost and will often regenerate from the ground at lower temperatures. 'Feuerwerk' has striking nodding blooms.

Brugmansia suaveolens

Tender / Sun or light shade

Generally the most commonly available brugmansia. Vigorous small shrub or tree 1.8–4.5 m or more tall. Leaf shape is ovate to narrowly elliptic with smooth margins. Funnel-shaped flowers are 20–30 cm long, nodding, occasionally horizontal, intensely scented, normally white to cream and occasionally yellow or pink. Flowers in bursts. 'Frosty Pink' has salmon pink blooms. 'Goldtraum' has golden yellow flowers. 'Jamaica Yellow' has soft yellow blooms. 'Pink Delight' has large pink blooms. 'Tropical Sunset' has yellowish blooms with darker orange edges.

Brugmansia versicolor

Tender / Sun or light shade

From tropical regions of Ecuador, bush or small tree 2.5–4.5 m tall, with elliptic to oblong smooth-edged leaves. Trumpet-shaped flowers, largest of all brugmansia flowers, 30–50 cm long with extended filaments, are drooping, strongly scented, usually white, becoming peach or pink with age, appearing in impressive bursts. 'Apricot Queen' has rich peach blooms. 'Creamsickle' has long white double blooms fading to soft creamy peach. 'Ecuador Pink' has intense pink blooms.

Brugmansia vulcanicola

Tender / Sun or light shade

Rarest of the brugmansia species and the most tender, shrub or small tree up to 3.5 m tall with ovate to elliptic, softly hairy, toothed or smooth-edged leaves, 15–25 cm long. Small flowers are 15–22 cm long, nodding to horizontal, often green at the base, changing to light red, then fading to a shade of yellow near the mouth. *Brugmansia* 'Roter Vulkan', a hybrid between *B. sanguinea* and *B. vulcanicola*, has small brick red blooms. There are several multi-coloured forms of *B. vulcanicola* in shades of yellow, pink, and red. As with *B. sanguinea*, *B. vulcanicola* and its hybrids prefer a cool climate. They should be kept at 10°C or higher over the winter.

Brugmansia hybrids

Tender / Sun or light shade

There are some very beautiful *Brugmansia* hybrids. The shape of the flower is often an intermediate between funnel and trumpet; some may even resemble *B.* ×*candida*, like the beautiful hybrid 'Day Dream' with large, pendent, double to triple pink blossoms, or 'Magnifique' with large triple white flowers. 'Edna' has large double white flowers. 'Fandango' has large, pendent, double cream-apricot flowers, while 'Bolero' with its trumpet-shaped, nodding, double, triple, quadruple, or sometimes even quintuple cream-yellow flowers almost resembles *B. aurea*. 'L'Amour', a hybrid between *B. aurea* and *B. versicolor*, has dark salmon blooms. 'Rosamond' has intense pink blooms. Almost all hybrids with golden yellow flowers belong in this group, such as 'Primrose Yellow', which is easy to obtain, and 'Herbstgold' with small double flowers in a bright golden yellow. Single and double flowers can be found in one flush. 'Herbstfeuer' has nodding double flowers in golden yellow.

Caesalpinia (Fabaceae, subfamily Caesalpiniaceae)

Tropical to warm-temperate regions worldwide

This is a genus of some 150 species of shrubs, a few of which seem to be fairly hardy in cool-temperate gardens with a little help. They need sandy, gritty soil that drains well. As with other plants in this cutting-edge style of gardening, these are worth trying outside, especially if you have a warm microclimate.

Caesalpinia gilliesii

Yellow bird-of-paradise
Frost-hardy / Full sun

Rather open and irregularly branched shrub with delicate feathery bipinnate foliage, hailing from Argentina and Uruguay, and now widespread in southern North America. Showy yellow flowers—not as vivid in colour as those of *C. pulcherrima* but nonetheless really tropical looking—have long red stamens through most of the summer. Try outside

Caesalpinia gilliesii, flowers

in a sheltered spot against a warm wall in a dry position. As with the other caesalpinias, as the plant matures and the wood ripens, it should withstand temperatures down to −12°C and lower.

Caesalpinia japonica

Frost-hardy / Full sun

Very twiggy, fast-growing, deciduous, scrambling, scandent shrub from Japan and China with vicious prickles 10 mm long. Bipinnate leaves 20–40 cm long have dull green leaflets that are whitish beneath. Alluring flowers 25–35 mm across in a strong rich yellow are formed in terminal racemes 20–30 cm long in late spring. Upper petal is smaller and striped with red. Has been known to endure −11°C in its stride.

Caesalpinia mexicana

Mexican poinciana
Frost-hardy / Full sun

From Texas and Mexico, another caesalpinia worth trying against a warm, south-facing wall, where it can grow up to 3.5 m tall if there is a run of mild winters; otherwise much shorter. Flowers are bright yellow and deliciously fragrant. Hardy to about

−8°c or lower with protection, especially in a favourable microclimate. Like all caesalpinias must be grown in very well-drained gritty soil.

Caesalpinia pulcherrima

syn. *Poinciana pulcherrima*
Barbados pride, red bird-of-paradise
Half-hardy / Full sun

From the West Indies, shrub with feathery bipinnate leaves offering a lush, fernlike appearance. In a hot summer becomes a blaze of colour with terminal clusters of fiery orange-red with a tinge of gold on the edges. Although not particularly hardy, worth trying against a warm, south-facing wall. Can reach 3 m or more, depending on how it coped with the previous winter. Hardy to about −1°c and a few degrees colder if covered with fleece; otherwise grow as a container plant. If cut back by frost, will probably regrow from the base if mulched heavily during the winter.

Callistemon (Myrtaceae)

Bottlebrush
Australia and Tasmania

There are about twenty species in the genus *Callistemon*, woody evergreen shrubs ranging from 50 cm to 4 m tall with spectacular flowers that are pollinated by birds in the wild. Until recently considered half-hardy and grown as conservatory plants in the British Isles, they deserve to be tried outside more often. Many species will take a fair amount of frost, especially if protected from the prevailing winds by a wall or hedge. In their first year out, young plants should be protected with horticultural fleece or something similar. Once established they will tolerate drought and limited maintenance. They grow well in a wide variety of soils except strongly alkaline. Callistemons grown in full sun produce the best flowers.

The flower spikes of bottlebrushes, made up of a number of individual flowers, form in spring and

Callistemon viminalis hybrid, flower spikes

Callistemon
'Mauve Mist',
flower spike

summer. The pollen of the flower forms on the tip of a long, coloured stalk called a filament. It is these filaments that give the flower spike its colour and distinctive shape. The filaments are usually red or yellow and sometimes the pollen also adds a bright yellow flush to the flower spikes. If you are concerned about hardiness in your area, bottlebrushes can be grown in tubs and containers that can be brought under cover in winter.

Callistemon citrinus

Lemon bottlebrush
Frost-hardy / Full sun

Shrub growing 1.5–2 m tall and 1.5 m wide with narrow, oblong, midgreen leaves and mauve-pink flowers that fade with age in summer. Crushing its leaves produces a delicious lemon scent. 'Splendens' is a form with brilliant scarlet flowers. Best planted in full sun on well-drained soil, preferably against a south-facing wall. Protect it from frosts below −5°C; will endure lower temperatures for short periods.

Callistemon linearis

Frost-hardy / Full sun

Shrub reaching a height and spread of 2 m with narrowly elliptic evergreen leaves. Flower spikes are a rich matte red and appear in late spring and summer. Prefers full sun and well-drained soil. Hardy to −8°C. Grows well near the sea and tolerates windy conditions.

Callistemon 'Mauve Mist'

Frost-hardy / Full sun

Shrubby evergreen that is slightly deciduous and grows to around 2 m tall by 1.5 m wide. Covered in spring and summer with bright pink brushes, set off well by dark green foliage. Although considered hardy to about −5°C, has been known to survive temperatures as low as −11°C. Prefers a slightly acid soil.

Callistemon pallidus

Frost-hardy / Full sun

Upright shrub with slender, spreading branches, growing to a height of 2–3 m. Pale lemon flowers produced in profusion contrast well with grey-green foliage. Leaves are tapered, up to 10 cm long, and dotted with oil glands. Young growth is often attractively covered with dense silky hairs, later becoming smooth. Flowers are borne from autumn to winter in profuse cylindrical spikes 50–100 cm long. Responds well to periodic pruning, which encourages a bushier growth habit. Although considered hardy to about −5°C, has been known to survive temperatures as low as −11°C.

Callistemon pityoides

Alpine bottlebrush
Hardy / Full sun

Rather dense-growing evergreen shrub 1.5 m high and 1 m wide with sharply pointed dark green leaves. Yellow flowers 4 cm long appear in summer. Reputed to be hardy down to −15°C. Like all callistemons, must be planted in well-drained soil.

Callistemon 'Red Clusters'

Australian bottlebrush
Hardy / Full sun

Very vigorous and rounded evergreen shrub growing to 2.5 m tall and 2 m wide with lanceolate leaves 6 cm long. Newly emerging shoots are pink. Abundant flowers are crimson red spikes with gold anthers that appear in spring and autumn. Hardy to around −7°C.

Callistemon rigidus

Hardy bottlebrush
Frost-hardy / Full sun

Evergreen shrub growing to 2 m tall and 1.5 m wide. Cylindrical dark red flowers appear from midsummer to early autumn. Prune after flowering to keep its bushy habit. Hardy to around −8°C although I have heard reports of it taking temperatures of −15°C for short periods; the leaves will become burnt if there is strong wind chill. As its common name describes, will grow happily in most gardens given a little protection. Ideal for coastal gardens as it tolerates salt and wind well. Stake new plants to stop wind rock; I have seen plants literally take off in high winds!

Callistemon salignus

Frost-hardy / Full sun

Spreading shrub to 3 m or more tall and wide with white or greenish, sometimes pale yellow or pink, flowers in summer and early autumn. Hardy to −7°C.

Callistemon sieberi

Alpine bottlebrush
Hardy / Full sun

Thought by some growers to be the hardiest callistemon in cultivation. Foliage is dense and narrow, suggesting flattened conifer needles rather than leaves. Flower spikes appear creamy white with just a hint of lemon and are more rounded than elongated.

Callistemon subulatus

Hardy / Full sun

Ornamental callistemon with narrowly elliptic leaves and masses of very attractive bright crimson bottlebrush flowers 10 cm long by 3 cm wide in summer. Prefers well-drained, slightly acid soil. Hardy to −10°C once established.

Callistemon viminalis

Weeping bottlebrush
Frost-hardy / Full sun

This large bottlebrush is widely cultivated. Evergreen arching shrub producing bright red flower spikes redolent of a 'bottle brush,' in early summer. *Callistemon viminalis* occurs naturally on the east coast of Australia from Cape York to northeastern New South Wales, where it grows from 5 to 7 m tall. For optimum results it should be planted in moist, well-drained soil in full or partial sun, though will take drought once established. The species is susceptible to frost damage while small and suitable protection is necessary.

Catalpa (Bignoniaceae)

Eastern Asia and North America

Members of this genus of eleven species of deciduous shrubs and trees, grown for their leaves and flowers, are short-lived but tolerate hot weather and city pollution well. They tend to grow rapidly at first and then slow down with age, and can reach 27.5 m tall, though 15 m would be more typical. They prefer a sunny position in well-drained, moist, rich soil. The foxglovelike flowers, white with yellow and purple markings, are scented and very ornamental, appearing in panicles in early summer. In autumn, fruit appears in the shape of long pods. All are hardy to −15°C and lower.

Catalpa bignonioides

Indian bean tree, southern catalpa
Hardy / Full sun

Handsome, exotic-looking tree from the southeastern United States, reaching a height and spread of 15 m when mature and 2.5 m when pollarded yearly, which it takes well. One of the last trees to come into leaf, producing large heart-shaped pale green leaves in late spring, larger when pollarded. When mature, produces flower heads of white with gold and purple markings in midsummer. Beanlike seedpods up to 40 cm long remain throughout the winter, giving rise to its common name. Leaves are likely to be damaged in

windy positions. 'Aurea' (golden Indian bean tree) is a shrub to 2.5 m with large golden yellow leaves that look dramatic against a dark blue sky and become greener as the season progresses. Flowers are 5 cm long, white with yellow and purple markings, frilled at the mouth on upright 20-cm spikes in early summer. 'Variegata' (variegated Indian bean tree) grows to a height and spread of 5 m with heart-shaped green leaves with creamy white markings that turn green with maturity. Flowers are white with yellow and purple markings and appear from late spring to early summer.

Catalpa ×erubescens 'Purpurea'

Purple Indian bean tree
Hardy / Full sun

Growing to around 3.5 m tall, this handsome catalpa produces intensely purple, almost black foliage that turns dark green with age. In July panicles of white flowers appear.

Catalpa speciosa 'Pulverulenta'

Speckled Indian bean tree
Hardy / Full sun

This interesting catalpa grows to around 2.75 m high. Leaves are green and heavily speckled with white markings. Panicles of white flowers appear in early summer.

Cercis (Fabaceae)

Judas tree, redbud
North America, eastern Asia, and Europe

The six or seven species in the genus *Cercis* are quite old plants on the evolutionary scale. Fossils that date back as far as the Cretaceous period some one hundred million years ago have been found in France. These deciduous, generally small shrubs and often multistemmed trees are grown for their attractive broadly ovate leaves and abundant

Catalpa bignonioides 'Aurea'

Cercis siliquastrum

pealike flowers that emerge in spring before the leaves. Often they don't come into leaf before mid-spring, thus avoiding frost damage. They prefer moderately fertile, well-drained soil.

Cercis canadensis

Eastern redbud

Hardy / Full sun

Deciduous, often multistemmed tree to a height and spread of 10 m with bright green, broadly ovate, heart-shaped leaves that turn yellow in autumn and purple-red pealike flowers that appear in spring before the leaves unfurl. 'Forest Pansy' is a beautifully exotic form with flowers that are magenta in bud, opening to pale pink, followed by handsome dark reddish purple leaves.

Cercis siliquastrum

Judas tree

Attractive, spreading, often multistemmed tree growing to a height and spread of 10 m, though usually less. Heart- to kidney-shaped, glaucous, bluish green leaves up to 10 cm long are bronze when juvenile and turn yellow in autumn. Conspicuous clusters of pink flowers are produced before and during leaf growth, in mid to late spring.

Choisya (Rutaceae)

Mexican orange blossom
Mexico

This genus of seven species was introduced from Mexico by Jacques Deis Choisy in 1825. All members are evergreen with delightful flowers that resemble orange blossoms in spring. All prefer well-drained soil. Most will take lows of −10°c for short periods.

Choisya ternata

Mexican orange blossom
Frost-hardy, full sun

Medium-sized, round shrub with glossy dark green leaves pitted with numerous oil glands that give off a pungent scent when crushed. Leaves are produced in clusters of three leaflets, giving rise to the species name. Five-petalled, star-shaped white flowers are borne in terminal clusters of three to six, 2.5–3 cm across and sweetly scented, appearing from spring throughout the summer and often well into the autumn. Grows to 3 m high and 2.5 m wide. Plant in the lee of a taller shrub or wall to protect from wind and prune after flowering to keep in shape or cut back to the ground in spring to force new shoots. 'Sundance', with a height and spread of 2.5 m, has golden yellow leaves that turn slightly green with age, best in full sun. 'Aztec Pearl', a species cross with *C. arizonica*, is a very compact shrub that is useful for low hedging, with leaves divided into much more slender five-fingered leaflets. Flowers appear in spring and are pink in bud, opening to white, and almond scented. Will take full sun or dappled shade.

Citrus (Rutaceae)

China to India, Southeast Asia, New Guinea, and Australia

This genus comprises about twenty species of mostly evergreen shrubs and small trees, grown in warmer countries for their edible fruit, including oranges, lemons, limes, grapefruit, mandarins, and clementines. They are highly ornamental plants with their dark, glossy leaves and deliciously scented starlike white flowers. The twigs are green and often thorny. The leaves when crushed give off a strong citrus aroma. They make excellent tub and

Choisya ternata
'Sundance'
(bottom) with
Lilium 'Pink
Perfection'

Clerodendrum
bungei

Clerodendrum
bungei, flower
detail

Right

Clerodendrum
trichotomum

container plants and look especially good when trained as a standard. A fruit-laden tree is a sight to behold, giving a strong Mediterranean feel to the garden. Although they tend to be expensive, they will give you a lifetime of pleasure. Many will take a light frost, though it is advisable to store them during the winter somewhere that stays above freezing and kept on the dry side. They make excellent conservatory plants, especially as you can pick the fruit in winter! A few varieties will be available in your local garden centre, though specialist nurseries will have a far greater choice of named forms.

Clerodendrum (Verbenaceae)

Tropical and subtropical regions of Asia and Africa

Most of the members of this large genus of four hundred species of evergreen and deciduous small trees, shrubs, and subshrubs are tropical, and some of these can be grown as container or conservatory plants. They need well-drained soil that is humus-rich. Clerodendrums are good for attracting butterflies to the garden.

Clerodendrum bungei

Cashmere bouquet, glory flower
Frost-hardy to hardy / Dappled or full shade

Deciduous, aggressively suckering shrub from China and northern India, with large, coarsely serrated, greenish purple leaves on upright stems to a height and spread of 2 m. Domes of tightly clustered, small, fragrant, deep pinkish purple flowers appear in late summer and early autumn. Since it blooms on current season's growth, pruning stems that come through the winter will make it bushier. Leaves have a rather peculiar odour of peanuts or burning rubber! Although hardy, may be cut back to ground in severe winters, although I have been growing it for more than fifteen years in Norwich without any dieback. Suitable for growing in the shade of large trees or shrubs. Takes −12°c and lower.

Clerodendrum trichotomum

Hardy / Sun or dappled shade

Bushy shrub or small tree from Japan, growing to 7 m or more though usually a lot smaller, with large dark green leaves up to 23 cm long and 13 cm wide that are tinted bronze when young. Most revered feature is the deliciously scented cymes of pure white flowers that appear in late summer. Steel blue fruit appears after flowering in the middle of the red calyx and remains attractive for a long period of time, provided it is not all consumed by birds, who also find it attractive! Hardy to −15°c.

Clianthus (Fabaceae)

Glory pea, lobster claw, parrot's beak, parrot's bill
Australia and New Zealand (North Island)

Clianthus consists of two species of tender semi-evergreen plants. Although these are tropical plants, they will grow in sheltered microclimates with protection in cold weather; otherwise grow them as container plants that can be brought into a frost-free place for the winter.

Clianthus puniceus

Frost-hardy / Full sun

Climbing shrub for a south-facing wall in full sun, where it can grow up to 1.8 m tall with a similar spread. Dramatic flowers appear in midsummer that are scarlet red and reminiscent of a parrot's beak in shape. 'Albus' is a white-flowering form. Best grown in well-drained soil. Hardy to around −6°C for short periods, but if you live in a cold area should be grown in a greenhouse or conservatory.

Clianthus puniceus var. maximus 'Kaka King'

Frost-hardy / Full sun

Variety with fernlike shining leaves and deep red flowers borne in late winter to early spring, so planted in a very sheltered part of the garden, preferably against a warm wall in well-drained soil. Grows to 1.8 m with a similar spread in ideal conditions but much less in a cool summer. Water during dry periods. Hardy to −5°C for short periods. If cut to the ground by frost, usually reshoots from the base, especially if well mulched.

Corylus (Betulaceae)

Hazel

Europe, northern Africa, and western Asia

This genus encompasses about fifteen species of suckering shrubs and trees grown for their habit, catkins, and edible nuts. Although hazels are considered dead common, I have included here a few that are very useful for background colour and form in the exotic garden. They are easy to grow and hardy and will thrive in well-drained soil in full sun or dappled shade. They can be pollarded yearly or biennially to keep the shrubs small and to keep the brilliant new growth nearer the ground.

Corylus avellana

Hardy / Sun or dappled shade

Common hazel. 'Aurea', the golden form, grows to a height and spread of 4.5 m though much smaller and more manageable when regularly pollarded. Leaves are oval, greenish yellow. 'Contorta' forms a dense, slow-growing shrub with bizarre, heavily twisted branches and sharply toothed, midgreen, plain leaves. Pendent yellow catkins in winter.

Corylus maxima 'Purpurea'

Hardy / Sun or dappled shade

Vigorous, deciduous, open shrub growing to 6 m tall and 5 m wide, though much smaller and more manageable when regularly pollarded. Purplish catkins with yellow anthers hang from bare branches in late winter. Leaves are oval, toothed, deep bronze-purple. Edible nuts appear in late summer.

Cotinus (Anacardiaceae)

Smoke bush, smoke tree

North America and southern Europe to central China

This genus of three species of trees and shrubs is closely related to sumac (*Rhus*). All the smoke bushes are sharply rounded shrubs or small trees grown for their summer interest and often dramatic autumn colour. Try to avoid contact with the sap when pruning as it is very sticky and resinous! Most are hardy to around −15°C and lower in a sheltered situation.

Cotinus coggygria

Hardy / Full sun

Deciduous shrub-tree usually as wide as high, with roundish leaves and flower plumes forming a dramatic haze resembling puffs of smoke. Prefers a sunny location with well-drained soil but seems content with most soil conditions. Can be kept in shape with light pruning to prevent it from getting leggy, especially if space is restricted. 'Golden Spirit' is a medium-sized shrub of broadly upright habit, growing to 2.5 m high and 2 m wide, with leaves that are brilliant golden yellow throughout the summer and explode into shades of orange and red in autumn. 'Grace' is a vigorous shrub reaching 3–6 m high with large leaves that are wine red when

Cotinus coggygria

Cotinus coggygria
'Golden Spirit'

young, darkening to plum red by summer and turning orange-scarlet in autumn; bears large, conical, deep pink flower clusters in profusion during summer. 'Royal Purple' has purple foliage, turning a spectacular fiery red before falling in autumn, and soft pink flower plumes; eventually forms a small tree up to 3.5–4.5 m high with a similar spread. 'Young Lady' grows to a height and spread of 3–4.5 m with midgreen leaves that turn a stunning yellowish red in autumn; flowers very freely, with huge plumes of smoky pink flowers from mid to late summer.

Cupressus (Cupressaceae)

Northern Hemisphere

I have listed two conifers in this book, including this one, because I think they are very . . . exotic! By that I mean that they are unusual in a temperate landscape, that they are redolent of hot places, and *Cupressus* fits this description. This is a genus of about twenty-five species of evergreen conifers often found growing on dryish slopes and in hillside forests.

Cupressus cashmeriana

Kashmir cypress
Frost-hardy / Full sun

Beautiful and mysterious tree, found in wild stands in Bhutan, that as it grows develops curtains of blue pendulous foliage that flows like a waterfall. In ideal conditions can reach 30 m tall by 10 m wide, though usually less in temperate cultivation. May be a juvenile form of *C. torulosa* (Himalayan cypress) or *C. corneyana* (Bhutan cypress). Best grown in mild areas with few winter frosts; otherwise should be grown in a large container overwintered in a frost-free location. Gets hardier with age.

Cupressus sempervirens

Italian funeral cypress
Frost-hardy / Full sun

Tall, narrow, columnar evergreen, often used in formal landscaping or planted in a row 1 m apart for a fast-growing screen. Will reach 7 m tall rather quickly and then continue to grow more slowly to 12–18 m tall or more in a favourable location. Cultivated since ancient times in the Mediterranean region, can live up to a thousand years. Hardy to −10°C and lower when mature. Prefers well-drained sandy soil; should be staked when planted, as it blows over easily until fully rooted. 'Glauca' is a tight columnar form with blue-green foliage. 'Stricta' is extremely narrow. 'Swane's Gold' is a narrow form with golden foliage. 'Totem' is a seedling selected from 'Stricta' that produces an extremely narrow spire.

Cytisus (Fabaceae)

Europe, northern Africa, Canary Islands, and western Asia

This genus in the pea family consists of about thirty-three species of small prostrate evergreen shrubs and small trees. The following is a stunning species for the exotic garden.

Cytisus battandieri

syn. *Argyrocytisus battandieri*
Moroccan broom, pineapple broom, silver broom
Frost-hardy / Full sun

Fairly lax, upright shrub up to 3.5 m tall by 3.5 m wide, hailing from the Rif and Atlas mountains of Morocco. Leaves are divided into three silvery leaflets with a dense covering of fine reflective hairs. Pineapple-scented flowers are formed in racemes from early summer to midsummer. Can be trained against a wall and responds well to regular pruning after flowering to keep in shape. Hardy to −10°C in a sheltered position with well-drained soil. A beautiful broom that looks especially good in a Mediterranean-style garden.

Daphniphyllum
(Daphniphyllaceae)

Eastern Asia

This genus contains some fifteen species of evergreen trees and shrubs found in woodlands in their native habitats. They are grown for their handsome foliage with somewhat rhododendron-like leaves. Only one species, *D. macropodum*, is generally grown. This very gardenworthy plant looks highly attractive at any time of year, though especially when the young stems emerge deep crimson with bright apple green new foliage in spring. Unlike rhododendron, it thrives on alkaline soils.

Daphniphyllum macropodum

Frost-hardy / Sun or dappled shade

Small, handsome evergreen shrub or small tree with dense foliage, hailing from Japan, China, and Korea. In the wild can reach a height and spread of 6 m eventually, but grows slowly, reaching about 1.5–2 m in ten years. Leaves are narrowly oblong, leathery, rich dark green, glaucous, pale greyish green underneath, up to 20 cm long, often with red leaf stalks and midribs. Prefers moist (though it will take dry conditions once established), well-drained soil. Hardy to −8°C and probably lower.

Embothrium (Proteaceae)

Central and southern Andes of South America

Embothrium is a small genus of eight species of evergreen shrubs or small trees with long willowy branches and flowers in flamboyant terminal clusters.

Embothrium coccineum

Chilean fire bush
Frost-hardy / Full sun

Slender, upright, evergreen tree that reaches 7–9 m tall in ideal conditions, though usually much smaller in cultivation and rather slow growing at first. Deep green, lance-shaped foliage sets off exquisite fiery red tubular flowers held in loose clusters in early summer to midsummer. Requires soil that is poor, neutral to acid, and should be sheltered from cold, drying winds. Hardy to −10°C.

Eriobotrya (Rosaceae)

Loquat
Eastern Himalaya to Southeast Asia and Japan

Embothrium coccineum

There are about twenty-six species of trees and shrubs in this genus, all with tough leaves that are felted underneath. *Eriobotrya japonica* is probably the hardiest; it was introduced by Sir Joseph Banks in 1787 from southeastern China and the most southerly parts of Japan. Both it and *E. deflexa* have a good subtropical appearance.

Eriobotrya deflexa

Bronze loquat
Frost-hardy / Sun or partial shade

Small, low-branching tree growing to 6–9 m tall or more. Young leaves of this Taiwanese species are attractively tinted bronze and turn green with age, hence the common name. Widely planted in warmer regions, though it should take at least −5°C in a protected corner of the garden. Works well as a container plant overwintered in a cold greenhouse. Takes well to pruning to keep in shape.

Eriobotrya japonica

Erythrina crista-galli, flowers

Eriobotrya japonica

Frost-hardy / Sun or partial shade

Evergreen that is an essential for any exotic garden, having luxurious, glossy, corrugated dark green leaves, 30 cm long. In its native habitat grows up to 9 m high; attains a more sedate 3.5–4.5 m in cool-temperate climates. New spring growth is pale silvery green and very attractive. Round creamy orange-yellow fruits are formed in bunches at terminal ends of branches after small white flowers. Rarely produces fruit in cool-summer locales. Prefers humus-rich soil. Hardy to −10°c and lower. Branches break easily under snow, so snow should be carefully knocked off.

Erythrina (Fabaceae)

Brazil, Argentina, Uruguay, Asia, and Africa

Members of this genus of 112 species of deciduous or semi-evergreen trees, shrubs, and perennials are not particularly hardy but are worth trying for their spectacular flowers and interesting foliage.

Erythrina ×bidwillii

Coral tree

Half-hardy / Sun or partial shade

Deciduous, narrow, multistemmed shrub with green leaves and narrow 5-cm-long dark red flowers on long 60–90-cm spikes that arch out and above the foliage. In a good summer grows 1.8 m high. Although hardy to 0°c can be tried in warm favourable locations against a wall with protection.

If frost-damaged will usually reshoot from base if well mulched. Can be slow growing and nonflowering in cool summers.

Erythrina crista-galli

Cockspur, coral tree, fireman's cap
Frost-hardy / Sun or partial shade

Deciduous upright shrub that forms a woody base and grows to 1.8 m high or more in a hot summer, less in a cool-summer climate. Leaves have three-lobed blue-green leaflets and leafy terminal racemes of dramatic deep crimson red flowers in summer and autumn. Hardy to −5°c with protection for short periods. Most winters will kill it to the ground, so in cold areas is best grown in a pot and brought into frost-free conditions during the winter to maintain height.

Eucalyptus (Myrtaceae)

Australia

Eucalyptus is a very large and fascinating genus comprising more than seven hundred species and accounting for more than two-thirds of Australia's vegetation. They can be found growing in a range of habitats from high snowy mountains to arid deserts and tropical rainforests. Most eucalyptus go through a change from juvenile foliage, which is usually round and stem-clasping, to long and willowy foliage when mature. Many eucalyptus can be coppiced yearly, creating a bushy shrub up to 2 m tall. They are often considered as not reliably hardy outside the subtropics; fortunately there are several that are gardenworthy in temperate climes. They are not fussy as to soil, taking conditions from moist—but not wet—to dry and from fertile to impoverished.

Eucalyptus coccifera in the wild

Eucalyptus coccifera

Tasmanian snow gum, Mt. Wellington peppermint gum
Frost-hardy / Full sun

Fast-growing attractive tree to 25 m that will grow in a wide range of soil types and situations. Juvenile leaves smell of peppermint. Young shoots glisten and flower buds are also silvery. Adult leaves are blue and willowlike. Bark is a patchwork of grey and white. Hardy down to −10°C and below.

Eucalyptus dalrympleana

Mountain gum
Hardy / Full sun

Stunning, fast-growing tree with pale grey to white mottled bark turning a spectacular pink and grey in late summer and with a canopy that is thin and graceful. Adult leaves are blue-grey and scythelike, often showing reddish tints when older. Will endure −15°C and probably lower.

Eucalyptus debeuzevillei

Hardy / Full sun

Fine robust specimen with interesting bark patterns in mottled shades of grey and white, growing to a height of 10 m or more. Smaller twigs have a distinct bluish white blush and leaves are also a glaucous bluish white. Hardy to −15°C. Suitable for growing on the coast.

Eucalyptus erythrocorys

Candle bark gum
Frost-hardy / Full sun

Though not particularly hardy, this one is included because it is one of the most spectacular flowering gums. Grows to around 4 m high in its native habitat, less in cool-summer climates. Yellow flowers up to 7 cm across are preceded by large rectangular scarlet buds and followed by large helmet-shaped fruit that can weigh the branches down. Foliage is dark green and sickle-shaped. Bark is creamy with mottled brownish patches. Hardy to −5°C, so suitable only for the mildest areas. Can be grown as a container plant and brought in during frosty spells.

Eucalyptus glaucescens

Tingiringi gum

Frost-hardy / Full sun

Substantial eucalyptus growing to 12 m tall. Strikingly silver, round juvenile leaves are packed closely on the stems and have a fruity aroma. Young adult leaves are glaucous, pink, and sickle-shaped. Bark is green when young, turning white-silver when mature. Like many eucalyptus, coppices well. Hardy to −10°C.

Eucalyptus gunnii

Cider gum

Hardy / Full sun

Best-known gum in the British Isles, growing to 27.5 m tall or more, eventually developing a spreading crown. Juvenile leaves are round and may be blue, silvery white, or green. Adult leaves are short and usually blue or green; bark is often brown or grey with greenish and pink patches. Common name is derived from the fact that it produces an edible cider that can be tapped from the trunk in the same manner as maple syrup. Tolerates most soil conditions. Takes −15°C and lower.

Eucalyptus nitens

Shining gum

Frost-hardy / Full sun

Extremely fast-growing ornamental eucalyptus used as a timber crop in Australia, to 40–60 m tall.

Juvenile bark is green and turns a smooth shiny grey on maturity. Hardy to −11°C and lower.

Euonymus (Celastraceae)

Spindle tree

Mostly Asia

This is a genus of about 175 species of deciduous, semi-evergreen, and evergreen shrubs, trees, and climbers indigenous to woodlands and thickets. They are cultivated for their often brightly variegated foliage and rival many variegated tropical plants in the exotic garden, especially with the many hybrids now available. They prefer full sun to dappled shade in moist, well-drained soil, although many will take dry conditions once established. Many are worth trying, though only a few cultivars of *E. fortunei* are mentioned here.

Euonymus fortunei

Hardy / Sun

Broad-leaved evergreen vine or shrub that trails or climbs by rootlets. 'Emerald Gaiety' is a small, compact form to a height of about 1 m and a spread of 1.5 m, with bright green leaves with white margins that are tinted pink during the winter months. 'Emerald 'n' Gold' is a small bushy shrub up to 90 cm high and wide, with bright green leaves with rich yellow margins tinted pinkish red during the winter months. 'Silver Queen' is an upright bush up to 2.5 m high or more as a climber, with dark green leaves and irregular white margins tinted pink with age.

Fatsia (Araliaceae)

Japan, Taiwan, and South Korea

Fatsia is a genus of just three species of evergreen autumn- and winter-flowering plants grown for their exotic foliage and flowers. Although they are frost-hardy, they prefer to be grown in a sheltered corner away from desiccating winds. They can grow in full sun and are drought tolerant once established, but the foliage tends to be more lush in dappled shade with well-drained, moist soil.

Eucalyptus gunnii in the wild

leaves irregularly and heavily marked with white to pale green-yellow following the leaf veins. 'Moseri' is a more compact form, growing to a maximum of 2 m high with a slightly larger spread; the foliage is rather compact although the leaves can reach up to 43 cm across. 'Variegata' is a variegated form, a rather slow-growing but architectural shrub that reaches 45–75 cm in height and width, with leaves tinged with cream along the edges. 'Spider's Web' from Plant Delights Nursery in Raleigh, North Carolina, United States, has dark green leaves that become progressively speckled white toward the edges. Mature fatsias sucker from the base. All grow well as container plants. Most are drought tolerant. Hardy to −10°c when established.

Fatsia polycarpa

Frost-hardy / Sun or shade

Recent introduction collected at high altitude in Taiwan by Bleddyn and Sue Wynn-Jones of Crûg Farm Plants in northern Wales, with a spread and height of up to 3.5 m. Dark matte green, palmate leaves are deeply (to half their length) five- to seven-lobed. Long spikes of rounded clusters of creamy white flowers are held on heavily brown stems covered with fine hairs. Hardy to −10°c in a sheltered position.

Fremontodendron
(Sterculiaceae)

California, northern Baja California, central Arizona

Large and showy flowers characterise the three species of evergreen to semi-evergreen shrubs in this genus named after Major General John C. Frémont, an explorer and amateur botanist in California in the mid-nineteenth century. These plants are also known to cause dermatitis and eye irritation because of the fine hairs on the flowers buds and leaves. They are best grown in free-draining, poor soil, simulating their natural habitat.

Fatsia japonica

False castor-oil plant, Japanese aralia
Frost-hardy / Sun or shade

Fast-growing, dramatic, dense, rounded evergreen shrub, reaching 1.5–3.5 m high with spears of a similar height. Common name refers to its resemblance to the true castor-oil plant, *Ricinus communis*. Shoots are stout with large, palmate, deeply lobed, shiny dark green leaves, 30 cm across. Dense panicles of small white flowers appear in midautumn, followed by small black fruit. 'Aurea' has dark green

Fremontodendron californicum

California fremontia, flannel bush
Frost-hardy / Full sun

Fast-growing, semi-evergreen shrub with a fairly upright habit that reaches 2–5 m tall with a similar spread. Leaves are a matte olive-grey-green, 4–8 cm long, usually three-lobed. Rich yellow flowers are in fact petal-like cup-shaped sepals, 5 cm across or more, appearing in late spring and then sporadically throughout the summer. Can be grown free-standing in warm locations; otherwise grow against a sunny wall, tying the branches in and pruning to keep in shape. Hardy to −10°C and lower for short periods.

Griselinia (Cornaceae)

New Zealand and Chile

This genus encompasses seven species of evergreen trees and shrubs grown for their exotic, shiny evergreen foliage. They make good mild coastal plants as they are very wind and salt resistant; they are common in gardens of Northern Ireland, especially in town gardens and near the coast. They prefer full sun and fertile, well-drained soil. They make good wind-resistant hedging and are often clipped like privet, and make fine specimen plants for the exotic garden, adding winter colour and form.

Griselinia littoralis

Griselinia littoralis 'Dixon's Cream'

Fremontodendron mexicanum, flowers

Fremontodendron mexicanum

Southern flannel bush
Frost-hardy / Full sun

Very similar to *F. californicum*, though the leaves are five-lobed as opposed to three-lobed and have narrower sepals. Flowers for a longer period, although blooms are obscured by the denser foliage. Marginally less hardy.

Griselinia littoralis

Broadleaf, kapuka, papauma, New Zealand privet

Frost-hardy / Full sun

Grows to 8 m high by 4.5 m wide in its native habitat, considerably less in cool-summer gardens, with leathery, oval, glossy bright green leaves. 'Dixon's Cream' has green leaves splashed an attractive creamy white. 'Green Jewel' has green, slightly crenulated leaves edged in creamy yellow. 'Variegata' has foliage variegated with green and cream. Hardy to −8°C and maybe lower.

Griselinia lucida

Akepuka, puka

Half-hardy / Full sun

In New Zealand this species often starts its life epiphytically, eventually forming a wide, spreading tree up to 4.5 m tall and wide; in cultivation it is considerably smaller, as it is only marginally hardy. Leaves are rich green above, with a paler underside, and can become large, up to 20 cm long. Will stand only a few degrees of frost so has to be grown in warm locations or as a container plant brought into frost-free conditions for winter. 'Variegata' is a stunning variegated form with oval to slightly elongated midgreen leaves, with paler green markings and very conspicuous, variable, creamy white edges.

Hibiscus syriacus 'Bluebird', flower

Hibiscus (Malvaceae)

Tropical, subtropical, and warm-temperate regions worldwide

Plants in this genus of more than two hundred species of evergreen and deciduous trees, shrubs, perennials, and annuals are mostly grown for their extravagant flowers. All need full sun and humus-rich soil kept moist in dry weather.

Hibiscus syriacus

Rose of Sharon

Hardy / Full sun

Deciduous, upright shrub growing to 3 m high and 2 m wide, with lobed, deep green leaves and large, trumpet-shaped, lilac-blue flowers with red centres, 7 cm across, from late summer to midautumn. Can be tip-pruned to maintain bushiness. Hardy to −15°C. There are many hybrids available, of which the following are a few. 'Aphrodite' has mauve-pink single flowers with a dark magenta eye. 'Ardens' is a double form with mauve-purple flowers. 'Bluebird' has single lavender-blue flowers with a dark magenta eye. 'Minerva' has single mauve-lavender flowers with a red eye. 'Woodbridge' has large, rich pink, trumpet-shaped flowers up to 10 cm across with a contrasting maroon eye.

Kalopanax (Araliaceae)

Eastern Asia

This genus in the ivy family consists of a single species of tree native to the cool deciduous forests of eastern Asia, grown for its luxuriant leaves.

Kalopanax septemlobus

Hardy / Full sun

Sparingly branched, round tree 6–18 m high by 3–9 m wide. Five- to seven-pointed, palmate, lobed dark green leaves on long stalks look like a cross between a sycamore and an ivy leaf in shape and are lighter on the underside. Large rounded clusters of small white flowers appear in late summer followed by clusters of bluish black berries. Var. *maximowiczii* is a large, variable shrub or small tree from Japan, armed with ferocious prickles. Glossy, deeply lobed leaves form from swollen buds in late winter. Large clusters of small white flowers are produced in autumn.

Laurus (Lauraceae)

Bay laurel, bay tree
Southern Mediterranean region

This genus contains two species of evergreen shrubs grown for their foliage and highly aromatic leaves. The leaves and berries of bay laurel contain the essential oils eugenol, cineol, and geraniol, which account for the distinctive spicy aroma and make this a popular culinary seasoning. Bay trees are grown commercially worldwide. Bay laurel is the true laurel of Greek and Roman mythology.

Laurus nobilis

Bay laurel, bay tree
Frost-hardy to hardy / Sun or dappled shade

Evergreen, broadly conical tree to 12 m by 10 m, though usually much smaller as a garden shrub. Leaves are dark green, narrowly ovate, glossy, and leathery. Foliage is compact. Prefers a sheltered position in moist, well-drained soil. Foliage can be scorched by extremely cold winds. Works well as a container plant and takes clipping well, hence is used as a topiary plant.

Liriodendron (Magnoliaceae)

Eastern United States, China, Taiwan, and northern
  Vietnam

This genus in the magnolia family was originally believed to comprise a single species of tree from the United States until a second similar species was discovered in central China in 1875. These plants are grown for their interesting foliage and exotic-looking tuliplike flowers.

Liriodendron chinense

Chinese tulip tree
Hardy / Full sun

Fast-growing, broad, deciduous tree with a long, straight trunk to 25 m tall and 12 m wide. Four-lobed leaves are deep green and turn a translucent yellow in autumn. Flowers are green outside with yellow-green veins inside, appear in midsummer, and are carried high up in the tree where they are not always easy to see. Hardy to −15°c and lower.

Laurus nobilis in
standard form

Liriodendron tulipifera

Hardy / Full sun

Fast-growing, deciduous, spreading tree with proportions similar to *L. chinense*. Interesting tulip-shaped flowers are greenish yellow with an orange band. Leaves are deep green and turn a blazing golden yellow in autumn. Hardy to −15°c and lower.

Magnolia (Magnoliaceae)

Himalaya to Japan, Borneo, Java, eastern United States to the West Indies and Venezuela

Magnolia is a genus of deciduous and evergreen trees and shrubs, comprising approximately one hundred species and countless cultivars, grown for their dramatic flowers. Magnolias have the largest leaves and flowers of any trees in the temperate region. They are the oldest flowering plants in the world and were around when dinosaurs roamed the earth some 100 million years ago. The primitive flowers are pollinated by beetles, because they evolved before bees and other flying pollinators existed. The flowers do not have true petals or produce nectar but instead attract beetles with a sugary secretion. Most magnolias prefer acid soils that are rich in humus, though many will grow in neutral soil with a mulch of well-rotted manure. Wind and late frost can damage the flowers, so magnolias are best grown in a sheltered position. The roots tend to be shallow, so the trees should be planted where they will not be disturbed. The name "magnolia" was given by Linnaeus in honour of Pierre Magnol, a French professor of botany during the late seventeenth and early eighteenth centuries. The magnolias listed here were selected for either their large leaves or their flowers.

Magnolia delavayi

Evergreen Chinese magnolia
Frost-hardy / Full sun

Charming, evergreen, round tree or dense shrub from Yunnan, China, 8–10 m high and wide. Oblong dark green leaves are silvery green underneath and 15–35 cm long. Large, night-flowering, short-lived, creamy white, bowl-shaped flowers up to 18 cm across appear from late summer to early autumn. Hardy to −10°c and lower.

Magnolia grandiflora

Bull bay / Southern magnolia
Hardy / Full sun

Evergreen, broadly pyramidal tree growing to at least 10 m by 10 m, though can be pruned to keep to a more manageable size. Takes well to being trained up against a wall, as in the garden at Sissinghurst Castle in Kent. Oblong glossy leaves are 13–20 cm long and dark green. 'Exmouth' is velvety, light matte brown underneath. Bears large, fragrant, bowl-shaped white flowers, 20–30 cm across, intermittently from midsummer to early autumn. Hardy to −15°c and lower.

Magnolia delavayi

Left

Liriodendron tulipifera, flower detail

Magnolia macrophylla

Great-leaved magnolia
Hardy / Full sun

Deciduous tree growing to a height and spread of 10 m with stout, brittle, twiggy stems. Can be pruned for a small garden. Has the largest simple leaf that can be grown in temperate zones, bright green, thin, and very large at 30–100 cm long by 15–30 cm wide, with a slight blue-grey bloom. Prefers a sunny, sheltered location.

Magnolia tripetala

Elkwood, umbrella tree
Hardy / Full sun

Deciduous spreading tree to a height and width of 10 m, conical when young. Large, simple, dark green leaves, 30–60 cm long, grey-green and felted beneath, with an unpleasant odour, are clustered at shoot tips. Flowers are 15–25 cm across, narrow and creamy white in spring and early summer. Prefers moist, deep soil.

Mahonia (Berberidaceae)

Asia, North America to Central America

This genus contains about seventy species of evergreen shrubs grown for their foliage and fragrant racemes of yellow flowers. Several make good exotic garden plants, especially as they are winter flowering. Large mahonias make excellent architectural specimen plants with their spiky, somewhat holly-like foliage. All prefer humus-rich soil.

Mahonia japonica

Hardy / Full sun

Evergreen, upright shrub from Japan, growing to 1.8 m high and 3 m wide, with long, leathery, dark green spiny leaflets. Sprays of fragrant yellow flowers are held in upright, arching racemes from late autumn to spring. Hardy to −15°c and lower.

Mahonia lomariifolia

Hardy / Sun or partial shade

Evergreen shrub with upright stems, from western China, growing to 3 m high by 2 m wide, with whorls of dark green, spiny, hollylike leaflets. Erect spikes of fragrant yellow flowers appear from autumn to spring, followed by attractive, glaucous, blue-black fruit. Dramatic plants that give backbone to the garden in winter.

Mahonia ×media 'Charity'

Hardy / Full sun

Evergreen, vigorous, upright shrub with dark green spiky foliage, hailing from western China. Long, erect racemes of arching, deliciously scented yellow flowers are borne from early to late winter. Stems have very tactile, deeply fissured, corklike bark when mature. Magnificent flowering shrub for the winter months, bringing a touch of spring to the garden.

Melaleuca (Mytaceae)

Honey myrtle, paperbark
Mostly Australia, with several in Indonesia, New
  Guinea, and Malaysia

Members of this genus of approximately 250 species in the myrtle family are found along watercourses and along the edges of swamps and are widely used in Australia as landscaping plants. Melaleucas are grown for their stunning flowers and are closely related to *Callistemon* (bottlebrush), differing in the fact that their stamens are united into bundles whereas *Callistemon* stamens are generally free. Included here are several that are gardenworthy in warmer areas or microclimates. All prefer acidic well-drained soil in sun to partial shade. Most will stand only light frost, though several are slightly hardier. Can be grown as container plants in cooler areas.

Melaleuca armillaris

Bracelet honey myrtle
Frost-hardy / Sun or partial shade

Fast-growing evergreen shrub to 4 m by 2 m depending on location. Forms a spreading canopy of narrow dark green leaves. White flowers in cylindrical heads appear from late spring to summer. Leaves are damaged below −5°c.

Melaleuca bracteata

Frost-hardy / Sun

A very exotic-looking evergreen shrub or small tree growing to 5 m tall by 3 m across with soft, linear, bright green leaves. Profuse terminal spikes of creamy white flowers are produced in spring.

Melaleuca bracteata

Prefers well-drained soil. Has endured −6°C at Trevena Cross Nurseries in Cornwall, England.

Melaleuca lateritia

Robin redbreast bush
Frost-hardy / Sun or partial shade

Evergreen shrub reaching 1.5–2 m tall and 1–1.5 m wide with arching branches and linear, light green leaves that are aromatic when bruised. Soft spikes of orange-scarlet flowers are borne mostly on older wood in midsummer. Grows well in a container. Hardy to −5°C when mature.

Melaleuca thymifolia, flowers

Melaleuca thymifolia

Thyme honey myrtle
Frost-hardy / Sun

Melianthus major

Pretty, freely branching shrub growing to about 1 m tall. Young twigs are lined by narrow bluish green leaves. Small clusters of mauve-pink blossoms appear in summer. Reportedly hardy down to −10°C in very well-drained soil.

Melaleuca wilsonii

Frost-hardy / Sun

Dense, spreading form growing up to 2 m high with a similar spread, with linear grey-green leaves. Bottlebrush flowers are pink. Reportedly hardy down to −10°C in very well-drained soil.

Melianthus (Melianthaceae)

South Africa

Melianthus is a genus of six often lax evergreen shrubs and perennials grown for their attractive, deeply serrated leaves, which give form and character in the exotic garden. *Melianthus* comes from the Greek *meli* (honey) and *anthos* (flower), meaning that it has abundant nectar. The long stems can be shortened in spring or cut to the ground for a flush of new growth. Mulch around the base in autumn with a thick layer of straw to protect the new growth. All require sun and fertile soil in a sheltered position.

Melianthus comosus

Half-hardy / Full sun

Evergreen, multistemmed shrub with large, greyish, mostly green leaves clustered toward the tips of the branches, with heavily toothed edges. As with *M. major*, foliage has a peculiar odour, between peanut butter and burnt rubber, when bruised. Needs a warm location against a sunny wall, like *M. major*.

Melianthus major

Honey flower, honey bush
Frost-hardy / Full sun

Evergreen, vigorous, sparsely branched, lax shrub 2–3 m tall and wide in ideal conditions, though often far smaller in cool climates. Stunning, powdery silver-blue leaves, 25–45 cm long, are divided into seven to thirteen toothed, oval leaflets and look beautiful when early morning dew collects along each tooth. Terminal flower spikes are brownish red, up to 30 cm long, from midsummer to autumn. Stems can be tied to canes if they become too floppy. Takes −5°c for short periods. If cut down by frost will reshoot from the base if well mulched.

Melianthus minor

Half-hardy / Full sun

Evergreen shrub with large grey-green leaves. More tender than *M. major* so should be planted near a warm wall, or in gardens that get little frost in winter. Occasionally bears greenish flowers with red bracts.

Melianthus pectinatus

Half-hardy / Full sun

Evergreen shrub with greyish green leaves and occasional scarlet flowers. Tolerates 0°c for short periods only.

Melianthus villosus

Half-hardy to frost-hardy / Full sun

Similar to *M. minor* but with hairy leaves, occasionally producing purple-black flowers. Reportedly will take a few degrees of frost in a warm protected location.

Myrtus (Myrtaceae)

Mediterranean region

This is a genus of evergreen shrubs, often treelike, grown for their flowers, fruit, and aromatic foliage. They give the garden a strong Mediterranean feel, especially in hot weather when their pungent scent wafts through the air.

Myrtus communis

Myrtus communis

Common myrtle
Frost-hardy to hardy / Full sun

Evergreen, bushy shrub from the Mediterranean region, growing to a height and spread of 3 m in ideal conditions. Highly aromatic, shiny, dark green leaves. Flowers are white and fragrant, from mid-spring to early summer, followed by purplish black berries. Subspecies *tarentina* grows to a height and spread of 1.8 m, with small, shiny, dark green, narrowly ovate leaves. Fragrant saucer-shaped white flowers, each with a dense cluster of stamens, appear from midspring to early summer. 'Variegata' has a conspicuous cream margin to the leaves. Hardy to −10°C for short periods.

Myrtus luma

syn. *Luma apiculata*
Frost-hardy to hardy / Full sun

Extremely vigorous, evergreen, upright shrub or multitrunked small tree, growing to 4 m high by 3 m wide with attractive, peeling, golden brown and greyish white bark that looks stunning in evening light. Small leaves are dark green, contrasting well with the cup-shaped white flowers. 'Penwith' is a variegated form. Hardy to −10°C for short periods.

Nerium (Apocynaceae)

Mediterranean region and Asia

This genus contains a single species, a roadside shrub much used in the Mediterranean region that tolerates drought. The common pink form is generally available, often as specimen plants at specialist nurseries. They are often on sale in the houseplant section in garden centres. As yet, there are no nurseries experimenting with hardiness, though they are definitely worth trying, preferably against a south-facing wall or in warmer areas. They make fine conservatory plants that can be brought into the garden for the summer months.

Nerium oleander

Oleander
Frost-hardy / Full sun

Small-to-large evergreen shrub that can be trained as a single or multistemmed tree, 1–7 m tall and 1–3.65 m wide in its native habitat. Leaves are 7.5–15.5 cm long, dark grey-green, stiff, leathery, narrow, lighter underneath with a prominent midrib. Flowers form in terminal clusters and can be white, red, pink, or yellow, single or double, blooming from late spring to early autumn. Hardy to −7°C in a sheltered sunny position on well-drained soil. A pink form has been growing in my garden on the east coast of England for five years, enduring frosts

down to −7°C for short periods with minor leaf burn; although 1.5 m tall, it has hardly grown in the last few years, although it does flower. I also have one that has been out for a similar period of time and has survived −6°C in a fairly exposed position with little leaf burn; it is reluctant to flower, though, needing a hot summer to flower well. In the United States there has been more experimentation with hardiness, hence there are several hybrids that appear to have proven hardiness.

Olea (Oliaceae)

Mediterranean, Africa, Asia, and Australia

Plants in this genus of about twenty species of evergreen trees and shrubs are grown for their fruit and decorative foliage. With age, the trunk and branches become superbly knurled and contorted. Many gardeners like to grow these plants even if they don't fruit, because they are so redolent of the Mediterranean. They need the protection of a south- or west-facing wall or warm microclimate in a sunny position in very well-drained soil.

Olea europaea

Olive tree

Frost-hardy / Full sun

Evergreen, slow-growing, long-lived tree from the Mediterranean region, to a height and spread of 10 m, though much less in cool-temperate gardens. Leaves are narrowly oblong, greyish green above, silver beneath. Small fragrant flowers are borne in late summer followed by green, becoming dark purple, fruit, commonly known as olives. Fruit needs a very hot summer to ripen, so trees are mainly grown for their foliage in cool-summer areas. Occasionally old specimens can be purchased at great expense, though young sapling trees are more common and relatively cheap. Hardy to −10°C for short periods in a sheltered position in very well-drained soil.

Nerium oleander

Paulownia tomentosa

Foxglove tree

Hardy / Full sun

Fast-growing, deciduous, spreading tree to 15 m tall by 9 m wide with bark that is grey-brown, interlaced with shiny smooth areas. Large leaves are lobed, rounded, soft, velvety, midgreen, 13–30 cm long, arranged in pairs along the stem, with terminal sprays of fragrant, showy pinkish lilac flowers in spring. Makes an excellent specimen plant for a sheltered corner of the garden. Alternately, for much bigger leaves cut down to one bud from the ground in spring. One large stem will grow up to 3 m high in one season, somewhat resembling a sunflower, with very large leaves, up to 46 cm across. Do this every year to maintain the larger leaves.

Photinia (Rosaceae)

Himalaya to Japan, Sumatra, and Indonesia

Photinia is a genus of about sixty evergreen and deciduous trees and shrubs (in the rose family) grown for their foliage, which is often strikingly coloured in spring, and, with the deciduous species, in autumn. In Japan they are widely used as hedging plants, especially beside motorways. They also work well as standard plants in containers. They prefer full sun to dappled shade. Some prefer acid soil.

Photinia ×fraseri

Hardy / Sun or dappled shade

Group of hybrid evergreen shrubs with new leaf growth that is attractive over a long period. Oblong leaves are resistant to late frost. 'Birmingham' is an upright, dense, bushy shrub growing to 6 m tall by 4 m wide, though it can be kept much shorter with regular pruning. Glossy dark green leaves are bright reddish purple when young. Heads of small white flowers appear in spring. 'Red Robin' is a popular form, being upright and dense, with a size similar to 'Birmingham', with glossy dark green leaves that are brilliant red when young.

Paulownia tomentosa

Paulownia (Scrophulariaceae)

Empress tree, princess tree, royal paulownia
Eastern Asia

This genus comprises six species of deciduous trees, grown for their large leaves and attractive foxglovelike flowers, which appear before the foliage. Historical records in China describe their use for medicinal, ornamental, and timber purposes for more than three thousand years; they are still in demand today as they grow quickly.

Pinus (Pinaceae)

Europe, northern Africa, West Indies, North and
Central America, and Asia

You are probably wondering why I have included
pines in this book. I have selected forms with beautiful drooping needles that hang from the branches
in curtains, giving a very soft flowing appearance
reminiscent of a living waterfall. Although eventually reaching massive proportions, they can be
carefully pruned to keep them to a scale suitable
for a smaller garden. If you have the room, let them
grow to full height. They work well in Mediterranean-style gardens.

Pinus engelmannii

Apache pine, Engelmann pine
Frost-hardy / Full sun

Hailing from Mexico and the western United
States, tree growing to 30 m tall by 6 m wide. Often
found in dry situations, has a rounded open crown
with grey-green needles up to a staggering 38 cm
long. Bark on mature trees ranges from dark grey to

Photinia × fraseri
'Red Robin'

Left

Photinia × fraseri

black-grey and is thick, rough, and deeply furrowed into scaly ridges. Hardy to −12°C and lower.

Pinus montezumae

Mexican weeping pine
Frost-hardy / Full sun

From the mountains of Mexico, tree growing to 21.3 m tall with green needles up to 30 cm long. Bark on mature trees is thick, dark greyish brown, divided by deep vertical and horizontal fissures into rough, scaly plates. On young trees the bark is reddish brown, rough, and scaly. A very handsome pine that appears to flow like a waterfall from youth to maturity and is also very tactile. Hardy to −12°C and lower.

Pinus montezumae

Pinus palustris

Longleaf pine, pitch pine
Frost-hardy / Full sun

Hailing from the southern United States, tree growing to 30 m tall by 4.5 m wide, with highly attractive green needles up to a colossal 45 cm long. Bark is quite scaly, orange-brown to grey, eventually developing plates. Hardy to −15°C and lower.

Pinus patula

Frost-hardy / Full sun

Rather striking pine, slowly growing to about 15 m tall with handsome drooping needles up to 30 cm long or more that hang in fans almost straight down. Bark reddish and flaky. Hardy to −10°C in sheltered location.

Pittosporum (Pittosporaceae)

Asia, Africa, Australia, and New Zealand

This genus encompasses about 150 species of trees and shrubs grown for their ornamental, evergreen, usually glossy foliage. They are often grown in warmer parts of cool-temperate areas, though many are hardier than might be thought. In exposed areas, plant near a south- or west-facing wall or in a suitably warm microclimate. They also work well in containers and tubs as specimen plants, or as evergreen hedging. All need well-drained soil with added organic matter.

Pittosporum crassifolium

Frost-hardy / Full sun

Medium to large evergreen shrub, with thick, deep green, leathery leaves, white felted beneath, bearing in early summer clusters of deep purple flowers, each 1 cm or so across, that are richly fragrant and can fill the air of a calm evening with their alluring perfume. Grows well in coastal gardens. Hardy to about −5°C and lower for short periods.

Pittosporum ralphii

Frost-hardy / Full sun

Medium-sized shrub or small tree growing 3–4.5 m tall. Leaves are glossy dark olive green, densely woolly underneath. Sweet-scented flowers in a rather unusual shade of deepest maroon are borne in clusters. Hardy to about −8°c for short periods.

Pittosporum tenuifolium

Frost-hardy / Full sun

Large shrub or small tree of columnar habit, capable of reaching 4–6 m tall though usually smaller, with purple-black twiggy growth and glossy, midgreen, undulating-edged leaves that make a striking contrast against the dark twigs. Small, bell-shaped, honey-scented reddish black flowers appear in late spring to early summer. Works well as an informal hedge. Hardy to about −8°c for short periods, maybe lower. 'Eila Keightley' (syn. *P. tenuifolium* 'Sunburst') is a very showy form growing to 1.5 m high with leaves conspicuously blotched bright greenish yellow in the centre; variegation is most prominent on older foliage. 'Purpureum' grows to a height of 1.5 m or more with pale green leaves that gradually change to deep purple-bronze with maturity; more tender than the green form. 'Silver Queen' is a very showy shrub that works well as an informal hedge, growing 1–4 m high by 2 m wide, forming a compact plant with leaves suffused silver-grey, narrowly margined in white.

Many more cultivars of *P. tenuifolium* are available, including 'Abbotsbury Gold', with yellow leaves with irregular green margins; 'Elizabeth', with cream and green leaves with a distinctive pink edge; 'French Lace', with an upright habit and foliage that turns an attractive plum colour in autumn; 'Gold Star', with variegated leaves with a gold star in the centre; 'Limelight', with deep gold leaves edged with green veining; 'Margaret Turnbull', with dark green leaves heavily variegated with a gold centre; 'Moonlight', with yellow leaves with deep green edges; 'Stevens Island', with dark green leaves with white variegation; and 'Victoria', with pale silvery green leaves edged in white, becoming tinged with dark pink in winter.

Pittosporum tobira 'Variegata'

Japanese mock orange
Half-hardy / Full sun

Dense, compact shrub growing 1.5–3.5 m tall with pale grey-green leaves with irregular creamy white margins. Flowers are creamy white and smell like orange blossoms. Less cold-hardy than the species. Works well as a container plant brought into frost-free conditions in autumn.

Pittosporum tenuifolium

Pittosporum tobira 'Variegata'

Poncirus (Rutaceae)

Northern China and Korea

This is a genus of one species of spiny deciduous shrub or small tree, grown for its flowers, foliage, and fruit. Although not the most spectacular of shrubs, it nevertheless does produce inedible orangelike fruit and looks like a real citrus! Some intrepid enthusiasts are experimenting with citrus in Europe with apparent success, but few are yet available in general cultivation, so that makes this look-alike particularly valuable in the exotic garden. It is very useful as an impenetrable hedge, as well as a specimen shrub.

Poncirus trifoliata

Bitter orange, Chinese citron, hardy orange, Japanese bitter orange, mock orange
Hardy / Full sun

Shrub or tree growing to 8 m high. Twigs and vicious spines are green, giving the plant the appearance of being evergreen even though it is deciduous. Leaves are dark green and composed of three oval leaflets that turn butter yellow in autumn, looking visually pleasing against the green stems. Flowers are four- to five-petalled in spring with a delightful citrus scent, followed in early autumn by small, sour citrus fruits 2.5–4 cm across that are slightly furry. Although bitter, fruits can be used for making marmalade. Takes pruning well, so can be kept at a size that suits the garden. Also suitable as an impenetrable hedge, especially as it is covered in visciously sharp spines. 'Flying Dragon', a decorative form with twisting branches, is often used as an ornamental shrub.

Populus (Salicacaceae)

Northern temperate regions

Populus is a genus of thirty-five species of fast-growing deciduous trees. I have only included one poplar that has very exotic large leaves and is useful if you want a large tree rapidly. Poplars in general have large root systems so should not be planted close to a building, as they can damage the foundations.

Populus lasiocarpa

Chinese necklace poplar
Hardy / Full sun

Very ornamental Chinese tree growing to 15 m tall with large heart-shaped leaves, often up to 30 cm long, with conspicuous red veins and leaf stalks. Drooping yellow catkins are produced in spring. Can be coppiced every year to produce much bigger leaves, as with *Paulownia tomentosa*. Will grow in any soil.

Protea (Proteaceae)

Tropical Africa to South Africa

This genus of more than one hundred species of evergreen shrubs and trees, grown for their stunning and colourful bracted flower heads, is named after the sea god of classical mythology, Proteus, who could change his form at will. They are generally considered difficult to grow unless you can offer ideal conditions—that is, hot summers, full sun, and well-drained soil that is neutral to acid and low in phosphates and nitrates. They are mostly tender, withstanding only a few degrees of frost, hence are best suited to warm areas. Some amazing specimens can be seen at the Tresco Abbey Garden in southwest England. I will not be mentioning any particular species here, as I do not want to oversimplify their growing requirements. The excellent book *The Protea Book: A Guide to Cultivated Proteaceae* (2002) by Lewis Matthews covers the family Proteaceae in great depth.

Prunus (Roseaceae)

Northern temperate regions of the world and mountainous parts of northern Africa

This genus comprises more than two hundred species of evergreen and deciduous shrubs and trees that are grown mainly for their ornamental flowers, fruit, and leaves. I will be dealing here only with *P. laurocerasus*, as the luxuriant foliage is well suited to the exotic garden, making a good backdrop for other exotic plants. This underrated plant should

be used in preference to Leyland cypress as hedging. Laurels are a common shrub in parks and gardens, where they form huge, dense thickets or medium-sized trees. They prefer moist but well-drained, moderately fertile soil.

Prunus laurocerasus

Cherry laurel, English laurel

Hardy / Full sun

Dense, evergreen, bushy shrub or small tree from southeastern Europe to Iran, Asia, and the Balkans, growing to a spread and height of 6 m, becoming spreading and open with age. Large, oblong, glossy leaves, 13–20.5 cm long, are somewhat reminiscent of the rubber plant, *Ficus elastica*. They can be used as a single specimen shrub or, by removing the lower branches, a very handsome tree. The profuse, fragrant, creamy white flowers are borne in racemes, 5–6.5 cm long, in spring, followed by dark purple stoned fruits much loved by blackbirds. 'Marbled White' is a variegated form. A smaller variety, 'Otto Luyken', grows to about 1–1.5 m tall, being a good shrub for the more restricted situation. 'Castlewellan' is an unusual and stunning variety with leathery evergreen leaves that are heavily marbled creamy white. 'Magnoliifolia' (large-leaved evergreen cherry)—sometimes listed as 'Latifolia', 'Macrophylla', or 'Magnifolia'—is best grown as a tree to 7.6 m tall; alternatively, it can be trained into an attractive standard tree. The leaves are large, smooth, and glossy, up to 30 cm long by 10 cm wide, mostly hanging downward and looking very imposing, somewhat resembling *Magnolia grandiflora* foliage. Fragrant white flowers are held in vertical racemes borne in early spring, followed by black fruit.

Prunus laurocerasus 'Marbled White'

Pseudopanax
ferox

Pseudopanax
laetus

Pseudopanax (Araliaceae)

syn. *Neopanax*
New Zealand, Tasmania, Australia, and Chile

This small group of twelve or more species of shrubby *Aralia* allies are grown for their thick ever-green leaves of various sizes and shapes, which make them excellent foliage plants for the exotic garden. Their insignificant flowers appear in summer. They thrive in sun or dappled shade in most garden soils and make good container plants. The tips can be pinched out to make them bushier.

Pseudopanax arboreus

Five-finger
Frost-hardy / Sun or dappled shade

Shrub growing to 8–10 m tall, though more like 2–3 m in cool-temperate gardens. Large glossy dark green leaves are divided into five to seven oblong leaflets. Tiny honey-scented green flowers are fol-lowed by rounded purplish black fruits on female plants in autumn. Although not considered particu-larly hardy, has survived −11°C in Norwich, Nor-folk, with only minor leaf burn.

Pseudopanax crassifolius

Lancewood
Frost-hardy / Sun or dappled shade

Rather interesting if not unusual, slowly grow-ing shrub to 2.5 m high and similar width, though usually less in cool-temperate gardens. As a juve-nile (which can last many years), grows as a single upright stem. Leaves are up to 60 cm long by 2 cm wide, stiff, dark bronze-purple with a distinct orange midrib. Leaf edges are sharply serrated and hang down at a 45-degree angle when young. As plant matures, leaves become smaller and lift upward. Hardy to −10°C.

Pseudopanax ferox

Savage lancewood
Frost-hardy / Full sun

Bizarre plant that looks as though it has been planted upside down! With few branches on very erect stems, grows slowly to about 2 m high in its native habitat, though much less in cool-temperate gardens. Stiff, thin, mottled bronze-brown leaves are jagged, sharply toothed, and hang at a 45-degree angle to the stems, widely spaced apart, reaching a length of up to 45 cm. Prefers well-drained soil in a sunny corner of the garden. Cover with fleece in very cold weather. Hardy to around −8°c for short periods.

Pseudopanax laetus

Frost-hardy / Full sun

Forms a very tropical-looking, round tree, with a height and spread of 3 m, with large leathery, glossy, palmate dark green leaves, composed of five to seven oblong, deep green leaflets with prominent midribs, up to 30 cm long. Tiny greenish purple flowers appear in summer, followed by round black fruit. Protect from cold desiccating winds. Hardy to −5°c and lower in a protected corner.

Pseudopanax lessonii

Frost-hardy / Full sun

Very ornamental shrub with an erect, bushy habit, with bright green, thick, leathery, usually five-palmate leaves borne on stout branches. 'Black Ruby' is a rather attractive shrub growing to around 5 m tall in its native habitat, though more like 1–2 m in cool-temperate gardens. The handsome, glossy, dark bronze-purple, three-lobed leaves become even darker when planted in full sun. 'Gold Splash' is an ornamental shrub, growing to a height and spread of 3 m with a dense, bushy habit, with striking, thick, leathery, usually five-palmate midgreen leaves with a strong golden yellow central variegation. 'Purpureus' is a very ornamental shrub with a bushy habit, growing to about 2.5 m tall by 1.5 m wide, with palmate, glossy, leathery, toothed, bronze-tinged, three- to five-lobed leaves up to 7 cm long. In winter the foliage turns a delicious deeper bronze-purple. 'Trident' is an excellent and very ornamental evergreen shrub with a columnar spreading habit, growing to 5 m tall by 3 m wide, though usually much less in cool-temperate climes. Attractive dark green leaves are tough, leathery, with prominent pale veins. Often carries single-,

double-, and triple-lobed leaves on the same plant. All are hardy to about −5°c and probably lower, provided they are grown in a corner of the garden protected from prevailing winds.

Quercus (Fragaceae)

Quercus ilex

Oak

Northern Hemisphere

Members of this genus of about six hundred species of deciduous and evergreen trees and shrubs are grown for their habit and form, many living to a great age. All have simple leaves that are often toothed and deeply lobed. Some produce spectacular autumn colour. I have picked three that fit into the exotics category, as they have large leaves or are evergreen and are hardy. Most oaks prefer deep alluvial soil, though some are tolerant of poor, dry soil.

Quercus dentata

Japanese emperor oak

Hardy / Full sun

Tree growing to 20 m tall by 12 m wide, with horizontal branches that arise from a short trunk. Large leaves are green, up to 38 cm long by 20 cm wide. Foliage turns brown and stays on the tree over the winter.

Quercus ilex

Holm oak

Hardy / Full sun

Evergreen oak growing to about 25 m tall by 20 m wide with comparatively smooth dark grey bark. Leaves are ovate to lance-shaped, entire or toothed, shiny, rich dark green, greyish and felted underneath, up to 8 cm long. Whole tree has a very dense appearance and creates a lot of shade, hence needs positioning wisely. Looks tremendous when planted in avenues, especially if you own a baronial estate!

Quercus rubra

Northern red oak, red oak

Hardy / Full sun

Fast-growing and spreading deciduous tree with large green lobed leaves to 20 cm long, with seven to eleven bristle-tipped lobes that turn fiery red in autumn. Fabulous oak tree that deserves to be more widely grown.

Rhododendron (Ericaceae)

Europe, northern India, China, Burma, Tibet, New Guinea to the northern tip of Australia, Japan, and North America

This is a genus of about 850 species of deciduous, semi-evergreen, and evergreen shrubs grown mainly for their flowers, though here we will be dealing with those that fit into the exotic garden category by virtue of having large leaves, with flowers as a bonus. Most grow well in a temperate climate and prefer dappled shade. They require neutral to acid soil that is well-drained and humus-rich. Yellowing of the leaves is caused by poor drainage or soil that is too alkaline. The following should be grown in a protected corner away from chilling winds.

Rhododendron macabeanum

Frost-hardy / Dappled shade

Rhododendron reaching up to 15 m tall in the wild, though more like 3 m in temperate gardens. Grows at 2400 to 2700 m in the Naga Hills, Assam, and

Manipur in northern India, among birches or as compact forests on its own. Enormous leaves are broadly ovate to elliptic, up to 38 cm long, deep green, shiny, leathery, with a hairy white-fawn indumentum underneath. Bell-shaped yellow flowers have a purple blotch and bright red stigma and appear only on large, mature plants, in trusses of twelve to twenty blooms in early spring. Hardy to about −12°C, preferring a sheltered situation.

Rhododendron rex subsp. fictolacteum

Hardy / Dappled shade

Hardiest of the big-leaved rhododendrons, growing to 3.5 m high by 3 m wide and capable of reaching tree-sized proportions. Leaves are up to 30 cm long, shiny, dark green, while the underside is covered with rusty-brown indumentum, an attraction of the plant when not in flower. Pale creamy white flowers with a crimson blotch at the base of the petals are formed in trusses of twelve to twenty. Hardy to

about −15°C, making this the hardiest of the large-leaved forms.

Rhododendron sinogrande

Hardy / Dappled shade

One of the most aristocratic of the large-leaved species, introduced from China by the renowned plant collector George Forrest. Grows to around 3 m, with very large, oblong to lance-shaped, glossy dark green leaves, 80 cm long, silvery below. Wide bell-shaped pale yellow to creamy white flowers are borne in large imposing trusses. Hardy to about −10°C.

Robinia (Fabaceae)

North America

Members of this genus of about twenty species of deciduous shrubs and trees grow well in poor soil and prefer a sunny aspect. The branches are rather brittle and break in high wind. *Robinia pseudoacacia*

Robinia pseudoacacia 'Frisia'

often forms thickets by root suckering and has become invasive in some parts of the United States. It is commonly called black locust or false acacia. A light and airy canopy allows light to filter through, so it can be grown in places where other trees might cast too dense a shadow.

Robinia pseudoacacia 'Frisia'

Hardy / Full sun

Much more exotic tree than the species, with an eventual height of 15 m and a spread of 8 m. Luxuriant leaves are composed of nineteen leaflets that are golden yellow when young (and look stunning against a dark blue sky), turn greenish yellow through the summer, and then turn orange-yellow in autumn. Always remove suckers as they revert to the species, which is green. Takes well to pruning and can be pollarded and kept as a bush, making a bright backdrop to darker-leaved plants. Whole tree has a light and airy appearance.

Sambucus (Caprifoliaceae)

Elder

Most of the members of this genus of about twenty-five species of perennials, shrubs, and small trees are deciduous. They are grown for their foliage, flowers, and fruit. In this case I will be dealing with the coloured-leaf forms. For superlative foliage, prune all shoots to the ground each winter. If you only want foliage, you can remove the flowers and the fruit. Elders prefer sun and moist, fertile soil.

Sambucus canadensis 'Aurea'

Hardy / Sun

Deciduous, upright shrub, growing to a height and spread of 4 m, though more like 1.5–1.8 m tall when regularly pollarded. Large golden yellow leaves have oblong leaflets. In midsummer, domed heads of small star-shaped white flowers are produced, followed by red fruit.

Sambucus nigra

Hardy / Sun

Grows to larger proportions than *S. canadensis* 'Aurea', more like 1.8–2.5 m when pollarded yearly. *S. nigra* 'Aurea' has stout, corky shoots with golden yellow leaves composed of five oval leaflets, followed by fragrant creamy white flowers in early summer and later by clusters of small, round, black fruits. 'Aureomarginata' has pale variegated foliage. 'Guincho Purple' foliage matures to a dark, lustrous purplish black. 'Plumosa Aurea' has finely cut leaves that are bronze when young, maturing to a rich golden yellow.

Tetrapanax (Araliaceae)

Southern China and Taiwan

This is a genus of one species of evergreen shrub, part of the ivy family. The plant looks somewhat similar to a large *Fatsia japonica*, though far more handsome and striking. This is an absolutely essential shrub for the temperate exotic garden, preferring a mild climate in moist, humus-rich soil, with a mulch of well-rotted manure in spring.

Tetrapanax papyrifer

Rice-paper plant
Frost-hardy / Sun or dappled shade

Upright, vigorous, suckering shrub growing to 2–4.5 m tall, evergreen in mild areas only, with powder-covered stems. Common name is derived from the fact that a type of fine rice paper is made from the pith of the stems. Leaves on long stalks, to 90 cm across, are heavily felted when young, deeply lobed with five to ten fingers, dark green, borne mainly at terminal ends; they overlap to form a dense canopy. Large panicles of small creamy white flowers develop in early autumn, though usually cut back by first

frosts. Needs careful positioning, as it will come up among your other plants! New plants can be propagated from 6-cm root sections. Take more than you need, as they are tricky to propagate. Keep young plants under cover for the first winter, then plant out the following spring. Hardy to −8°C for short periods. Will reshoot from the base if cut down. In cold areas wrap the stem with straw and surround with fleece or sacking. The elusive 'Variegata' is a less hardy form with cream-edged leaves.

'Rex' is a fairly recent introduction to British cultivation, notable for being hardier and more vigorous than *T. papyrifer*. Leaf lobes are more deeply cut, pointed, and tend to droop more than the more common form, with leaves growing to a staggering 1.2 m across; the shrub can grow up to 2 m in one season. A form in the United States sold under the name 'Steroidal Giant' seems to be identical in growth to 'Rex'. 'Rex' is hardier than the form, taking −10°C in its stride. Another form named 'Empress' that promises to be even hardier was recently collected; its leaves have a slightly purple blush and are similar in size to those of 'Rex'.

Above

Tetrapanax papyrifer with *Agapanthus* Ardernei hybrid (underneath, center) and *Euonymus fortunei* 'Silver Queen' (underneath, to the left)

Below

Tetrapanax papyrifer 'Rex' with *Colocasia esculenta* (underneath, to the left), *Cyperus involucratus* (center left), and *Dicksonia antarctica* (above right)

Right

Trevesia palmata with *Colocasia esculenta* 'Mammoth' and *Persicaria microcephala* 'Red Dragon' beneath

Trevesia (Araliaceae)

Himalaya to southern China and southern Asia

This genus includes twelve species of trees and shrubs, members of the ivy family. They are highly attractive and desirable plants with stunning architectural form. The shrubs are often dense and clump-forming, and sometimes have prickly stems.

Trevesia palmata

Semi-tender / Dappled shade

Grows unbranched or as a wide-crowned shrub or tree to 9 m tall by 3.5 m wide in its native habitat, although much smaller in a container. Leaves are grey-green, indescribably exotic, intricately cut into snowflake patterns and palmately lobed to 90 cm. Minimum temperature 5°C. Makes an excellent container plant for a conservatory, which can be brought out for the summer months. Prefers moisture-retentive, fertile soil.

Trochodendron
(Trochodendraceae)

Japan, South Korea, and Taiwan

This genus contains one species of evergreen tree, grown for its exotic foliage and flowers.

Trochodendron aralioides

Cartwheel tree

Frost-hardy to hardy / Dappled shade

Small evergreen tree that grows slowly and reaches 3–5 m tall in cool-temperate climates, with whorled branches. Growth habit is considerably more open in shade than in sun. Leaves are bold, rubbery, long-stalked, ovate or obovate, 8–15 cm long, often glossy, dark green. Flowers are greenish, produced in erect terminal racemes 6–8 cm long, mostly in early summer. Prefers organically rich soil in dappled shade. Prune as necessary to emphasise the whorled branch structure. Bark is pleasantly aromatic. Takes lows down to −10°C and probably lower.

Vestia (Solanaceae)

Chile

Vestia is a genus of one species of evergreen shrub in the nightshade family, grown for its foliage and flowers. Found in woodland areas in its native habitat, it prefers dappled shade, although it will grow in full sun.

Vestia foetida

Frost-hardy / Sun or dappled shade

Attractive, evergreen, upright, open shrub, growing fast to a height and spread of 1.5 m. Tightly packed, glossy, dark green, oblong, ovate, pointed leaves up to 7 cm long have a fetid scent when crushed. Flowers are tubular, pendent, solitary, pale yellow, from midspring to midsummer, followed by bright green seed capsules that turn brown. Hardy to −5°C for short periods.

Viburnum (Caprifoliaceae)

Europe, Asia, and North America

Plants in this genus of more than 150 species of evergreen, semi-evergreen, and deciduous trees and shrubs are grown for their foliage (and their autumn colour, in the deciduous species). They prefer sun or dappled shade in deep, rich soil. The evergreen species make superb exotic garden plants

Viburnum davidii

with their interesting foliage and make good back-bone plants, visually settling the garden by giving the appearance of age.

Viburnum davidii

Hardy / Sun or dappled shade

Compact evergreen shrub forming a dome shape to 1 m high by 1.5 m wide. Dark green, glossy, leathery leaves, narrowly oval, are marked with three distinct veins. Terminal clusters of small off-white flowers appear in late spring. If both sexes are grown, female shrub produces attractive turquoise metallic-blue fruit. Plant en masse for a low-maintenance, shrubby ground cover or grow as a single specimen for its year-round structural contribution.

Viburnum rhytidophyllum

Hardy / Sun or dappled shade

Open, upright, vigorous evergreen shrub, grow-ing to a height and spread of 3.5 m. Long, narrow, wrinkled dark green leaves up to 18 cm long are velvety greyish yellow on the underside. Terminal clusters of creamy white flowers are borne from late spring to early summer, followed by red fruits that turn black with age. 'Aldenhamense' has leaves with a sulphur-yellow tinge.

Viburnum tinus

Hardy / Sun or dappled shade

Another good, dense, evergreen backbone shrub, growing to a height and spread of 2.4–3 m. Dark green glossy to matte leaves are oblong-oval and pointed, to 9 cm long. Flattish heads of small, pink-ish white, fragrant flowers appear from winter to early spring, followed by blue-black berries. Can be clipped after flowering to keep in shape and can also be used as a loose hedging plant. 'Eve Price' is a bushy, compact form with elongated leaves and light pink flowers. 'Lucidum' has very glossy leaves. 'Purpureum' has attractive bronzed new growth.

Viburnum rhytidophyllum

Conversion Tables

inches	cm
1/10	0.3
1/6	0.4
1/4	0.6
1/3	0.8
1/2	1.3
3/4	1.9
1	2.5
2	5.1
3	7.6
4	10
5	13
6	15
7	18
8	20
9	23
10	25
20	51
30	76
40	100
50	130

feet	m
1	0.3
2	0.6
3	0.9
4	1.2
5	1.5
6	1.8
7	2.1
8	2.4
9	2.7
10	3
20	6
30	9
40	12
50	15
60	18
70	21
80	24
90	27
100	30
200	60

temperatures

$$°C = 5/9 \times (°F - 32)$$
$$°F = (9/5 \times °C) + 32$$

Where to Find Exotics

British Nurseries

Abacus Nurseries (dahlias)
Drummau Road
Skewen
Neath SA10 6NW
tel: 01792 817 994
www.abacus-nurseries.co.uk

Abbotsbury Sub Tropical Gardens
Abbotsbury
Weymouth
Dorset DT3 4LA
tel/fax: 01305 871 344
www.abbotsburyplantsales.co.uk

Amulree Exotics (palms, bamboos, bananas,
      cacti, and exotics)
The Turnpike
Norwich Road
Fundenhall
Norfolk NR16 1EL
tel: 01508 488 101
www.turn-it-tropical.co.uk

Architectural Plants
Cooks Farm
Nuthurst
Horsham
West Sussex RH13 6LH
tel: 01403 891 772
fax: 01403 891 056
www.architecturalplants.com

Big Plant Nursery Limited
Hole Street
Ashington
West Sussex RH20 3DE
tel: 01903 891 466
fax: 01903 892 829
www.bigplantnursery.co.uk/index.htm

Cotswold Garden Flowers
Browns' Nurseries
Gibbs Lane
Offenham
Evesham
Worcestershire WR11 8RR
tel: 01386 422 829
www.cgf.net

Burncoose Nurseries (wide range of
  exotic and hardy plants)
Gwennap
Redruth
Cornwall TR16 6BJ
tel: 01209 860 316
fax: 01209 860 011
www.burncoose.co.uk

Chapel House Exotics
Chapel House
County Road
Leeswood
Flintshire CH7 4RF
tel: 07840 868 271
www.chapelhouseexotics.co.uk

Crûg Farm Plants (outstanding and
  unrivalled selection of plants)
Griffith's Crossing
Caernarfon
Gwynedd LL55 1TU
tel: 01248 670 232
www.crug-farm.co.uk

Dibleys Nurseries (coleus and others)
Llanelidan
Ruthin
North Wales LL15 2LG
tel: 01978 790 677
fax: 01978 790 668
www.dibleys.com

Eucalyptus Nurseries
Allt-y-Celyn
Carrog Corwen
Denbighshire LL21 9LD
tel/fax: 01490 430 671
www.eucalyptus.co.uk

Hardy Exotics Nursery
Gilly Lane
Whitecross
Penzance
Cornwall TR20 8BZ
tel: 01736 740 660
fax: 01736 741 101
www.hardyexotics.co.uk

Hart Canna (cannas)
27 Guildford Road West
Farnborough
Hants GU14 6PS
tel: 01252 514 421
fax: 01252 378 821
www.hartcanna.com

Holly Gate Cactus Nursery and Cactus
  Garden
Billingshurst Road
Ashington
West Sussex RH20 3BB
tel: 01903 892 930
www.hollygatecactus.co.uk

Hyde Cottage Palms and Exotics
Church Road
Crowle
Worcestershire WR7 4AT
tel: 01905 381 632
fax: 01905 381 632
www.palmsandexotics.co.uk

Jungle Giants (bamboos and large things)
Ferney
Onibury
Craven Arms SY7 9BJ
tel: 01584 856 200
fax: 01584 856 663
www.junglegiants.co.uk

Jungle Seeds and Gardens
P. O. Box 45
Watlington SPDO
Oxon OX49 5YR
tel: 01491 614 765
fax: 01491 612 034
www.junglegardens.co.uk

KobaKoba Nursery
Ashcott
Somerset TA7 9QT
tel: 01458 210 700
www.kobakoba.co.uk

Madrona Nursery (unusual trees, shrubs,
  and perennials)
Pluckley Road
Bethersden
Ashford
Kent TN26 3DD
tel: 01233 820 100
fax: 01233 820 091
www.madrona.co.uk

Mulu Nurseries (wide range of exotics)
Longdon Hill
Wickhamford
Evesham
Worcestershire WR11 7RP
tel: 01386 833 171
fax: 01386 833 136
www.mulu.co.uk

Newington Nurseries ("Specialists in the
    unusual")
Newington, nr. Stadhampton
Oxon OX10 7AW
tel: 01865 400 533
www.newington-nurseries.co.uk

Northern Exposure Hardy Exotics
P.O. Box No. 25
Wilmslow
Cheshire SK9 2FU
tel: 01625 530 866
fax: 01625 531 979
www.northernexposureexotics.com

The Old Walled Garden (exotic plants)
Oxon Hoath
Oxon Hoath Road
Hadlow
Tonbridge
Kent TN11 9SS
tel: 01732 810 012
fax: 01732 810 856
www.ep-d.co.uk/index.htm

The Palm Centre (palms and other exotics)
Ham Central Nursery
Ham Street
Ham
Richmond
Surrey TW10 7HA
tel: 02082 556 191
fax: 02082 556 192
www.thepalmcentre.co.uk

The Palm House (palms and other exotics)
8 North Street
Ottery St. Mary
Devon EX11 1DR
tel: 01404 815 450 or 07815 673 397
www.thepalmhouse.co.uk

Pantiles Garden Centre (semi-mature
    containerised plants)
Almners Road
Lyne
Chertsey
Surrey KT16 0BJ
tel: 01932 872 195
fax: 01932 874 030
www.pantiles-nurseries.co.uk

Premier Plants UK (specimen wholesale
    plants)
Ongar Road West (A414)
Writtle
Chelmsford
Essex CM1 3NT
tel: 01245 422 525
fax: 01245 422 566
www.premierplantsuk.com

PW Plants (large selection of bamboos and
    more)
Sunnyside
Heath Road
Kenninghall
Norfolk NR16 2DS
tel/fax: 01953 888 212
www.hardybamboo.com

Rare Exotic Plants UK
tel: 01227 711 897
www.Rare-Exotic-Plants.co.uk

Reads (conservatory plants)
Hales Hall
Loddon
Norfolk NR14 6QW
tel: 01508 548 395
fax: 01508 548 040
www.readsnursery.co.uk

Secret Seeds Garden Nursery (echiums)
Cove
Tiverton
Devon EX16 7RU
tel/fax: 01399 331 946
www.echiums.com

Shrubland Park Nurseries (conservatory,
    succulents, tender and hardy perennials)
Coddenham
Ipswich
Suffolk IP6 9QJ
tel: 01473 833 187
www.shrublandparknurseries.co.uk

Trevena Cross Nurseries (diverse variety of
    plants, including restios)
Breage
Helston
Cornwall TR13 9PS
tel: 01736 763 880
fax: 01736 762 828
www.trevenacross.co.uk

Urban Jungle (large range of exotics)
Ringland Lane
Old Costessey
Norwich
Norfolk NR8 5BG
tel: 01603 744 997
fax: 07092 366 869
www.urbanjungle.uk.com

Continental European Nurseries

Monika Gottschalk (brugmansias)
Diebsteinweg 18
D-36358 Herbstein
Germany
tel: +49 6643 1794
fax: +49 6643 799 671
www.monika-gottschalk.de/index.htm

Anne Kirchner-Abel (brugmansias)
Schützenstr. 24
47229 Duisburg
Germany
tel: +49 02065 49271
fax: +49 02065 421339
www.kirchner-abel.de

Plantsman Nursery (exotic climbing plants)
Clos St Jacques
Route de Coutras
Sablons 33910
France
tel: +33 6035 81460
www.plantsman.com

Tropica Flore (subtropical and exotic plants)
10 Rue de la Vigne aux Vieux
77710 Treuzy-Levelay
France
tel: +33 1607 34747
fax: +33 1642 90475
www.tropicaflore.com

Winter Hill Plants (exotic, rare, and unusual plants)
France
homepage.ntlworld.com/dia.smith

U.S. Nurseries

Aloha Tropicals (subtropical and exotic plants)
P.O. Box 6042
Oceanside, CA 92054
tel/fax: (760) 631-2880
www.alohatropicals.com

Asiatica (international rare plant resource)
P.O. Box 270
Lewisberry, PA 17339
tel: (717) 938-8677 (no phone orders, please)
fax: (717) 938-0771
www.asiaticanursery.com

Bamboo Sourcery
666 Wagnon Road
Sebastopol, CA 95472
tel: (707) 823-5866
fax: (707) 829-8106
www.bamboosourcery.com/catalog.cfm

The Banana Tree (tropical plants, bananas, palms,
    and seeds)
715 Northampton Street
Easton, PA 18042
tel: (610) 253-9589
fax: (610) 253-4864
www.banana-tree.com

Bird Rock Tropicals (bromeliads)
P.O. Box 231458
Encinitas, CA 92023
tel: (760) 436-3088
fax: (760) 436-2998
www.birdrocktropicals.com

Bromeliad Specialties
28001 SW 197th Avenue
Homestead, FL 33030
tel: (800) 874-9892 or (305) 247-5990
fax: (305) 247-5519
www.tillandsia.com

Cloud Jungle Epiphytes
4909 Sadies Place
Wingate, NC 28174
www.cloudjungle.com

Gerry's Jungle (cold-hardy palms and other exotics)
P.O. Box 314
Scottsmoor, FL 32775
tel: (321) 264-8917
www.neotropic.com

Glasshouse Works (plants for home,
  conservatory, and garden)
Church Street
P.O. Box 97
Stewart, OH 45778
tel: (740) 662-2142
fax: (740) 662-2120
www.glasshouseworks.com

Gossler Farms Nursery (hardy broad-leaved
  evergreens and unusual plants)
1200 Weaver Road
Springfield, OR 97478
tel: (541) 746-3922
fax: (541) 744-7924
www.gosslerfarms.com

Karchesky Canna Collection (cannas and
  brugmansias)
558 South Ridge Road
Coal Center, PA 15423
tel: (724) 466-0979
www.karcheskycanna.com

Kartuz Greenhouses (rare and exotic plants)
1408 Sunset Drive
Vista, CA 92081
tel: (760) 941-3613
fax: (760) 941-1123
www.kartuz.com

Logee's Greenhouses (tropical container plants
  for home and garden)
141 North Street
Danielson, CT 06239
tel: (888) 330-8038
fax: (888) 774-9932
www.logees.com

Mesogeo (Mediterranean and hardy tropical
  plants suited to the Pacific Northwest climate)
12364 Miller Road
N.E. Bainbridge Island, WA 98110
tel: (206) 855-9017
www.mesogeogarden.com

Natural Selections Exotics ("The collector's
  plant source")
Mail order only
www.naturalselections.safeshopper.com

New England Bamboo Company (large array
  of temperate bamboo species)
5 Granite Street
Rockport, MA 01966
tel: (978) 546-3581
fax: (978) 546-1075
www.newengbamboo.com

Plant Delights Nursery (exotic and unusual
  plants)
9241 Sauls Road
Raleigh, NC 27603
tel: (919) 772-4794
fax: (919) 662-0370
www.plantdelights.com

Stokes Tropicals (wide range of subtropical
  and exotic plants)
4806 E. Old Spanish Trail
Jeanerette, LA 70544
tel: (337) 365-6998
www.stokestropicals.com

Top Tropicals Botanical Garden (retail and
  wholesale nursery)
47770 Bermont Road
Punta Gorda, FL 33982
tel: (941) 575-6987
fax: (954) 252-4442
www.toptropicals.com

TyTy Nursery (cannas and other exotics)
4723 U.S. Hwy. 82 West
P.O. Box 130
TyTy, GA 31795
tel: (800) 972-2101
www.tytyga.com

YuccaDo Nursery (arid and semi-arid plants)
P.O. Box 907
Hempstead, TX 77445
tel: (979) 826-4580
fax: (979) 826-4571
www.yuccado.com

Seed Companies

B and T World Seeds
Route des Marchandes
Paguignan
34210 Aigues-Vives
France
tel: +33 4689 12963
fax: +33 4689 13039
www.b-and-t-world-seeds.com

Chiltern Seeds
Bortree Stile
Ulverston
Cumbria LA12 7PB
United Kingdom
tel: 01962 820 431
www.edirectory.co.uk/chilternseeds

Jungle Seeds and Gardens
P.O. Box 45
Watlington SPDO
Oxon OX49 5YR
United Kingdom
tel: 01491 614 765
fax: 01491 612 034
www.jungleseeds.co.uk/index.html

rarepalmseeds.com
Tizianstr. 44
80638 Muenchen
Germany
tel: +49 8915 77902
fax: +49 8915 704284
www.rarepalmseeds.com

Silverhill Seeds
P.O. Box 53108
Kenilworth 7745
Cape Town, South Africa
tel: +27 21 762-4245
fax: +27 21 797-6609
www.silverhillseeds.co.za

Thompson and Morgan
Poplar Lane
Ipswich
Suffolk IP8 3BU
United Kingdom
tel: 01473 695 200
fax: 01473 680 199
www.thompson-morgan.com

Thompson and Morgan Seedsmen
220 Faraday Avenue
Jackson, NJ 08527
United States
tel: (800) 274-7333
fax: (888) 466-4769
seeds.thompson-morgan.com/us

Whatcom Seed Company
Oregon
United States
www.seedrack.com

References and Further Reading

Books

Beckett, Kenneth A. 1987. *The RHS Encyclopedia of Houseplants*. London: Century Hutchinson.

Billington, Jill. 1991. *Architectural Foliage*. London: Ward Lock.

Bown, Deni. 2000. *Aroids: Plants of the Arum Family*. 2nd ed. Portland, Oregon: Timber Press.

Branney, Tim M. E. 2005. *Hardy Gingers*. Portland, Oregon: Timber Press.

Brickell, Christopher, ed. 2003. *The Royal Horticultural Society A–Z Encyclopaedia of Garden Plants*. 3rd rev. ed. London: Dorling Kindersley.

Challis, Myles. 1988a. *The Exotic Garden*. London: Fourth Estate.

———. 1988b. *Exotic Gardening in Cool Climates*. London: Fourth Estate.

Cooke, Ian. 1998. *The Plantfinder's Guide to Tender Perennials*. Portland, Oregon: Timber Press.

———. 2001. *The Gardener's Guide to Growing Cannas*. Portland, Oregon: Timber Press.

Darke, Rick. 2007. *The Encyclopedia of Grasses for Livable Landscapes*. Portland, Oregon: Timber Press.

Dunnett, Nigel, and Noël Kingsbury. 2004. *Planting Green Roofs and Living Walls*. Portland, Oregon: Timber Press.

Gibbons, Martin. 2000. *Palms: The Illustrated Identifier to Over 100 Palm Species*. Hove, East Sussex, England: Apple Press.

Graf, Alfred Byrd. 1978. *Tropica*. East Rutherford, New Jersey: Roehrs.

Graham, Martyn. 2002. *Hardy Palms and Palm-like Plants*. Lewes, East Sussex, England: Guild of Master Craftsman Publications.

Grenfell, Diana, and Mike Shadrack. 2004. *The Color Encyclopedia of Hostas*. Portland, Oregon: Timber Press.

Heims, Dan, and Grahame Ware. 2005. *Heucheras and Heucherellas: Coral Bells and Foamy Bells*. Portland, Oregon: Timber Press.

Hemsley, Alan. 2002. *Tropical Garden Style with Hardy Plants*. Lewes, East Sussex, England: Guild of Master Craftsman Publications Ltd.

Hill, Susan, and Susan Narizny, eds. 2004. *The Plant Locator Western Region*. Portland, Oregon: Black-Eyed Susans Press/Timber Press.

Hillier Nurseries. 1991. *The Hillier Manual of Trees and Shrubs*. 6th ed. Newton Abbot, Devon, England: David and Charles.

Hogan, Sean, ed. 2003. *Flora: A Gardener's Encyclopedia*. Portland, Oregon: Timber Press.

Hoshizaki, Barbara Joe, and Robbin C. Moran. 2001. *Fern Grower's Manual*. Revised and expanded edition. Portland, Oregon: Timber Press.

Irish, Mary, and Gary Irish. 2000. *Agaves, Yuccas, and Related Plants: A Gardener's Guide*. Portland, Oregon: Timber Press.

Iversen, Richard R. 1999. *The Exotic Garden*. Newtown, Connecticut: Taunton.

Large, Mark F., and John E. Braggins. 2004. *Tree Ferns*. Portland, Oregon: Timber Press.

Latymer, Hugo. 2001. *The Mediterranean Gardener*. Paperback ed. London: Francis Lincoln.

Mabberley, D. J. 1997. *The Plant-Book: A Portable Dictionary of the Vascular Plants*. 2nd ed. New York: Cambridge University Press.

Matthews, Lewis. 2002. *The Protea Book: A Guide to Cultivated Proteaceae*. Portland, Oregon: Timber Press.

Nelhams, Mike. 2000. *Tresco Abbey Garden: A Personal and Pictorial History*. Truro, Cornwall, England: Truran Books.

Phillips, Roger, and Martyn Rix. 1989. *Shrubs*. London: Pan Books.

———. 1989. *Bulbs*. London: Pan Books.

———. 1991. *Perennials*. Vol. 1, *Early Perennials*. Vol. 2, *Late Perennials*. London: Pan Books.

———. 1998. *Conservatory and Indoor Plants*. 2 vols. London: Pan Macmillan.

Preissel, Ulrike, and Hans-Georg Preissel. 2002. *Brugmansia and Datura: Angel's Trumpets and Thorn Apples*. Richmond Hill, Ontario, Canada: Firefly Books.

Rickard, Martin. 2003. *The Plantfinder's Guide to Garden Ferns*. Portland, Oregon: Timber Press.

Riffle, Robert Lee. 1998. *The Tropical Look: An Encyclopedia of Dramatic Landscape Plants*. Portland, Oregon: Timber Press.

Riffle, Robert Lee, and Paul Craft. 2003. *An Encyclopedia of Cultivated Palms*. Portland, Oregon: Timber Press.

Robinson, William. 1871. *The Subtropical Garden*. London: Murray.

Ross, Thomas, and Jeffrey Irons. 1997. *Australian Plants: A Guide to Their Cultivation in Europe*. Wirral, England: J. Irons.

Rowlands, Gareth. 1999. *The Gardener's Guide to Growing Dahlias*. Portland, Oregon: Timber Press.

Royal Horticultural Society. 2006. *RHS Plant Finder 2006–2007*. London: Dorling Kindersley.

Shaw, Christine. 2003. *Architectural Plants*. New York: Collins.

Snoeijer, Wim. 2004. *Agapanthus: A Revision of the Genus*. Portland, Oregon: Timber Press.

Stearn, William T. 2002. *The Genus Epimedium and Other Herbaceous Berberidaceae*. Portland, Oregon: Timber Press.

Steens, Andrew. 2003. *Bromeliads for the Contemporary Garden*. Portland, Oregon: Timber Press.

Stephenson, Ray. 1994. *Sedum: Cultivated Stonecrops*. Portland, Oregon: Timber Press.

Sunset Editors. 1996. *Sunset Western Garden Book*. Menlo Park, California: Sunset Books.

Tebbitt, Mark C. 2005. *Begonias: Cultivation, Identification, and Natural History*. Portland, Oregon: Timber Press.

Ulmer, Torsten, and John M. MacDougal. 2004. *Passionflowers of the World*. Portland, Oregon: Timber Press.

van Dijk, Hanneke. 2004. *Agapanthus for Gardeners*. Portland, Oregon: Timber Press.

Whittaker, Paul. 2005. *Hardy Bamboos: Taming the Dragon*. Portland, Oregon: Timber Press.

Electronic Sources

Much information on exotic plants has been gathered from the online catalogues of North American as well as British plant retailers, of which there are far too many to mention. Other online sources consulted include the following:

American Brugmansia and Datura Society. http://www.abads.net/abadssitemap.htm (description and identification of *Brugmansia* species and hybrids).

Botanical Dermatology Database. http://bodd.cf.ac.uk/BotDermFolder/BotDermA/ARAC-1.html (information on the family Araceae).

Botany, the Encyclopedia of Plants and Gardening. http://www.botany.com (general information from the Encyclopedia of Plants).

Brugmansia Growers International. http://www.brugmansias.org (information on brugmansias).

CoolTropiX.com. http://www.cooltropix.com (site covering everything from palms and cycads to bananas, giving excellent information about every aspect of growing exotics in cool-temperate, often chilly, climates).

Forums, Chat Groups, and Boards

North America

Aroid Forum
forums.gardenweb.com/forums/aroid

Bromeliad Forum
forums.gardenweb.com/forums/bromeliad

Brugmansia Forum
forums.gardenweb.com/forums/brug

Canna Forum
forums.gardenweb.com/forums/canna

Hardy Palm and Subtropical Board
members3.boardhost.com/HardyPalm

International Palm Society, North American Chapters
www.palms.org/chapters/north.htm

Moss, Ferns, and Cryptogams Forum
forums.gardenweb.com/forums/crypto

Northwest Palms Discussion Board
www.cloudforest.com/northwest/index.html

Pacific Northwest Palm and Exotic Plant Society
www.hardypalm.com

Palms and Cycads Forum
forums.gardenweb.com/forums/palms

PalmTalk: International Palm Society forum
palmtalk.org

Passiflora Forum
forums.gardenweb.com/forums/passiflora

Great Britain and Europe

Allegras Englestrompeten Forum (brugmansias)
www.allegras-foren.de/phpbb/sitemap.php

Canna group
tech.groups.yahoo.com/group/canna

European canna exchange
tech.groups.yahoo.com/group/CannaExchangeEU

Palm Centre Discussion Forum
www.thepalmcentre.co.uk/index_forum.html

UK Oasis Discussion Board
p206.ezboard.com/fukoasisfrm1

Index of Plant Names

Italicised page numbers refer to illustrations.

sweet corn. See *Zea mays*

sweet potato. See *Ipomoea batatas*

Swiss chard. See *Beta vulgaris*

Swiss cheese plant. See *Monstera deliciosa*

sword fern. See *Polystichum*

Syngonium 31, 49

Syngonium podophylla 49

Syngonium podophylla 'Variegatum' 49

T

tannia. See *Xanthosoma*

tara vine. See *Actinidia arguta*

Tasmanian snow gum. See *Eucalyptus coccifera*

tatting fern. See *Athyrium filix-femina* 'Frizelliae'

Telanthophora grandifolia. See *Senecio grandifolius*

Tetrapanax 409-10

Tetrapanax papyrifer 409-10, *410*

Tetrapanax papyrifer 'Empress' 410

Tetrapanax papyrifer 'Rex' 410, *410*

Tetrapanax papyrifer 'Steroidal Giant' 410

Tetrapanax papyrifer 'Variegata' 410

Tetrastigma 197

Tetrastigma voinierianum 197

Thamnocalamus 70-72

Thamnocalamus aristatus. See *T. spathiflorus*

Thamnocalamus crassinodus 'Kew Beauty' 70, *70*

Thamnocalamus crassinodus 'Lang Tang' 70, *71*, 72

Thamnocalamus spathiflorus 72, *72*

thread palm. See *Washingtonia robusta*

Three Kings cabbage tree. See *Cordyline kaspar*

Thunbergia 222-3

Thunbergia alata 222-3, *223*

Thunbergia grandiflora

Thunbergia mysorensis 222, *223*

thyme honey myrtle. See *Melaleuca thymifolia*

Tibouchina urvilleana 189

tiger flower. See *Tigridia pavonia*

Tigridia 137

Tigridia pavonia 137, *137*

Tillandsia 22, 112-13

Tillandsia aeranthos 112

Tillandsia bergeri 112

Tillandsia cyanea 112, *112*

Tillandsia usneoides 112-13, *113*

tingiringi gum. See *Eucalyptus glaucescens*

Tithonia 224

Tithonia rotundifolia 224

Tithonia rotundifolia 'Aztec Sun' 224

Tithonia rotundifolia 'Fiesta del Sol' 224

Tithonia rotundifolia 'Goldfinger' 224

Tithonia rotundifolia 'Torch'

toad lily. See *Tricyrtis* 224, *224*

tobacco. See *Nicotiana tabacum*

tobacco plant. See *Nicotiana*

toetoe grass. See *Cortaderia richardii*

toitoi. See *Cortaderia richardii*

torch lobelia. See *Lobelia laxiflora*

Tovara virginiana. See *Persicaria virginiana*

Trachelospermum 197-8

Trachelospermum asiaticum 197

Trachelospermum jasminoides 197-8, *197*

Trachelospermum jasminoides 'Tricolor' 197

Trachelospermum jasminoides 'Variegata' 197, *198*

Trachelospermum jasminoides 'Waterwheel' 197

Trachycarpus 286-9

Trachycarpus fortunei 12, *15*, 21, 24, 275, 287, *287*

Trachycarpus latisectus 287

Trachycarpus nanus 288

Trachycarpus sikkimensis. See *T. latisectus*

Trachycarpus takil 288

Trachycarpus wagnerianus 288, 289

Tradescantia 22, 247, 270-3

Tradescantia albiflora. See *T. fluminensis*

Tradescantia blossfeldiana. See *T. cerinthoides*

Tradescantia cerinthoides 271, *271*

Tradescantia fluminensis 272

Tradescantia fluminensis 'Albovittata' 271

Tradescantia fluminensis 'Maiden's Blush' *270*, 272

Tradescantia fluminensis 'Variegata' 272, *272*

Tradescantia pallida 272, *273*

Tradescantia spathacea 272

Tradescantia spathacea 'Variegata'. See *T. spathacea* 'Vittata'

Tradescantia spathacea 'Vittata' 272

Tradescantia zebrine 273, *273*

Transvaal daisy. See *Gerbera*

tree celandine. See *Macleaya*

tree poppy. See *Romneya*

Trevesia 410

Trevesia palmata 410, *411*

Trichocereus affinis 'Pascana' *16*

Trichocereus bruchii. See *Echinopsis bruchii*

Tricyrtis 338-9

Tricyrtis formosana 338

Tricyrtis hirta 339, *339*

Tricyrtis hirta var. *alba*

Tricyrtis hirta 'Miyazaki' 339

Tricyrtis hirta 'Miyazaki Gold' 339

Tricyrtis hirta 'White Towers' 339

Tricyrtis japonica. See *T. hirta*

Tricyrtis stolonifera. See *T. formosana*

Trithrinax 289-90

Trithrinax acanthocoma 289, *289*

Trithrinax campestris 289-90, *289*

Trochodendron 412

Trochodendron aralioides 412, *412*

Tropaeolum 198-200

Tropaeolum ciliatum 198, *198-9*

Tropaeolum majus 198, *199*

Tropaeolum peregrinum 200

Tropaeolum speciosum 200

Tropaeolum tricolor 200, *200*

Tropaeolum tuberosum 200

Tropaeolum tuberosum 'Ken Aslet' 200

tropical lizard vine. See *Tetrastigma voinierianum*

true maidenhair fern. See *Adiantum capillus-veneris*

trumpet flower. See *Bignonia capreolata*

Tulbaghia 137-8

Tulbaghia natalensis 137

Tulbaghia simmleri 138

Tulbaghia simmleri 'Alba' 138

Tulbaghia violacea 138, *138*

Tulbaghia violacea 'Silver Lace' 138

Tulbaghia violacea 'Variegata'. See *T. violacea* 'Silver Lace'

Tweedia 224

Tweedia caerulea 224

U

umbrella bamboo. See *Fargesia murielae*

umbrella plant. See *Cyperus involucratus*

umbrella tree. See *Magnolia tripetala*

Uncinia 348-9

Uncinia rubra 349

Uruguayan firecracker plant. See *Dicliptera suberecta*

V

variegated Indian bean tree. See *Catalpa bignonioides* 'Variegata'

variegated Japanese ginger. See *Zingiber mioga* 'Dancing Crane'

variegated Japanese sedge grass. See *Carex hachijoensis* 'Evergold'

variegated Japanese silver grass. See *Miscanthus sinensis* 'Variegatus' variegated shell ginger. See *Alpinia zerumbet* 'Variegata'

Verbena 189, 339

Verbena bonariensis 19, 339, *339*

Verbena hastata 12

vervain. See *Verbena*

Vestia 412

Vestia foetida 412, 412

Viburnum 412-13

Viburnum davidii 413, 413

Viburnum rhytidophyllum 413, 413

Viburnum rhytidophyllum 'Aldenhamense' 413

Viburnum tinus 413

Viburnum tinus 'Eve Price' 413

Viburnum tinus 'Lucidum' 413

Viburnum tinus 'Purpureum' 413

vine lilac. See *Hardenbergia violacea*

Virginia creeper. See *Parthenocissus quinquefolia*

Virginia potato. See *Apios americana*

virgin palm. See *Dioon edule*

Vitis 201

Vitis coignetiae 201, 201

Vitis coignetiae 'Claret Cloak' 201

Vitis pulchra 201

Vitis vinifera 'Purpurea' *175*

voodoo lily. See *Sauromatum*

Vriesea 113

Vriesea philippo-coburgii 113

Vriesea splendens 113

W

walking fern. See *Woodwardia unigemmata*

Wallich's wood fern. See *Dryopteris wallichiana*

wandering Jew. See *Tradescantia fluminensis, T. zebrina*

Washingtonia 290

Washingtonia filifera 290, 290

Washingtonia palm. See *Washingtonia filifera*

Washingtonia robusta 290, 290

Watsonia 138-9

Watsonia beatricis 138

Watsonia borbonica 138, 139

Watsonia pillansii. See *W. beatricis*

Watsonia fourcadei 138

Watsonia meriana 139, 139

Watsonia pyramidata. See *W. borbonica*

Wattakaka. See *Dregea*

wattle. See *Acacia*

wedge-leaf wattle. See *Acacia pravissima*

wheki. See *Dicksonia squarrosa*

wheki-ponga. See *Dicksonia fibrosa*

white bird-of-paradise. See *Strelitzia alba*

white paintbrush. See *Haemanthus albiflos*

white skunk cabbage. See *Lysichiton camtschatcensis*

wild bean. See *Apios americana*

wild dagga. See *Leonotis, L. leonurus*

wild garlic. See *Tulbaghia*

wild passionflower. See *Passiflora incarnata*

wild potato. See *Apios americana*

Windermere palm. See *Trachycarpus latisectus*

windmill palm. See *Trachycarpus fortunei*

wine palm. See *Butia*

wolf milk plant. See *Euphorbia stygiana*

wood fern. See *Dryopteris*

woodrush. See *Luzula*

wood spurge. See *Euphorbia amygdaloides*

Woodwardia 240

Woodwardia fimbriata 240

Woodwardia radicans 240, 240

Woodwardia unigemmata 240

woolly tree fern. See *Dicksonia antarctica*

X

Xanthorrhoea 349

Xanthorrhoea glauca 349

Xanthorrhoea johnsonii 349, 349

Xanthosoma 50

Xanthosoma nigrum 50

Xanthosoma sagittifolium 50, 50

Xanthosoma violaceum. See *X. nigrum*

Y

yautia. See *Xanthosoma*

yellow bird-of-paradise. See *Caesalpinia gilliesii*

Yucca 168-71

Yucca aloifolia 168

Yucca aloifolia 'Marginata' 168, *168*

Yucca aloifolia 'Tricolor' 168

Yucca carnerosana 169

Yucca elephantipes 169

Yucca elephantipes 'Variegata' 169

Yucca faxoniana 169, 169

Yucca filamentosa 169

Yucca filamentosa 'Bright Edge' 169

Yucca filamentosa 'Golden Sword' 169

Yucca filamentosa 'Ivory Tower' 169

Yucca filifera 169

Yucca glauca 170

Yucca gloriosa 170

Yucca gloriosa 'Variegata' 170, *170*

Yucca recurvifolia 170, 171

Yucca rostrata 171, 171

Yucca whipplei 171, 171

Yushania 72

Yushania anceps 72, 73

Yushania maculate 72-3

Z

Zantedeschia 31, 50-1, 51

Zantedeschia aethiopica 31

Zantedeschia aethiopica 'Crowborough' 50

Zantedeschia aethiopica 'Green Goddess' 50, *51*

Zantedeschia 'Cameo' 51

Zantedeschia 'Crystal Blush' 51

Zantedeschia elliottiana 50-1

Zantedeschia 'Firebird' 51

Zantedeschia 'Flame' 51, *51*

Zantedeschia 'Garnet Glow' 51

Zea 225

Zea mays 225

Zea mays 'Harlequin' 225

Zea mays var. *japonica 225*

Zea mays var. *japonica* 'Quadricolor' 225, *225*

Zea mays 'Variegata'

zebra grass. See *Miscanthus sinensis* 'Zebrinus'

zebra plant. See *Aphelandra squarrosa*

Zebrina pendula. See *Tradescantia zebrina*

Zingiber 100-1

Zingiber mioga 100-1

Zingiber mioga 'Dancing Crane' 101

Zingiber officinale 100

Zingiber zerumbet 'Darceyi' 101, *101*

Zulu daisy. See *Arctotis*